Puerto Rican Jam

Puerto Rican Jam

RETHINKING COLONIALISM AND NATIONALISM

Frances Negrón-Muntaner and
Ramón Grosfoguel, editors

University of Minnesota Press

Minneapolis

London

Grateful acknowledgment is made for permission to reprint from the following: Norma Alarcón, "The Theoretical Subjects(s) of *This Bridge Called My Back* and Anglo-American Feminism," in *Making Face, Making Soul/Haciendo Caras: Creative and Critical Perspectives by Feminists of Color*, ed. Gloria Anzaldúa (San Francisco: Aunt Lute Books, 1990), copyright 1990 by Gloria Anzaldúa, by permission of Aunt Lute Books; Chandra T. Mohanty, "Introduction. Cartographies of Struggle: Third World Women and the Politics of Feminism," in *Third World Women and the Politics of Feminism*, ed. Chandra Talpade Mohanty, Anna Russo, and Lourdes Torres (Bloomington: Indiana University Press, 1991); Gayatri Chakravorty Spivak, "Subaltern Studies: Deconstructing Historiography," in *Selected Subaltern Studies* (Delhi and New York: Oxford University Press, 1988); Manuel Zeno Gandía, *La charca* (Caracas: Biblioteca Ayacucho, 1978); Greg Tate, excerpt from "What Is Hip-Hop?" copyright 1995 Great Tate; Vico C, lyrics quoted from "Tradución," by permission of Prime Publishing; Wiso G, lyrics quoted from "Me levanto los domingos," by permission of Musical Productions, Inc.; Jenaro Díaz, lyrics quoted from "Puerto Rican in the U.S.A." by permission of Jenaro Díaz; Irie Boy, lyrics quoted from "Acapella," by permission of U Records.

Every effort has been made to obtain permission to reproduce copyrighted material in this book. The publishers ask copyright holders to contact them in writing if permission has inadvertently not been sought or if proper acknowledgment has not been made.

Published by the University of Minnesota Press
111 Third Avenue South, Suite 290, Minneapolis, MN 55401-2520
Printed in the United States of America on acid-free paper

Library of Congress Cataloging-in-Publication Data

Puerto Rican jam : rethinking colonialism and nationalism / Frances Negrón-Muntaner and Ramón Grosfoguel, editors.
    p. cm.
    Includes index.
    ISBN 0-8166-2848-3 (alk. paper). — ISBN 0-8166-2849-1 (pbk. : alk. paper)
    1. Puerto Rico—Politics and government—1952– 2. Nationalism-Puerto Rico—History. 3. Ethnicity—Puerto Rico. 4. Identity (Psychology)—Puerto Rico. 5. Puerto Rico—Relations—United States. 6. United States—Relations—Puerto Rico. I. Negrón-Mutaner, Frances. II. Grosfoguel, Ramón.
F1976.P585   1997
972.9505—dc21   97-9569

native of nowhere

stranded between vanishing islands
floating on an endless sea of receding coasts
my body is my only land
my hands navigate my skin
mapping the currents with my fingers
abysses fields mountains deserts oceans
so many oceans
echoes and cemeteries

transnational orphan
with feet full of memories
of running barefoot along volcanic cliffs
lightning between my breasts
of sitting on hot asphalt in the rain
watching the steam and the fog exchanging masks
of hurting somewhere
deep outside
everywhere

my feet
the corridors to places i lived places i died places i never went places
    i can't remember
populated by voices of missing people
some dead some i killed some gone some i left behind some i never met
nor did i touch
nor did i caress
people i never traveled

native of nowhere
a ticket to the wind on my back
i swallow hurricanes
my skeleton floats wildly in my body of floods
earthquakes vibrate through my limbs
reconfiguring my desires

my body
a disaster zone of erotic wastes
a white wooden house lies wrecked
my father pulls the curtains

my body is my only land
a land without homes nor hosts
a land of humidity, edges and edges
a land of volcanoes submerged in quicksand
a land of roaming scars

my land
a body from which i remove the earth with each step
i travel that territory called myself
before i become extinct

once again

Chloé S. Georas

Contents

Acknowledgments

This book began as a series of conversations among scholars and friends in Puerto Rico and the United States through a period of several years. These exchanges left a significant intellectual and personal imprint on the collection that we would like to publicly acknowledge and express our gratitude for to some of the participants. In Puerto Rico, we thank Miriam Muñiz, María Milagros López, Madeline Román, Carlos Pabón, and Juan Duchesne. On both sides of the Atlantic, Chloé S. Georas was a continuous source of ideas, support, and encouragement throughout the process of conceiving, writing, and preparing the book for publication.

Ramón Grosfoguel has had the privilege of the intellectual, professional, and personal support of colleagues Immanuel Wallerstein, Giovanni Arrighi, and Mark Selden at Binghamton University, as well as Beverly Silver from the Johns Hopkins University. Carmen Lydia Grosfoguel was a constant source of emotional sustenance for Ramón throughout the process. Frances Negrón-Muntaner's parents, scholars Mariano Negrón and Ada Muntaner, colleague Chon Noriega, and Maggie de la Cuesta have all provided unfailing encouragement and rigorous intellectual challenges.

Once the manuscript made its way to the University of Minnesota Press, Doris Sommer and Julio Ramos provided us with the first reading of the collection, solid suggestions, and energetic enthusiasm. Former editor Biodun Iginla and editorial assistant Elizabeth Knoll Stomberg embraced the book and took the first steps with us toward transforming the manuscript into a book. Mary Byers and Mary Keirstead, managing editor and copy editor, respectively, patiently and caringly made sense of and respected our particular forms of English but helped us to render it accessible to English-speaking readers.

Our appreciation goes to George Yúdice, Juan Flores, and Jean Franco, who generously shared with us many insightful comments, particularly about the book's introduction, and also contributed financially to the translation of Raquel Rivera's essay "Rapping Two Versions of the Same Requiem" from the Spanish original. Our deep thanks to Marianne Negrón, who gracefully translated hip-hop from Spanish to English and back.

There are hardly any words to express our thanks to Lisa Freeman, director at the University of Minnesota Press. Her support, patience, critical insight, and invaluable advice transformed a potentially exhausting experience into an enjoyable process. Finally, we thank the book's collaborators for their patience, solidarity, and common interest in stimulating debate about Puerto Rico and Puerto Ricans.

Beyond Nationalist and Colonialist Discourses: The *Jaiba* Politics of the Puerto Rican Ethno-Nation

Ramón Grosfoguel, Frances Negrón-Muntaner, and Chloé S. Georas

> *Ultimately, the native intellectual's life depends upon his ability to imitate the other perfectly, without a trace of parody; it depends, in short, upon his ability to mime without the perception of mimicry.*
> Diana Fuss, "Interior Colonies"

> *Americanicémonos, para no ser americanos.*
> Fernando Ortiz, *Orbita de Fernando Ortiz*

Intellectual Nomads

Like all anthologies, this collection of essays emerges within a specific set of personal and social contexts. The immediate context is the encounter of three island Puerto Rican graduate students during the late 1980s in Philadelphia, who shared a sense of intellectual and political isolation from both mainstream and "left" Puerto Rican cultural/political practices in the United States and the island.

Superficially we were undergoing what many middle-class intellectuals from the island already saw as routine—going up to *el norte* to buy a prestigious (or not so prestigious degree) *en inglés* and returning home to an always already present space in academia. But we knew that for different and complex reasons for each of us, we were not going back "home."[1] In fact, as Alberto Sandoval Sánchez points out in his essay "Puerto Rican Identity Up in the Air: Air Migration, Its Cultural Representations, and Me 'Cruzando el Charco,'" home, from now on, was going to be right here. Or, more accurately, here and there.

The motivation to produce this book stems from both an intellectual crisis of political orphanhood and a crisis for us as "national" intellectu-

1

als turned "ethnics" in the United States. We soon realized that this supposed "demotion"—so feared by many Puerto Rican intellectuals—was
in fact one of the many effects of posing Puerto Rico's political struggles
as a colonial/national dichotomy, a framing that only allows political
agency in terms of the consolidation of a nation-state (that is, national
"liberation"). It seemed evident that the apparent transparency of signification of the nationalist/colonialist dichotomy had to be reexamined in
order to map more effective strategies of political participation.

A useful starting point in articulating the inadequacy of the binary
suggested here is José Quiroga's essay "Narrating the Tropical Pharmacy."
In this text, Quiroga suggests that part of this conceptual *tranque* (dead
end) within Puerto Rican historiography relates to a discursive tendency
to construct colonialism as "illness" and nationalism as its "cure." Within
this logic, the illness and the cure are mutually implicated sides of the
same coin that do not allow other potentially more "salutary" options to
be articulated. In light of this historically consistent but currently limited
understanding, we partially conceived this collection as a way of creating
a dialogue that we hope will generate fresh ways of posing the political
challenges faced by Puerto Ricans beyond the reverse discourses of colonialism and nationalism. Hence, the introduction's title is not dismissive
of these discourses' effects. Instead, it extends an invitation to rethink the
constraints imposed on Puerto Rican political and cultural possibilities
by articulating complex histories and subjectivities as a unidimensional
confrontation between colonialist and nationalist discourses and political projects.

Although this is the first anthology to explicitly challenge this dichotomy as an epistemological stumbling block, the line of questioning
proposed here has produced over the last two decades some of the most
insightful commentary on Puerto Ricans. Essays by José Luis González,
Juan Flores, and Arcadio Díaz-Quiñones;[2] collective efforts such as the
journals *Postdata*, *Bordes*, and *Nómada*; and a growing body of feminist
criticism and women's literature (e.g., Rosario Ferré, Ana Lydia Vega,
Magali García Ramis) and gay and lesbian literature (particularly Manuel
Ramos-Otero) have helped to create a context where a collective statement regarding the need to reimagine Puerto Rican history and expand
or dismantle the hegemonic notion of the "national" is possible. Still, different from many of these writers, we are not necessarily suggesting a
new "content" for a national project (under the guise, for example, of a
new revolutionary subject). On the contrary, we are posing a set of ques-

tions that propose that the resistance to a nation-state project by the majority of Puerto Ricans partly speaks to a discursive terrain of heterogeneity that is alien to nationalism as a political strategy leading to the founding of a state. In other words, Puerto Ricans are bound by nationalist ideologies. Yet, the national often refers to ethnic culture and solidarity strategies, and rarely does it entail a mass demand to administer the chaos left behind by five hundred years of colonial and neocolonial relations.

The strategy of rethinking nationalist and colonialist discourses in a moment of "crisis" is, of course, historically consistent in Puerto Rican intellectual production during the twentieth century. In this sense, Kelvin Santiago-Valles's "The Discreet Charm of the Proletariat: Imagining Early-Twentieth-Century Puerto Ricans in the Past Twenty-Five Years of Historical Inquiry" serves as a reflexive space for this collection. As Santiago points out, the project of rethinking historical relations in Puerto Rico is always a political endeavor that constitutes an intimate relationship between the way that Puerto Rico is historicized and the ways it is politically imagined. Our purpose here, however, is not to "solve" colonialism through a single political program (that is, "cure" the colony). Instead, we propose a critical stance toward the colonial/national discursive dichotomy through a variety of strategies that we hope will lead to other political and theoretical proposals. These textual strategies include the examination of events and processes ignored by previous scholarship, rereadings of "classic" historiographical topics by new social subjects and frameworks, and the articulation of radical democratic perspectives not assumed by either nationalist or colonial discourses. Within the book's space we acknowledge Santiago's provocative question: "What is the relationship between the way societies are organized and the ways they are studied?" We affirm that as Puerto Rican intellectuals, our theories are our politics, and this relationship must be critically examined.

Although the anthology constructs a dialogue among the texts, we acknowledge that not all participants share a common political project or necessarily share every point presented in this introductory text. It is important to emphasize that our reading of the essays can also be considered a "misreading" that neither represents nor fixes the multiple implications of each text. We consider the potential of these essays as important interventions in other fields and contexts by no means exhausted by this space and encourage further reading, writing, and debate about the different perspectives included here.

The Crisis of Colonial and Nationalist Discourses

The current urgency of rearticulating Puerto Rico's colonial/nationalist dichotomous paradigm to facilitate the mapping of a fresh course is partly linked to the current ongoing process of Caribbean restructuring and U.S. economic decline. Historically, Puerto Rican intellectuals have adopted one of two discursive poles (supportive of the colonial relationship or anticolonial/nationalist). However, as the island's economy continues to deteriorate, intellectuals and other sectors supporting the colonial status quo have faced a crisis of legitimation. For the first time in fifty years, state intellectuals have publicly accepted that the Estado Libre Asociado (ELA, or literally Free Associated State)[3] is obsolete as an institutional framework to promote the island's economic "development."

During the 1950s and 1960s, the ELA was able to supply U.S. industries with cheap labor, to grant federal tax exemption to American corporations, and to stimulate free trade between the island and the mainland. Today these incentives have lost all bargaining power. The shift to labor-intensive industrialization in peripheral regions with cheaper labor forces, such as the Dominican Republic, as well as the creation of the North American Free Trade Agreement (institutionalizing Mexico's northern border as a low-wage haven for U.S. transnational corporations) has displaced Puerto Rico as a central location for U.S. capital investments. Moreover, the fiscal crisis of the metropolitan state has forced significant cuts in programs favoring corporate investments in Puerto Rico.[4] The effect has been a fast deindustrialization of the island, structural unemployment, deterioration of basic infrastructure, and massive migration. Simultaneously, the state's fiscal crisis has reduced the amount of federal transfers to the island. Hence, the processes that allowed a relative improvement in the quality of life for most island residents during the past decades are at their limits. The notion that islanders have a radically different insertion into the American political and economic structures than U.S. Puerto Ricans is increasingly questionable as Puerto Rico threatens to become the shining "scar"—not star—of the Caribbean.[5]

At the same time that pro-colonial discourses are in crisis, nationalist discourses in Puerto Rico (capitalist or socialist versions) are virtually defeated. The decline of popular support for independence or for measures that in any way create obstacles to American incorporation suggests that nationalism as a massive (not symbolic) political ideology is only powerful among elite minorities. The popular rejection of nationalism as a pro-independence (separatist) ideology (only 4 percent of the votes were pro-independence in the "status" referendum of November 1993) can be read not as a symptom of a colonized "mind" but as a reaction against several regional and world processes that Puerto Ricans tend to be critically aware of.[6]

Contrary to other twentieth-century colonial experiences where the local elites hegemonized subordinated social groups against foreign powers, in Puerto Rico the latter have struggled against the interests of the local elites by mobilizing the democratic and civil rights discourses of the metropolitan center.[7] From the moment of the American invasion of Puerto Rico in 1898, different social groups (organized around class, race, and/or gender categories) have attributed different meanings to U.S. colonialism on the island. Some sectors quickly understood the invasion as a disaster since it shattered (at least for nearly forty years) any hope of local political hegemony. Other sectors, particularly among the peasantry and working classes, welcomed the invaders as the agents of a new order that would extend democratic guarantees to all Puerto Ricans. In this sense, the invasion allowed an unprecedented "national" class struggle to assume public dimensions.

In "Surviving Colonialism and Nationalism," Mariano Negrón-Portillo details the paternalism (at best) of the creole elites, their autonomist political project during the nineteenth century, and the increased possibilities of political intervention by formerly marginalized groups after the invasion. Negrón-Portillo focuses on the discontent of most subordinated social groups (against both the creole elites and the Spanish regime) as one of the central elements in the lack of cohesion of a nationalist ideology during the early part of the century. Once the peasantry began its process of proletarianization and the urban working classes grew in number and organizational capacity, Negrón-Portillo stresses, large sectors of these groups articulated a political project of modernization in alliance with U.S. interests and in opposition to the local elites (their class enemies). For many among the organized working class, discourses anchored around *la puertorriqueñidad* (Puerto Ricanness) were often perceived as obstacles in the process of achieving a certain degree of social and economic protections such as the right to strike, freedom of speech, and a minimum wage. Also, the Hispanicist orientation of the elites' nationalist discourse overlooked the social resentment that many among the peasantry and working classes still held against the

Spanish regime, its allies, and its descendants. Contrary to what the majority of island intellectual opinion during this century sustains, most Puerto Ricans did not (and still do not) perceive the central political contradiction to be one between colonizer/colonized but rather to be between different class/race/gender interests not mechanically determined by nationality.

Although most political conflicts were publicly played out by men of different class and cultural identities, one of the groups that sought to take advantage of the new regime were women (of all classes). While many working-class women advocated feminism (including suffrage) within (mostly pro-American) worker's organizations, middle-class women were also articulating strategies to deploy American colonialist discourse in winning some basic rights for themselves. One of the most provocative essays in this collection regarding the often contradictory effect of American colonialism in Puerto Rico is Gladys Jiménez-Muñoz's "So We Decided to Come and Ask You Ourselves: The 1928 U.S. Congressional Hearings on Women's Suffrage in Puerto Rico." In this account, Jiménez-Muñoz traces the complexities of gender, ethnicity, and colonial administration in an attempt to explore the interplay of power relations within that context. On the one hand, Puerto Rican feminist suffragists sought an alliance with American feminists, who in turn appealed to American congressmen (white and male) to intervene on behalf of Puerto Rican women by extending them the vote in local elections. At the same time, this strategy (against Puerto Rican men) articulates an alliance between middle-class (Puerto Rican and white American) women and a call for further colonial (imperial) intervention in local matters (on behalf of some women) by American men. In this sense, the suffragists used the same discourse circulated by the metropolis (the imperialist notion that the United States came to bring progress to the island) and pitted colonized versus colonialist men in a struggle to gain the vote for middle-class women. The intricacies of the strategy and its effects suggest that totalizing categories such as nationality and gender do not exhaust the complexity of colonial power relationships experienced in Puerto Rico.

The fact that different groups saw U.S. colonialism on the island as a context for increased political participation is deeply related to the particularities of colonialism practiced in Puerto Rico, particularly after the 1940s. In Ramón Grosfoguel's essay "The Divorce of Nationalist Political Discourses from the Puerto Rican People: A Sociohistorical Perspective," he proposes a historical periodization of the diverse structuring logics (capitalist accumulation, geopolitical military/security considerations, symbolic/ideological strategies) that have governed U.S. interests in Puerto Rico during the past century. The interplay of alliances and concessions from the metropolis have produced the context for a non-nationalist political constituency in Puerto Rico. Contrary to traditional political-economy approaches, Grosfoguel argues that capitalist accumulation has not always dominated the structural relationship between the metropolis and the colony because U.S. interests have shifted throughout the century. At certain historical junctures, these shifting interests have in fact contradicted capitalist accumulation processes, thus directly affecting U.S. corporations established on the island. The extension of rights and federal transfers to Puerto Rico, particularly during the second half of the twentieth century, is a clear example of the hegemony of the symbolic in U.S. policy regarding Puerto Rico. Puerto Rico's postwar incorporation was determined by the United States' symbolic strategy of "showcasing" the island as the American model of development for the Third World as opposed to the Soviet model. According to Grosfoguel, the outcome of this strategy was a colonial reform that eliminated the old type of colonialism and transformed the island into a "modern colony."[8] He concludes the essay with a call to de-essentialize the island's status debate and with a proposal to reconstruct a new left alternative beyond colonialist and nationalist discourses.

The analysis proposed by the essays discussed here is of great importance to a nondichotomous frame of reference since it significantly and productively complicates the various power struggles along more than one axis (colonial subjects/metropolis). At the same time, it examines how different racial, class, and gender groups have been (often simultaneously) oppressed or have benefited from U.S. intervention. Without an understanding of these dynamics, it is virtually impossible to understand how American hegemony functions in Puerto Rico and how Puerto Ricans resist colonial power(s). Thus, the weakening of a political nationalist agenda in Puerto Rico was partially produced by the metropolitan oscillation between making "good" on their promise of bringing "progress" to Puerto Rico—civil liberties, a minimum wage, welfare programs—and their colonial needs such as economic exploitation and military maneuvering. This conceptualization has enormous consequences for political participation because it seriously questions the premises upon which contemporary oppositional (nationalist) island politics are built.

The Nation-Building Processes in the Caribbean Region

Although Puerto Rico has never had a massive pro-independence move-ment, Puerto Ricans hold a vicarious knowledge of other postcolonial re-alities, particularly in Latin America and the Caribbean. What Puerto Ri-cans have witnessed very close to home has not been seductive: regimes of state-orchestrated terror, International Monetary Fund intervention, pauperization of the population, illegal emigration, foreign debt, and a lack of strength to forcefully negotiate with the economic centers. As Patrick Baker suggests:

> As the world system developed, metropolitan centres found that they could obtain Third World resources through the economic structures that had emerged, and that the need for costly administration of their colonies was no longer necessary, efficient, or desirable. Thus, the met-ropolitan powers were ready to divest themselves of their colonies, and they took advantage of local efforts to centre peripheries to rid them-selves of the administrative responsibility for them.[9]

Puerto Ricans—in a more dramatic way—have taken note that the most economically and socially vulnerable social groups are among the most affected by postcolonial economic realities as Haitians, Domini-cans, and Cubans risk their lives to reach Puerto Rican or American shores.[10] This comment does not imply that Puerto Ricans do not have legitimate economic claims in relation to the metropolitan center— Puerto Rico's per capita income, for example, is half of the poorest U.S. state—which should form part of any anticolonial political program. Within the context of transtatal capitalism in the Caribbean, however, Puerto Ricans can count on more resources to maneuver capitalist re-structuring in the region by its relationship to the center as a "modern colony" than as a Caribbean nation-state.[11] Moreover, capitalist transta-tialization has made nation-states' structures obsolete in attempting to control economic processes within their borders. In short, Puerto Ricans have experienced a process of nation building without creating a nation-state, in part because the United States, unlike in other intervened coun-tries of the region (which are nation-states), continues to reluctantly fi-nance its own economic and political failure in Puerto Rico.[12]

A more recent contextual element in relation to the decline of nation-alist, particularly socialist, discourses in Puerto Rico relates to the fall of the authoritarian Soviet bloc and its illusion of constructing a so-ciety "outside" of capitalism. The revolutionary experiences of diverse

Caribbean and Central American nations, where attempts to construct alternate economic arrangements have been crushed militarily (Grenada), defeated through United States-financed warfare (Nicaragua, El Salvador), or strangulated economically (Nicaragua, Cuba), have also contributed to widespread skepticism regarding Puerto Rico's ability to combat U.S. economic hegemony in its own sphere of influence. Even revolutionary movements such as the FMLN (Frente Farabundo Martí para la Liberación Nacional) in El Salvador have been forced to recognize the impossibility of an "outside" to capitalism and have modified their intervention tactics:

> To this end, all the five organizations within the FMLN have established profit-making enterprises, ranging from agricultural co-ops and import-export companies, to the conversion of the legendary guerrilla radio station, Radio Venceremos, into a commercial radio station in which ideology and politics have been replaced by non-stop Latin pop and inane DJ patter.[13]

The FMLN experience shows not only that there is no outside to capitalism but also the impossibility within the present historical conditions of frontally challenging U.S. capitalist hegemony in the region (even in its weakened shape). The Sandinistas in Nicaragua have arrived at similar conclusions, even within a developmentalist discourse. Victor Tirado López, one of the nine Sandinista commanders, comments:

> I believe that the cycle of anti-imperialist revolutions is coming to a close; understanding these to mean total, military, and economic confrontations with imperialism. We have to look for other options. The underdeveloped world cannot resist to live in perpetual war.... Underdeveloped countries like ours cannot endure conflicts which undermine our economic base.... I think the best thing we can aspire to is a peaceful co-existence with imperialism, even if it hurts us to say it. Just have good relations with them so we can develop ourselves.[14]

Following this state of affairs, both Sandinistas and the FMLN have negotiated a transition to "democratic" politics without fully abandoning a more radical democratic or revolutionary project.

In the case of Puerto Rico, preliminary plebiscite hearings conducted in San Juan during the late 1980s involving all major political parties made it clear that the United States would keep its military bases on the island and would not tolerate potential alliances between Puerto Rico and American enemies, regardless of the status chosen by the majority. It was also evident that the American independence or autonomous "solution" for Puerto Rico constitutes a form of colonialism without any of its benefits (in the form of metropolitan transfers and basic democratic rights). Puerto Rico would still be a subordinated part within an American sphere of influence in the region. As Orlando Patterson has noted in regard to the independent island nations of the West Indies:

> The flow of American capital, technology and mass culture to the islands, far from promoting self-sustained national development—as was once innocently hoped—has thoroughly disrupted their traditional economies and cultures and is, in fact, the main reason for the current migration to America. The sad truth is that these island economies are, in the long run, simply not viable—they are too small, too poor in natural resources and too close to America's overwhelming post-industrial culture. They are, de facto, already part of NAFTA, and it's only a matter of time before they are de jure.[15]

Unfortunately, Puerto Rican nationalist pro-independent discourses continue to ignore the fact that Puerto Rico, given its historical relationship to the United States, its lack of a national economy, and its disadvantaged insertion in the world economy, cannot become "independent."[16] The experience of the Palau Islands, which proclaimed independence from the United States in October 1994, supports the assumptions outlined here for Puerto Rico. (The Palauans status is that of a "Compact of Free Association" between the United States and Palau.) Under the agreement, the U.S. military has access to the island for fifty years and may exercise "strategic denial" in perpetuity to forbid access to Palau by any U.S. "enemy" country, and Palau will receive only $517 million from the federal government.[17] The right to migrate to and from the United States and work in the United States granted to Palauans would most likely not be offered to Puerto Ricans born under the "Associated Republic."

Ambiguous Identities

In general, most intellectuals frame Puerto Rican struggles within a nineteenth-century model of colonialism in which the colonized lived in daily confrontation with the invader on their own soil and thus are unable to properly contextualize Puerto Rican cultural practices. It is often the case that these intellectuals suspect that Puerto Ricans are not independent—assuming independence to be a sign of national maturity and real territorial power, a condition to claim nationhood—because they have been brainwashed by American colonialism to desire "dependency." This position fails to understand our specificity as a colonial experience different from that of Latin America and some parts of the Caribbean, producing a narrative that constitutes our experience as aberrant and our hybrid culture as corrupt.

During the early twentieth century, the United States attempted with limited success to "assimilate" Puerto Ricans to "American culture" by coercion. Colonial authorities in Puerto Rico proceeded to impose English as the primary language in several public institutions, particularly in primary and secondary education, and banned the display of emerging nationalist symbols such as the Puerto Rican flag. Within this assimilationist project, any sign of collective (even if minority) national affirmation was considered to be subversive and was actively persecuted. The political cost of this form of domination, the ineffectiveness of these policies (due to resistance and inadequate implementation), and the metropolitan need to maintain domestic peace during the Cold War forced the United States to devise a formula to reinvent Puerto Rico's colonial subordinated status, thus conveniently recognizing an autonomous and different cultural "heritage."

The formation of the Estado Libre Asociado (ELA) marked a definitive rupture with traditional assimilationist colonial practices, inaugurating the opposite strategy as a way to contain potentially anti-imperialist sentiments against the United States. The ELA constituted the institutional apparatus that managed to reproduce Puerto Rican national subjectivity at the same time that it created both an illusion of political autonomy and concealment of the subordinated economic absorption of the island by the United States.

Carlos Pabón[18] suggests that the ELA discourse marked the beginning of a metamorphosis in the political meaning of the "national" itself. Luis Muñoz Marín, the leading architect of the ELA, successfully neutralized the nationalist forces lead by Albizu Campos during the critical decade of the 1930s by making a particular version of nationalism an integral part of its political ideology. Because of this mutation—which resignified the meaning of the national in Puerto Rico—the U.S. state apparatus managed by Puerto Ricans on the island was/is able to reproduce a discourse that has effectively constituted "national" subjects (at least culturally). In this sense, neonationalist forces that continue to insist that the basic cultural contradiction in Puerto Rico is between those who are pro-statehood and those who defend *la puertorriqueñidad* fail to recognize that cultural nationalism has already been institutionalized by the U.S. state apparatus as reproduced in Puerto Rico. Given this process of taming the national by U.S.-Puerto Rico-administered colonial state, the potential of calling on Puerto Ricans' nationalism for a separatist political program is canceled out. Thus, "nationality" is not a question in Puerto Rico but rather a *cienpiés* (centipede) of proposals and possibilities.

Just as the creation of the ELA produced national subjects without a state, it also produced a context of illusory autonomy from the metropolitan center. We call Puerto Rico's autonomy "illusory" not because there is no Puerto Rican agency in this process but because the cultural and political discourses of autonomy have obscured how (subordinately) integrated Puerto Ricans are to the United States' economic and political structures (e.g., Puerto Ricans on the island cannot elect congressional representation or vote for the president, and are under the territorial clause). The U.S. Congress has absolute authority over Puerto Rico's local political structures.

As Jaime Benson-Arias argues in his essay "Puerto Rico: The Myth of the National Economy," Puerto Rico is a colony only in the political sense because the island has been completely absorbed into the U.S. economy. Puerto Rico's economic structures are a regional extension, although subordinated and unequal, of the mainland. The ELA's successful representation of Puerto Rico as an autonomous nation and economy has resulted in a political terrain where both colonialist and nationalist discourses participate in the same illusory assumptions that define both an internal "national economy" and an external U.S. economy.

Due to its overt hybrid character, the ELA in Puerto Rico is a striking example of how national ideological apparatuses can produce the sense that a "nation" (even when it has not consolidated a "state") is controlling an internal space "outside" international capitalist hegemonic control. An ideological tenet of the capitalist world-system is that each nation-state develops independently from the others. This developmentalist ideology represents hierarchical relations of inequality and subordination as if all participants were "equal," that is, nations. According to Immanuel Wallerstein,

> A central ideological theme of the capitalist world-economy was that every state could, and indeed eventually probably would, reach a high level of national income and that conscious, rational action would make it so. This fit very well with the underlying Enlightenment theme

of inevitable progress and the teleological view of human history that it incarnated.[19]

Similarly, the ELA reproduced a developmentalist ideology by arguing that Puerto Ricans struggled and achieved an autonomous status from the United States, and that its (current) economic development was a product of its own efforts (the industrialization program was adequately named "Operation Bootstrap"). Puerto Rico's early success in transforming and improving the quality of life on the island was sold to "developing countries" as "living proof" that they too could achieve development, if only they worked "hard" and opened their markets to U.S. transtatal capitalist investments. The failure of the developmentalist discourse in Puerto Rico ultimately suggests that an awareness of unequal power relations between the United States and Puerto Rico and of the economic absorption of the island into the metropolis is a more productive premise from which to map future political interventions than the illusion of autonomy (nation-state or any other variant), an illusion that continues to hinder the creation of a public political sphere where a discussion (beyond nationalism) is able to articulate a politically effective critique of world political and economic dynamics as they affect the lives of Puerto Ricans.

The ELA has fostered a "misrecognition"[20] of Puerto Rico's colonial positioning in relation to the United States that is shared neither by other "nations" nor the U.S. Congress. This misrecognition is often exemplified in "cultural" debates where a given claim of autonomy contradicts political structures and cultural practices. Thus, it is misrecognition that allows former Senator Ronaldo "Rony" Jarabo, for example, to claim that the "Spanish Only" legislation in Puerto Rico will "protect" all Puerto Ricans from the "English Only" threat, while the legal fact is that any measure taken by the Puerto Rican legislature can be unilaterally invalidated by the U.S. Congress. It is also a misrecognition that permits island intellectuals to represent the island's territory/population as the only Puerto Rican "nation," thus rendering invisible the fragmentation of the Puerto Rican body politic spilled over onto the U.S. mainland. These contradictory claims do not always limit cultural debate or practice. Instead, they often make "culture" a hotly contested and slippery terrain.

Puerto Rico's disadvantaged and ambiguous political and economic integration into the United States has not resulted in a loss of cultural identity, as supporters of "cultural imperialism" theories claim, but in an overt hybridization and multiplication of Puerto Rican identities played out by different subjects. As Celeste Olalquiaga writes in relation to Latin America in general, "Accustomed to dealing with the arbitrary imposition of foreign products and practices, this culture has learned the tactics of selection and transformation to suit the foreign to its own idiosyncrasy, thus developing popular integration mechanisms that are deliberately eclectic and flexible."[21]

Raquel Rivera, in her essay titled "Rapping Two Versions of the Same Requiem," challenges supporters of cultural imperialism theories by examining how rap culture and music in Puerto Rico give voice to urban, black, and poor youth against state and nationalist discourses that tend to negate or criminalize them. Rap culture also realigns solidarities beyond the colonial/national discursive dichotomy by recognizing class and race as important elements in the building of solidarities. This essay proposes that despite the colonial reforms experienced on the island during this century, the racial/colonial power relationships between the local Puerto Rican (white) elites and black Puerto Ricans have not substantially changed. Based on color and not on origin, racism is still an important mechanism of exclusion on the island, with its particular set of political challenges.

In contrast to U.S.-style racism, Puerto Rican blacks and mulattoes are promised the possibility of "racial mobility" for their offspring through racial intermixing and economic advancement.[22] Hence, a light-skinned subject with African ancestry may be accepted as "white" in Puerto Rico if he/she exhibits "white" looks. Simultaneously, despite the widespread understanding that blackness constitutes the most undesirable racial identity among Puerto Ricans, both colonialist and nationalist discourses subscribe to the myth of racial democracy. According to this ideology, all Puerto Ricans regardless of "race" are the mixture of the same ethnic ingredients—Spanish, African, Indian—and therefore equal. This superficially more benign form of racist ideology is often as, if not more, effective than more overt racist discourses in preventing racism from being socially and politically challenged in public discourse.

As the example of rap music suggests, the so-called products of global culture can have a radicalizing impact on class and racial struggles on a local level, creating new communities beyond traditionally determined national boundaries. In "Contending Nationalisms: Culture, Politics and Corporate Sponsorship in Puerto Rico," Arlene Dávila radically questions the premise that the globalization of culture will inevitably result in the dissolution of cultural differences. Dávila contends that in Puerto Rico, contrary to nationalist claims on "cultural imperialism," American corporate sponsorship has become a major player in shaping and reproducing nationalist discourses through its financing of popular and elite cultural events and the commodification of national representations, for example, the flag, landscapes, and architecture. Different from most U.S. marketing strategies in the world, capitalist interests operating in Puerto Rico have realized that Puerto Rican cultural representations sell products and hence must be deployed rather than ignored. Interestingly, cultural representations promoted by corporations are often based on popular—rather than elitist or nostalgic—conceptions of "culture," such as salsa concerts, that can be at odds with other forms of Puerto Rican culture considered to be more "authentic" by the island's middle and upper classes.

The reframing of the question of Puerto Rican "culture" is, then, not whether Puerto Ricans even "have" a culture or if that culture is corrupt or "penetrated," but rather in what ways do Puerto Ricans imagine themselves in culture as part of communities. As Benedict Anderson says, "Communities are to be distinguished not by their falsity/genuineness, but by the style in which one is imagined."[23]

"Puerto Rico" has been (and continues to be) imagined in many ways: as a sovereign nation, as a nation within a nation, as an ethnic group with a regional identity in alliance with a nation, or as several combinations of these formulations. In addition, "Puerto Rico" is not always conceived as a geographically specific space but as a symbolic claim of belonging to a community of fellow members. As Agustín Lao poetically argues in his essay "Islands at the Crossroads: Puerto Ricanness Traveling between the Translocal Nation and the Global City," Puerto Ricans form part of a "transnation" or translocal nation, a web of possibilities, flows, and broken-English dreams between the island and the United States. Given the contradictory political relationships with the United States that Puerto Ricans must engage in daily, the sign of "Puerto Rican" sometimes serves as a way of maintaining critical distance within oppressive contexts of unequal exchange. Thus, in Puerto Rico, after a failed attempt to produce "American" cultural subjects on the island during the early twentieth century, "Puerto Ricans" are reproduced by widely circulated and repeated narratives of belonging that sometimes function oppositionally through specific institutions (e.g., schools, family, media) and sometimes as complementary to American "identity."

Concurrently, in the United States Puerto Ricans are reproduced by a combination of racist American structures and ethnic community formations mostly in large northeastern cities. Third-generation Puerto Ricans in the United States continue to identify themselves as Puerto Ricans without the hyphenated "Puerto Rican-American." Puerto Ricans are the only group in the United States that after several generations keep using a nonhyphenated identity. On the island as well as in the United States, however, the ambiguity of Puerto Ricans' relationship to the United States creates a slippery semantic context where sometimes "Puerto Rican" is claimed as a sign of difference, for example, cultural identity and language, while at other times, the same sign is equated with being part of the "United States" (citizenship, welfare entitlements). This double strategy was spectacularly performed during the intense debates around language policy in Puerto Rico during the early 1990s. The legislative imposition of Spanish as the single official language of Puerto Rico in 1991 was met with intense resistance by various sectors who saw the measure as an obstacle to the discussion of permanent and/or full political integration in the United States. The reversal of the decision by the pro-statehood administration in 1993 and the reinstitution of English and Spanish as official languages were a triumph of the majority political strategy of maintaining a doubleness to Puerto Rican "identity." As Frances Negrón-Muntaner argues in her essay "English Only Jamás but Spanish Only Cuidado: Language and Nationalism in Contemporary Puerto Rico," the language debates intermittently brought to public attention during the twentieth century in Puerto Rico are modes of imagining the collectivity's limits and hierarchies while rehearsing alliances and testing the viability of political projects. A close look at the metaphors and performances enacted throughout the past five years in relation to "Spanish First "and "English Also" suggests that the political ambiguity and flexibility signaled by an official bilingual language policy represented a more inclusive political project than the linguistic nationalist proposition, even when advocates on both sides made essentialist assumptions about the relationship between power and language (English = progress, Spanish = tradition). Yet, the fact that nationalist ideologies of different stripes are part of public discourses at all levels and by all sectors of the population underlines the fact that the "national question" is no question at all in Puerto Rico. The more relevant question is, On behalf of whose interests are "national" discourses mobilized for?

A Puerto Rican Ethno-Nation?

The multiple and contesting notions of the concept of "nation" alluded to in the previous discussion are, however, not indeterminate. A clear majority of the population (as gauged by popular elections, media, and popular culture) articulates Puerto Rico as both an ethnic group with partial or no desire to control its own state apparatus and as a distinct cultural identity autonomous from the United States and/or "complementary" to the United States. In Puerto Rico, it has been possible for a significant number of the population to imagine the "nation" without a "Puerto Rican" state and to view the United States' state apparatus as a more beneficial structure to advance the "nation's" interests. By the same token, although many Puerto Ricans on the island are willing to give up (at least formally) claims to territorial power, all Puerto Rican political formulas are articulated on behalf of a group of people imagined to belong to a well-defined territory. Ambivalence among pro-statehooders in calling this collectivity a nation is probably as linked to ideological differences in their imagining of Puerto Rico as to political pragmatism. All sectors of the pro-commonwealth and pro-statehood political elites are keenly aware that a nationalist discourse will seriously impede pro-statehood negotiations with Congress. Thus, it can be argued that to the extent that Puerto Ricans make political (territorial) claims on behalf of Puerto Ricans, Puerto Ricans constitute a national formation. At the same time, to the extent that a political claim is made on behalf of Puerto Ricans formally relinquishing state power, Puerto Ricans constitute a partially territorialized ethnic group (islanders). Since both tendencies not only coexist between groups but also simultaneously in social and subjective contexts, Puerto Ricans imagine themselves as an "ethno-nation," with different emphasis on both sides of the hyphen. This ambiguity and double consciousness are not born out of political opportunism. Instead they are the result of strategies developed under conditions of colonial domination. As Rajagopalan Radhakrishnan, an Indian postcolonial critic, said,

> I would argue that there is a distinction between ambivalence as a
> given conditioning and the agential politization of ambivalence. We
> cannot forget that double consciousness and ambivalence are mutually
> constitutive, and peoples and cultures that have been coerced into
> more than one history through domination, slavery, and colonialism
> have the ethicopolitical need and authority to make their presence felt

in all of these histories. Ambivalence gives these cultures a double di-
rectionality: a here or the present home, and a there or the elsewhere
in terms of which metropolitan contemporaneity can be interrogated
and transformed. Call this the anthropologization of the West (Spivak)
or the ethnicization of America. The diasporic reterritorialization of
postcoloniality into ethnicity has the potential to represent the third
world within the first world not through easy assimilationalism or
strategic opportunism, but through a fundamental questioning of the
manner in which dominant regimes play and dictate the identity game
to subaltern groups on the basis of a rigged and stacked text.[24]

The ambiguity of this articulation is evidenced by the fact that even
when many Puerto Ricans in the United States imagine themselves pragmatically as an "ethnic group" with no territorial (state) claim in the
United States, Puerto Rico is at least claimed symbolically as the territorial site where ethnics become nationals through the magical operation
of the air bridge. The instability of the concept of ethnic group to refer
to Puerto Ricans is also rooted, for example, in assumptions about how
ethnicity is reproduced in the working classes. Some suggest that the
persistence of ethnicity in the capitalist world economy's metropolises
is mostly related to the reproduction of a cheap labor force or industrial
reserve army. This is partially true in the Puerto Rican case. Yet, as
María Milagros López suggests,[25] many Puerto Ricans are not effectively
reproduced as capitalist labor force, but instead, under conditions of
colonial postindustrial expulsion from the labor force, Puerto Ricans developed postwork strategies within the system (informal jobs, hustling of
diverse state-generated incomes, or a combination of both) in order to
survive without renouncing access to capitalist mass consumption. In
this sense, Puerto Rican "ethnicity" cannot be reduced to the sphere of
labor reproduction.

The hegemony of ethnicity over nation or nation over ethnicity depends on the geopolitical and historical context of the Puerto Rican communities in question, and what objectives are sought at any particular
juncture. For example, most Puerto Ricans consider Puerto Rico a "nation" when Olympic competition or the Miss Universe Pageant is involved but an ethnic community when claims to civil rights or access to
federal programs is concerned. Military service is another example.
Puerto Ricans have fought and died in all the wars the Americans have
fought during this century. When it comes to wars, the United States has
been ready to recognize Puerto Ricans as full U.S. citizens and to recruit
them for military service. Puerto Ricans have participated in these wars

as a U.S. ethnic group. However, in the Vietnam War, many Puerto Ricans resisted "ethnic identity" and claimed "national identity" in order to question their participation in a war of aggression against a Third World country.

Hence, the discursive demarcation of a Puerto Rican specificity points to a strategy of resistance that defies easy categorization within contemporary theoretical debates. Because of a multiplicity of factors, Puerto Rican politics and cultural practices are neither entirely "inside" the American mainstream nor "outside" it. We conceptualize Puerto Ricans' self-representation as both an increasingly deterritorialized "ethno-nation" in the United States and a territorialized "ethno-nation" in Puerto Rico.[26] Although there are differences of location and participation between Puerto Ricans living in the United States and Puerto Rico, some of these differences become remarkably more overt or negligible when the main category of analysis is not "national identity" but a more complex understanding of how social identities are constructed, resisted, and represented.

The proposed conceptualization of Puerto Ricans as an ethno-nation is a self-conscious effort to recognize that the majority of Puerto Ricans tend to oscillate between understanding themselves (self-representing) as an ethnic group, a nation within a nation, and a sovereign nation. We suggest that given the limits imposed on Puerto Rican locations, effective political strategies should include both incorporation (with critical distance) and differentiation. The breaking of the binary is already a step in another direction that facilitates looking beyond nationalist and colonialist discourses to recognize other political agendas (women, gays, Afro-Puerto Ricans) not organized along the colonized/metropolis axis, which may facilitate the production of a more inclusive body politic for Puerto Ricans residing anywhere. By this last comment we do not mean to suggest that Puerto Rico's colonial insertion is irrelevant to these other political subjectivities. Instead, we suggest that the dichotomy fails to explain these locations' complexities and thus fails to provide them with transforming possibilities.

Puerto Ricans as Racial/Colonial Subjects

In the United States, the hierarchization of ethnic groups has been hegemonized by male elites of European descent ("Whites") throughout a long historical process of colonial/racial domination of Native Americans, enslaved Africans, and migrant populations.[27] Even after independence, when the formal juridical/military control of the state passed from the imperial power to a newly independent state, white elites continued to control economic and political structures. This continuity of power from colonial to postcolonial times allowed these hegemonic groups to exclude people of color from the categories of full citizenship in the imaginary community of the "nation," thus affirming a "coloniality of power"[28] within the existing and expanding borders of the new state. The civil, political, and social rights that citizenship provided to the members of the nation were selectively expanded over time to the white working classes and to white middle-class women. However, groups with colonial histories in the United States remained as "second-class citizens," never having full access to citizen rights, despite a formal recognition of these rights as naturalized in legal discourse.

 During the first half of the twentieth century, the word *ethnic* referred to cultural differences among white European groups (e.g., Italian, Irish, German) while *race* was used to refer to distinct cultural (as well as ethnic and/or national) groups from non-European origins (e.g., Blacks, Asians). Since the 1960s, *ethnic* in the United States has become a code word for race as a result of the civil rights movement.[29] Rather than characterizing groups along racial lines (which had been linked to racist and antidemocratic practices of segregation), the more conciliatory terms of *ethnic* and *migrant* were used instead. This emerging dominant discourse was elaborated by Nathan Glazer and Daniel P. Moynihan in their now classic *Beyond the Melting Pot: The Negroes, Puerto Ricans, Jews, Italians, and Irish of New York City.*[30]

In Glazer and Moynihan's formulation, the experiences of people of color in the United States are equated to the white European migrations dating from the beginning of the twentieth century. The main assumption is that by transmuting the terms of discrimination from racial to ethnic, groups such as Puerto Ricans and African Americans will suffer the ordinary pressures of any incoming European ethnic group and eventually become economically incorporated as were earlier waves of white migrants. This approach obliterates the history of racial/colonial oppression experienced by, for example, African Americans and Puerto Ricans and ignores each group's specific colonial incorporation into the U.S. body politic.[31] In the African American case, barriers to full social, economic, and political participation stem from a long colonial history of slavery and subsequent marginalization under a segregationist regime.

Puerto Ricans were submitted to a colonial regime that expropriated the most desirable land and incorporated the people as cheap labor in sugar plantations during the first half of the century and as low-wage manufacturing workers in Puerto Rico and the United States during the past four decades. In this sense, Puerto Ricans and African Americans are not simply migrants or ethnic groups but rather colonial/racialized subjects in the United States.[32]

At the same time, Puerto Ricans present a puzzle to the rigid racial definitions structuring American social and political relationships. A mixed racial community ranging in "color" from white to black—and everything in between—Puerto Ricans cannot be fixed as a single racial category (White or Black). Despite this racial ambiguity, increased contact with Puerto Ricans in large cities like New York provided the context to redefine Puerto Ricans as a racialized Other of a different kind.[33] Thus, Puerto Ricans became a *new* racialized subject (Spanish-speaking, racially hybrid), different from Whites and Blacks, but sharing with the latter a subordinate position to the former.[34] This shift of perception was represented and projected onto mainstream culture by Hollywood films during the late 1950s and through the 1970s, and famously articulated by *West Side Story*.[35] Through this tale of the perils of miscegenation, Puerto Ricans were transformed into a nationally recognized racialized minority, no longer to be confused with Asians, Blacks, or Chicanos.[36]

The racialization of Puerto Ricans was the result of a long historical process of colonial/racial subordination on the island and the mainland.[37] Although the racism experienced by Afro-Puerto Ricans in many instances can be more overt than that experienced by light-skinned Puerto Ricans, "white" Puerto Ricans are also racialized as an inferior group[38] by at least two mechanisms: open identification with the group, and/or by assumption of origin as registered through the use of Spanish, surname, and/or accent. This highlights the social rather than biological character of racial classifications. Regardless of phenotype, all Puerto Ricans are considered a racial group in the social imaginary of most Americans, accompanied by racist stereotypes such as laziness, violence, stupidity, and dirtiness.[39] The derogatory naming of Puerto Ricans as "spiks" in the symbolic field of New York designates the negative symbolic capital attached to identifying, or being identified, as a Puerto Rican.[40]

The racialization of Puerto Ricans in the United States is also intimately connected with the labor migrations during the second half of the century to New York City and other northeastern and midwestern cities.

In New York's racial/ethnic division of labor, Puerto Ricans occupied the economic niche of low-wage manufacturing jobs. By 1960, more than 50 percent of Puerto Ricans in New York were incorporated as low-wage labor in this sector. During the 1960s, Puerto Ricans' successful struggles for labor rights made them "too expensive" for the increasingly informalized manufacturing sector; simultaneously, the deindustrialization of New York led to the loss of thousands of manufacturing jobs. Most of these manufacturing industries moved to peripheral regions around the world, while those that stayed in New York operated in a more informal way. The manufacturing industry, in constant need of cheap labor, relied heavily on new Latino immigrants, legal or illegal, that counted on even fewer citizenship rights than internal colonial subjects such as Puerto Ricans. The expulsion of Puerto Ricans from manufacturing jobs and the racist educational system that excluded Puerto Ricans from the best public schools produced a redundant labor force that could not reenter the formal labor market. This led to the formation of what some have called the Puerto Rican "underclass," which we prefer to call a displaced racialized/colonial population.[41] Unable to find jobs, many Puerto Ricans developed survival strategies, legal or illegal, to overcome the crisis.

Concurrently, it is important to highlight that for many Americans living outside cities with large Puerto Rican populations, who do not have an awareness of the diversity of Latino migrations, Puerto Ricans can sometimes be confused or homogenized into other ethnic groups or simply referred to by the generic "Latino" (a racialized term as well but with no cultural or historical specificity). In contrast to the awareness of African Americans, for example, a group invested with great symbolic value as part of nation-building "historical" metanarratives (e.g., the Civil War, the civil rights movement), general unawareness concerning American colonial history, particularly the enormous impact of the Spanish-American War and the civil rights struggles of Puerto Ricans in the United States, has historically contributed to a context of Puerto Rican invisibility. In this sense, it may sometimes be more accurate to suggest that in most American cultural and political spaces, Puerto Ricans are rendered invisible as an internal colonial population despite one hundred years of shared colonial history. Conversely, when Puerto Ricans are recognized as distinct, they are represented as racialized subjects, with little—if any—understanding of the group's distinct relationship to the United States as a colonial possession under congressional jurisdiction. This lack of symbolic relevance is one of the greatest political problems facing Puerto Rican self-determination today, since very few Americans will contest an imposed unilateral "solution" by Congress to legally resolve the question of Puerto Rico's status.

Puerto Rico's Double Coloniality of Power

While all Puerto Ricans suffer from different degrees of racialization and exclusion as second-class citizens in the United States, subordinated social groups in Puerto Rico suffer from a double coloniality of power. The first coloniality of power—supported by racist structures and exercised from the metropolis—severely constrains the possibility of self-government and allows Congress to unilaterally determine all aspects related to Puerto Rico. The second, and much less discussed form, is a coloniality of power enforced by the local elites (the "blanquitos" or "little whities") over local hegemonic political, cultural, and economic spaces, sometimes under the banner of a nationalist ideology. The fact that an end to colonial relationships between countries does not entail the dismantling of class, racial, and gender hierarchies within the frontiers of the new state (internal colonialism) constitutes one of the greatest challenges to decolonizing projects at the close of the twentieth century.

The Latin American experience of the past two centuries shows that an independent state does not guarantee a radical transformation of the old colonial racial and class hierarchies. As Richard Harvey Brown has written:

> The political and cognitive processes go on between elites and others *within* states much as they did between colonizers and colonized. Indeed, colonists from old nations and state builders within new ones both operate at a critical ideological juncture, for nowhere are the notions of normal, familiar action and given systems in greater jeopardy than at the external frontier of the empire or the internal frontier of the state. . . . Thus, the process of state formation may be seen as a kind of internal colonization, a maintenance of identity and authenticity through cultural labeling and suppression.[42]

After the wars of independence that took place throughout Latin America during the nineteenth century, there was a transfer of power from the metropolis to the white creole elites but little transformation of the relations between classes, races, and genders. In the few contexts where a call for social revolution was part of the independence struggle, such as in Cuba during the late 1890s, a U.S. intervention made sure that independence was nominal and social revolution impossible. A similar process occurred in Puerto Rico after World War II. The colonial reforms allowed Puerto Ricans to elect their own governor rather than be ruled by a white American governor appointed by the president. However, this reform not only did not transform the colonial control of the U.S. Congress over the island but left Puerto Rico's racial and class hierarchies largely intact. The initial possibility of social revolution opened up by the 1898 invasion was eventually narrowed down as the Puerto Rican white elites monopolized the new local political and economic spaces. Although racial exclusion has not been exercised in Puerto Rico through apartheid mechanisms, such as in the South in the United States, Afro-Puerto Ricans and mulattoes are excluded from, or subordinated to, racist, classist, and gendered power structures. Ironically, some of the few (even if extremely limited) mechanisms of class and social mobility available for all Puerto Ricans, including Blacks, are those mandated by the colonial state such as the public school system.

The historical continuity between the first (colonialist/colonized) coloniality of power and the second (internal colonialism) demands a need to redefine what is meant by decolonization. Contemporary nation-states such as Guatemala represent pointed examples of persistent colonial relationships. The demands of militant and internally colonized "ethnic" Mayas are often aimed at the racist structures that legitimize social inequities within the state's borders. In this sense, the decolonization of the Mayas and their access to full citizen rights require the inclusion of indigenous people at all levels of political participation and the resistance to co-optation under the guise of identity politics. Rigoberta Menchú has commented:

> Recently, the FDNG [Guatemala Democratic Front] proposed creating an indigenous ministry in Guatemala. We all came out against it. Why? Because it would be returning to apartheid Guatemala. The Ministry of Defense and all other ministries would be in the hands of non-indigenous people, and there would be a tiny bureaucratic office for Maya peoples. This would be a mistake.[43]

A decolonization project in the Caribbean cannot be understood only as a process of self-determination at a formal political level, but must be seen as a process of radical transformation of the old colonial hierarchies, that is, the eradication of the racial, gender, sexual, and class hierarchies built throughout a long colonial history.

Postmodernist Strategies: Rican Style
New Political Subjects

The emergence of a postmodern state of affairs has inaugurated new political subjects whose agenda is often not contemplated by traditional nationalist (or colonial) political discourses. Intellectuals invested in a political project critical of the unfulfilled promises and hierarchies of modernity (the "posmodernos" in island terminology) are also becoming more visible. Thus, new cultural and political practices, social movements, and countercolonial and national discourses are questioning the patriarchal, racist, and homophobic premises of much nationalist political thinking and practice, including those of the metropolitan state itself.

The fissures between subjects assumed to hold identical subject positions (that is, "women") are investigated in Yolanda Martínez's "Deconstructing Puerto Ricanness through Sexuality: Female Counternarratives on Puerto Rican Identity." This essay explores some of the tensions among Puerto Rican women on the basis of class, race, and political ideology, referred to in Jiménez-Muñoz's text, through the literary texts of two women novelists of diverse class and ideological positions. Martínez follows a double strategy in the reading of these texts in order to foreground the difficulties of incorporating "women" into hegemonic national narratives during the early twentieth century. The first strategy focuses on comparing the texts of working-class internationalist Luisa Capetillo and bourgeois nationalist Ana Roque. Capetillo as an internationalist worker organizer is a dissenting voice in the articulation of the "nation," but the explicitly nationalist narrative by Roque is also incapable of assigning one (unitary) subject position to all women. The second strategy reads women's previously ignored voices against the canonical male literary proto-nationalist production (exemplified by Antonio S. Pedreira and novelist Manuel Zeno Gandía), thus calling into question the alleged continuity of a national project in Puerto Rico from the late nineteenth century to the mid-1930s.

The texts by Martínez and Jiménez propose that Puerto Rican women have made use of a wide range of representational (textual and political) practices without restricting themselves to nationalist discourses. In this process, women's locations, desires, and subjectivities are revealed as multiple, contradictory, and not reducible to the colonial and nationalist discourses that have historically sought to contain them (that is, the reproductive, the body to be seduced). In this sense, even when it can be argued that Puerto Ricans constitute a national formation of a specific kind, national narratives often collide with each other. Thus, while each narrative may have the attributes and continuity of the subject,[44] they often articulate different subjects altogether or contradictions within the subject, only superficially equated by the categories of language.

In part fostered by a relatively large "sexilio"[45] to the metropolis and a growing public discourse around sexuality generated by the AIDS epidemic, Puerto Rican gay and lesbian cultural production and scholarship are currently producing some of the most challenging readings of cultural identity, nationalism, colonialism, gender, and migration. Thus, in Manuel Guzmán's "Pa' La Escuelita con Mucho Cuida'o y por la Orillita," the strategies for Latino cultural resistance are articulated through the experiences of Latino gays and lesbians who patronize New York's most long-lasting bar, "The Little School." At the same time, Guzmán's analysis of La Escuelita as a site of resistance is intertwined with a personal narrative of identity, producing a new form of narrative in Puerto Rican historiography that refers to multiple levels of experience usually articulated as dichotomous (high culture/popular culture, the personal/political, Puerto Rican/gringo). Through writing the subject as unstable, Guzmán ultimately abandons the category of "Puerto Rican realness" (discarded as a social "malaise") in order to affirm an ethnic/sexual hyphenated identity not contemplated by either hegemonic accounts of migration or national identity. Within this formulation, Latino gay codes of resistance can articulate other forms of cultural syncretism, including the formation of a multi-Latino cultural imaginary (that is, through the use of drag as an encoder of sexual and cultural memory), further stretching the borders of Latin American (queer) "nations" beyond nationalism.

Puerto Ricans' *Jaiba* Politics

The crisis of both nationalist and pro-colonial discourses, the potential American disavowal of its responsibility in (re)producing deteriorating Puerto Rican possibilities, the emergence of new social movements, and the hegemony of transtatal capitalism beg the burning question of participation and transformation. What are some strategies for effective and transformative political participation? How can we begin to deconstruct the colonialism/nationalism dichotomy in our political praxis in order to open other possibilities? Are broad-based coalitions beyond nationalism and colonialism possible? We think so. Majority responses to both nationalist and colonialist discourses during the past fifty years have insisted on an ambiguous and guarded position that articulates a politics of caution that can serve as the basis for a different kind of anticolonial politics. This practice, often referred to locally as *jaibería*, anticipates current postmodern debates and concepts such as "mimicry without identification"[46] and "postmodernist parody."[47]

Decades before the emergence of postmodernism, Puerto Rican popular sectors developed political strategies very close to what today some theorists refer to as "postmodernist" politics and culture. It can be argued that Puerto Ricans during the twentieth century have often deployed a strategy of "mimicry" (adoption of "American" discourses and styles) to struggle against the most oppressive elements of colonial rule. In using this term, we do not mean to erase historical junctures of confrontations with the U.S. regime, particularly during the 1930s and 1970s, when pro-independence nationalist organizing was a crucial part of setting the tone for later negotiations between the United States and the Popular Democratic Party. What we aim to point out, however, is that the strategy of mimicry has been historically and consistently successful in obtaining political concessions that have resulted in the improvement of everyday life for Puerto Ricans.

According to Diana Fuss in her essay on Frantz Fanon,[48] there is a tendency within postcolonial and psychoanalytic discourse to distinguish between the practices of mimicry and masquerade. While in psychoanalysis, masquerade is understood as the unconscious assumption of a role, mimicry, according to Homi K. Bhabha, is understood as a colonial strategy of subjugation. Fuss, however, stresses that there can be a mimicry of subversion where the deliberate performance of a role does not entail identification. The performance's contexts thus become crucial in determining its subversive potential:

> But the point to be registered is that imitation may either institute or gratify an unconscious identification, it can and does frequently exceed the logic of that identification. Put another way, identification with the other is neither a necessary precondition nor an inevitable outcome of imitation. For Fanon, it is politically imperative to insist upon an instrumental difference between imitation and identification, because it is precisely politics that emerges in the dislocated space between them.[49]

It is significant for our proposals that in both Fanon's and Fuss's texts, the most powerful example of subversive mimicry is that of the Algerian nationalist woman militant who "passes" as a Europeanized subject in order to advance the cause of national liberation. We can associate this mimicry of subversion with women not because women necessarily do it more often (or better) than men but because femininity itself is coded as artifice while masculinity is the "natural" (non-imitative) term of the polarity. Thus, to suggest a "feminization" of Puerto Rican politics at this juncture is to suggest that neither confrontation nor a rational discourse of the benefits of Puerto Rico to the United States will result in any positive changes to the current situation. We are affirming that those strategies associated with women by the patriarchal imagination are part of the anticolonialist discursive arsenal for rethinking a reflexive and seductive Puerto Rican politics. As Grosfoguel has written elsewhere,

> Rather than seeking to violently impose its will in sterile confrontations that lead to self-destruction, a feminization of political practices would deploy a pragmatic and realistic style of politics which stems from the recognition that peripheral countries are in an unequal relationship of power, constraining the possibility of achieving every objective.[50]

"Feminization" here is not inscribed in the traditional colonial discourses' binary opposition of colonial subjects/feminine versus imperial power/masculine. Instead, feminization refers to a nonessentialist political strategy that has been practiced by many oppressed subjects (organized through different categories such as men, women, gays, lesbians, Afro-Americans, Afro-Caribbeans) in diverse contexts of extreme subordination and repression in the metropolis as well as in the periphery. In the Caribbean context, a patriarchal imaginary of virility and confrontational politics has mediated left-wing political strategies whose outcomes have normally been political defeat and economic disaster. Thus, a "feminization" of political practices refers to a positive resignification, generalization, and extension of political strategies such as seduction, ambiguity, and negotiation, associated historically with women in patriarchal discourses, to a wide range of political struggles.[51] It is the strategy of those forced to struggle in the terrain of the adversary. This strategy is especially relevant in the present context of globalization where there is no absolute "outside" to transtatal capitalism.[52]

A strategy of Puerto Rican "mimicry" without identification is perhaps one of the most viable means of demanding U.S. responsibility and decolonization without losing a sense of autonomy from the United States. The recent devastation of the AIDS epidemic, commented on by Alberto Sandoval Sánchez, is also an important context in which to examine how Puerto Ricans have used colonialist resources and discourses for their benefit at the same time that radical transformation faces the limits of colonialism.[53] It is, however, precisely within these ambiguities and tensions that political theories for new political projects must be sought, not in the master narratives of independence and nationalism— except if they prove to be useful, which at this point they have not.

The notion of postmodern parody holds a similar allure as a trope for Puerto Rican politics since, according to Linda Hutcheon, this concept allows for a complicitous critique (or in Grosfoguel's term, "subversive complicity")[54] where cultural practice articulates a critique of capitalist societies within the terms of that society:

> What I mean by "parody" here—as elsewhere in this study—is *not* the ridiculing imitation of the standard theories and definitions that are rooted in eighteenth-century theories of wit. The collective weight of parodic *practice* suggests a redefinition of parody as repetition with critical distance that allows ironic signalling of difference at the very heart of similarity.[55]

Puerto Rican political practice does not posit an "outside" to capitalist and consumer relations but rather parodies them through the articulation of diverse postwork subjectivities, illegal forms of work, and hustling of diverse state-generated incomes.[56] Puerto Rican postwork subjectivity is created by the confluence of lacking access to salaried work, high consumption habits generated by an increased standard of living, and the United States' need to maintain Puerto Rico as a showcase for the rest of the world, even when they must subsidize the show. The fact that Puerto Ricans feel "entitled" to federal transfers entails both a recognition that "work" is increasingly unavailable in postindustrial societies and that under capitalist organization work is in fact a somewhat "undesirable" activity offering low wages and little satisfaction. Within this context, diverse claims to "enjoyment" rather than work may (there is no guarantee) become a proposal for a postwork, postcapitalist society. Another proposal is to reduce labor time from eight to six hours per day, without a reduction in salary. This could reduce unemployment by increasing the availability of jobs.[57]

Entitlement and a postwork attitude among Puerto Ricans do not remit us to racist perceptions of Puerto Ricans as lazy and therefore reluctant to exercise citizenship rights. It is instead a stance against a capitalist division of work in which it seems preferable to fake an illness to obtain Social Security benefits than to become sick or to age prematurely working at a polluting factory or maddening Fordist assembly line, and to claim citizenship rights to obtain some state income than to continue unemployed searching for a fictitious or nonexistent job in a deindustrialized city. This pragmatic assertion is not a celebration—it does not necessarily entail a practice of collective transformation—but it refers to some of the specific strategies used by Puerto Ricans in negotiating the system in its own terms. Social rights are an important component of citizen's rights that in a postindustrial/postwork society should be expanded in order to include a social salary for those marginalized from the labor force. Unable to produce new sources of jobs, deindustrialized countries such as France, where the RMI (Revenue Minimum d'Insertion) program provides a social salary for the unemployed, recognize social rights. However, in a Protestant-work-ethic society like the United States, not only do these programs not exist, but those few programs that exist to ameliorate the social conditions of the marginalized population are under a constant threat of eradication. In this sense, Puerto Rican entitlement attitudes and postwork subjectivity imply a pragmatic resistance to capitalism and colonialism and an assumption that there is no outside/inside dichotomy nor an outside to consumer culture. Yet, this pragmatic recognition has made survival *and* subversion possible, despite its contradictions. As Hutcheon suggests,

> It must be admitted from the start that this is a strange kind of critique, one bound up, too, with its own complicity *with* power and domination, one that acknowledges that it cannot escape implication in that which it nevertheless still wants to analyze and maybe even undermine.[58]

Lastly, the popular tradition of *jaibería* provides us with an indigenous metaphor for an attitude toward negotiation and transformation. The word *jaibería* has its origins in the term *jaiba*, or mountain crab, who in going forward moves sideways. Within the Puerto Rican usage, *jaibería* refers to collective practices of nonconfrontation and evasion (the "*unjú*," roughly translated as "sure . . . no problem"), of taking dominant discourse literally in order to subvert it for one's purpose, of doing whatever one sees fit not as a head-on collision ("winning" is impossible) but a bit under the table, that is, through other means. This form of addressing power has been the subject of much enraged nationalist writing. Antonio S. Pedreira referred to it as a "verbal contraband" and "ill-intentioned malice."[59] Puerto Rican patriot José de Diego, for example, deplored the lack of virility implicit in the Puerto Rican's inability to say "no" as a reprehensible Puerto Rican political and cultural habit:

> Generally, a Puerto Rican never . . . knows how to say NO: "We'll see," "I'll study the issue," "I'll deal with it later." When a Puerto Rican uses these expressions one must understand that he is saying NO, although at most, he is linking the YES to the NO, and making from an affirmative and a negative adverb a conditional conjunction, ambiguous, nebulous, in which the will fluctuates . . . like an aimless bird without a nest over the plains of a desert.[60]

Mid-twentieth-century writer René Marqués popularized this ambiguity as a negative "trait" in his infamous essay "El puertorriqueño dócil" ("The Docile Puerto Rican").[61] In this sense, ambiguity, lack of virility, and ambivalence have often all been noted by nationalist writers to explain Puerto Ricans' inability to form a nation-state. In our formulation, these three traits are revalorized as useful resources in negotiating colonialism and subordination, although often with less than ideal results. As Doris Sommer has argued, "Why is it political only to resist? Are deals never struck, concessions never made? . . . Is there no—perhaps post-modern—politics that acknowledges insoluble tensions as dynamic sites of construction?"[62] It is also important to note that there can be purely complicit uses of *jaibería* that fail to advance any collective agenda. Yet, *jaibería* as a form of complicitous critique or subversive complicity points to an acknowledgment of being in a disadvantaged position within a particular field of power. A nonheroic position, *jaibería* favors endurance over physical strength, and privileges ambiguity over clarity. Although it has been mistaken for docility, it is instead an active, low-intensity strategy to obtain the maximum benefits of a situation with the minimum blood spilled.

The proposed reframing of these questions is advanced not only by "postmodernist" theorists but also by other scholars such as Immanuel Wallerstein[63] when he criticizes the old left liberal ideology of acquiring state power and rationally managing the difficulties of the system for the benefit of all. This liberal strategy has tended to destroy antisystemic social movements, transforming them into conservative nation-state institutions trapped in a developmentalist illusion. Given the failure of socialist liberalism, Wallerstein suggests other ways to contest capitalist hegemony:

> A multi-front strategy by a multiplicity of groups, each complex and internally democratic, will have one tactical weapon at its disposal which may be overwhelming for the defenders of the status quo. It is the weapon of taking the old liberal ideology literally and demanding its universal fulfillment . . . one can push on every front for the increased democratization of decision-making, as well as the elimination of all pockets of informal and unacknowledged privilege. What I am talking about here is the tactic of overloading the system by taking its pretensions and its claims more seriously than the dominant forces wish them to be taken. This is exactly the opposite of the tactic of managing the difficulties of the system.[64]

The tactic of taking the old liberal ideology "literally" and demanding its universal fulfillment is a form of parodic or mimetic politics. It is the strategy practiced today not only by the Sandinistas in Nicaragua and the FMLN in El Salvador but also in Puerto Rico since the turn of the century.[65] Many social movements in Puerto Rico during the twentieth century practiced such a "postmodern" or *jaibería* strategy by literally adopting metropolitan discourse and demanding civil rights already recognized in the metropolitan constitution.[66]

The notions of *jaibería*, parody, and mimesis, however, all point to strategies that are most effective in contexts where Puerto Ricans are by far the most disempowered part of the equation.[67] The adoption of these practices is also a way of acknowledging the contemporary (worldwide) political defeat of alternative political and cultural propositions "outside capitalism" that are potentially more egalitarian.[68] If mass movements contesting the current geopolitical and economic hegemonies throughout the world existed, our reading of the situation would clearly be different. Unfortunately, given the current coordinates of power, Puerto Ricans must develop strategies to address the growing deterioration of everyday life, both on the island and in the United States, by seeking increased representation within the centers of power. Puerto Rico's complex set of problems, unlike the political parties seem to suggest, will not be solved by the victory of any "ideal" (Commonwealth, independence, or statehood). None of the dominant political "solutions" (or "formulas" as they are interestingly called) scratch the surface of the power inequities that will remain after any political change in definition. These proposals will only rearrange the current players' ability to administer a colony, neocolony, or impoverished U.S. state.

The task of reimagining Puerto Rican politics is, of course, not free of particular ideologies or contextual constraints. A further difficulty is the sense among postmodernist intellectuals that in some ways Puerto Ricans have the dubious honor of being "postcolonial" colonial subjects. Thus, how can a postcolonial politics be imagined as a basis for a political practice without falling into the trap of altogether ignoring the fact that Puerto Rico is a colonial configuration? In this sense, intellectuals invested in a decolonization project for Puerto Ricans must seek models that speak to the specific ambiguities of our location. The essays in this collection contribute to this ongoing and inconclusive debate.

Notes

We would like to thank Doris Sommer, Ada Muntaner, Mariano Negrón-Portillo, and Julio Ramos for their thoughtful comments on and recommendations for this introductory text.

1. For a cinematic treatment and partial pretexts to this book, see Frances Negrón-Muntaner's films/videos *Brincando el charco: Portrait of a Puerto Rican* (1994, distributed by Women Make Movies and the Independent Television Service), *Puerto Rican I.D.* (1995, distributed by Signal to Noise and the Independent Television Service), and *Homeless Diaries* (1996, distributed by Receding Coastline Pictures).

2. Arcadio Díaz Quiñones, *La memoria rota* (Río Piedras: Huracán, 1993).

3. The Estado Libre Asociado, founded in 1952, made Puerto Rico a self-managed colonial possession. It created a parliament (house of representatives and senate) and allowed for popular elections for all local government posts. However, Puerto Rico's insertion into the American body politic is determined by its inclusion in the Constitution's territorial clause, which clearly states that all local decisions can be mandated by Congress. The sole Puerto Rican representative in Congress had (and still has) no vote.

4. An example of this is the recent eradication of the 936 Section of the U.S. Internal Revenue Code exempting U.S. corporations from paying federal taxes on profit remittances from the island to the mainland. The program will phase out by the year 2006.

5. This is an ironic pun on the official slogan affirming that Puerto Rico is the "shining star of the Caribbean." For a critique of this official ideology, see Poli Marichal, *Burundanga Boricua*, video, 1987.

6. Ramón Grosfoguel, "Plebiscitos, 'colonias modernas,' y el Caribe," *Diálogo*, Mar. 1996, 27.

7. Ramón Grosfoguel, "Feminizando la política," *El Nuevo Día*, July 24, 1990, 51.

8. For a further discussion of this conceptualization, see Ramón Grosfoguel, "Caribbean Colonial Immigrants in the Metropoles: A Research Agenda," *Centro* 7, 1 (1995): 82–95.

9. Patrick L. Baker, *Centring the Periphery: Chaos, Order and the Ethnohistory of Dominica* (Montreal and Kingston: McGill-Queen's University Press, 1994), 59.

10. Grosfoguel, "Plebiscitos, 'colonias modernas,' y el Caribe."

11. Ramón Grosfoguel, "El Caribe y la 'Independencia realmente existente,'" *Diálogo*, May 1996, 26.

12. Miriam Muñiz, "Más allá de Puerto Rico 936, Puerto Rico USA y Puerto Rico INC: Notas para una crítica al discurso del desarrollo," *Bordes* 1 (1995): 54–66.

13. Matthew Carr, "El Salvador: Two Cheers for Democracy," *Race and Class* 36, 1 (1994): 6.

14. As quoted in Ramón Grosfoguel, "Suicidio o Redefinición," *El Nuevo Día*, June 25, 1990, 55; and Grosfoguel, "Feminizando la política," 51.

15. Orlando Patterson, "The Culture of Caution," *New Republic*, Nov. 27, 1995, 26.

16. Ramón Grosfoguel, "Confesiones de un Alienado," *El Nuevo Día*, July 24, 1990, 51.

17. William Branignin, "Palau Independent of United States," *Philadelphia Inquirer*, Oct. 3, 1994, 8.

18. Carlos Pabón, "De Albizu a Madonna: Para armar y desarmar la modernidad," *Bordes* 1 (1995): 22–40.

19. Immanuel Wallerstein, "The Concept of National Development, 1917–1989: Elegy and Requiem," *American Behavioral Scientist* 35, 4/5 (Mar.–June 1992): 517.

20. Jacques Lacan, *Ecrits* (New York: W. W. Norton and Co., 1977), 1–7.

21. Celeste Olalquiaga, *Megalopolis: Contemporary Cultural Sensibilities* (Minneapolis: University of Minnesota Press, 1992), 84.

22. For further discussion regarding different articulations of racist ideologies, see Darcy Ribeiro and Mercio Gomes, "Ethnicity and Civilization," *Dialectical Anthropology* 21 (1996): 217–38.

23. Benedict Anderson, *Imagined Communities* (London: Verso, 1983), 15.

24. Rajagopalan Radhakrishnan, *Diasporic Mediations: Between Home and Location* (Minneapolis: University of Minnesota Press, 1996), xxiv.

25. María Milagros López, "Post-Work Selves and Entitlement Attitudes in Peripheral Post-Industrial Puerto Rico," *Social Text* 38 (spring 1994): 111–33.

26. A few decades ago, Puerto Ricans in the Northeast could claim a sense of "territory" within the metropolis since most migrants settled in New York. New migration patterns, however, are destabilizing these spatial correlations, thus making the migratory experience increasingly deterritorialized/reterritorialized.

27. For a discussion on colonial/racial domination as it applies to Puerto Ricans in the United States, see Ramón Grosfoguel and Chloé S. Georas, "The Racialization of Latino Caribbean Migrants in the New York Metropolitan Area," *Centro* 8, 1–2 (1996): 190–201.

28. Aníbal Quijano, "América Latina en la economía mundial," unpublished manuscript, 1993. For a discussion on the use of Quijano's concept "coloniality of power" as it applies to Puerto Ricans on the island, see Kelvin Santiago-Valles, "On the Historical Links between Coloniality, the Violent Production of the 'Native' Body, and the Manufacture of Pathology," *Centro* 7, 1 (1995): 108–18; as it applies to Puerto Ricans in the United States, see Grosfoguel and Georas, "The Racialization of Latino Caribbean Migrants."

29. Grosfoguel and Georas, "The Racialization of Latino Caribbean Migrants."

30. Nelson Glazer and Daniel P. Moynihan, *Beyond the Melting Pot: The Negroes, Puerto Ricans, Jews, Italians, and Irish of New York City* (Cambridge: MIT Press, 1963).

31. Grosfoguel and Georas, "The Racialization of Latino Caribbean Migrants."

32. Ibid.

33. Ibid.

34. The literature on migration and ethnic relations has traditionally treated Puerto Ricans as an ethnic group. The conceptualization of Puerto Ricans as a new racial category in the social imaginary of white Americans distinct from Asians, Blacks, or Native Ameri-

cans is developed in Grosfoguel and Georas, "The Racialization of Latino Caribbean Migrants."

35. For a critique of Puerto Rican representations in a variety of mediums, including mainstream and independent films during the past four decades, see Frances Negrón-Muntaner, *Passing Memories: Puerto Ricans and Assimilation to American Culture and Politics*, unpublished manuscript. For a more in-depth look at *West Side Story*, see Alberto Sandoval, "A Puerto Rican Reading of 'America': *West Side Story*," *Jump Cut* 39 (1994): 59–66.

36. Grosfoguel and Georas, "The Racialization of Latino Caribbean Migrants."

37. See Kelvin Santiago, *Subject People and Colonial Discourses* (Albany: State University of New York Press, 1994); and Blanca Vázquez, "Puerto Ricans and the Media: A Personal Statement," *Centro* 3, 1 (1991): 5–15.

38. This point is developed in Grosfoguel and Georas, "The Racialization of Latino Caribbean Migrants."

39. Ibid.

40. Ibid.

41. Ibid.

42. Richard Harvey Brown, "Cultural Representation and State Formation: Discourses of Ethnicity, Nationality, and Political Community," *Dialectical Anthropology* 21 (1996): 265–97.

43. "An Interview with Rigoberta Menchú Tum," *NACLA*, 29, 6 (May/June 1996): 6–10, 8.

44. Etienne Balibar, "The Nation Form: History and Ideology," in Etienne Balibar and Immanuel Wallerstein, eds., *Race, Nation, Class: Ambiguous Identities* (New York: Verso, 1988).

45. The term *sexile*, coined by Manuel Guzmán, refers to a specifically gay and lesbian island migration to the United States. These migrants point to homophobia as part of their decision to migrate.

46. Diana Fuss, "Interior Colonies: Frantz Fanon and the Politics of Identification," *Diacritics* 24 (summer-fall 1994): 20–42.

47. Linda Hutcheon, *The Politics of Postmodernism* (London: Routledge, 1989).

48. Fuss, "Interior Colonies."

49. Ibid., 28–29.

50. Grosfoguel, "Feminizando la política," 51; translation by the author.

51. Ibid.

52. Ibid.

53. The AIDS crisis underlines both Puerto Rico's colonial situation in relation to the United States and the possibility of transferring resources from the United States to Puerto Rico to combat the epidemic. Thus, the "air bridge" functioned in multiple ways: migration of HIV-positive Puerto Ricans to the United States in search of better medical treatment and support networks, formation of activist communities linking U.S. and island-based AIDS activists, sharing of resources and information, and return migration of people with AIDS from the United States to Puerto Rico. For further discussion of the ACT-UP/San Juan air-bridge phenomenon, see Frances Negrón-Muntaner's interviews with Robert Vázquez and Juan David Acosta, "Surviving Cultures: A Dialogue on AIDS and Gay Latino Politics," *Centro* 6, 2/3 (1994): 115–27; Luis "Popo" Santiago, "Twenty Years of Puerto Rican Gay Activism," *Radical America* 25, 1 (1993): 39–51; and Moisés Agosto's intervention in the film *Brincando el charco: Portrait of a Puerto Rican*.

54. Grosfoguel, "Feminizando la política," 51.

55. Linda Hutcheon, *A Poetics of Postmodernism: History, Theory, Fiction* (London: Routledge, 1988), 26.

56. María Milagros López, "Post-Work Selves and Entitlement Attitudes in Peripheral Post-Industrial Puerto Rico."

57. For a discussion on new technologies, joblessness, and new postwork alternatives, see Stanley Aronowitz and William DiFazio, *The Jobless Future* (Minneapolis: University of Minnesota Press, 1994).

58. Linda Hutcheon, *The Politics of Postmodernism*, 4.

59. Antonio S. Pedreira, *Insularismo* (Río Piedras: Editorial Edil, 1973).

60. José de Diego, "No," in *Obras Completas Tomo II* (San Juan: Editorial del Instituto de Cultura, 1966), 18. Translated by the authors.

61. René Marqués, *Ensayos* (Río Piedras: Editorial Antillana, 1972).

62. Doris Sommer, "Puerto Rico: A flote desde Hostos hasta hoy," unpublished paper.

63. Immanuel Wallerstein, "The Collapse of Liberalism," in Ralph Miliband and Leo Panitch, eds., *The Socialist Register 1992* (London: Merlin Press, 1992).

64. Ibid., 110.

65. For a discussion of this strategy in the context of Latin America, see Ramón Grosfoguel, "From Cepalismo to Neoliberalism: A World-Systems Approach to Conceptual Shifts in Latin America," *Review* (Journal of the Fernand Braudel Center) 14, 2 (1996): 131–54.

66. Grosfoguel, "Suicidio o Redefinición," 55; and "Feminizando la política," 51.

67. Ibid.

68. Grosfoguel, "From Cepalismo to Neoliberalism."

PART ONE

Challenging Nationalism

CHAPTER ONE

Puerto Rico: Surviving Colonialism and Nationalism

Mariano Negrón-Portillo

During the latter part of the nineteenth century, the Puerto Rican elite, struggling against the authoritarian Spanish rule, slowly began to articulate a political project that would serve to overcome its political and economic subordination. Although some of the Puerto Rican proprietors and professionals were either *independentistas* or annexationists,[1] the majority of the creole elite favored some form of self-government for the island during the final decades of the century. Autonomy thus appeared to be the most adequate political project for these cautious and relatively weak social sectors that lacked the cohesion and the strength to assume more radical stances.

The primary goal of the *autonomista* elite rested on displacing the local Spanish bureaucracy and obtaining a relative degree of control over the local government. Meeting this goal would hence facilitate the advancement of its own vested interests and do away with the privileges traditionally enjoyed by the Spanish proprietors, who not only were important landowners but also controlled commerce and credit.

At the core of the *autonomista* strategies lay liberalism that promoted principles such as administrative decentralization, individual rights, and separation of church and state. Liberal intellectuals were also concerned about the wretched conditions of the peasants—their misery and ignorance, and their so-called vices were stressed—and thought them in need of a social rebirth to be carried out by the creole elite. Salvador Brau, one of Puerto Rico's most distinguished nineteenth-century writers, emphasized in his essays the need to improve the "moral" and living conditions of the *campesinos*. In several essays, he addressed what he considered some of the worst social ills of the peasantry, for example, gambling, illiteracy, and concubinage. He rejected the traditional view that the *campesinos* were lazy, and emphasized the need for advancing their social regeneration through instruction and organization. By training them, Brau reasoned, the proprietors would have an educated, healthier labor force at their call: "Our working classes need instruction, moral education, professional guidance, . . . rejection of vices must be inspired among them, respect of property . . . and lastly, a deep understanding that work is not a punishment but a duty."[2] The task of regenerating the peasants, Brau stressed, was the responsibility of the proprietors.[3]

Alejandro Tapia y Rivera, one of the most progressive and better-known Puerto Rican writers of the second half of the nineteenth century, also considered the working classes to be in need of moral and social rebirth. In his *Memorias*, Tapia remarked, "what can be expected of people without instruction, even rudimentary, or moral education . . . with an enervating climate and government?"[4] In 1895, Mariano Abril, a prominent intellectual of his time, charged that the *campesinos* were being exploited by the Spaniards and reduced to hunger, weakness, and ignorance.[5] Luis Muñoz Rivera, the leader of the Partido Autonomista in the 1890s, was distressed about the hungry masses and the moral laxity displayed by the "popular conscience."[6]

This concern about the living conditions of the peasantry was not accompanied by any widespread discussion about social, "racial," or cultural characteristics of the population. Popular culture was usually described in terms of some distinctive customs or traditions, which on many occasions were considered a burden to the life of the *campesinos*.

In the late nineteenth century, liberal autonomists proposed to reform the colonial condition of the island, which would allow them to control the local government, overcome Spanish privileges in the economy, open markets, increase the availability of capital, and assist the peasants in their social rebirth. Puerto Rican unity played a key role in the cultural discourse of the *autonomistas*. When autonomy was granted in 1897–98, they were ready to mold and lead this emerging society into the future. Supposedly, it was the moment of unity of *la gran familia puertorriqueña* (the great Puerto Rican family).

But were the working classes just a pitiful mass of impoverished and passive peasants who in order to improve their lives needed the guidance of the Puerto Rican elite? Apparently this was the case when one examines the *autonomistas'* view of society. Reality, however, was much more complex. During the latter part of the century, it became evident that in the *ruralía* active social discontent was widespread, and in the larger urban centers groups had adopted belligerent forms to express some of their collective concerns.

It was not by chance that the Spanish government reinforced those institutions dealing with social and political vigilance. The introduction of the infamous Civil Guard in the early 1870s, the continuous persecution of supposedly vagrant peasants and other so-called suspicious characters, and the opening of the asylum for the mentally disturbed and the Prison of San Juan (1888) were concerted measures to deter the growing social unrest and deal with its most obvious symptoms.

The various forms of repression and the isolation that characterized the lives of many *campesinos* help explain why most of the expressions of discontent were fragmented and limited in their repercussions. Desertions, acts of arson, and other manifestations of delinquent behavior were common forms of resistance. In 1898, within the political context of the Spanish-American War and the United States' invasion of Puerto Rico, changes started to take place rapidly.

1898: Social Ruptures and New Identities

The sociopolitical context created by the United States' invasion had immediate effects on various social groups on the island. These groups saw the military conflict as an opportunity to assume a political role long denied by the authoritarian Spanish regime.

After July 25, 1898, several groups and communities expressed their dissatisfaction with the Spanish regime and their high expectations of the incoming one. A massive civilian turnout welcomed the North American troops, and many people helped the invading soldiers by harassing the Spanish forces. Incursions into various towns, to facilitate the invasion or to display the symbols of the invaders, were more than enough to confuse the Spanish.

A clear example of the attitude of the lower classes—both urban and rural—was observed in Arecibo during the transfer of authority to the U.S. military government. When the Spanish forces were departing and the U.S. flag was raised to a thunderous applause, "a black man, very excited, riding a small horse, appeared leading a mob and swinging a flag of the Union. That parade, made up of people of the worst type, went through the town, seemingly possessed by the spirit of the anarchist mobs."[7] But most striking were the activities held by numerous groups of peasants who quickly engaged in acts of civil violence and destruction against a good number of proprietors. These acts may have been the first massive insubordination in Puerto Rican history.[8] The attacks carried out by these groups were mainly directed against Spanish landowners and merchants who were singled out by the peasants as the main beneficiaries of the predominant economic system. Puerto Rican proprietors, however, were not excluded from the onslaught.

This impressive social upheaval made it clear that among the working classes antagonistic ways of expressing social aspirations and animosities would no longer be easily silenced. Although the peasants' insubordination came to an end in 1900—for various reasons that primarily included the harsh measures adopted by the government—the unexpected activism initiated a transformation in the way political and social differences were expressed and debated in Puerto Rico. After 1900, new outlets for political expression and organization were explored constantly.

The traditional patterns of coerced deference that had a shaky hold on social relations on the island during the nineteenth century were radically altered. If there was any element of truth in the conception proposed by nationalist leader Pedro Albizu Campos of *la vieja felicidad colectiva* (the old collective happiness) during the Spanish regime, it was shattered in 1898. A historical discontinuity had just started.

At this point, and before the new groups are discussed, it is necessary to examine briefly the emergence of annexationism as a force of cardinal importance in the history of Puerto Rico. Annexation sympathizers were present in many of the struggles against Spanish authoritarianism in the late nineteenth century. Most of their political incursions, as well as their conspiracies against the regime, were carried out under a mantle of disguise that allowed them to protect their identities.

In 1899, several annexationists who had enjoyed a relatively long relationship with the United States joined the most progressive group of the *autonomistas*[9] and founded the Partido Republicano, a pro-statehood party, which became the second most important political force on the island.

Although many leaders of the Partido Republicano, as well as other politicians and intellectuals of different political backgrounds, had a limited understanding of the principles of colonialism, they knew that the U.S. government recognized rights that they considered instrumental in achieving the modernization of the Puerto Rican society. Under the leadership of José Celso Barbosa, and particularly in the early twentieth cen-

tury, the *republicanos* came to expect a transformation of the existing social order in accordance with the liberal postulates of the U.S. system. Although conservative economic interests were present, the ideals of social
mobility, fundamental rights for all citizens, and the development of republican institutions of government continued to prevail in the Partido
Republicano up to the early 1920s.[10]

When the peasants' upheaval of 1898–1900 came to an end, political
activism and social discontent continued. After 1900, however, new and
more complex actors emerged. Whereas in rural municipalities riots,
shoot-outs, scuffles, and other acts of violence carried out by small
groups were still common, in urban areas groups of workers and "marginal" sectors organized to politically support the Partido Republicano
and the new government of Puerto Rico.[11]

Powerful images were produced in this period. For example, in
Ponce, a bastion of the most traditional sector of the elite, Antonio "el
negro" Guilbe, a leader of the boisterous "marginal" groups of the city,
used to walk the streets along with followers who foul-mouthed members of the elite. Astonished, the proprietors watched as this black man
paraded gun in hand, with the U.S. flag wrapped around his shoulders.
Incidents like this made for a forceful proclamation of change.

In San Juan, an organization made up of artisans and peasants who
had migrated to the city and "marginal" survivors of this precapitalist
urban center became deeply and aggressively involved in politics and
other aspects of daily life in the capital. This organization was commonly
known as the *Turbas Republicanas* (Republican mobs) and was a fundamental element in the consolidation of a social identity long ignored in
Puerto Rican history.[12]

The *turbas'* ideology clearly sustained that the people—as opposed
to the exclusionary stance of the ruling elites—should govern, and that
the heritage passed down by Spanish rule and hence those associated
with it, as, for example, the *autonomistas* of Muñoz Rivera, should be
banned from political structures on the island. They were determined to
reach their goals even with the use of violence.

In urban areas at the turn of the nineteenth century, several groups
of artisans had begun to organize the incipient working class and to elaborate an alternative social and cultural project. The consolidation of capitalist relations in Puerto Rico during the early twentieth century was
coupled by the emergence of a mainly agrarian working class that labored in the sugarcane plantations. Artisans were highly involved in the

long and arduous task of helping these workers organize into a strong social movement, which would eventually have a considerable influence in
Puerto Rican society.

The organized working classes viewed the North American government as a guarantor of fundamental civil rights in Puerto Rico. Workers
had a high regard for the political and teaching institutions in the United
States, as well as its economic development. Annexation to the metropolis was seen as a way of insuring democracy and government support
for social struggles.[13] Santiago Iglesias, the most important leader of
the working-class movement, summarized best the beliefs embraced by
many of his followers: "We are annexationists, because the American Republic in its womb and practices, performs equitable, fair and scientific
administrative and governmental procedures, and that there is nothing
in the country [Puerto Rico] that is more advantageous, even in theory."[14] The particular views of society promoted by those urban artisans
who helped shape the workers' movement in Puerto Rico were fundamentally opposed to the concept of the *patria* (as ruled by the elite) as
the supreme value.[15] The proposition of an alternative way of life based
on the concepts of internationalism, brotherhood, and solidarity characterized the discourses of the emerging working class in Puerto Rico.

Moreover, for those who shared the subjective meaning of the U.S.
government in Puerto Rico as one associated with democracy and the
possibility of a strong social and political presence, the *Patria del Criollo*
(the creoles' motherland) was a fearsome concept, and in many ways
identified with oppression.[16]

It did not sit well with the workers that some of the most prominent
leaders of the pro-autonomy party (*Unionista*)[17] openly vented their animosity toward organized labor in Puerto Rico. For example, José de
Diego, the Speaker of the House of Delegates, not only used to speak of
the "race" and to defend the role of the Catholic Church, which held little
appeal to the working class, but was also quick to criticize social initiatives that were not associated with the struggle for the independence of
the *patria*. The Program of 1913 of the Partido Unionista, brought forth
by *el Caballero de la Raza* (de Diego) and backed by Muñoz Rivera, stated
that the party "would not give its support to the doctrines of anarchy, or
to systems that could disturb coexistence and harmony among all social
elements."[18]

It is evident that several social identities emerged or gained strength
during the early 1900s. Some faded out fast or lost their cohesiveness,

while others, like the working class, became a permanent force in the country. All were considered antagonistic or troublesome by the political organizations of the *autonomistas* (and *independentistas*), which had a traditional and conservative view of Puerto Rican society. The new social identities could not conform to dominant representations of Puerto Ricanness.

The colonial power, whose intentions of integrating Puerto Rico as a territory were made evident from the beginning, was quite aware of the prevailing antagonisms between the *patriotas* and the emergent groups. It took government officials little time to take advantage of the circumstances and to establish that the Spanish regime, as most Puerto Ricans already knew, had been an authoritarian, repressive, and backward form of colonial domination with no positive political legacy to be remembered by. Consequently, those who were associated with the Spanish management of insular affairs (like the *unionistas*) were deemed adversaries of the transformations that were soon to take place in Puerto Rico. Moreover, it was stressed that the government of the United States represented the best opportunity for economic development and political democratization in Puerto Rico. The prevailing discourse was that Puerto Ricans were not ready for self-government and hence should undergo a period of readiness for any form of self-rule.

Discourses that supported these positions and served the colonial rulers to reinforce their control of the island rapidly emerged or developed. Furthermore, as previously mentioned, the *unionistas* displayed unabashed hostility toward individuals and groups who had set particular goals that interfered with their call for local rule by the elite. Since not everyone was in favor of these patriotic histrionics, which denied cultural and political authenticity to the new identities, the United States was able to attract widespread support from different sectors. In sum, the colonial power had two key factors on its side: first, the subjective meaning that U.S. rule had for many Puerto Ricans (political rights, democratization, prospects of economic prosperity, and so on), and second, that those promoting the virtues of *la puertorriqueñidad* were considered by nontraditional sectors as forces opposed to their independent self-affirmation and to the U.S. presence in Puerto Rico.

While the colonial regime wasted no time in establishing that to affirm the Puerto Rican nationhood was a political strategy of a conservative, authoritarian elite, the *unionistas* maintained that social antagonisms should be subordinated to the goals of the *patria*.

The *Autonomistas* (and the *Independentistas*) and the "National Identity"

As discussed earlier, up to 1898, the liberal *autonomistas* under the leadership of Muñoz Rivera had developed a reform-oriented project that corresponded to the economic, political, and intellectual aspirations of the Puerto Rican elite. The *criollos*, ignoring their share of responsibility, blamed ruling Spanish interests for the country's ills. Furthermore, they displayed a paternalistic concern for the masses, who were generally seen as peasants in dire need of a social regeneration. Muñoz Rivera, when discussing the peasants, found fit to mention that they also needed a strong dose of patriotism.

From the time of the invasion of 1898, the government of Puerto Rico made it very clear that the goals of the Puerto Rican elite had to be subordinated to U.S. interests. Hence, the island was to be rapidly integrated—although on an unequal footing—with the ruling state. Capital from the United States started to flow to the island and soon became the dominant force in most sectors of the economy.

At the same time, basic freedoms and rights were extended to the island accompanied by primary elements of North American culture. For example, the teaching of English became of paramount importance to the colonial power. The need to develop a comprehensive educational reform created major upheavals, particularly when a second language that sometimes acted more like a first language became part of the school curriculum.

Although language was the most sensitive issue for many who thought English would soon replace the island's vernacular, the incorporation of many North American traditions—fueled by the hiring of teachers from the mainland to oversee the school offerings—produced a political quagmire. These and other changes, in the view of the new government, did not require interlocutors, a role that the *autonomistas* had ascribed to themselves.

Both the military (1898–1900) and civil governors, as well as other local administrators and federal government officials, made it clear that their rule should be considered highly advantageous for Puerto Rico. Their main positions envisioned the extension of new institutions to Puerto Rico to obtain social improvements free of any form of attachments to old Spanish ways or to the kind of patriotism commonly exposed by some of the *autonomistas* and *independentistas*, that is, the "nationalists"[19] of the Partido Unionista.

As their old dream of assuming local control of the island's affairs began to diminish and the ideologies that justified the colonial or territorial condition began to circulate forcefully, the *autonomistas* and *independentistas*, in a defensive position against a powerful metropolis, started to articulate discourses of exclusion in order to face those aspects of the colonial regime they disliked.

The nationalists wasted no time in breathing life into their own definition of the Puerto Rican identity and thus proclaiming what they considered to be the essence of Puerto Rican culture. To achieve this goal, they needed to outline the political and social traits of the "people." It is important to point out that the liberalism displayed by the *autonomistas* practically disappeared along with the Spanish colonial regime. The much debated processes of "Americanization" and "disruptive" social fragmentation experienced in Puerto Rico, so frequently contended by the *autonomistas* and *independentistas*, had a fundamental consequence: these groups, and their party, began to conceptualize Puerto Rican society very differently. It was a position that would help this elite to challenge the ideology of colonialism and suppress or contain the political expressions or projects of the emergent social identities and classes. Shortly, it turned into a discourse that, with some modifications, continues to have a strong presence today.

The *autonomistas* thought that the main goal of all members of the Puerto Rican society (*la gran familia puertorriqueña*) should be to unite efforts to achieve local rule. The *independentistas*, in turn, would clamor for a broader sovereignty. Up to the 1930s, nationalist organizations developed a conception of Puerto Rican culture based on an integrated interpretation of the nationhood—that failed to understand differences— and on the principles of the unity of the people in support of the designs of the nationalist elite. The autonomous forms of political and social expression by emergent groups, for example, organized workers, led the *unionistas* to publicly oppose these groups for the first time, that is, in a continuous manner. Consequently, the early twentieth century gave rise to the emergence of characterizations (by the *unionistas*) that viewed the assertive and aggressive urban organizations as "riffraff" and the working class as "insubordinate."

The *puertorriqueñidad* in the nationalist discourse had a conservative core. The *unionistas*, for example, opposed women's rights, defended the Catholic Church (as a result of their concern about the emergence of Protestantism), and defined national identity by what they considered traditional cultural traits. Their discourse of exclusion and regression attempted to suppress differences and silence new subjectivities.

Puerto Rican culture was seen as fundamentally Hispanic. Mariano Abril, one of the main ideologists of the Partido Unionista, argued that Puerto Rico was "of Hispanic origin and, therefore, of Spanish soul." He pointed out that foreigners on the island had been few, and that the descendants of African ancestry were Spanish in their language, customs, and idiosyncrasy.[20] From then on, language (Spanish, of course) would be established as a key element in defining true Puerto Ricanness.

Moreover, in the nineteenth century the Puerto Rican elite viewed the peasants and their ways of life as in need of regeneration, while in the twentieth century the nationalists idealized the peasants (and rural life) and turned them into some sort of national emblem. Their music, dances, and customs assumed a pastoral veneer that greatly contrasted with the cultural changes that were taking place under U.S. rule. Going back to the rural areas in search of "good" traditional ways and values— our "cultural essence"—has been an important element of the nationalist imaginary in Puerto Rico.

Efforts to undermine all social or political projects of emergent groups were intense. It was not only during the early twentieth century that intellectuals and politicians like José de Diego, Muñoz Rivera, and Abril contributed to the development of a powerful frame of differentiation based on a particular cultural interpretation of Puerto Rican society. Other intellectuals, like Francisco Zeno (1920s), and Antonio S. Pedreira (1930s), tried to build on the unitary vision of a Puerto Rican nationhood (or "national identity") that excluded other social undertakings.

Zeno, nostalgic for the agrarian dream of a beneficent Puerto Rican rural elite, blamed plantations for introducing workers into the socialist doctrine and accused corporations of destroying the old system (during the Spanish regime) of small landholders.[21] A few years later, Pedreira faced what he consider the "problem" of the Puerto Rican identity and offered an essentially Hispanic definition of Puerto Rican culture. The contradiction of this culture, he asserted, was the United States and its civilization. Working classes had very little bearing on his conception.[22]

Non-Nationalist Discourses

Up to the 1930s, the groups that had struggled to maintain their own particular singularities, that is, those who had resisted the view of a common culture determined by the elite, did so by building on their own strengths, creating their own social imaginary, and in many cases adopting the subjective meaning of the presence of the United States in Puerto Rico. The new social identities resorted to their own projects in response to the views and activities of the *patriotas*, the oppression of the United States' and Puerto Rican bourgeoisie, and, on many occasions, the lack of capacity, sensibility, or goodwill shown by the Washington-appointed bureaucrats (and sometimes displayed by their local allies—officials of both the Partido Unionista and the Partido Republicano).

The organized working class produced its own political undertakings based on principles such as solidarity, social democracy, and equal rights. It would also generate cultural expressions primarily based on defiance. Regardless of the lack of understanding of the colonial intentions of the United States shown by many working-class leaders, workers traditionally demonstrated an inspired sense of affinity that was amply expressed in building and keeping alive their organizations for several decades. Two very good examples were the Federación Libre de Trabajadores and the Partido Socialista, which attracted great hostility from both government officials and part of the local elite. This sense of solidarity was also exemplified in the numerous strikes, protests, and political struggles carried out against economic forces (U.S. corporations and Puerto Rican agrarian interests of all political inclinations), local administrators, and the Partido Unionista.

The working-class organizations were also involved in the development of the feminist movement in Puerto Rico. Since the late nineteenth century, women's rights (the right to vote, equal work, equal pay, full participation in social life, and so on) had been part of the objectives of these organizations.[23] Tens of women's unions were organized during the 1900s, and their members had considerable participation at all levels in the Partido Socialista.

Although their position in the labor movement was of fundamental importance, some working-class feminists began to act independently as they became more aware of their particular condition. Since the 1910s there had been an active movement in Puerto Rico that included groups that supported women's rights and helped construct another political category: *la mujer trabajadora.*

These struggles, however, were not limited to working-class women. Social issues, women's suffrage in particular, were also part of the organized efforts of middle-class and professional women who struggled against male-dominated local politics. Their efforts lasted many years; limited voting rights for women were not enacted until 1929 and placed suffragists in constant antagonistic positions regarding local parties. The *unionistas* in particular opposed their stance of seeking support in the United States when it had not been forthcoming in Puerto Rico.[24]

The Nationalist Party

During the 1930s, the nationalist tradition adopted its most radical political expressions in the activities of the Partido Nacionalista. Under Pedro Albizu Campos, the party courageously and with an uncompromising sense of sacrifice defied forcefully, and sometimes violently, the colonial condition of the island and the inability of Washington to deal with a society mired in a deep economic and political crisis.

The *nacionalistas'* view of Puerto Rican society had some of its roots in the essentialism that had been circulating in various forms for decades. In their fight against colonialism, the *nacionalistas* promoted the idea of an independent capitalist development for the island. Shedding blame on foreign interests for the economic problems of the country, the *nacionalistas* were particularly concerned with the idea of protecting the Puerto Rican bourgeoisie and turning workers into small landholders. In part, it was the old nostalgic and questionable conviction that during the Spanish regime, Puerto Rico had been a "nation of proprietors." The truth of the matter was that concentration of land was an ever increasing problem in the late nineteenth century, and small landowners led a precarious existence.

This conception of society was also accompanied by many of the same principles that had characterized patriotic postures for decades. In a way, Albizu was just the most radical exponent of a long nationalist, elitist tradition. His discourse was based on the defense of *la Raza*, animosity toward North Americans (who were viewed as foreigners), assimilation of many elements of the Catholic conception of the world, reverence toward national heroes, Hispanism, and an authoritarian view of political and social struggles.

Albizu's and the *nacionalistas'* failure to lead the workers during the general strike of 1934 made evident the boundaries of their ideology. The fundamental positions of the *nacionalistas* made it impossible for them to recognize a social movement whose aspirations went far beyond the *intereses nacionales* and *la gran familia puertorriqueña*. For the workers, a better quality of life could be achieved without the need to sacrifice their views and aspirations in a struggle for the creation of a nation-state.

The Popular Democratic Party

In the late 1930s most of the *autonomistas* and *independentistas* joined Luis Muñoz Marín in his populist movement, Partido Popular Demo-crático (PPD). For the United States, the PPD became the best alterna-tive—within the limits of the colonial condition—for dealing with the crisis of the 1930s. In the context of a successful reform movement in the United States (the Roosevelt administration fully supported the PPD) and the unstable situation of both colonial and international capitalism, the PPD provided the United States with a satisfactory means to handle the political and social quagmire of the island. Although the PPD sus-tained pro-independence stances, in a matter of years it renounced its initial postures and was satisfied with reforming the colonial condition of Puerto Rico.[25] An array of measures garnished by the PPD paved the way for the creation of the much touted age of modernization of Puerto Rico. In 1952 the Estado Libre Asociado was founded.

The PPD, which had uninterrupted control of the local government until 1968, was not concerned with promoting the interests of the Puerto Rican agrarian bourgeoisie, defending the Catholic Church, or toying with concepts like *la Raza*. The culture of populism was essentially based on the concept of the unity of *el pueblo*, the promotion of Western values (*occidentalismo*), and the paternalistic idea that only the *autonomista* elite should be in charge of running the country.

It was a curious blend of principles that tried to transcend national-ism but maintained elements of the nationalist tradition. During the 1940s and 1950s, the *populares* fought hard to industrialize the country and to improve services. At the same time, other organizations that aimed to be independent movements were undermined or kept under the *populares'* control. The populist goal of the political elite to harmo-nize conflictive interests and subordinate them to its conceptions was present in the PPD from its beginnings. Moreover, the hundreds of thou-sands of people who migrated from the island to the United States in the 1950s and 1960s faced many difficulties in achieving cultural legitimacy as Puerto Ricans.

The affirmation of *puertorriqueñismo* was given some room, particu-larly through the Instituto de Cultura, while the *jíbaro* (white peasant)[26] remained an icon of the people. Nevertheless, the most important goal of the PPD appears to have been to achieve a higher form of "civilization" that transcended traditional nationalism.

The University of Puerto Rico played an important role in asserting the virtues of Western civilization. The lack of interest of many *populares* in adopting, at least in a comprehensive way, the most traditional and essential views of a Puerto Rican society as sponsored by the nationalists left the *independentistas* as the main advocates of this tradition. The *populares* were happy to reestablish the ancestral dream of political rule by the elite that had guided the *autonomistas* since the nineteenth century. Independent groups or historical identities were to subordinate their goals to the achievements of the great civilization that would pave the way to the future.

The promotion of the nationalist discourse of exclusion was embraced by cultural and political organizations that failed to inscribe differences and engaged in "saving the national identity." Their view of a nationhood continued to be saturated by elements like Hispanism, *ruralismo*, regressions, resurrection of "heroes," nostalgia, idealization of premodern middle-class social values, and so on.[27]

Nevertheless, some *independentistas* and *populares* have continued joining forces on different political fronts and in cultural institutions. Recently, particular activities like championing "Spanish Only" and sports sovereignty have turned into terror-inspiring strategies that work on establishing differentiations that, for example, openly ignore the hundreds of thousands of Puerto Ricans who have English as their vernacular and that treat with mistrust and even contempt those Puerto Rican athletes who are associated with U.S. Olympic teams.

The "Lumpen" and the "Sanitation" of Puerto Rican Society: The *Independentismo* in Recent Times

Historically, vast social sectors in Puerto Rico have struggled to remain outside of the labor market. During the nineteenth century there were continuous complaints from large landholders on this matter, which contributed to the initiatives spearheaded by the government to persecute and force "idle" peasants to work for the proprietors. One of the best known initiatives was the *Ley de la Libreta* of 1849.

The notion of laziness, as well as docility, has been a forceful one among the elite ever since. Some of the main leaders of the Partido Independentista Puertorriqueño (PIP) and a good number of intellectuals have been ardent advocates of a work ethic that will "straighten" the "marginal" way of life in Puerto Rico. Their views seem to be based on the premise that those outside the formal sectors of the economy make poor patriots, which may turn out to be true.

The *pipiolos* attribute many social ills to the excessive dependency on government handouts. According to Rubén Berríos and other PIP leaders, food stamps coupled with a high rate of unemployment have turned Puerto Rico into a ghetto. Independence, Berríos posits, will inspire Puerto Ricans to regain their dignity and pride;[28] a new work ethic will hence purge the country. Victor García San Inocencio views Puerto Rico as being on the verge of barbarism and calls for an effort to "civilize" it,[29] while PIP Representative David Noriega sponsors legislation that matches food stamps with jobs for those recipients who are able to work. According to Noriega, "Bread and Work" ("Pan y Trabajo") will help improve the work ethic on the island and will sanitize society.[30] This view turns out to be a real problem for the *pipiolos* and other *independentistas* if one considers that those that have been discharged from their discourse, because of their transgressive nature, may constitute the majority of Puerto Ricans.

Independentistas in general have remained anchored to the cultural, nationalist discourses of exclusion as a continuous reaction to the economic processes in Puerto Rico in recent decades that (partly through large assistance programs) have made consumption available to all segments of society. With little else to offer but an independence based on austerity and a tough judgmental work ethic that has little appeal to a large segment of the population, the *independentistas'* only remaining bastion for a final defiance is the cultural contest between the "real" Puerto Ricans and the "Others."

One good example has been the recent skirmish in favor of making Spanish the only official language of Puerto Rico. The "Spanish Only" initiative warrants a closer examination if one takes into account that the vernacular does not appear to be under siege in Puerto Rico, that a staggering number of Puerto Ricans living in the United States have English as their first language, that English is widely esteemed among Puerto Ricans not only for utilitarian reasons but for its intellectual and artistic importance, and lastly, that English is the language used by a number of countries that have different relationships with Puerto Rico.

Always turning to their own frame of differentiation, nationalist intellectuals continue to ignore questions regarding multilingual situations. At the close of the century, there should be no doubt in a country of so many confluences, travelers, and migrants that English "*is also ours.*"[31]

Final Comments

During the Spanish regime, most of the Puerto Rican elite struggled to reform the political system of the island by means of a liberal discourse that defined their aspirations to administer the local government, put an end to Spanish control of the island's economy, and regenerate the peasantry, who were seen as in need of a healthier tutelage and a sense of patriotism.

The invasion of 1898 showed that starting with the peasants' revolts of 1898–1900, workers and peasants were capable of their own political and cultural strategies. These opportunities to express their singularities were generally regarded as a consequence of the extension of political freedoms to Puerto Rico.

In the early twentieth century, the nationalist segment of the Puerto Rican elite, reacting against some colonial impositions, developed a conservative view of society that rejected the aspirations and initiatives of the independent groups and identities that emerged after 1898 and promoted a unifying, homogeneous conception of the Puerto Rican culture. Confusion and exclusion prevailed when dealing with the defiance of rural revolt, urban activism, organized workers, blacks who welcomed the invaders, and women who demanded their rights.

The identities that have surfaced recently—whose designs are based on rejecting a work-oriented ethic and maintaining a strong relationship with the Puerto Rican communities in the United States—as well as middle-class groups with an extended access to consumption and to services in general continue to have little in common with the *independentistas*.

Does this mean that Puerto Ricans are inextricably linked to the metropolis and that the construction of a Puerto Rican nation-state is only a distant possibility? The affinity of Puerto Ricans with the United States (both material—dependency on economic assistance, opportunities— and subjective—citizenship, constitutional rights) has tenaciously resisted penetration by nationalist discourses and promises of a local elite rule.

It does not seem probable that Puerto Ricans, given the extensive historical identities among them, will engage in a process of organizing a national state and ending their complex and long-standing ties with the

United States. As it is for many other nationalities, groups, and "countries" around the world, integration/accommodation into a larger national state will continue to be a familiar experience for Puerto Ricans.

Notes

1. In the nineteenth century Puerto Rico had considerable trade with the United States. Among the Puerto Rican elite, relationships with this country were not uncommon. The ideals of the U.S. political system had influenced a number of Puerto Rican intellectuals. While some members of the elite had commercial or professional links with the northern country, others had attended universities in various states. As a result, by 1898 the idea of the United States incorporating Puerto Rico had had a long and cautious— primarily because of the repression—presence on the island.

2. Salvador Brau, *Ensayos (Disquisiciones Sociológicas)* (Río Piedras: Editorial Edil, 1972; reprint), 66. Translated by the author.

3. Ibid.

4. Alejandro Tapia y Rivera, *Mis Memorias* (Río Piedras: Editorial Edil, 1971; reprint), 145. Translated by the author.

5. Mariano Abril, *La Democracia*, June 4, 1895, 2.

6. Luis Muñoz Rivera, *La Democracia*, Apr. 3 and 19, 1895, 2.

7. Commentaries by Lieutenant Edwards as quoted in Angel Rivero, *Crónica de la Guerra Hispanoamericana en Puerto Rico* (New York: Plus Ultra, 1973; reprint), 436. Translated by the author.

8. Numerous *haciendas* were raided and destroyed, houses and warehouses set on fire, proprietors and managers assaulted and even murdered. These activities took place in many municipalities, particularly in the mountainous region of the western part of the island.

9. In 1897, the autonomist movement was divided into two groups, which had distinct views not only on politics but also on society as a whole. Although the division has traditionally been attributed to disparate opinions regarding the best way to achieve self-government for the island, the matter was much more complex. One of the two groups, headed by Luis Muñoz Rivera, comprised the majority of the *autonomistas*. The other group, although smaller, represented more progressive and democratic positions. It was headed by José Celso Barbosa, a black physician educated in the United States. Barbosa clamored for a representative form of government and proposed a more advanced conception of Puerto Rican society that recognized, among other things, the existence of several social antagonisms. For Barbosa and his followers, Puerto Rico was not just a rural society with peasants in need of "regeneration"; it also included workers and urban people, who deserved wider social and political participation.

10. Aaron Gamaliel Ramos, *Las ideas anexionistas en Puerto Rico bajo la dominación norteamericana* (Río Piedras: Ediciones Huracán, 1987), 18.

11. The Partido Republicano showed strong electoral support in the main cities of the island from 1900, when elections were held for the first time under U.S. rule. Victories in San Juan, Ponce, and other urban areas were common for the *republicanos* early in the century.

12. Mariano Negrón-Portillo, *Las Turbas Republicanas, 1900–1904* (Río Piedras: Centro de Investigaciones Sociales and Ediciones Huracán, 1990).

13. Gervasio L. García and A. G. Quintero Rivera, *Desafío y solidaridad* (Río Piedras: Ediciones Huracán, 1982), 30–34.

14. Taller de Formación Política, *La cuestión nacional* (Río Piedras: Ediciones Huracán, 1982), 78. Translated by the author.

15. A. G. Quintero Rivera, "Clases sociales e identidad nacional: Notas sobre el desarrollo nacional puertorriqueño," in Angel G. Quintero Rivera et al., *Puerto Rico: Identidad nacional y clases sociales* (Río Piedras: Ediciones Huracán, 1978), 27–33.

16. Workers, as well as other groups, were not ignorant of the ruthlessness and oppression that characterized the regimes established by the dominant classes in Latin America. Naturally, they wanted no part of what they thought could be a similar reality if the island veered toward independence.

17. Until the 1940s, most *independentistas* remained as a vocal but relatively small group within the pro-autonomy organizations whose political struggles were basically geared to obtain local rule.

18. José de Diego, *Obras completas*, vol. 2 (San Juan: Instituto de Cultura Puertorriqueña, 1966), 158. Translated by the author.

19. This term should not be confused with the name later used by the members of the Partido Nacionalista, which was organized in the 1920s. For the purposes of this essay the term *nationalist* will be used to define those who favored political rule by the Puerto Rican elite and the unity of Puerto Rican society behind its project. Some of them favored the creation of a nation-state, whereas most of them accepted U.S. rule but demanded control of internal affairs. Both groups were characterized by a cultural nationalist and essentialist discourse of exclusion that failed to accept differences and new subjectivities. With some exceptions, the nationalists were members of the Partido Unionista until late in the 1930s. After the 1940s, differences between *autonomistas* and *independentistas* became more significant, as will be discussed later on in the essay.

20. Mariano Abril, *La Democracia*, Aug. 5, 1909, 1. Translated by the author.

21. Angel Quintero Rivera, *Patricios y plebeyos: Burgueses, hacendados, artesanos y obreros* (Río Piedras: Ediciones Huracán, 1988), 277–78.

22. Juan Flores, *Insularismo e ideología burguesa* (Río Piedras: Ediciones Huracán, 1979).

23. Alice Colón, Margarita Mergal, and Nilsa Torres, *Participación de la mujer en la historia de Puerto Rico* (Río Pedras: Centro de Investigaciones Sociales, 1986), 10–11.

24. Ibid., 44.

25. Many *independentistas* within the PPD were kicked out or left to organize the Partido Independentista Puertorriqueño in 1946.

26. Racial matters have long been ignored by the main political organizations in Puerto Rico. The black identity has apparently remained muzzled by the traditional cultural ideology.

27. For decades, many *independentistas* were the target of both local and federal authorities but were unable to generate much sympathy. The fundamentalist content of their discourses made it easier for some of them to be portrayed as dangerous people.

28. Rubén Berríos Martínez, "El futuro de la nación puertorriqueña," *Nueva Sociedad* 114 (1991): 57–62.

29. Victor García San Inocencio, "La salida fácil," *El Nuevo Día*, Apr. 18, 1993, 39.

30. "Diez por ciento de elegibles," *El Nuevo Día*, Feb. 15, 1993, 6.

31. This expression was used by Pedro Laín Entralgo in an article on the use of a second language in Spain. Pedro Laín Entralgo, "La España deseable," *El País*, Feb. 21, 1994, 8.

CHAPTER TWO

The Divorce of Nationalist Discourses from the Puerto Rican People: A Sociohistorical Perspective

Ramón Grosfoguel

The referendum of November 14, 1993, concerning the political status of Puerto Rico provides a critical opportunity to analyze the historically consistent rejection of independence by Puerto Ricans. More than 70 percent of the electorate participated in the referendum. The breakdown of the results by alternatives was as follows: 48 percent voted in favor of maintaining the Commonwealth (the current colonial status), 46 percent voted for statehood, and only 4 percent voted for independence. A significant feature of the outcome was the increase of the pro-statehood vote, which grew by 7 percent, as compared to the 1967 plebiscite where statehood received 39 percent of the vote. There can be no doubt that the great majority of the Puerto Rican people expressed an interest in consolidating some form of "permanent union" with the United States.

Historically, nationalist discourses have put forward several explanations to account for the failure of the independence movement. Certain discourses claim that traditional colonialist leaders have developed a campaign to misinform and instill fear about independence, some blame the "ignorance" of the Puerto Rican people, and still others point to the cultural/ideological colonization by, or assimilation to, the United States as the culprit. Even if we give these arguments the benefit of the doubt, the failure of the pro-independence movement cannot be reduced to a problem of "alienation." Elitist claims that people are "assimilated/alienated" obscure relevant questions such as: Why does independence have minimal support among the Puerto Rican people despite the offer of double citizenship? Why do the overwhelming majority prefer a political status that consolidates the union with the United States? Why has the pro-statehood alternative received massive support among Puerto Ricans despite the "English Only" precondition?

To understand the unpopularity of the independence movements in Puerto Rico, it is important to understand the shifting relationship of Puerto Rico to the United States since 1898. I propose that the United States has made political and economic concessions to working classes in Puerto Rico (which have rarely been made to any other colonial or post-colonial peoples) primarily because of the *military* and *symbolic* strategic importance of the island.

This essay attempts to address these questions and to suggest other ways of articulating the status issue within a radical democratic perspective. The first section consists of a historical overview of Puerto Rico's peculiar modes of incorporation to the United States. The second part critically places the unpopularity of independence discourses within the context of the postwar Caribbean "modern colonies." The last section is an attempt to provide a nonessentialist interpretation of the status alternatives.

Puerto Rico's Modes of Incorporation (1898–1995)

The colonization of Puerto Rico by the United States has had three dominant interests, namely, economic, military, and symbolic.[1] Despite the simultaneity of these three interests throughout the century, one interest has acquired priority over the others at times, depending on the historical context. It is important to note that these interests can either reinforce or contradict each other. Contrary to the economic reductionism of some dependency/mode of production approaches, the economic interests did not always dominate the core-periphery relationship between Puerto Rico and the United States. Instead, state geopolitical considerations such as symbolic or military interests have dominated the U.S.-Puerto Rico relations over extensive periods during the twentieth century.[2] The importance of these geopolitical interests was such that in some instances they actually contradicted corporate economic interests of the United States in Puerto Rico.

The economic interests have been embodied by U.S. corporations. The dominant industries have shifted through different historical periods. From 1898 through 1940, U.S. sugar corporations were the dominant economic actors. During the 1947–70 period, labor-intensive light industries (apparel, textiles, shoes, etc.) became dominant. As of 1973,

U.S. capital-intensive, high-tech, transnational industries (i.e., pharmaceutical and electronic) have controlled the production sphere.

Military interests are represented by the Pentagon. Puerto Rico has served as a beachhead for U.S. invasions and military operations in the Caribbean region. The island has been a naval training ground for joint exercises of NATO and Latin American naval ships. Because of the island's tropical weather, it has served as a training ground for counter-insurgency operations deployed in countries such as Vietnam, Grenada, and Haiti. U.S. military interests in Puerto Rico ruled from 1898 through 1945.

Symbolic interests were inscribed in the actions taken by the State Department and the Department of the Interior. For instance, Puerto Rico became a symbolic showcase of the capitalist model of development that the United States presented to the "Third World" vis-à-vis the competing Soviet model.[3] Thus, Puerto Rico became an international training ground for President Truman's Point Four Program. Through this program, thousands of members of the peripheral countries' elites visited Puerto Rico to receive technical training and learn firsthand the lessons of the first experiment in capital import-export-oriented industrialization. This model of development was based on attracting foreign capital through cheap labor, development of industrial infrastructure, and tax-free incentives for corporations. Billions of dollars in federal aid were transferred from the core state to the colonial administration in order to make Puerto Rico a "success story."[4]

The dialectical dynamics among the interests just outlined are crucial to understanding the specific relationship the United States has with Puerto Rico. For example, as will be discussed later, political concessions to the Puerto Rican population as a result of military or symbolic considerations sometimes clashed with U.S. corporations' economic interests during certain historical periods. Thus, I prefer to conceptualize Puerto Rico's modes of incorporation as the hierarchical articulation (harmonious and/or contradictory) between the economic, military, and symbolic interests of the United States spanning different historical contexts. The consequent periodization of Puerto Rican history during the twentieth century is, then, as follows: a period of agrarian capitalism in which the U.S. military interests predominated (1898–1940), a labor-intensive export-oriented industrialization period in which the U.S. State Department's symbolic interests were dominant (1950–70), a capital-intensive export-oriented industrialization period[5] in which both the transnational corporations and military interests shared the dominant position (1973–90), and an era of overtly economic interests dominating over all geopolitical interests, thus significantly reducing the strategic importance of the island (1991–?). Despite the predominance of one or two actors' interests (the Pentagon, U.S. corporations, the State Department) at a specific historical period, the three have been simultaneously present throughout these periods. The peculiar manifestations of each interest and the articulation among them has, however, changed historically.

Early-Twentieth-Century Puerto Rico (1898–1930)

The geopolitical strategies of core countries in the world interstate system have been crucial determinants of the peripheral incorporation of Caribbean societies. The interest of the United States in seizing Cuba and Puerto Rico from Spain in 1898 was a response mainly to state security interests. Several years before the Spanish-American War, American naval strategist Alfred T. Mahan stressed the strategic importance of building a canal in Central America in order to solve a major problem of U.S. mainland defense: the forced division of its naval fleet between the Atlantic and Pacific coasts. A U.S.-controlled canal in Central America would make possible a unified fleet. The fleet would move with greater speed and security from one ocean to the other by way of a canal, thus eliminating the trip around the tip of South America through the Strait of Magellan. Otherwise, 13,000 miles between San Francisco and Florida had to be navigated, taking more than 60 days.[6]

In addition to building and controlling a canal, Mahan added that it would be necessary to control the canal's eastern and western strategic maritime routes before construction. Mahan foresaw that the construction of a canal would attract the interest of other imperial powers, forcing the United States to enter international conflicts. According to Mahan, foreign control of the canal could be used as a beachhead to attack the United States. This foreign control would destroy the major U.S. asset against foreign aggression, namely, its geopolitical isolation.[7] As a means to achieve geopolitical control, he recommended the acquisition of Hawaii and the naval control of four Caribbean maritime routes before building the canal. The four routes were Paso de Yucatán (between Mexico and Cuba), Paso de los Vientos (the principal U.S. access route to the canal between Cuba and Haiti), Paso de Anegada (near St. Thomas, an island off Puerto Rico's eastern coast), and Paso de la Mona (between

Puerto Rico and the Dominican Republic).[8] Mahan advised that naval bases be established in each of these zones as necessary steps for the United States to become a superpower. Mahan's influence was strongly felt among key political elites headed by Theodore Roosevelt and Henry Cabot Lodge.[9]

The only islands with access to the four maritime routes mentioned by Mahan were Cuba and Puerto Rico. Moreover, they were more amenable to foreign control when compared to Haiti and the Dominican Republic, which had already become nation-states. Cuba and Puerto Rico were still colonies of Spain, a weak and declining imperial state. Because the United States feared other imperial countries would take advantage of Spain's weakness by seizing its last two colonies in the Western Hemisphere,[10] these islands became targets. At the time, this belief was not farfetched, because the Germans had a military plan to attack the United States wherein the first step was to seize Puerto Rico.[11] Another strategic consideration in terms of timing was to intervene before Cuban nationalist rebels defeated Spain in their war of independence. A sovereign nation-state could make the negotiation process difficult for the United States.[12] Thus, in the mid-1890s the United States began to plan a conflict with Spain. In 1898, Puerto Rico and Cuba were seized by the United States during the Spanish-American War.

The geopolitical interests of the United States and the local relation of forces in Puerto Rico and Cuba set the conditions for the different modes of incorporation of the two islands. The United States encountered important local differences between Cuba and Puerto Rico. Cuba had a strong nationalist movement pressuring for the departure of the Americans. The negotiations between the United States and Cuba established a protectorate treaty as well as the right of the United States to build a naval base in Guantanamo.

Two salient features of the internal power relations in Puerto Rico affected its mode of incorporation to the United States. First, all political parties supported the annexation of Puerto Rico to the mainland immediately after the 1898 invasion. Shortly after the landing of U.S. troops in Puerto Rico, General Nelson Miles proclaimed that the war against Spain occurred for humanitarian reasons such as justice and freedom.[13]

Second, Puerto Rico did not have a strong nationalist movement at the time of the U.S. invasion. This allowed the United States to make Puerto Rico a colonial possession without difficulties, thus providing the best conditions to safeguard the military strategic use of the island. Accordingly, the U.S. military prescribed that Puerto Rico remain a colonial possession and that a naval base be built off the northeastern coast of Puerto Rico in Culebra.[14]

A few years after the U.S. invasion, the Orthodox Party and Liberal Party exchanged political programs.[15] The Orthodox Party, linked to the sugar landowners who were radical autonomists under Spain, became an annexationist force under U.S. domination. This transition was marked by a name change from the Orthodox Party to the Puerto Rican Republican Party. The Liberal Party, linked to the coffee *hacendados* who were moderate autonomists under Spain, initially assumed an annexationist position with autonomist tendencies, but later, because of the U.S. pro-sugar policies,[16] became a radical autonomist party, ultimately flirting with pro-independence positions. These transitions were marked by name changes from the Liberal Party to the Federal Party and subsequently to the Union Party.

The Union Party represented those social forces with the greatest potential for building a pro-independence movement. However, the local *hacendados* were never supported by the popular classes. Because of the *hacendados'* alliance with the Spanish colonial administration's authoritarian repressive measures against the rights of peasants and workers, many among these sectors perceived the *hacendados* as their class enemies. Workers and peasants associated the *hacendados'* pro-independence positions with a romantic nostalgia for the forms of labor coercion and authoritarianism of the Spanish regime, under which the *hacendados'* social and economic position had not been threatened. Under U.S. domination, on the other hand, many workers saw an opportunity to establish civil and labor rights by pressuring the U.S. government to extend their legislative laws to the island. These sectors adopted the Americanization discourse promoted by the new imperial power as a strategy to weaken the political power of the local *hacendados* and gain democratic rights recognized in the metropolitan constitution. Despite the negative effects on U.S. sugar corporations of extending labor rights to Puerto Rico, the American state extended these rights to the Puerto Rican working class. The U.S. government wanted to gain popular support for the island's colonial incorporation. By extending labor rights to Puerto Rican workers, the pro-annexationist position of the labor movement was strengthened. This encouraged the formation of a pro-colonial bloc, which in turn impeded the possibility of a pro-independence alliance. The U.S. government's extension of civil and labor rights to Puerto Rico proved to be an important deterrent to the development of a collective national demand for self-determination.

The concessions to the Puerto Rican working classes by the U.S. government mark a distinctive feature of Puerto Rico's incorporation. Different from other U.S. military occupations of Caribbean countries such as Cuba, the Dominican Republic, and Haiti, where the U.S. government relied on authoritarian alliances with the landowners and/or the political/military elites to protect its interests, the U.S. strategy in Puerto Rico relied on a populist-democratic alliance with the working classes and progressive liberal middle-class sectors at the expense of the coffee landowners. The extension of democratic rights to the colony precluded the working classes sympathizing with a nationalist solution to the colonial question. The weakening of the *hacendados'* power base also debilitated the pro-autonomy forces and accelerated wage-labor relations in Puerto Rico. By contrast, the U.S. invasion in a country like Haiti relied on a class alliance with the local commercial elites and the coffee landowners, which strengthened noncapitalist forms of labor coercion.[17]

In sum, the evidence suggests that Puerto Rico's re-peripheralization from a Spanish possession to a U.S. colony was predominantly due to the American government's security interests. Puerto Rico's geopolitical location was strategically important for the U.S. government's defense against possible European aggression against the Panama Canal and the U.S. mainland. In contrast to the peripheral incorporation of other countries, where the economic interests in mining or agriculture were predominant, Puerto Rico's incorporation to the United States in the early twentieth century was primarily geopolitical. As illustrated earlier, the secondary status of the economic interests of the United States was such that certain state policies such as the extension of civil and labor rights to the local population contradicted the immediate interests of U.S. corporations investing in the island at the time.

The End of the Sugar Plantations (1930–45)

During the Great Depression, the United States developed the "Good Neighbor" foreign policy toward Latin America. The decline in sugar production, the spread of poverty, unemployment, and hunger throughout Puerto Rico, along with the emerging popularity of pro-independence ideas among many sectors had become shameful examples for U.S. foreign policy in the region. To counteract the impact of Puerto Rico's situation upon its international reputation, the United States extended to Puerto Rico certain New Deal reforms and supported an industrialization program (the Chardón Plan). This change of policy was marked by the transfer of the U.S. colonial administration in Puerto Rico from the Department of War to the Department of the Interior. However, the local power bloc hegemonized by U.S. sugar plantations presented many obstacles for the extension of these reforms. This period in U.S.-Puerto Rico relations (when symbolic interests of the United States dominated Puerto Rico's incorporation) was short-lived because of the imminent possibility of war, which made military interests dominant again.

During the late 1930s and early 1940s, the U.S. government supported a local populist power bloc at the expense of U.S. sugar corporations. The mortal blow to the sugar plantations, however, was the implementation of the 500-acre law in 1941. This law forced U.S. corporations to sell all land exceeding 500 acres to the colonial government. These lands were used to enforce the agrarian reform that eradicated the *agregados* (peasants forced to pay in rent, kind, or labor for living on the landowner's property) and mitigated the housing needs of thousands of peasants.

State military considerations during World War II fundamentally structured these policies. The state understood that a local population angry at the exploitation and abuses of U.S. sugar corporations was completely undesirable because it could represent a security problem for the military use of the island in times of war. The new governor of Puerto Rico in 1941, the reformist liberal Rexford Tugwell, confirms the military priority of Puerto Rico in his memoirs:

> My duty as a representative of my country in Puerto Rico was to shape civil affairs, if I could, so that military bases, which might soon (before they were ready) have to stand the shock of attack, were not isolated in a generally hostile environment.[18]

In short, the U.S. strategy in Puerto Rico was one of exchanging basic democratic rights for Puerto Ricans for the military exploitation of the island.

Postwar Puerto Rico (1945–95)

The U.S. symbolic interest in Puerto Rico gained dominance immediately after World War II. Puerto Rico became a token in the symbolic battleground between the Soviet Union and the United States, particularly in the United Nations. The Soviets claimed that Puerto Rico symbolized U.S. colonialist and imperialist aims in the world. Concerned about the image of the United States in the eyes of newly independent Third World countries, the State Department pressured for concessions to Puerto Rico. These concessions developed into a strategy to make Puerto Rico a showcase of democracy and capitalism during the 1950s and 1960s.[19] The first concession was the appointment of a Puerto Rican as governor in 1946. The right to elect a local governor was established shortly after, in 1948. Following this, the metropolis fostered the creation of a new status called Estado Libre Asociado (Commonwealth), which was approved in 1952. Lastly, a program of industrialization through massive foreign capital investments (i.e., the model of industrialization by invitation) was implemented, thus radically improving the island's infrastructure.

To enable the fulfillment of Puerto Rico's symbolic role and to foster a successful economic program, the U.S. government cooperated with local elites to support a massive labor migration of the marginalized Puerto Rican labor force.[20] The creation of the institutional framework to facilitate migration through the availability of cheap airfares between Puerto Rico and the United States as well as an advertisement campaign for jobs in the United States provided the conditions of possibility for Puerto Rico's "success story" during the 1950s and 1960s.

These transformations allowed the U.S. State Department to designate Puerto Rico in 1950 as the Point Four Program's international training ground for technical development of Third World elites. This program was more ideological than technical to the extent that these elites learned firsthand about the American model of development for "Third World" countries as opposed to the competing Soviet model.

Puerto Rico's important symbolic role during the Cold War explains the massive U.S. federal assistance given to Puerto Rico in areas such as housing, health, and education.[21] Puerto Rico was treated like any other state in need of federal assistance. The main difference between Puerto Rico and other states was that Puerto Rico's residents did not have to pay federal taxes. It is important to note that this "privileged" status was not granted to any other U.S. colonial territories.

Recent events have transformed once again the United States interest in Puerto Rico. The disappearance of the Soviet Union has changed the priorities of the core powers and the articulation among the different global logics. Today, U.S. economic interests have primacy over geopolitical considerations, and domestic economic concerns over foreign policy. As Anthony P. Maingot states in an excellent article about the Caribbean in the post-Cold War era, "geopolitics have given way to geoeconomics."[22] Therefore, the symbolic and military importance of Puerto Rico for the United States has become a secondary concern. In this sense, Puerto Rico is perceived by U.S. political elites more as an expense to the state than as an important military bastion or symbolic showcase. Economic crisis in the United States (such as the huge U.S. public debt) has created the context for Congress to eradicate 936 benefits for U.S. corporations in Puerto Rico, reduce federal transfers, and (among several factions of the U.S. political elites) articulate a sympathetic position toward a more autonomous status for the island. These trends suggest that a change in Puerto Rico's colonial status could result in the formation of a neocolonial relationship with the United States. If Puerto Rico becomes a neocolony, the United States would be relieved from the expenses of a modern colony, creating a "colony without any expenses." Particularly affected by this redefinition are Puerto Rican working classes.

Modern Colonies in the Postwar Caribbean

Modern colonialism is the term that addresses the dramatic change of the colonialism implemented by core countries in the postwar Caribbean.[23] In terms of standard of living and civil rights, postwar Caribbean colonial incorporations to the metropolises have been more beneficial to working classes than neocolonial relationships. This can be illustrated by comparing U.S., French, and Dutch postwar modern colonies to neocolonial republics.

Anticolonial struggles and Cold War geopolitical military and symbolic considerations forced western metropolises to make concessions to their colonies. While certain colonies became nation-states, such as Jamaica, Guyana, and most of the English Caribbean, other territories remained colonial possessions because of their strategic location and/or symbolic/ideological importance. U.S., French, and Dutch colonies such as Puerto Rico, Martinique, and Curaçao, respectively, were granted economic and democratic reforms in order to preclude the success of any potential anticolonial struggles. The benefits enjoyed by these modern colonial populations (vis-à-vis their neocolonial neighbors) include annual transfers of billions of dollars of social capital from the metropolitan state to the modern colony (e.g., food stamps, health, education, and unemployment benefits), constitutional recognition of metropolitan citizenship and democratic/civil rights, the possibility of migration without the risks of illegality, and the extension of Fordist social relations that incorporated the colonial people to metropolitan standards of mass consumption.

Given Puerto Rico's importance as a symbolic showcase and a strategic military location, the United States responded to the 1974 economic crisis with federal assistance aimed to guarantee political stability and the survival of the "industrialization by invitation" model of development. The federal transfers were increased by extending several programs to individuals on the island. Federal transfers to individuals increased from $517 million in 1973, to $2.5 billion in 1980, to $4 billion in 1989. Federal aid represented 8 percent of the GNP in 1973, 23 percent in 1980, and 21 percent in 1989. Federal transfers to individuals were 10 percent of personal income in 1973, 22 percent in 1980, and 21 percent in 1989. While approximately 60 percent of families in Puerto Rico qualified for food stamps, only 11 percent of families in the United States qualified for the same program. This countercyclical "shock absorber" is crucial to understanding how the Puerto Rican lower classes survived the crisis.

These economic benefits account in part for why hardly any significant segment of the population from Puerto Rico, Martinique/Guadeloupe, or Saint Martin/Curaçao is willing to renounce U.S., French, or Dutch citizenship.[24] The fact that half of the Surinamese population moved to the Netherlands when the Dutch imposed, for economic reasons, the formation of Surinam as a nation-state supports this argument.[25]

There is no doubt that the colonial administration of these modern colonies developed ideological and cultural colonization strategies. The people of these modern colonies, however, are neither passive recipients of colonial policies nor ignorant about what is happening in the region. On the contrary, observing the situation of neighboring neocolonial republics, speaking with immigrants from these countries (e.g., people from the Dominican Republic in Puerto Rico, from Grenada in Curaçao, and from Haiti and Dominica in Guadeloupe), and listening to the authoritarian and elitist discourses of pro-independence leaders, modern colonial peoples of the Caribbean fear the authoritarian and exploitative potential of a nation-state. It is not a coincidence that a constant comment made by Puerto Ricans, Guadeloupeans, and Martinicans in the streets is, "To be independent like Haiti or the Dominican Republic, better to be a colony."

Although authoritarianism is not intrinsic to independence, these is-sues continue to worry those who enjoy democratic and civil rights under modern colonial arrangements vis-à-vis neocolonial relationships. Their preoccupation should not be underestimated in light of the clien-telistic/*caudillista* political traditions and the weak peripheral economies of small Caribbean islands. The possibilities of a dictatorship under these conditions are relatively high, especially considering the long-term dicta-torships of Cuba, Haiti, and the Dominican Republic during this century. Moreover, even the recently formed independent Caribbean states like Surinam, Dominica, Guyana, and Grenada have suffered military coups and/or authoritarian regimes.

The anti-independence and pro-permanent union political posi-tions of most modern colonial peoples of the Caribbean should not be caricatured as the product of a "colonized" or "ignorant" people. Given the drastic difference between the situation of working classes in modern colonies and neocolonial nation-states of the region, these people prefer a modern colony that benefits from metropolitan transfers over a neo-colonial nation-state with the same colonial exploitation of a modern colony but no benefits from the metropolitan state. Rather than the as-sumption that modern Caribbean colonial peoples are "alienated" or "as-similated," their position suggests a political pragmatism rooted in con-ditions where options are extremely limited. In the current Caribbean context there is no space external to U.S. hegemony over the region. Even the most "independent" republic cannot escape U.S. control. Any at-tempt to subvert this order is militarily or economically destroyed, as oc-curred in Grenada, Nicaragua, and Jamaica.

The Puerto Rican people's strategy has been pragmatic rather than utopian; that is, they are not struggling to be freed from imperialist op-pression (which is highly improbable and perhaps even undesirable under the present circumstances) but are instead attempting to struggle for a milder version of this oppression. They would rather be exploited with some benefits (as in Curaçao and Martinique) than be exploited without any benefits (as in the Dominican Republic and Haiti). In this sense, the unpopularity of the independence movement is a pragmatic rejection of a neocolonial independence. Puerto Rican workers in many instances throughout the century have followed a strategy of *subversive complicity* with the system. This is a subversion from within the domi-nant discourses. A good example is the use and abuse of the discourse of

Americanism by the early-twentieth-century working class movement in Puerto Rico. As a Puerto Rican pro-statehood worker recently stated,

> In the name of democratic and civil rights as citizens of the United States we should struggle for equality by becoming the 51st state. We cannot let the Americans enforce an independence status on us in order to cut their budget deficits. Through independence they will keep controlling us but without the commitment to extend welfare benefits and civil rights. After destroying our economy and exploiting the best energies of the Puerto Rican workers during this century, now they want to get rid of us. That is unacceptable. After the Americans ate the meat, let them now suck the bones.[26]

I am not suggesting that colonialism is the solution to Third World problems nor that we should stop struggling against colonial oppression. These islands are no paradise.[27] Instead, I am trying to understand, without resorting to traditional nationalist moralization or colonialist explanations, why the people from modern colonies like Puerto Rico, Curaçao, and Martinique prefer a status of permanent union with the metropolis to independence. Considering the history of imperialist exploitation and destruction of the local economies, it is legitimate to pose the following questions: On whose shoulders would the sacrifices required by the economic reconstruction for an independent state fall? Whose salaries and wages would be reduced for local and transnational industries to compete favorably in the world economy? Who would be affected by the reduction of state assistance (e.g., food stamps, housing subsidies) in favor of the republic's economic reconstruction? Obviously, the sacrifice will not be made by the lawyers, merchants, doctors, and professors of the pro-independence leadership but instead will be made by the working classes. Does the rejection of this scenario imply a "colonized" mentality?

When people ask pro-independence militants how they will survive if Puerto Rico becomes a nation-state, the response usually refers to the new equality and justice for all that will be achieved under the republic. This vague response does not address the legitimate concern that Puerto Rico imports approximately 80 percent of its food. Those who demand a serious answer are aristocratically accused of being colonized, assimilated, or ignorant. However, people eat neither flags nor hymns; nor do they outlive the eternity of sacrifices necessary to reach the future "paradise republic."

The romantic rhetoric of the pro-independence movement cannot conceal the dire reality awaiting a future republic. In the contemporary world system, where no space is external to global capitalism,[28] the transition toward an independent nation-state will entail overwhelming sacrifices for the working classes.

Toward a Nonessentialist Treatment of the Status Question: Challenges and Options

Irrespective of whether Puerto Rico becomes an independent republic, a reformed commonwealth, the fifty-first state, or an associated republic, the island will remain under U.S. hegemony. Thus, the relevant question is, Which status alternative will be more favorable to the protection, deepening, and expansion of the social and democratic rights already recognized under the current colonial status (e.g., federal minimum wage, unemployment benefits, social security, abortion rights, civil rights)?

The failure of the independence movement in the past referendum (only 4 percent of the votes) manifests the historical divorce between nationalist discourses and the Puerto Rican people. If the pro-independence movement[29] wants to convince the Puerto Rican people of their project, they need to offer a political-economic-ecological-sexual program superior to that of other status alternatives. Their alternative program would have to significantly improve the standard of living and the democratic and civil rights that Puerto Ricans already enjoy. This challenge is difficult to meet, however, within the present context of global capitalism. The free-trade agreement between Mexico and the United States, the increased opening of Cuba, the incorporation of the Central American economies after a decade of civil wars, the absence of a Puerto Rican "national" economy, the island's extreme dependence on federal assistance, and the competition of other low-wage countries in the Caribbean region make the economic viability of an independent Puerto Rico extremely questionable in this historical conjuncture. An independent Puerto Rican nation-state would have to pauperize its population in order to compete in the capitalist world economy by reducing the minimum wage and government transfers to individuals, by submitting to neoliberal policies of the International Monetary Fund to subsidize the trade and balance of payment deficits, and by reducing environmental controls. Thus, given the impossibility in the present historical conjuncture of offering a pro-independence project superior to that of the other status options at this moment in history, the progressive forces within the pro-independence movement have three alternatives. First, they can continue to support the independence project but can speak openly to the people about the necessary sacrifices and risks of a transition to an independent state. Second, they can abandon the independence project and support one of the two remaining status alternatives, submitting to their currently conservative programs and leadership. Third, they can stop understanding the status issue in essentialist terms or as a question of principle. Instead, the movement could struggle for a "democratization of democracy" in all spheres of everyday life, pressure the other parties to develop progressive programs, and open the pragmatic question of which status alternative will do better (or the least evil) in protecting and improving the island's ecology, quality of life, and democracy. This could channel their efforts beyond the limits set by the status debate. Although it is important to assume a position concerning the status issue, progressive forces should not reify it at the expense of democratic struggles. The reification of the status question precludes the emergence of alternative forms of radical politics.

Given the unconvincing platform of the pro-independence movement, the third option, that is, a radical democratic project,[30] could become a more viable alternative than the second alternative, which basically supports the traditional conservative programs and colonialist leadership of the pro-commonwealth and pro-statehood options. The political practice of a radical democratic project would privilege the improvement of oppressed subjects' quality of life in the present rather than in a distant future "paradise." This movement would include a multiplicity of projects to promote and support the struggles of diverse oppressed subjects such as blacks, women, youth, gays, lesbians, and workers. Coalitions between these groups can only be possible if differences and organizational autonomy are respected without privileging the demands of one group at the expense of another.

Although these demands may not entail the destruction of capitalism, they can at least weaken the power bloc and improve the quality of life of different social groups. I call this strategy subversive complicity with the system against capitalism, patriarchy, racism, heterosexism, and authoritarianism. A meta-narrative (totalizing discourse) articulated to struggle against the system from the vantage point of a utopian space beyond capitalism makes the movement vulnerable to an authoritarian response from the state. By contrast, the strategy of subversive complicity would imply the radical resignification of the symbols of U.S. hegemonic discourses in the Caribbean region such as democracy, civil rights, and equal opportunities. This means using a democratic discourse rather than a socialist discourse but resignifying it in a radical democratic direction.

A radical democratic project in Puerto Rico would "democratize democracy" through the deepening of democratic and civil rights for oppressed subjects and the increasing of their control over the conditions of everyday life. Several struggles could exemplify a radical democratic project:

1. A struggle against environmental pollution. Currently, the colonial government's Junta de Calidad Ambiental (Board of Environmental Control), in alliance with transnational capital, has a pernicious effect on the island's environment. The Junta overlooks pollution increases and allows the destruction of the island's natural resources. A radical democratic project could struggle for the right to a healthy life by demanding legal measures that criminalize harmful industrial practices. The focus would be the democratization of political power over the environment.

2. A struggle for women's rights. Stronger social measures to transform the sexual division of labor that subordinates thousands of women could be developed in the name of equality of opportunities. For instance, the creation of child-care centers combining public and private funds would significantly reduce the amount of work women do in Puerto Rico.

3. Struggles to improve the quality of life. Two measures that would radically improve the quality of life are the construction of a monorail in the major cities and a train route throughout the whole island. This form of transportation would decrease the use of cars (Puerto Rico has one of the highest numbers of cars per capita in the world) and would in turn immediately improve the quality of life by eradicating traffic jams, lowering pollution levels, and indirectly increasing salaries due to the decrease in car expenses (e.g., gas, auto parts, insurance, and loans).

4. A struggle to decrease the crime rate. Most homicides and robberies in Puerto Rico are a result of two factors: unemployment and drugs. First, the legalization of highly addictive drugs (e.g., heroin) and the free distribution of drugs among the addicted population would eliminate the need to kill or steal to gather the necessary money to maintain a heroin addiction. Experimental programs in England and the Netherlands have had impressive results using this strategy. Second, the reduction of the workday while keeping constant the eight-hour workday salary would increase the job supply, enabling the massive incorporation of unemployed workers in the formal economy. Given the trend toward automation and technological development,

global capitalism cannot continue to expand or create new jobs indefi-
nitely. Thus, it is meaningless to plead for the creation of new eight-
hour workday jobs. Moreover, these measures would decrease the importance of illegal informal economic activities (e.g., selling drugs) for
a large number of unemployed workers. These activities, criminalized
by the state, constitute the economy of a large unemployed and underemployed sector of Puerto Rican society.

To gain legitimacy, the Left needs to dissociate itself from essentialist
discourses regarding the status issue, namely, to stop defending independence as a matter of principle. Contrary to the discourses and practices
of Puerto Rican political culture, status alternatives are not essentially
progressive or reactionary. The progressive or reactionary character of a
status alternative is contingent on the relation of forces, the strengths or
weaknesses of social movements, and the discourses articulating the status options in a specific conjuncture of the global capitalist system. Just
as nation-states can be either reactionary or progressive, states or associated republics can be either reactionary or progressive. For instance,
compare Hawaii's or Vermont's progressive health-care policies to Pennsylvania's reactionary policies in the United States, or compare the Russian state's authoritarian control over the "autonomous" republics to the
democratic autonomous regions of Spain.

The pro-statehood movement in Puerto Rico has been hegemonized
by conservative and right-wing factions.[31] However, the statehood alternative is not inherently reactionary. One can imagine an antimilitarist
and a radical-democratic pro-statehood movement in Puerto Rico that
makes alliances with and defends the democratic struggles of other oppressed groups (e.g., Latinos, African Americans, women, gays and lesbians) in the United States The early-twentieth-century movement of
Puerto Rican workers is a good example. This socialist pro-statehood
movement built coalitions with U.S. workers' unions and defended
Americanism as a strategy to make civil and labor rights recognized in
the mainland extend to Puerto Rico.

Similarly, we can imagine an autonomous status, called the Associated Republic, that could eliminate certain federal laws to improve the
quality of life of the population instead of pauperizing it. Examples are
increased autonomy from federal environmental laws so that stricter reg-
ulations could be developed, and the elimination of the federal minimum wage so that it could be increased.

In a more progressive direction, the transformation of the Puerto

Rican party system, traditionally organized in terms of status alternatives, presupposes the development of a popular radical democratic movement that defies the boundaries of current debates by undoing the correspondence between status alternatives and political parties. This movement could garner people with diverse political positions regarding the status issue who want to protect and expand the existing democratic, sexual, civil, and social rights. They could struggle for the decolonization of the island by demanding the right of self-determination for the Puerto Rican people without imposing a status option that would unnecessarily divide the movement. This mass democratic movement could struggle against any potential turn toward authoritarianism irrespective of the eventual political status of the island. All in all, the status is not a matter of principle and, consequently, remains secondary in relation to the primacy of radical democratic struggles.

Discourses warning against the threat of losing our "national" identity and language under the actual colonial status or statehood are mainly employed by nationalist groups in Puerto Rico to justify their defense of independence as a matter of principle. To speak Spanish at school and in public administrative life was achieved through the struggles of the Puerto Rican people more than fifty years ago. Moreover, the Quebecois in Canada, the Catalans in Spain, Guadeloupeans under France, and the Curaçaoans under the Netherlands are also "nations" without independent states. These "nations" without nation-states have not lost their languages or their "national cultures" although their cultures and languages have been transformed by the influence of the metropolises. This transformation can be seen, however, as an enrichment rather than a hindrance. Thus, statehood or some other form of union with the metropolis does not necessarily entail cultural or linguistic genocide. Puerto Ricans can be part of the struggle, together with other Latinos, for the recognition of cultural and linguistic diversity in the United States.

The Puerto Rican people share a feeling of nationhood that has not translated into traditional nationalist claims to form a nation-state. Puerto Ricans have formed an "imaginary community" with an imaginary belonging to a territory that spans the island as well as certain areas on the mainland (e.g., South Bronx, Spanish Harlem, North Philadelphia). This imaginary community oscillates between feelings of nationhood and ethnicity; that is, Puerto Ricans simultaneously imagine themselves as a nation and as an ethnic group. Puerto Ricans' self-perception does not fit either the concept of a "nation" or that of an "ethnic group." I believe the concept of "ethno-nation"[32] accommodates the Puerto Ricans' diverse and peculiar subject positions better than that of "nation."

Pro-independence ideologies that attempt to equate the status debate to a matter of principle constitute the political project of a minority seeking to become a national elite and/or bourgeoisie. This movement's emphasis upon the purportedly inevitable cultural and linguistic genocide has precluded a serious discussion of the socioeconomic consequences of independence for working classes today. Their struggles could be more effective if they concentrated on the development of a radical democratic movement that protects, expands, and improves the quality of life and the democratic and civil rights Puerto Ricans have today.

Notes

1. Ramón Grosfoguel, "World Cities in the Caribbean: The Rise of Miami and San Juan," *Review* (Journal of the Fernand Braudel Center) 17, 3 (summer 1994).

2. Ramón Grosfoguel, "Puerto Rico's Exceptionalism: Industrialization, Migration and Housing Development" (Ph.D. diss., Temple University, 1992).

3. Ibid.

4. Ibid.

5. Public Law 936 (passed in 1976) enabled transnational corporations in Puerto Rico to repatriate their profits to the mainland without paying U.S. federal taxes.

6. María Eugenia Estades Font, *La presencia militar de Estados Unidos en Puerto Rico: 1898–1918* (Río Piedras: Ediciones Huracán, 1988), 27–28.

7. Ibid.

8. Ibid., 29.

9. See Estades Font, *La presencia militar de Estados Unidos en Puerto Rico*, 31; and Jorge Rodríguez-Beruff, *Política militar y dominación* (Río Piedras: Ediciones Huracán, 1988), 149.

10. See Estades Font, *La presencia militar de Estados Unidos en Puerto Rico*, 40.

11. Helger Herwig, *Politics of Frustration: The United States in Naval Planning* (Boston: Little, Brown and Company, 1976), 61–65, 86–87.

12. Wilfredo Mattos Cintrón, *La política y lo político en Puerto Rico* (Mexico: Serie Popular ERA, 1980), 58.

13. See Estades Font, *La presencia militar de Estados Unidos en Puerto Rico*, 89–90.

14. Estades Font, *La presencia militar de Estados Unidos en Puerto Rico*, 36; and Alfred T. Mahan, *Lessons of the War with Spain and Other Articles* (Boston: Little, Brown and Company, 1899), 28–29.

15. Mattos Cintrón, *La política y lo político en Puerto Rico*.

16. Mattos Cintrón, *La política y lo político en Puerto Rico*; Angel Quintero Rivera, *Conflictos de clase y política en Puerto Rico* (Río Piedras: Ediciones Huracán, 1976).

17. Suzy Castor, *La ocupación norteamericana de Haití y sus consecuencias (1915–1934)* (Mexico: Siglo XXI, 1972).

18. Rexford G. Tugwell, *The Stricken Land* (New York: Doubleday, 1947), 148.

19. Grosfoguel, "Puerto Rico's Exceptionalism."

20. Ramón Grosfoguel, "The Geopolitics of Caribbean Migration: From the Cold War to the Post-Cold War," in *Security Problems and Policies in the Post-Cold War Caribbean*, ed. Jorge Rodriguez-Beruff and Humberto García-Muñiz (London: Macmillan Press, 1996).

21. Grosfoguel, "Puerto Rico's Exceptionalism."

22. Anthony P. Maingot, "Preface," *Annals of the American Academy of Political and Social Sciences* 533 (May 1994): 8–18.

23. Gerald Pierre Charles, *El Caribe Contemporáneo* (Mexico: Siglo XXI, 1981).

24. The most absurd campaign recently pursued by some pro-independence leaders is the rejection of their U.S. citizenship. This "revolutionary" luxury can only be enjoyed by individuals with enough income to sustain their families without working or who do not depend on the welfare state. This campaign shows the elitist character of the pro-independence leadership and their "alienation" from the Puerto Rican people. See also "E.U. impediría ingreso Mari Bras a Puerto Rico," *Claridad*, Feb. 18–24, 1924, 12.

25. Grosfoguel, "The Geopolitics of Caribbean Migration." In a referendum held on Nov. 19, 1993, 76.3 percent of the people of Curaçao voted for the present status. Only 0.5 percent voted for independence.

26. This quote is taken from ethnographic work done by the author in Puerto Rico during the summer of 1990.

27. There has been a cost to this special relationship. In the Puerto Rican case, the high crime rate suggests an acute social polarization.

28. Immanuel Wallerstein, "Dependence in an Interdependent World: The Limited Possibilities of Transformation within the Capitalist World Economy," in *The Capitalist World Economy*, essays by Immanuel Wallerstein (Cambridge and Paris: Cambridge University Press and Editions de la Maison des Sciences de l'Homme, 1979).

29. Although the Left and nationalist movements are not inherently equivalent, they have been linked in Puerto Rico since the founding of the Nationalist Party during the 1920s.

30. Ernesto Laclau and Chantal Mouffe, *Hegemony and Socialist Strategy* (London: Verso, 1985).

31. The only exception has been the socialist pro-statehood movement of the 1910s and early 1920s.

32. For a discussion of the concept of "ethno-nation," see the introduction to this volume.

CHAPTER THREE

Puerto Rico: The Myth of the National Economy

Jaime E. Benson-Arias

As an economic entity, Puerto Rico has been conceptualized in the literature of political economy in basically two ways: as an economic region of the United States[1] or as a separate, self-contained, autonomous economy.[2] Most treatments of Puerto Rico as a regional economy, with the exception of Frank Bonilla and Ricardo Campos's, leave out the island's unique social struggles and configuration. On the other hand, treating Puerto Rico as a separate national economy omits the specificity of its economic space with respect to two key political economy phenomena: capitalist accumulation and capitalist reproduction.[3]

Does Puerto Rico have its own capitalist accumulation process or regime, which is then articulated to the United States' accumulation process? Or is Puerto Rico integrated into the process of capital accumulation in the United States? Does Puerto Rico have its own national capitalist reproduction scheme? Or is Puerto Rico integrated into the United States' reproduction scheme? Does mass consumption in Puerto Rico reproduce a distinct national capitalist accumulation regime articulated with the United States' regime of capitalist accumulation? Or does insular mass consumption reproduce capitalist accumulation in the United States? These are some of the key questions that arise when the concrete capitalist accumulation and reproduction processes for Puerto Rico are considered.

In this essay, I will argue that Puerto Rico has become a differentiated region of the U.S. economy as an effect of "Operation Bootstrap" policies since the end of World War II. Underlying my analysis is the assumption that during the postwar period Puerto Rico has been unequally integrated to the United States' process of capitalist accumulation and reproduction, and that as such it is irrelevant to talk of a "Puerto Rican economy" in the sense of a distinct "national economy." I will argue that Puerto Rico constitutes a "regional armature"[4] of the United States regime of accumulation and mode of regulation.[5] Before I develop this argument, I will discuss the main contending theoretical approaches to the Puerto Rican spatial economic configuration.

Contending Theoretical Approaches to Puerto Rico's Economic Space

Neoclassical regionalists[6] revindicate the structural advantages of being an economic region of the United States. They claim that such advantages include the free and unobstructed movement of factors of production and merchandise between Puerto Rico and the United States without the structural balance of payments problems and consequences that most national economies face. Under this rationale, a free-trade, outward-looking model of development—consisting of incentives to export-oriented U.S. firms—was pursued from the early 1950s to the present, with only minor modifications. This model became known as "Operation Bootstrap" and was adopted to capitalize on the institutional advantages of being an economic region of the United States.

Although there are definitely some advantages in being part of the U.S. market (especially with respect to avoiding the major inconveniences related to balance of payments disequilibrium), this type of conventional thinking overlooks the asymmetry of the island's insertion into the mainland economy and some of the most dramatic socioeconomic consequences of the policies pursued within this context.[7] The flaws in the dominant orthodox modernization analysis, together with the crisis of its growth model in the early 1970s, led to the critique offered by the "Dependency School."

The *dependentistas* emerged as critics of the "Puerto Rican model of industrialization." Specifically, they denounced the model as one of "dependent industrialization" based on foreign investment, import dependence, and narrow market orientation to the United States for the sale of goods. Dependent growth, according to this view, has blocked the formation of a national industrial bourgeoisie, impeded the optimal use of internal resources, and, in the long run, led to a drainage of capital from the domestic economy.[8]

They argued, in opposition to conventional analysis, that the crisis of the dependent model of growth in the early 1970s was not circumstantial, and that its solution needed more than just a few policy adjustments. For the *dependentistas* it was a structural crisis: it was caused by the exhaustion of the export-led dependent-growth model and required a complete redefinition of the development strategy. Import substitution, support of local capital initiatives geared to the domestic market to generate forward and backward internal linkages and create labor-intensive activities, and either greater political autonomy or independence were some of the key pieces of a new overall inward-looking development strategy.

The *dependentistas'* main contribution is their critique of the Puerto Rican industrialization model. They were successful in pinpointing its shortcomings and inconsistencies. However, it is in characterizing the island's political economy and spatial configuration that their greatest weakness lies. *Dependentistas* mainly view Puerto Rico as an autonomous, dependent, and peripheral economy.[9]

Some consider it an extreme case of transnational-associated dependent development[10] in the tradition of the Latin American "Dependency School."[11] Others[12] emphasize the asset ownership dimension (i.e., the fact that nationals possess physical and financial wealth) in visualizing Puerto Rico as a national economy, with a "national financial position." These characterizations are misleading in the formulation of an accurate assessment of the current configuration of the island's political economy. This is especially true with regard to the particular process of capitalist accumulation and reproduction that the island participates in.

In response to the insufficiencies of orthodox development theory, dependency theory, and variants of Marxist orthodoxy theories in explaining the situation of underdevelopment in "Third World" countries, James Dietz builds on Lenin's approach of monopoly capitalism or imperialism as a distinct historical phase of capitalism in order to make sense of peripheral uneven industrialization. He makes a distinction between contemporary capitalist development in center countries (i.e., monopolist capitalism) and "imperialist-dominated capitalist development" in peripheral countries. Imperialist-dominated capitalist development, although it spreads capitalist relations and generates industrialization, at the same time "is in the interests of foreign capitalists to attempt to maintain a degree of underdevelopment and backwardness, in industry and agriculture, to protect their monopoly interest by thwarting the spread of capitalist social relations and blocking and distorting the development of the forces of production."[13]

Dietz chooses Puerto Rico as a case study of the effects of imperialist-dominated capitalist development in the Third World. Because of the high level of U.S. capital investment, Puerto Rico has become, according to Dietz, an urban, industrial, capitalist, and service-based economy. However, capitalist industrialization on the island has been disarticulated, with virtually no links between local supply and local demand. Agriculture and industrial sectors geared at supplying local demand have collapsed as a result of their exposure to unrestricted competition from U.S. agribusiness and consumer-goods conglomerates. Puerto Rico then, in Dietz's view, fits the case of imperialist-dominated capitalist development where capitalist industrialization coexists with retarded development of local agriculture and industrial sectors and generalized social marginalization.

But what is evident from Dietz's own analysis of Puerto Rico is that Puerto Rico is not a typical case of imperialist-dominated capitalist development. If anything Puerto Rico is a very atypical case. As Dietz himself admits, "This strengthening of pre-capitalist forms is not as evident in Puerto Rico as it is in Mexico, Colombia, Peru and other *independent* but imperialist dominated nations. This would seem to be due to Puerto Rico's *colonial status and its function as a tax haven for US transnationals.*"[14]

Furthermore, the uniqueness of Puerto Rico's situation raises the question whether it should be considered at all as a case of imperialist-dominated capitalist development as Dietz has defined it. Perhaps considering it as a differentiated part or region of what Dietz calls a monopoly capitalist formation is more fitting to the case under scrutiny. Dietz himself points in this direction:

> the island became little more than an extension of the U.S. economy, and while it is not meaningless to refer to the Puerto Rican economy, its distinctiveness has become blurred as a result of its nearly full integration with the mainland market, banking system, manufacturing methods, and labor, environmental, and juridical regulations.[15]

Edwin Meléndez,[16] for his part, depicts Puerto Rico as a national, autonomous economy with its own postwar Social Structure of Accumulation (SSA),[17] which he denominates as "Populismo," intermingled with elements of the United States' SSA. He views the economic interaction between the island and the mainland as one of economic integration between two distinct social formations. This economic integration forms part of both SSAs (i.e., Puerto Rico's and the United States') and entails their articulation.

Meléndez presents Puerto Rico as a small, open, national, autonomous economy with its own SSA; by means of economic integration with a bigger autonomous economy (i.e., the U.S.) with its own SSA, both SSAs are articulated. In the articulation between both SSAs, the mainland's SSA permeates all of the constituting elements or pillars of the island's structure at the same time that all of the domestic and international components of the United States' SSA form one of Populismo's constitutive pillars.

Rather than describing the articulation of two autonomous processes of capital accumulation and reproduction, this proposal, describes a single autonomous accumulation and reproduction process unevenly spread through two integrated social formations: the United States and Puerto Rico. Instead of the articulation of two distinct SSAs, we are witnessing the SSA of a dominant social formation, the United States, unevenly absorbing a subordinated social formation, Puerto Rico.[18]

Furthermore, none of the constitutive elements of Populismo could account for a Puerto Rican national, autonomous process of capitalist accumulation and reproduction or an SSA in its own standing. On the contrary, they all form differentiated parts or uneven integration mechanisms to the mainland's SSA. Thus what Meléndez considers a distinct Puerto Rican SSA (i.e., Populismo) is really a set of institutions that has facilitated the island's uneven participation in the mainland's SSA. It could be argued that in specifying the intermingling of the island's SSA with the mainland's SSA, Meléndez is recognizing the absorption of the island into the U.S. economy. Paradoxically the level of economic absorption that he describes weakens his case for an autonomous Puerto Rican SSA.

For Emilio Pantojas,[19] the incentives of section 936 (a section of the U.S. Internal Revenue Code that provides federal corporate tax exemption to U.S. corporations located in Puerto Rico), present since the mid-1970s, have greatly accelerated Puerto Rico's incursion into the high-technology and high-finance stage of industrialization, becoming as of late a case of "peripheral postindustrialization."

At first glance, the similarities between Puerto Rico and those countries that, according to Pantojas, could be considered cases of peripheral postindustrialization, such as Ireland, Singapore, and Hong Kong, are not few, especially with respect to the role of transnational high-technology manufacturing, services, and financial activities. Nonetheless, considering Puerto Rico as a case of peripheral postindustrialization because of these similarities plays into the delusion of conceptualizing the island as a national or autonomous economy.

Peripheral economies are those located commercially and institutionally at the outskirts of the most industrialized economies. They are mostly autonomous colonies or national states outside of the institutional range of the national markets in the advanced capitalist countries. Thus, although this may certainly be true for Hong Kong, Ireland, and Singapore, it does not hold for Puerto Rico. As I will argue later, Puerto Rico in the postwar period has been asymmetrically incorporated into the United States economy, both into its capitalist accumulation circuits and its capitalist reproduction institutional mechanisms.

These are not merely semantic or trivial issues; these are critical assessments of Puerto Rico's current political economy configuration with derived policy implications.

The work of Frank Bonilla and Ricardo Campos has the unquestionable merit of pioneering the analysis of the process of unequal integration of the island's labor market into the mainland's segmented labor market as an effect of the policies of Operation Bootstrap. In this sense, Bonilla and Campos have presented the case of Puerto Rico's uneven integration into the United States' internal capitalist labor reproduction process. They describe Puerto Rico as "a regional extension of the US economy that still preserves features of a national formation."[20] Bonilla and Campos have laid the foundation for the analysis of Puerto Rico's unequal integration into the United States' capitalist accumulation circuits and reproduction mechanisms that I am going to pursue.

Puerto Rico as a Regional Armature of the U.S. Model of Development

Accumulation regimes and modes of regulation[21] develop within nation-states: "In reality, struggles and institutional compromises take place mainly in the national framework, and thus methodological priority should be placed on the study of each particular social formation together with its external linkages."[22] Within each national formation a "model of development" comprises an industrial paradigm, stabilizing itself in a regime of accumulation, and guaranteed by a mode of regulation. Puerto Rico, however, within its colonial relationship with the United States has not developed into a nation-state, even within the relative autonomy gained in 1952 under the Commonwealth arrangement. In other words, Puerto Rico lacks "the archetypical form of any regulation," a complete national state with its regulation tools: control over the movement of capital, goods, services, and people, and the capability of engaging in effective anticyclical policy. Puerto Rico is actually unequally integrated into mainland production circuits and regulation institutional mechanisms. The island constitutes a differentiated part of the United States' economic space.

At this stage of the analysis an important caveat is appropriate. The lack of a national state constitutes a necessary but not a sufficient condition for Puerto Rico's trajectory as a differentiated U.S. economic region. The political defeat in the 1940s of the sociopolitical sectors that pursued an autonomous capitalist path within the institutional colonial political context entailed the triumph of a growth strategy within the institutional confines of the U.S. market that unevenly transferred mainland-based intensive accumulation activities and monopoly regulation networks to the island.[23]

It was the adoption of this particular growth strategy (the colonial political condition played an important supporting role, though an auxiliary one) that contributed to the insertion of Puerto Rico's economic space into the production circuits and capitalist reproduction institutions of U.S. capitalism. Thus, from this perspective, the adoption at the time and even today of an economic strategy that entails greater levels of self-reliance and diversification of the local economic structure is conceivable, even within colonial political parameters.

The "development by invitation" course adopted by the local hegemonic classes and political sectors led to the partial extension to Puerto Rico of specific phases (assembly of final products and processing of intermediate goods) of global vertically integrated manufacturing circuits headquartered in the United States. Under this arrangement, the island unit imports raw materials and intermediate goods and later exports its output, generating very few backward or forward industrial linkages with local-based enterprises.[24] Monitoring, research and development, and strategic decisions are realized in mainland headquarters.[25]

Likewise, portions of the mainland welfare state are extended to the island, entailing the partial transfer of the mainland's government-citizen accord. The defeat of the independent and most militant sectors of the local labor movement and the predominance of government-controlled and mainland industrial unions extended the logic of mainland capital-labor relations to Puerto Rico and hence the U.S. capital-labor accord.

The evolution of local financial institutions under the umbrella of the Federal Reserve System gradually integrated local capital markets to those of the mainland. Local banks and other financial intermediaries have favored home mortgages and consumer loans in their lending activities,[26] just as the mainland financial sector has. The entrance into the local market of the U.S. credit card establishment and of the big retail and consumer-credit conglomerates contributed to Puerto Rico's integration into the mainland's consumer-credit network. The entry of the big retail conglomerates also shaped the local retail market into the oligopolistic structures characteristic of mainland markets for final goods.[27]

This gradual integration into U.S. institutional regulation networks facilitated the local adoption of the mainland's social norm of mass consumption, characterized by the generalization of home ownership and purchases of automobiles and electric appliances.[28] With the exception of the stimulation of the local construction, cement, distribution, and banking sectors, Puerto Rico's mass consumption norm mainly supported mainland and global capital accumulation, as reflected by an annual average import coefficient for durable goods during the 1970s and 1980s of 45.7 percent.[29]

The launching of Operation Bootstrap fostered the transition from an extensive accumulation regime[30] characteristic of the sugar plantation, tobacco industry, and home needle labor processes, coexistent with a competitive regulation mode lacking a social safety net and the enforcement of labor protection laws and contracts, to an intensive accumulation regime and monopolist regulation mode via a gradual and uneven integration into mainland production and macroeconomic institutional networks. Puerto Rico during the postwar became a location for phases of mainland intensive accumulation activities and a U.S. consumer market backed by mainland institutional stimulants of aggregate demand.

Because of all of these factors, I describe the island's sociopolitical-economic space as a "regional armature" of the U.S. model of development. Alain Lipietz[31] defines a regional armature as a regional articulation of social relations that does not possess a complete state apparatus but in which secondary contradictions between dominant local classes are nonetheless resolved. Bob Jessop, on the other hand, offers a more elaborate definition, based on a more recent article by Lipietz. A regional armature

is a space "for itself" where the dominant classes of the local hegemonic bloc control their own political and ideological apparatus enabling them to regulate on a local scale some social and economic conflicts. It differs from the national state in having no universalistic legal
system, no monetary unit, and no monopoly of violence.[32]

Because Puerto Rico lacks a complete national state but contains its
own sociopolitical struggles with their particular national expression, it
is a regional armature whose insertion into the U.S. economic space is
asymmetrical in at least three instances:

1. The productive sphere: Only certain production activities of global
vertically integrated production circuits controlled and monitored by
the parent corporation in the mainland are located in Puerto Rico.
Most research and highly skilled employment remains external to
Puerto Rico.

2. The political-regulation-consumption sphere: Not all of the social
support programs of the U.S. government are extended to the island,
and some of the programs that are extended are extended only partially.

3. The labor-market-consumption sphere: Puerto Rico's labor force
forms part of the lowest layers of the U.S. segmented labor market,
that is, the layers with the highest unemployment rates and lowest
earnings. Although all sectors of the population take part in mass consumption, the integration into the mainland's social norm of consumption is unequal, representing a social norm below the mainland's
average.

The Crisis of U.S. Fordism as the Crisis of the Puerto Rican Model of Development

The end of the postwar "Golden Age" of growth and stability in the early
1970s with the breakout of the crisis of Fordism in the United States assumed the form in Puerto Rico of the crisis of the "Puerto Rican model
of growth."[33] A resurgence of worker resistance, the formation of new
militant unions, squatter land takeovers, student unrest, mass movements against the environmental impact of the expanding oil refining-
petrochemical complex characterized the local sociopolitical dynamics
of the crisis of Fordism.

In the mid-1970s federal and local authorities tried in basically two
ways to avert the crisis: through drastic increases in the amounts of federal aid granted to the island and by enhancing the package of fiscal in-

centives offered to mainland manufacturing firms that opened operations on the island.

In the early 1980s a complete policy reversal took place in Washington. In early 1981, Ronald Reagan took office, implementing across-the-board cuts in government social expenditures. The expansive monetary and welfare policies of the 1960s and 1970s were abandoned for greater monetary discipline and increases in military spending.

Puerto Rico's Social Norm of Consumption

Puerto Rico's social norm of consumption has been shaped since the postwar by its participation in mainland accumulation and regulation activities. Initially, during what has been described as the "Golden Age," Puerto Rico took part in continental intensive accumulation and Keynesian regulation processes that generated economies of scale in the production of durable and Fordist goods, leading to increases in real and social wages that made possible the island's incorporation into the mainland's norm of mass consumption.

Later on, in the midst of the crisis of intensive accumulation and stagnant output, Puerto Rico's participation in mainland defensive Keynesian policies by means of transfers and loose credit made it possible for Puerto Ricans to partially maintain the mass norm of consumption and continue to form part of the U.S. consumption norm. The reversal of Keynesian regulation in the early 1980s entailed the island's participation in the more competitive type of regulation and extensive accumulation processes prevalent on the mainland during the 1980s. In spite of the regressive income redistribution that took place during this period, the norm of mass consumption on the island was maintained, as on the mainland, through greater levels of consumer indebtedness.[34]

Puerto Rico in the 1980s: A Regional Armature of U.S. Extensive Accumulation and Competitive Regulation

The crisis of capitalist intensive accumulation entailed the resurgence of capitalist extensive accumulation as expressed by an increase in average working hours in the United States during the 1980s. The productivity slowdown in mass-production firms was compensated through increasing work time and "speed ups." Juliet Schor[35] estimates the increase in work time for the average American worker during the 1980s to have been 163 hours or the equivalent of one more month of work per year.

Puerto Rico as a location of certain U.S. capitalist extensive accumulation activities also experienced significant increases in average work time in manufacturing. Average work time in manufacturing increased by 4.5 percent during the 1980s compared to the combined average work time for the previous two decades. The average growth rate in labor time from the 1960s to the 1970s was approximately 1.2 percent.[36] This symmetrical pattern in average work time for both countries during the most recent decades reinforces the hypothesis that as a differentiated economic region of the United States, Puerto Rico constitutes an integral part of the process of capitalist extensive accumulation that was consolidated in the United States during the 1980s.

Likewise, the reductions in the social wage and the weakening of labor unions by the Reagan and Bush administrations during the early 1980s contributed to the reinforcement of a competitive regulation mode in the United States and by affiliation in Puerto Rico as well. Greater wage flexibility in the United States during the 1980s entailed greater polarization of the labor market between those with full-time relatively stable jobs, good wages, and considerable fringe benefits and a growing number of Americans and Puerto Ricans who are contingent workers, part-year workers, and, increasingly, part-time workers with low wages and almost no fringe benefits.

Since 1982, temporary employment in the United States has grown at a rate three times the growth rate of total employment.[37] In Puerto Rico a conservative estimate of the percentage of total employment that is temporary employment shows an increase from 11.6 percent in the 1970s to 15 percent during the 1980s to early 1990s.[38] If the most recent trends in employment growth during the most recent economic recovery in the United States are taken into account, 60 percent of the new jobs created are part-time jobs.[39] In Puerto Rico, part-time employment as a proportion of total employment increased from a combined decade average of 18.6 percent in the 1960s and 1970s to 28.3 percent in the 1980s.[40]

The rate of unionization of the labor force in the United States dropped from 26.2 percent in 1977 to 15.8 percent in 1993.[41] The rate of unionization of the labor force in Puerto Rico also dropped from 20 percent in 1970 to 7 percent in 1994.[42] Twelve years of anti-union appointments to the National Board of Labor Relations by the Reagan and Bush administrations have made their dent in the mainland segmented labor market, of which Puerto Ricans on the island and the continent constitute the lowest layer.[43] The same pattern of wage flexibility and greater segmentation in the mainland labor market experienced during the most recent decades has been reproduced in the Puerto Rican regional labor market as a differentiated part of the former, the basic distinction being that the higher rates of labor idleness in Puerto Rico entail greater levels of wage flexibility and competition for the regional labor market. All of this suggests that since the 1980s, Puerto Rico has made the transition as a differentiated part of U.S. capitalist intensive accumulation and monopolistic regulation during the postwar "Golden Age" period to an unequal part of U.S. capitalist extensive accumulation and competitive regulation.

Policy Implications of the Spatial Configuration of Puerto Rico's Political Economy

As I stated before, the characterization of the island's spatial configuration is not trivial, because it defines the structural parameters of the insular economy that help guide local economic policy and social and political goals. Those who have propagated the myth of the existence of a Puerto Rican national economy have contributed to an overstatement of the local levels of self-reliance and economic self-determination attained under the growth path pursued since the late 1940s. The net effect is the creation of a false sense of national economic achievement and an exaggeration of the degree of local economic maneuvering space for crisis management.

It bellifies the status quo under the current Commonwealth arrangement by reinforcing the myth of the existence of a Puerto Rican national economy with the benefits of a common market, currency, and citizenship with the United States. Thus, the policy prescription under this false scenario does not vary through time: incentives to U.S. investment are to be maintained or enhanced so that investment trickles down to satellite Puerto Rican industries that service and supply the transnational firms operating in Puerto Rico, resulting in the best of the two worlds, a Puerto Rican industry with the benefits of U.S. investment, government transfers, and free access to the continental market.

A similar assumption lay behind the policy prescriptions of the radical Left during the 1970s; the existence of a Puerto Rican national economy or industry made possible the abrupt delinking from the United

States economy without major long-term consequences for the population, who could reach a higher standard of living through the redistribution of wealth under a socialist republic. It was basically a matter of nationalizing the transnational segments of industry, which would be kept running under the new republic by the workers and specialists that worked for the firms during colonial times while they continued to be serviced and supplied by the national (i.e., Puerto Rican) sector of the economy.

On the other hand, the conventional regionalists either continue to hail the advantages of a free-trade, export-based growth strategy within the institutional confines of the mainland economy or to advocate the island's full political incorporation as a state so as to remove the only institutional barrier that inhibits Puerto Rico's full development as an economic region of the United States. Both policy prescriptions are founded on the false assumption that the island is a region integrated symmetrically into the U.S. economy.

Some of the most pressing problems that Puerto Rico currently faces as a regional armature of U.S. capitalist accumulation and regulation are the high unemployment levels that are a consequence of its asymmetrical insertion into U.S. accumulation circuits, which has resulted in a lopsided, disarticulated local industrial structure with a very low employment multiplier for new direct investment and in the current participation in U.S. competitive regulation and U.S. extensive accumulation. An outcome of these two effects has been the continued heavy reliance on U.S. treasury revenues, high dependence on U.S. capital and on imports of intermediate and consumer goods, the lack of dynamic autonomous economic institutions that could foster local autonomous economic development initiatives, stagnant overall productivity, a skyrocketing consumer debt, and greater social polarization.

In the context of the current fiscal crisis of the U.S. welfare state, Puerto Rico's high reliance on U.S. Treasury revenues in light of its legions of idle workers and numerous families living below the poverty line has become a burden on U.S. taxpayers, notwithstanding the slower growth rate in the flow of federal entitlements to the island during the most recent decade. Thus, no matter what political solution to Puerto Rico's current colonial situation is pursued, be it greater autonomy, statehood, or independence or even the continuation of the status quo, a concerted effort to promote more local initiatives and foreign investment in those sectors of local agriculture, manufacturing, and services with greater internal industrial linkages and hence greater employment spin-offs is required.

As paradoxical as it may seem, colonialists, autonomists, *independentistas*, and statehooders could all benefit from a more self-centered development effort that leads to greater self-reliance. The continuation of the current commonwealth status with its drainage of the U.S. Treasury by means of entitlements and foregone 936 corporate tax revenues is unsustainable in the medium to long run. Likewise, the admission of a beggar state faces strong opposition in a Congress faced with massive budget deficits. I do not need to make the case for greater autonomous development and self-reliance in the transition toward an independent Puerto Rico.

Notes

1. See J. C. Ingram, *Regional Payments Mechanisms: The Case of Puerto Rico* (Chapel Hill: University of North Carolina Press, 1962); Jorge Freyre, *El modelo económico de Puerto Rico* (Río Piedras: Interamerican University Press, 1979); and Frank Bonilla and Ricardo Campos, "Up by the Bootstraps: Ideologies of Social Levitation," in *Industry and Idleness*, ed. Frank Bonilla and Ricardo Campos (New York: History and Migration Task Force-Centro de Estudios Puertorriqueños, 1986).

2. James L. Dietz, *Economic History of Puerto Rico: Institutional Change and Capitalist Development* (Princeton, N.J.: Princeton University Press, 1986); Elias Gutiérrez, "The Transfer Economy of Puerto Rico: Toward an Urban Ghetto?" in *Time for Decision*, ed. Jorge Heine (Lanham, Md.: North-South Publishing Co., 1983); Joaquín Villamil, "Puerto Rico 1948–1979: The Limits of Dependent Growth," in Heine, ed., *Time for Decision*; Edwin Meléndez, "Accumulation and Crisis in the Postwar Puerto Rican Economy" (Ph.D. diss., University of Massachusetts-Amherst, 1985); and Emilio Pantojas, *Development Strategies as Ideology: Puerto Rico's Export-Led Industrialization Experience* (London: Lynne Rienner Publishers, 1990).

3. By capital accumulation I signify a real increment in both the fixed (i.e., productive equipment, intermediate goods, and productive facilities) and variable (i.e., amount of waged labor employed) components of capital in its Marxist sense. Capitalist reproduction should be understood as all the individual, social, and institutional activities and processes that ensure, facilitate, and support a particular form of capitalist accumulation.

4. Alain Lipietz, *El capital y su espacio* (Mexico: Siglo XXI, 1977).

5. I will be using the concepts of the "French School of Regulation." I will define and elaborate on these concepts as I develop the argument.

6. See Ingram, *Regional Payments Mechanisms*; and Freyre, *El modelo económico de Puerto Rico*.

7. Productive denationalization, unemployment, social marginalization, and mass immigration are some of the most dramatic consequences.

8. Jenaro Baquero, "La importación de fondos y la capacidad absorbente de nuestra economía," *Revista de Ciencias Sociales* 7 (1963): 79–92; and Elias Gutiérrez, *Factor Proportions, Technology Transmission and Unemployment in Puerto Rico* (Río Piedras: Editorial Universitaria, 1977).

9. A dependent economy is one that relies heavily on the technology, productive equipment, intermediate goods, and financial resources of another economy. An interdependent economy is one that has effective control over the development of its own technological, productive, and financial resources in close commercial and political interaction, either symmetrical or asymmetrical, with the rest of the world.

10. Villamil, "Puerto Rico 1948–1979."

11. See Fernando Enrique Cardoso, "Las contradicciones del Desarrollo-Asociado," *Revista Paraguaya de Sociología* 11, 29 (Jan.–Apr. 1974): 34–77; and Osvaldo Sunkel, "Transnational Capitalism and National Disintegration in Latin America," *Social and Economic Studies* 22, 1 (1973): 72–93.

12. Gutiérrez, "The Transfer Economy of Puerto Rico."

13. James L. Dietz, "Imperialism and Under-development: A Theoretical Perspective and a Case Study of Puerto Rico," *Review of Radical Political Economics* 11, 4 (winter 1979): 23.

14. Ibid., 23; emphasis mine.

15. Dietz, *Economic History of Puerto Rico*, 240.

16. Meléndez, "Accumulation and Crisis in the Postwar Puerto Rican Economy."

17. A Social Structure of Accumulation (SSA) comprises all the institutions that support a long wave of capital accumulation at a determined historical period and place. See Samuel Bowles, David Gordon, and Thomas Weisskopf, *Beyond the Wasteland: A Democratic Alternative to Economic Decline* (London: Verso, 1983).

18. In adopting a noneconomistic definition of what a social formation is, one has to incorporate the distinct social struggles and cultural expressions of a people to the particular articulation of modes of production within which they interact. Considering that Puerto Ricans constitute a distinct nationality with their own history of sociopolitical struggles and culture, Puerto Rico is a distinct social formation unequally integrated into the United States social formation.

19. Pantojas, *Development Strategies as Ideology*.

20. Bonilla and Campos, "Up by the Bootstraps," 102.

21. I use in my analysis some key concepts of the French Regulation School found in the work of some members of its Parisian branch. See Michel Aglietta, *A Theory of Capitalist Regulation: The US Experience* (London: Verso, 1979); Lipietz, *El capital y su espacio*; Alain Lipietz, "New Tendencies in the International Division of Labor: Regimes of Accumulation and Modes of Regulation," in *Production, Work, Territory: The Geographical Anatomy of Industrial Capitalism*, ed. Allen J. Scott and Michael Stopper (London: Allen and Unwin, 1986); and Robert Boyer, *The Regulation School: A Critical Introduction* (New York: Columbia University Press, 1990). A regime of accumulation is defined by the prevalence in capitalist societies of certain types of socio-technological relations of production that entail greater or lower levels of industrial productivity, which account for a particular allocation of resources between consumption and investment that makes possible a relatively longer stable or shorter unstable period of growth. A mode of regulation is comprised by the totality of institutional forms that materialize the social accords and the implicit norms that assure the consistency of behaviors and expectations that permit capitalist reproduction within a regime of accumulation.

22. Lipietz, "New Tendencies in the International Division of Labor," 22.

23. The Fordist regime of accumulation prevalent in the United States from the 1920s to the early 1970s was an intensive regime of accumulation based on the use of automatic assembly-line operations that made possible economies of scale in the mass production of standardized commodities. Monopoly regulation, on the other hand, takes the form of oligopolistic mark-up pricing in product markets, collective bargaining in labor

markets entailing "sticky wages," and an active Keynesian "welfare state" providing a social wage and managing aggregate demand through fiscal and monetary policies.

24. Dietz, *Economic History of Puerto Rico.*

25. U.S. Department of Commerce, *Economic Study of Puerto Rico*, vols. 1 and 2 (Washington, D.C.: Government Printing Office, 1979).

26. Rita Maldonado, *The Role of the Financial Sector in the Economic Development of Puerto Rico* (Washington, D.C.: Federal Deposit Insurance Corporation, 1970).

27. Jaime Benson, "Capitalist Regulation and Unequal Integration: The Case of Puerto Rico" (Ph.D. diss., University of Massachusetts, 1993), 82.

28. Ibid., 94, 95.

29. Ibid., 86. This relatively high figure underestimates the real magnitude of the relative participation of mainland and global accumulation activities in the island's durable consumption expenditures because the portion of local consumer demand supplied by nonresident transnational firms located on the island is not taken into account.

30. Capitalist extensive accumulation is characterized by the increase in work time or the work load of individual workers in order to enhance the levels of absolute surplus value. In Marxist terminology the prevalence of absolute surplus value extraction productive processes defines extensive accumulation.

31. Lipietz, *El capital y su espacio*, 43.

32. Bob Jessop, "Regulation Theories in Retrospect and Prospect," *Economy and Society* 19, 2 (May 1990): 209.

33. See Meléndez, "Accumulation and Crisis in the Postwar Puerto Rican Economy"; Pantojas, *Development Strategies as Ideology*; and Benson, "Capitalist Regulation and Unequal Integration."

34. Benson, "Capitalist Regulation and Unequal Integration."

35. Juliet Schor, *The Overworked American: The Unexpected Decline of Leisure* (New York: Basic Books, 1992), 29.

36. Jaime Benson, "Empresas de especialización flexible y autogestión obrera en un contexto institucional de mercado de trabajo competitivo en Puerto Rico: El compacto de empresa como arreglo institucional alternativo" (paper presented at the Twentieth Conference of the Caribbean Studies Association, Curaçao, May 22–27, 1995): 12.

37. Bennet Harrison, "The Dark Side of Flexible Production," *Technology Review* (May–June 1994): 40.

38. Benson, "Empresas de especialización," 16.

39. Harrison, "The Dark Side of Flexible Production," 40.

40. Benson, "Empresas de especialización," 15.

41. Aaron Bernstein, "Why America Needs Unions but Not the Kind It Has Now," *Business Week*, May 23, 1994, 70.

42. Benson, "Empresas de especialización," 13.

43. Bonilla and Campos, "Up by the Bootstraps."

PART TWO

Thinking Textually

The Discreet Charm of the Proletariat: Imagining Early-Twentieth-Century Puerto Ricans in the Past Twenty-Five Years of Historical Inquiry

Kelvin A. Santiago-Valles

> *It is as if it was particularly difficult, in the history in which men retrace their own ideas and their own knowledge, to formulate a general theory of discontinuity, of series, of limits, of unities, specific orders, and differentiated autonomies and dependencies. . . . As if we were afraid to conceive of the* Other *in the time of our own thought.*
>
> Michel Foucault, *The Archaeology of Knowledge*

> *The violence which has ruled over the ordering of the colonial world . . . will be claimed and taken over by the native at the moment when, deciding to embody history in his own person, he surges into forbidden quarters. To wreck the colonial world is henceforward a mental picture of action which is very clear, very easy to understand and which may be assumed by each one of the individuals which constitute the colonized people. To break up the colonial world does not mean that after the frontiers have been abolished lines of communication will be set up between the two zones. The destruction of the colonial world is no more and no less tha[n] the abolition of one zone.*
>
> Frantz Fanon, *The Wretched of the Earth*

How have the new historical studies of the past twenty-five years understood and interpreted the Puerto Rican reality of the first half of the twentieth century? How have social transgressions been defined, and how has social change been conceptually appraised? What difference have colonial differences made in researching the impact of capitalism on most Puerto Ricans? What was the place, if any, of textual analysis within this historical inquiry? And what was the sociohistorical/conceptual space—the episteme[1]—that constituted this particular historiographical order?

Until the late 1960s and early 1970s, traditional anticolonialist historiography had been represented by scholars such as Lidio Cruz Monclova, Loida Figueroa, Aida Negrón de Montilla, Manuel Maldonado Denis, and Robert Anderson. At that time, a different type of anticolonialist research arose,[2] eventually becoming known as the "New Historiography" and prevailing up to the early 1990s. Like other emergent Western(ized) sociohistorical trends, the Puerto Rican variant (often Marxist or broadly social-liberal) emphasized a history "from below," primarily focusing on the political-economic forces shaping poor majorities on the island and their migrations during the nineteenth and early twentieth centuries.[3] These new approaches soon influenced the ways in which Puerto Rican history was studied insofar as they compelled some of the old anticolonialist school's adherents to adopt elements of social history; additional research also surfaced combining (deliberately or not) the concepts and methods of both the older and the emergent tendencies.[4]

The Centro de Estudios de la Realidad Puertorriqueña (CEREP) and its formal members tended to predominate within this "school." From its inception, this trend was well represented within the unevenly ascendant "Puerto Rican Studies" in the U.S. academy: for instance, many of these perspectives coincided with those of the History and Migration Task Force of the Centro de Estudios Puertorriqueños at Hunter College-CUNY.[5] But from very early on, there was a comparable intellectual production occurring outside of, in no way connected to, and sometimes strongly critical of CEREP. Prominent examples of such critiques were the island publications and U.S. Ph.D. dissertations of the members of the Taller de Formación Política. Islandwide, U.S.-based, and broader international social strife and political upheavals during the late 1960s and early 1970s had a direct impact on this type of analysis.[6] But, eventually, this new historiography found a respectable niche within scholarly spaces (official and extra-academic) in Puerto Rico, the United States, Latin America, and Europe.[7]

I offer two caveats: First, since I am dealing mainly with historical descriptions of how the Puerto Rican laboring-poor majorities have been socially constituted during the early twentieth century, I emphasize the similarities between these populations on the island and their existence on the U.S. mainland. I realize that these two populations and the ways they have been socially constituted have diverged during this period; I am also aware of the need for further (and truly in-depth) historiographies of these processes and populations. Here, rather, I am focusing on their common origins, asymmetrical linkages, and—most of all—the enduring colonial(ist) context in which these origins and linkages unfold.

In this sense, the present analysis is a continuation of part of my previous investigations.[8] Second, all generational demarcations are arbitrary, and mine is no less so. And just as "pre-'New Historiography'" historical studies continue to be produced to this very day—although by different authors—so it is with the investigations of the "CEREP generation" and of its critics, all nevertheless belonging to the same methodological/thematic cohort.[9] What follows is my particular sketch of this generation's epistemic physiognomy. Like other postwar Caribbean and Latino students of Puerto Rican history, I have operated within this same intellectual heritage. Therefore, being able to examine its specific rules of formation[10] simultaneously entails a criticism of my own work.[11]

Economic Accents and the Invisible Domains of Colonialism

This historiography conceptually sutured the development and effects of capitalism in Puerto Rico with the development of U.S. colonialism by illustrating in great detail just how such links surfaced during the 1898–1950 period.[12] I believe the political-economic and discursive construction of "native" space in general and of the subaltern subject of colonial capitalism in particular[13] are issues intimately related to the various ways in which colonized laborers reacted to the process that brought them into being even as it transformed their lives. The scholarship of the late 1960s to early 1990s described the high social costs of this early-twentieth-century transformation, this being an obvious reaction to the emphases of the older historical studies on the actions of isolated individuals and on the force of powerful ideas. However, the newer studies were epistemically guided by the narrow economic dimensions of laboring-class formation (regardless of the explicit topic being examined).[14] Within this conceptual grammar, the advent of capitalism on the island and the subsequent demographic dislocations were primarily read as simply one manifestation—a vernacular form—of capitalism in general, that is, of European and Euro-American economic expansionism. As I have abundantly illustrated elsewhere,[15] we should take advantage of the approach and focus in some recent South Asian historiographies and cultural critiques. These would suggest several crucial similarities between, on the one hand, the nineteenth- and twentieth-century histories of the subcontinent and, on the other hand, the early-twentieth-century histories of Puerto Ricans. Gyan Prakash has pointed out (in the case of Indian historiography) that critical history cannot simply document the process by which capitalism becomes dominant, for that amounts to repeating the history we seek to displace; instead, criticism must reveal the difference that capitalism either represents as the particular form of its universal existence or sketches it only in relation to itself. . . . My point is that making capitalism the foundational theme amounts to homogenizing the histories that remain heterogenous to it.[16]

Any emphasis on the more economic and general aspects of how capitalism became dominant among Puerto Ricans eclipses *this* historical capitalism's structural-colonial qualities, its limits, and its disputed sign systems,[17] thereby hindering a more complex understanding of subaltern resistances.

This historiography did take into account the chronically low wages and the grueling working and living conditions; the trials and tribulations of the sugarcane *tiempo muerto* and of depression-era New York City; the penalties of the usurer, the plantation store, the loan shark, and the slumlord; the widespread use of police coercion; the dismal situation in the sweatshops; the paternalistic relief agencies and devious development programs; the food shortages and disease; and so on. But if and when the colonialist character of such cruelty was documented and interpreted, it tended to surface either as an excess of the existing institutions and/or as the workings of perverse individuals,[18] for example, U.S. personnel, white/Anglo entrepreneurs, and their "native" sycophants. Wilfredo Mattos Cintrón, for example, portrays the actions of Blanton Winship, island governor during the late 1930s, in the following manner:

> The yankee government named Blanton Winship as governor. By mid 1937, after having spent almost a year in an Island prison, victims of a kangaroo court, the nationalist leadership directed by Don Pedro Albizu Campos left Puerto Rico headed for the federal prison of Atlanta in the state of Georgia. Subsequently, under the inspiration of Winship, on March 21, 1937, an unarmed demonstration of nationalists was gunned down in the city of Ponce. This event has come to be known as the Ponce Massacre. Winship was following the orders issued to him.[19]

There are three important, structurally colonial-capitalist, and overlapping processes that fall outside the conceptual order of this school. The first is the coercive, regulatory, and disciplinary use of force and misery—intentional or not—that unfolded as a persistent, prominent, and vital element of the ways in which useful labor was created, organized, and regulated within and by rising capitalist and distressed noncapitalist forms of exploitation. The second is the impoverished majorities' harsh everyday life as a fundamental element of their subaltern condition. And the third is the ideological mechanisms that constituted the entire colonized space and these "native" laborers by, among other things, inscribing as wayward many of their responses and resistances to these hardships. Within most of the historical work that we were—and many are still—producing, it is as if capitalism operated on the island or on the U.S. mainland independently of colonialism and its technologies of representation; or, in Foucaultian terms, it is as if colonial capitalism had no political anatomy. From such an episteme, colonialism is visible mainly as a juridico-political ornament that periodically makes its presence felt in impertinent and unfortunate ways. The adversity endured, negotiated, and resisted by these laboring classes is conceptualized as a problem belonging to two separate categories that practically never intersect at the level of the everyday, socioeconomic, and semiotic realities of the poor majorities: on the one hand, capitalism, and on the other hand, colonialism. The prevailing research has not examined these destitute peasants, island urban and coastal workers, and U.S. ghetto residents—together with their families and communities and the corresponding social practices—qua partial effects of colonial economic relations because colonialism was not perceived as an economic reality.

In turn, these social classes mainly emerged as the result of a "poverty" and a "capitalism" far removed from the distinctly colonial framework of specific ideological representations. The socioeconomic composition of these subaltern subjects was rarely understood as being structured simultaneously by a colonialist textuality and by a textual colonialism. As Nicholas Dirks has pointed out in a broader context, the problem is that

> colonialism not only has had cultural effects that have too often been either ignored or displaced into the inexorable logics of modernization and world capitalism, it was itself a cultural project of control. Colonial knowledge both enabled colonial conquest and was produced by it; in certain important ways, culture was what colonialism was all about.... Sexuality in Sumatra, torture in the Congo, terror in the Mirabar caves [of India]—were all displacements of the fault lines of expanding capitalism at the same time that they became fundamental moments in the unfolding narrative of the modern.[20]

For the "New Historiography," on the contrary, the blindly economic deployment of this colonialist coercion, the structural logic of this colonialist misery, and the normative discourses that frame both were unthinkable as economic (colonial) forces. Colonialism seemed to be a perpetually extraneous, juridical, and political force: the corollary processes of signification and discursive construction are missing altogether. The resulting functionalism runs counter to the anticolonialist claims of these historical analyses—therein the need to search for and reconstruct human agency as a counterbalance to the economic emphases.

Mainstream Sociohistorical Studies and the Search for "Real" Politics

Overlooking the historical specificity of how this capitalism affected Puerto Ricans has hampered a more nuanced understanding of the anticolonialist responses of the working classes. Which is not to say that such (re)search has not taken place—quite the opposite. The relationship between, on the one hand, the resistance practices carried out by laboring poor Puerto Ricans everywhere and, on the other, opposition to colonial conditions during this period has been one of the most hotly disputed topics within (and outside) this scholarship. The controversy has mainly been about identifying trade-union leaders who made public statements in favor of Puerto Rico's independence, contesting the exact role that various pro-independence political parties played with respect to different labor conflicts, measuring local election results, trying to figure out why the only mass labor party in island history was eventually in favor of having Puerto Rico join the federal union as an incorporated province, debating the role and influence of the (colonialist) U.S. trade-union federation (the AFL), and so on.[21]

This accent represented a disavowal of "native" popular resistance forms (formally anticolonial or not, U.S.-based or not) that went beyond what most of us—and our older predecessors—continued to perceive as the consummate traditional-liberal expressions of sociopolitical opposition. There were a few paltry efforts to comb the archives and oral-history sources for traces of different countersystemic disruptions: on-the-job pilfering, odd-jobbing, use-value oriented reciprocal practices, and other early manifestations of the "informal economy." The same was true for sexual-outlaw practices, anti-Western cultural displays, and social violence that (at an individual or collective level and in whatever contradictory ways) contested the capitalist-colonial order's monopoly over physical force and its racist, masculinist, heteronormative, and property-based foundations. Another question not usually addressed was how such unruly subaltern practices unsettled the patrician and Eurocentric moralism of the creole elites and their artisan and/or peasant homologues in Puerto Rico and in the United States.

In this manner, the New Historiography inadvertently shouldered two burdens. First, to paraphrase Ranajit Guha, anticolonial politics were primarily identified with those institutions introduced, expanded, or legitimized by the colonial social order,[22] namely, political parties, activities that influence "public opinion," journalism and other literary forms, and trade-union ventures. Second, these terrains of social contest were, per se, the privileged domain of literate "natives" (i.e., a small portion of the Puerto Rican population): this last question was rarely constituted as a research—or a political—question.[23] As Partha Chatterjee has observed in his critique of how traditional Indian historiography (both nationalist and Marxist) understands "native" oppositional practices, "Their meanings (the subaltern's actions) are only given *extraneously*, from the domain of 'real' politics. In other words, they are incomprehensible, 'spontaneous.' "[24]

In this manner, crucial resistances of the colonized majorities became epistemologically barred outside of "real" politics because "real" politics was the only site where anticolonial human agency could reside. By privileging Western respectability, such studies rendered invisible many of the normalizing discourses that construct and regulate all forms of popular transgression. Colonialism continued to be inscribed and imagined as a force that is endlessly external, juridical, and political (in the formal-traditional sense of "real" politics). Its specifically disobedient forms of difference—the social practices at odds with the colonial-capitalist social order—were rarely identified because such forms/practices primarily flourished outside (or below) conventional "politics."

What were the rules of formation of such scholarship? The overall proclivity to normalize colonialism, as well as the popular resistances to it, within the conventionally understood political arena could have been due, among other things, to the signature tendency of mainstream social history to disengage "politics" and "ideology" from "economics," only to reunite—later and if need be—both under the aegis of "economics" by means of the customary architectural/topographic paradigm: the "base-superstructure" model. The examples of this tradition are far too abundant to even responsibly attempt to list them, but their Marxist ancestry is unmistakable.[25] When "economics" is reasoned as an independent realm, "politics" and "ideology" need only interfere on special occasions, as it were, from the "outside" or from "above." However, this does not mean that the politico-ideological "outside" is irrelevant. Far from it, for "politics" is understood to be the very site of power: the "modern representative state," according to *The Communist Manifesto*, is the rallying site of the "committee for managing the common affairs of the whole bourgeoisie." Likewise, the prevalent "ideology" of an era tends to be accepted as the ideas of the ruling class.[26] Within these conceptual parameters, the Lukácsian notion of "false consciousness" is usually not far behind.

I am aware that the capitalist state is structurally vital, not only as a social relationship of power, but even more so as the unstable condensation of all other power relations at a given moment.[27] The problem, rather, is that most Marxists (including Marx and Engels) do not understand power—and, hence, the entire realm of politics—as being in and of itself already inherent to capitalist relations of economic organization.[28] This is how and why most Marxisms reduce all power relations to the state, concurrently disregarding the chains of signification that do not simply reproduce modernity and/or ruling-class culture.

Inside the conceptual continent of mainstream Marxism and its gnoseological protocol, spontaneous labor resistances are expected to materialize only within the institutional province of "economics." Laborers alone, per se, are allegedly incapable of seriously confronting this thing called "power"—as may be seen in the Taller de Formación Política's *¡Huelga en la caña!* Such historiographies reduce not just capitalist power relations but, even more so, colonial-ideological power relations to a creature that inhabits the realm of the "superstructure." Colonialist power and ideology were only conceivable as a double "externality" with respect to most Puerto Ricans. Such power and ideology were located in the social stratosphere, and they ultimately resided outside subaltern communities (e.g., in Washington, D.C.), being only periodically delegated to and recycled through colonial emissaries in the local legislature, governorship, courts, police force, federal government, political parties, newspapers, and so on.

Evolutionism and the Teleology of Marxist Historiography

The distinctive scholarship of the late 1960s to early 1990s tended to produce the "emergent proletariat" (qua object of study)—particularly its active industrial component—as a historically necessary and progressive instance among Puerto Ricans. The proletariat would be the primary site of significant human agency in Puerto Rican historical evolution. This is why such studies lamented the persistence of enormous majority contingents of semiproletarian and nonproletarian peasants, agrarian wage-workers, and/or urban unemployed, underemployed, and nonemployed laborers among the working classes during most of the first half of this century. For example, the Taller de Formación Política described one of the key conditions that—according to them—limited anticolonial change by arguing that

> imperialist penetration in Puerto Rico constituted the proletariat in the Island as a fundamentally agrarian and rural one. The rural prole-tariat has a limited capacity for resistance with respect to capital, [a limitation] which can only be counteracted by means of their organizational association with the industrial proletariat. Imperialism, on the one hand, legalized the trade unions, but, on the other hand, impeded the formation of a broad industrial proletariat that could serve as an organizational axis for the working class. *The labor movement was born mutilated, deprived of its fundamental support.*[29]

Such reservations are usually informed by Marx and Engels's apprehensions about an aimless or misdirected peasantry and other not fully pro-letarian members of the laboring classes.[30]

The discussions of the 1898 U.S. invasion and its immediate aftermath are a good example of this conceptual universe and its evolutionist laws. Many of these historical analyses insisted that 1898 embodied a shift to a higher stage of democratic rights than what most of the population enjoyed under Spanish colonialism. The U.S. invasion strongly propelled Puerto Ricans up the path of capitalist economic relations, resulting in the creation of a Puerto Rican proletariat. In addition to the obvious and unfortunately exploitative character of capitalism, the only perceived drawbacks were the North American republic's control over Puerto Rican economic transformation, as well as U.S. hegemony over Puerto Rican politics—state affairs, in particular. But because the anticapitalist battle is the highest stage of historical conflict, socialist/proletarian struggles constitute its only authentic and legitimate anticapitalist forms. Such struggles become possible solely through the advent of a proletariat—particularly an industrial one—which, in turn, can only come about through the implantation and/or development of capitalism.[31]

This historical scholarship on early-twentieth-century Puerto Ricans did not invent the teleology of evolutionary progress. Although framed within the investigation of a different time period, one of the most extreme examples of this same evolutionism comes from some of my own previous work. On that occasion I explained and defended the implantation of noncapitalist relations of exploitation in Puerto Rico (debt-peonage and chattel slavery) during the nineteenth century arguing that "objectively speaking" and "in historical perspective," this "unfortunately painful and brutal" process nevertheless "represented as necessary a step forward . . . as did slavery in Classical Antiquity."[32] The latter statement, of course, was directly informed by Engels's *Anti-Dühring*.[33] No, they/we did not invent but instead drew and further elaborated on the foundational philosophies of history and antecedent "Sciences of Man" that emerged in the West from the eighteenth to the early twentieth centuries—including the overwhelming majority of Marxisms. Tenets spanning the "Great Chain of Being," Social Darwinism, and beyond are racist, class-based, and sexist versions of this broader, much more pervasive metadiscourse of progress-through-stages.[34]

According to this conceptual order, History and Humanity (i.e., "Mankind"), as coherent totalities, move through ascending levels, each one more advanced than its predecessor, each one the forerunner of the subsequent stage. The different schools of thought mainly differ on *which* historical agents personify (the spirit of) each phase or era—ideas, individuals, classes, genders, races, sexualities, cultures, religions, nationalities, grand formations, or transcendent patterns, and so on—and/or on *which* historical agents enable social change or guard existing achievements from perversion. The knowledge-power effects of such questions are rarely interrogated. This is what Gyan Prakash calls "foundational" historiography, whereby "history is ultimately founded in and representable through some identity—individual, class, structure—that resists further decomposition into heterogeneity."[35]

This metahistory, even—or, perhaps, particularly—in the case of its dialectical variants, is a history that ultimately moves ahead and upward. The latter is firmly located within the same Enlightenment, stage-ist, and modernist terrain shared by many of the artisan and trade-union activists, whose writings and lives are being recovered from oblivion by the historiographies that set the standard from the late 1960s to early 1990s.[36] This generation celebrated, absorbed, and built upon earlier artisan visions, as in the case of Quintero Rivera's 1988 study, which insists that

> in the face of the "four-hundred years of ignorance and servitude" of
> the Spanish era, . . . the North American presence was the closest thing

to a bourgeois revolution given the existing class configuration. It represented the modernization of the economy: oppressive and alienating due to its capitalist wage relations, but positive with respect to the development of the productive forces, especially free wage labor, *the element that made possible the socialist agenda.*[37]

What is hardly ever asked is, "how is it possible to write a critical account of capitalism unless we also estrange, disfigure, and deconstruct its colonization of history?"[38] In this sense, proletarian agency remains locked into the general and teleological episteme of most Marxisms: reading history as capitalist development and its effects.

I am not defending medieval obscurantism but, rather, attempting to problematize the historicity of "obscurantism," "pre-history," "development," and so on. This means not just criticizing the Eurocentric, propertied, and elitist parameters of such notions, as Juan Flores did in his study of the famous 1930s creole intellectual Antonio S. Pedreira.[39] Further, it means questioning the masculinism and infantilization that necessarily accompanies all evolutionist conceptual orders, including most Marxisms. I am not exhuming the "old-school" historiographic (and sociocultural) nostalgia for the alleged pre-1898 "Golden Age" that the late-1960s to early-1990s generation conceptually and empirically dismantled so thoroughly. Instead, my criticism aims to historicize the evolutionist modernism grounding even this/our generation's critique of older schools. The Puerto Rican nineteenth century was not an inferior stage of the twentieth century; both centuries/moments were not steps forward or backward in some teleological March of Progress. Instead, both centuries/moments were "just" different from each other: for subaltern Puerto Ricans, for the propertied and educated classes (creole and non-Puerto Rican), as well as in terms of the overall diachronic effects of each colonialist enterprise (particularly in the contested processes of subject formation) during both periods. I cannot go into the details of such distinctions here,[40] though I will say that they are grounded, to some extent, in the abstractions we deploy to make sense of—and, thus, imagine and partially produce/transform—the material conditions of our sociohistorical "heritage." The deceptively uncomplicated unity and homogeneity of both centuries are but neatly misleading theoretical tools and analytical parameters enabling us to grasp, designate, and recognize social processes and lived experiences that are extremely arbitrary, heterotopically spliced, and discontinuously linked.

The conceptual effects of modernist historiography are inescapable, albeit not always conspicuously. Within this evolutionist mise-en-scène—however lamentable some of its consequences—the implantation of capitalism unfolds as a positive and progressive stage of human maturation, Puerto Ricans included. The way capitalist development affects Puerto Ricans is only thinkable within the same traditional-political parameters within which such inquiry has defined colonialism. Hence, the historical landscape mapped by these historiographies (in their search for truly advanced anticolonial resistances) continues to echo the moralism and "respectability" of the more conventionally—and narrowly—delineated realm of " 'real' politics." Why look elsewhere—for example, to the "native" illegalities[41]—for popular resistances to this social order? Why bother with its signifying patterns?

But producing knowledge in this way has had additional—and equally inescapable—implications for those of us once or still working within the New Historiography's regime of truth. Unfortunately, I cannot examine these other effects here (that would be a whole other article), but not mentioning them would be even more remiss on my part. We have seen how Western(ized) Marxisms contextualized the emergence and unfolding of the late-1960s to early-1990s generation, a process further influenced by already alluded to societal turmoil and political struggles in Puerto Rico, in the United States, and internationally. Now I am referring to political practices that do not substantially interrogate the social conditions prevailing among most Puerto Ricans: throughout the island and in the U.S. ghettoes, the upstanding industrial proletariat continues to be glaringly diminutive, while the colonized majorities vie against, negotiate, and taunt the prevailing dispossession. Not questioning these conditions confirms an epistemic investment in modern economic development, moralism and "respectability," and " 'real' politics."[42] And despite the formally anticolonial or well-meaning intentions of its proponents, such investments betray the dead-end nature of modernity (including late, global "post"-modernity) and its inherent Eurocentrism.

The Emergent Historico-Textual Studies

None of this is meant to imply that the social history of Puerto Ricans has not been textually examined at all. There is now a small but growing body of inquiry studying the discursive production of Puerto Ricans.[43] These studies include some of the most incisive explanations of the sign systems structuring social conditions among Puerto Ricans during the twentieth century. Nevertheless, most of these analyses (particularly those focusing on the island) study the cultural work of the creole propertied and educated classes; such analyses are carried out within primarily Eurocentric conceptual parameters. Even in the few cases in which the dispossessed are studied, there is a strong inclination to focus on more traditionally defined, morally upright, and Western(ized) "politics."[44]

Additionally, the incursions that these studies have made into socioeconomic analysis are usually general in the extreme. This vagueness may be partially due to the fact that most of this scholarship originated in the humanities, particularly literary criticism. Their dependence on the economic histories and historical sociologies that characterized the late 1960s to early 1990s is evident and, in many cases, very explicit.[45] Unfortunately, this influence has been one-sided: most sociohistorical studies have not been analogously enriched by the theoretical frameworks of the new literary histories and textual analyses. Although some economic historiographies address part of the discursive production emanating from the laboring classes, such research customarily centers on the more "respectable" and modernist aspects of artisan and/or peasant everyday life.[46] The narratives of normalization that construct these practices, the corresponding mechanisms that textually fashion the colonized laboring classes, and the contested sign systems emanating from these transgressions have for the most part not been examined by the late-1960s to early-1990s generation of historiographies, taken as a whole. This generation has not deemed it necessary to explore, critically recuperate, much less transform, the epistemic shifts suggested by postcoloniality[47] and by poststructuralism as theoretical frameworks for sociohistorical inquiry.

Whereas, here, I have been carrying out a primarily conceptual critique, such a critique should not be simply dismissed to that limbo called "pure theory" or "mere text," that is, the diametrical opposite of something called "hard reality." I agree that in the final analysis the limits of Enlightenment-based horizons (including the Marxist mainstream) are not intellectual nor scholarly but closer to the politico-practical. These limits are personified ultimately by the proliferation of multifarious counterhegemonic movements all over the world, questioning—through their actions and ideological representations—all forms of statism, class/economic-reductionism, and modern politics in general: neoconservative, liberal, social-democrat, and Marxist. However, none of these practices or social spaces exist outside textuality. I agree with Gayatri Chakravorty Spivak that you will not get away from the text by deciding to join movements, or by deciding to stop reading books. A bullet in the chest, the fact of the death, might seem to stop textuality, but the reason why the bullet, the access to the bullet, why the bullet at all; who killed whom, why, how? . . . rather than simply advance it as an example of where the text stops—if we are going to *do* anything about the phenomenon, we have *no* alternative but to involve ourselves and mire ourselves in what we are calling the textuality of the socius. The real task here is to displace and undo that killing opposition between the text narrowly conceived as the verbal text and activism narrowly conceived as some sort of mindless engagement.[48]

On the other hand, neither am I ignoring the important discrepancies within and between postcoloniality and poststructuralism: for example, nationalisms versus localist expressions, masculinist anticolonialism versus feminism and queer theory, Eurocentric heterologies versus subaltern studies. Rather, I am emphasizing their affinities, specifically the ways in which recent postcolonial theorizations are rethinking historical "Third-World(ist)" nationalisms while profoundly transforming Western(ized) poststructuralist analyses of history and society. In historicizing the relationship between the study of culture, the social sciences, and colonialist/neocolonialist hegemony, Talal Asad argues that "right through modern imperial times and places, Western techniques for governing subjects have radically restructured the domain we now call society—a process that has reorganized strategies of power accordingly." He then says, "This process has been extensively written about (and not only by Foucault and his followers) in the context of modern European"—and, I would add, European-American—"history, but far less so in the context of Europe's"—and European-America's—"imperial territories. In fact the difference between the processes of transformation in the two contexts remains to be properly explored. Grasping that difference seems to me to require in part a closer examination of the emerging discourses of 'culture.'" Asad ends by saying, "Until we understand precisely how the social domain has been restructured (constituted), our accounts of the dynamic connections between power and knowledge during the colonial period will remain limited."[49]

I think this is the challenge for the Puerto Rican historical scholarship emerging now. The late-1960s to early-1990s generation did not— could not?—define itself/ourselves in terms of analyzing the dominant knowledges and power relations described by Edward Said in the case of the "Orient": the "corrective study" that turned Puerto Rico into "Porto

Rico" and transformed its impoverished majorities into "something one judges (as in court of law)," into "something one disciplines (as in school or prison), something one illustrates (as in a zoological manual)," and something that "is *contained* and *represented* by dominating frameworks." Said then immediately asks: "Where do these come from?"[50] Addressing this question would probably reposition the study of early-twentieth-century Puerto Ricans, as well as contribute, I hope, to an alternative, ex-"native" political imaginary.

Notes

1. I am using the concept of "episteme," here, according to Michel Foucault, *The Order of Things* (New York: Vintage, 1970), xxi–xxii, 168, 200.

2. As the then new generation was fond of pointing out, two of the rupture texts were Gervasio García's critique of Manuel Maldonado Denis, "Puerto Rico: Una interpretación histórico-social," *La Escalera* 4, 1 (June 1970): 23–31; and Angel Quintero Rivera, *Lucha obrera en Puerto Rico* (Río Piedras: CEREP, 1971), 5–12.

3. This investigation project has several important—but not always acknowledged—North American cofounders from the 1930s to the mid-1960s whose approach and focus is *the contemporary of* the late-1960s to early-1990s generation: for example, Justine and Bailey Diffie, Raymond Crist, and Sidney Mintz. Under the direction of Julian Steward, Mintz, together with Eric Wolf, Robert Manners, Elena Padilla Seda, and Raymond Scheele, participated in the variously influential historico-cultural study *The People of Puerto Rico* (Urbana: University of Illinois Press, 1956). The *diachronically incidental* gap between these intellectual siblings and the "New Historiography" was to some extent bridged by the work of Gordon K. Lewis, Edward Berbusse, and Eugenio Fernández Méndez.

4. An example of the first is Manuel Maldonado Denis, *Puerto Rico y los Estados Unidos: Emigración y colonialismo* (Mexico: Siglo XXI Editores, 1976). Examples of the second include Truman Clark, *Puerto Rico and the United States, 1917–1933* (Pittsburgh: University of Pittsburgh Press, 1975); María Luque de Sánchez, *La ocupación norteamericana y la Ley Fóraker* (Río Piedras: Editorial Universitaria, 1980); and Miles Galvin, *The Organized Labor Movement in Puerto Rico* (Cranbury, N.J.: Associated University Presses, 1979).

5. See Frank Bonilla, Ricardo Campos, and Juan Flores, "Puerto Rican Studies: Promptings for the Academy and the Left," in *The Left Academy: Marxist Scholarship on American Campuses*, vol. 3, ed. Bertell Ollman and Edward Vernoff (New York: Praeger, 1985), 67–102.

6. Gervasio García, *Historia crítica, historia sin coartadas* (Río Piedras: Ediciones Huracán, 1985), 40–41; Roberto Rodríguez-Morazzani, "Political Cultures of the Puerto Rican Left in the United States: An Intricate History," paper presented at the First Conference of the Puerto Rican Studies Association, Waltham, Mass., Sept. 29–Oct. 2, 1994; and Agustín Laó, "Resources of Hope: Imagining the Young Lords and the Politics of Memory," paper presented at the First Conference of the Puerto Rican Studies Association, Waltham, Mass., Sept. 29–Oct. 2, 1994.

7. For an analysis of part of the broader context of this whole generation (within Puerto Rico), see Arturo Torrecilla, *El espectro posmoderno: Ecología, neoproletario, intelligentsia* (San Juan: Publicaciones Puertorriqueñas, 1995), 69–148.

8. In my book *"Subject People" and Colonial Discourse: Economic Transformation and Social Disorder in Puerto Rico, 1898–1947* (Albany: State University of New York Press, 1994), I define and extensively illustrate what I understand by "colonial conditions." Elsewhere I have explained briefly why such a concept/context suggests social and economic commonalities—throughout the entire twentieth century—between all dispossessed Puerto Ricans (on the island and in the United States) vis-à-vis such conditions among most North Americans: "Dances with Colonialism: The Current Plebiscite Debate in Puerto Rico as Crisis Management," *Centro* 4, 2 (spring 1992): 14, 19–20; " 'Looking at One's Self through the Eyes of Others': Coloniality and the Utopia of Identity," paper presented at the conference "Fixed Identities in a Moving World," sponsored by the Cultural Studies Program and the Doctoral Program in Comparative Literature, Graduate School of the City University of New York, Apr. 24, 1993; "La crisis contra los trabajadores," *Proceso* 5 (June 1982): 8–9.

9. Examples of this more recent historiographical work include María del Carmen Baerga, ed., *Género y trabajo: La industria de la aguja en Puerto Rico y el Caribe hispánico* (Río Piedras: Universidad de Puerto Rico, 1993); Edwin Meléndez and Edgardo Meléndez, eds., *Colonial Dilemma: Critical Perspectives on Contemporary Puerto Rico* (Boston: South End Press, 1993); and Guillermo Baralt, *Tradición de futuro, el primer siglo del Banco Popular de Puerto Rico, 1893–1993* (San Juan: CARIMAR, 1993). Additional examples may be found in Carlos Antonio Torre, Hugo Rodríguez Vecchini, and William Burgos, eds., *The Commuter Nation: Perspectives on Puerto Rican Migration* (Río Piedras: Universidad de Puerto Rico, 1994); Juan Manuel Carrión, Teresa Gracia Ruíz, and Carlos Rodríguez Fraticelli, eds., *La nación puertorriqueña: Ensayos en torno a Pedro Albizu Campos* (Río Piedras: Universidad de Puerto Rico, 1993); and Silvia Alvarez-Curbelo and María Elena Rodríguez Castro, eds., *Del nacionalismo al populismo: Cultura y política en Puerto Rico* (Río Piedras: Ediciones Huracán/Universidad de Puerto Rico, 1993).

10. The concept of "rules of formation" is being used here along the lines indicated in Michel Foucault, *The Archeology of Knowledge* (New York: Pantheon, 1972), 37–70, 158–59, 173.

11. For example, see Kelvin Santiago-Valles, "Algunos aspectos de la integración de Puerto Rico al interior del Estado metropolitano," *Revista de Ciencias Sociales* 23, 3–4 (July–Dec. 1981): 297–347; Kelvin Santiago-Valles, "Concentración y centralización de la propiedad en Puerto Rico, 1898–1929," *Hómines* 6, 2 (July–Jan. 1983): 5–14; Kelvin Santiago-Valles, "El Puerto Rico del siglo XIX: Apuntes para su análisis," *Hómines* 5, 1–2 (Jan.–Dec. 1981): 7–23.

12. My previous work operates within this same conceptual field. I still acknowledge the link between capitalist development and colonialism in Puerto Rico—see *"Subject People"*—so I will not belabor the point. Moreover, the New Historiography has already been critically appraised in greater depth from within its own ranks: Santiago-Valles, "El Puerto Rico del siglo XIX"; García, *Historia crítica*; Francisco Scarano, "La historia que heredamos," paper presented at the first Annual Research Seminar of CEREP San Juan, Puerto Rico, Mar. 11–12, 1983; Emilio González Díaz, "Historia y ciencia social: Propuesta limitada para un debate largamente postergado," paper presented at the first Annual Research Seminar of CEREP, San Juan, Puerto Rico, Mar. 11–12, 1983; Andrés Ramos Mattei, "New Trends in Puerto Rican History," *Newsletter: Conference on Latin American History* 20, 1 (Apr. 1984): 14; James Dietz, "Puerto Rico's New History," *Latin American Research Review* 19, 1 (1984): 210–22; Angel Quintero Rivera, *Patricios y plebeyos: Burgueses, hacendados, artesanos y obreros* (Río Piedras: Ediciones Huracán, 1988), 280–332; María de los Angeles Castro Arroyo, "De Salvador Brau hasta la 'novísima' historia: Un replanteamiento y una crítica," *OP.CIT.* 4 (1989): 9–56.

13. I use the term "native" as synonymous to "the colonized" and as the antonym of the Western notion of "(hu)man," that is, with the same irony that Sartre deploys in the opening sentences of his preface to Frantz Fanon's *The Wretched of the Earth* (New York: Grove Press, 1968): "Not so very long ago, the earth numbered two thousand million inhabitants: five hundred million men, and one thousand five hundred million natives" (7). The concept of "subaltern," on the other hand, denotes here only a portion of the colonized population, namely, the polymorphous, labile, and contradictory dispossessed classes and sectors—with all the heterogeneity and alterity they embody: sociocultural, racial, sexual, and so on. Thus, the term "subaltern" terminologically excludes propertied and educated "natives." My use of the concept borrows from the way recent South Asian historiography and cultural criticism have recuperated yet transformed Gramsci's original notion of the "subaltern." See Ranajit Guha, "On Some Aspects of the Historiography of Colonial India," in *Subaltern Studies*, vol. 1 (Delhi: Oxford University Press, 1982), 1–8; Gayatri Chakravorty Spivak, "Can the Subaltern Speak?" in *Marxism and the Interpretation of Culture*, ed. Cary Nelson and Lawrence Grossberg (Urbana: University of Illinois Press, 1988), 271–313; and Antonio Gramsci, *Selections from the Prison Notebooks* (New York: International Publishers, 1971), 52–55.

14. See, for instance, Angel Quintero Rivera, "La clase obrera y el proceso político en Puerto Rico-II," *Revista de Ciencias Sociales* 18, 3–4 (Sept.-Dec. 1974): 61–110; History Task Force, *Labor Migration under Capitalism: The Puerto Rican Experience* (New York: Monthly Review Press, 1979); Emilio Pantojas García, "Desarrollismo y lucha de clases: Los límites del proyecto populista en Puerto Rico durante la década del cuarenta," *Revista de Ciencias Sociales* 24, 3–4 (July-Dec. 1985): 355–92; Marcia Rivera Quintero, "Incorporación de la mujer al mercado de trabajo en el desarrollo del capitalismo," in *La mujer en la sociedad puertorriqueña*, ed. Edna Acosta Belén (Río Piedras: Ediciones Huracán, 1980), 49–65; Virginia Sánchez-Korrol, *From Colonia to Community* (Berkeley: University of California Press, 1983); Juan Baldrich, "Class and the State: The Origins of Populism in Puerto Rico, 1934–1952" (Ph.D. diss., Yale University, 1981); Adalberto López, "The Puerto Rican Diaspora: A Survey," in A. López, ed., *The Puerto Ricans* (Cambridge, Mass.: Schenckman, 1980), 313–44; Miriam Muñiz Varela, "Análisis del capital monopólico azucarero y el papel del Estado en el proceso de transición al capitalismo: 1898–1920," *Revista de Ciencias Sociales* 23, 3–4 (July-Dec. 1981): 443–96; Taller de Formación Política, *La cuestión nacional: El Partido Nacionalista y el movimiento obrero puertorriqueño* (Río Piedras: Ediciones Huracán, 1982); Yamila Azize, *La mujer en la lucha* (Río Piedras: Editorial Cultural, 1985), 40–57; Alice Colón, Margarita Mergal, and Nilsa Torres, *Participación de la mujer en la historia de Puerto Rico* (Río Piedras: Universidad de Puerto Rico, 1986); María del Carmen Baerga, "La articulación del trabajo asalariado y no-asalariado: Hacia una reevaluación de la contribución femenina a la sociedad puertorriqueña," in Y. Azize, ed., *La mujer en Puerto Rico* (Río Piedras: Ediciones Huracán, 1987), 89–111; Wilfredo Mattos Cintrón, *La política y lo político en Puerto Rico* (México: Editorial Era, 1980); James Dietz, *Economic History of Puerto Rico* (Princeton, N.J.: Princeton University Press, 1986); Edgardo Meléndez, *Puerto Rico's Statehood Movement* (New York: Greenwood, 1988); Luis A. Ferrao, *Pedro Albizu Campos y el nacionalismo puertorriqueño* (Río Piedras: Editorial Cultural, 1990).

15. See Santiago-Valles, "*Subject People,*" 5–14, 79–97, 106–9, 144–47, 172–83.

16. Gyan Prakash, "Postcolonial Criticism and Indian Historiography," *Social Text* 10, 2–3, 31/32 (1992): 13.

17. To some extent, Fernando Picó's work does not fit this general pattern: for example, *Los gallos peleados* (Río Piedras: Ediciones Huracán, 1983); *1898: La guerra después de la guerra* (Río Piedras: Ediciones Huracán, 1987); *Vivir en Caimito* (Río Piedras: Ediciones Huracán, 1990); *Al filo del poder* (Río Piedras: Universidad de Puerto Rico, 1993). Neither

do portions of Mariano Negrón-Portillo's *Las turbas republicanas, 1900–1904* (Río Piedras: Ediciones Huracán, 1990).

18. See, for example, Angel Quintero Rivera, "El Partido Socialista y la lucha política triangular," *Revista de Ciencias Sociales* 19, 1 (Mar. 1975): 47–100; Juan Angel Silén, *Apuntes: Para una historia del movimiento obrero puertorriqueño* (Río Piedras: Editorial Cultural, 1978), 59–63, 82; Virginia Sánchez-Korrol, "Survival of Puerto Rican Women in New York before World War II," in *The Puerto Rican Struggle: Essays on Survival in the U.S.*, ed. Clara Rodríguez, Virginia Sánchez-Korrol, and José Oscar Alers (New York: Puerto Rican Migration Research Consortium, 1980), 47–57; Taller de Formación Política, *¡Huelga en la caña!* (Río Piedras: Ediciones Huracán, 1982); José Sánchez, "Housing from the Past," *Centro* 2, 5 (spring 1989): 37–41; and Michael Lapp, "The Rise and Fall of Puerto Rico as a Social Laboratory, 1945–1965," *Social Science History* 19, 2 (summer 1995): 169–88.

19. Mattos Cintrón, *La política*, 83. All translations are mine.

20. Nicholas Dirks, "Introduction: Colonialism and Culture," in *Colonialism and Culture* (Ann Arbor: University of Michigan Press, 1992), 3, 4.

21. For example, see Arcadio Díaz Quiñones, *Conversaciones con José Luis González* (Río Piedras: Ediciones Huracán, 1976), 105–7; Benjamín Torres, "El Nacionalismo en Puerto Rico: 1922–1930, Apuntes para su interpretación," *Revista Puertorriqueña de Ciencias Sociales* 1, 1 (July–Dec. 1976): 41–47; Silén, *Apuntes*, 57–101; Ricardo Campos and Juan Flores, "Migración y cultura nacional puertorriqueñas: Perspectivas proletarias," in *Puerto Rico: Identidad nacional y clases sociales* (Río Piedras: Ediciones Huracán, 1979), 81–146; Félix Ojeda, *Vito Marcantonio y Puerto Rico* (Río Piedras: Ediciones Huracán, 1978); Mattos Cintrón, *La política*, 54–124; Taller de Formación Política, *La cuestión nacional*; Dietz, *Economic History*, 160–70; Quintero Rivera, *Patricios y plebeyos*, 129–79; and Georg Fromm, "El nacionalismo y el movimiento obrero en la década del 30," *OP.CIT.* 5 (1990): 37–103.

22. Guha, "On Some Aspects of the Historiography of India," 3–4.

23. One recent exception is Julio Ramos, *Amor y anarquía: Los escritos de Luisa Capetillo* (Río Piedras: Ediciones Huracán, 1992), 14–17, 40–44.

24. Partha Chatterjee, "Peasants, Politics, Historiography: A Response," *Social Scientist* (May 1983): 60; emphasis in the original.

25. For a recent critical summary of this whole question, see Michèle Barrett, *The Politics of Truth: From Marx to Foucault* (Stanford: Stanford University Press, 1991).

26. Karl Marx and Friedrich Engels, "Manifesto of the Communist Party," in *Karl Marx, The Revolution of 1848: Political Writings*, vol. 1, ed. David Fernbach (New York: Vintage Books, 1974), 69.

27. Nicos Poulantzas, "The Capitalist State: A Reply to Miliband and Laclau," *New Left Review* 95 (Jan.–Feb. 1976): 63–83.

28. Antonio Negri, *Marx beyond Marx: Lessons on the Grundrisse* (South Hadley, Mass.: Bergin and Garvey Publishers, 1984).

29. Taller de Formación Política, *La cuestión nacional*, 69; emphasis in the original. See also Quintero Rivera, "La clase obrera-II"; Campos and Flores, "Migración"; Mattos Cintrón, *La política*, 55–56, 66; Angel Quintero Rivera and Gervasio García, *Desafío y solidaridad* (Río Piedras: Ediciones Huracán, 1982), 93–98; Carlos Rodríguez-Fraticelli and Amilcar Tirado, "Notes towards a History of Puerto Rican Community Organizations," *Centro* 2, 6 (summer 1989): 35–38. One of the early works of Juan Flores partially departs from this norm: *Insularismo e ideología burguesa en Antonio Pedreira* (La Habana: Casa de Las Américas, 1979), 46–47.

30. In addition to the extensive foreboding that Marx repeatedly expressed toward the European peasantry in *The Class Struggles in France* and in *The Eighteenth Brumaire*,

see, for instance, Marx and Engels, "Manifesto," 77; Marx and Engels, "The Demands of the Communist Party of Germany," in Fernbach, ed., *Political Writings*, vol. 1, 109–11; Marx and Engels, "Address of the Central Committee of the Communist League (June 1850)," in Fernbach, ed., *Political Writings*, vol. 1, 333–34; Marx, *Historia crítica de la teoría de la plusvalía*, vol. 1 (Buenos Aires: Ediciones Brumario, 1974), 349, 353. It is still an open question whether Marx's last studies of the Russian peasant commune constituted a qualitative shift in his overall perspective on "the agrarian question."

31. See Silén, *Apuntes*, 58–59; Mattos Cintrón, *La política*, 54–65, 67–69, 74–84; Santiago-Valles, "Concentración y centralización"; Colón, Mergal, and Torres, *Participación de la mujer*, 21–24; Dietz, *Economic History*, 98–112; Frank Bonilla and Ricardo Campos, "Imperialist Initiatives and the Puerto Rican Worker: From Foraker to Reagan," *Contemporary Marxism* 5 (1982): 1–9; Rivera Quintero, "Incorporación de la mujer," 49–51, 60–61; Taller de Formación Política, *La cuestión nacional*, 67–79; Quintero Rivera, *Patricios y plebeyos*, 111–13.

32. Santiago-Valles, "El Puerto Rico del siglo XIX," 13–14.

33. Friedrich Engels, *El anti-Dühring* (Buenos Aires: Editorial Claridad, 1970), 193–94.

34. See Winthrop Jordan, *White over Black: American Attitudes toward the Negro, 1550–1812* (Chapel Hill: University of North Carolina Press, 1968), 220–28, 304–5, 482–511; Arthur O. Lovejoy, *The Great Chain of Being* (Cambridge: Harvard University Press, 1978); Foucault, *The Order of Things*, 46–387; Nancy Leys Stepan, "Race and Gender: The Role of Analogy in Science," in *Anatomy of Racism*, ed. David T. Goldberg (Minneapolis: University of Minnesota Press, 1990), 38–57; Gayatri Chakravorty Spivak, "Subaltern Studies: Deconstructing Historiography," in *In Other Worlds* (New York: Routledge, 1988), 199–200, 202, 215–20.

35. Gyan Prakash, "Writing Post-Orientalist Histories of the Third World: Indian Historiography is Good to Think," in Dirks, ed., *Colonialism and Culture*, 368.

36. See, for example, César Andreu Iglesias, *Memorias de Bernardo Vega* (Río Piedras: Ediciones Huracán, 1977); Jesús Colón, *A Puerto Rican in New York and Other Sketches* (New York: International Publishers, 1982); Angel Quintero Rivera, "Socialista y tabaquero: La proletarización de los artesanos," *Revista Sin Nombre* 8, 4 (Jan.–Mar. 1978): 100–138; Campos and Flores, "Migración"; Amilcar Tirado Avilés, "Ramón Romero Rosa, su participación en las luchas obreras, 1896–1906," *Caribe* 2, 2–3 (1980–81): 3–26; Azize, *La mujer en la lucha*, 61–88; Rubén Dávila Santiago, *El derribo de las murallas y "El Porvenir de Borinquen"* (Río Piedras: CEREP, 1983); Norma Valle Ferrer, *Luisa Capetillo: Historia de una mujer proscrita* (Río Piedras: Editorial Cultural, 1990).

37. Quintero Rivera, *Patricios y plebeyos*, 110–11, my emphasis.

38. Prakash, "Writing Post-Orientalist Histories," 369.

39. Flores, *Insularismo e ideología*, 25–26. This study, however, still bears the marks of evolutionism: for example, its acritical usage of the narratives of "primitivism" when describing indigenous resistances and slave rebellions, and its depiction of "primitive" popular insurgencies as the "socio-historical legacy" of the "modern popular culture" of workers and peasants (46).

40. My first attempt at exploring the particulars of this process was *"Subject People."*

41. See my review essay, "The New Historiographies of Criminality and Social Disorder in Early Twentieth-Century Puerto Rico," *Journal of Historical Sociology* 6, 4 (Dec. 1993): 455–70.

42. Aspects of this epistemic investment are beginning to be critically explored and/or historicized in, for example, Juan Flores and George Yúdice, "Living Borders/Buscando America: Languages of Latino Self-Formation," *Social Text* 8, 2, 24 (1990): 57–84;

Santiago-Valles, "Dances with Colonialism"; Kelvin Santiago-Valles, "The Unruly City and the Mental Landscape of Colonized Identities: Internally Contested Nationality in Puerto Rico, 1945–1985," *Social Text* 12, 1, 38 (spring 1994): 149–63; Laura Ortíz, *Al filo de la navaja: Los márgenes en Puerto Rico* (Río Piedras: Centro de Investigaciones Sociales, Universidad de Puerto Rico, 1991); Torrecilla, *El espectro posmoderno*; Miriam Muñiz Varela, "Más allá de Puerto Rico USA, Puerto Rico 936, Puerto Rico, Inc. Notas para una crítica del desarrollo," *Piso 13* 1, 11 (Apr. 1993): 6–7; Gladys Jiménez-Muñoz, "'A Storm Dressed in Skirts': Ambivalence in the Debate on Women's Suffrage in Puerto Rico, 1927–1929" (Ph.D. dissertation, Binghamton University-SUNY, 1993); Rodríguez-Morazzani, "Political Cultures"; Laó, "Resources of Hope"; Madeline Román, "El Girlie Show: Madonna, las polémicas nacionales y los pánicos morales," *Bordes* 1 (1995): 14–21; Carlos Pabón," De Albizu a Madonna: Para armar y desarmar la nacionalidad," *Bordes* 1 (1995): 22–40.

43. See, for instance, Flores, *Insularismo e ideología*; José Luis González, *Nueva visita al cuarto piso* (Río Piedras: Libros del Flamboyán, 1985); Arcadio Díaz Quiñones, "Recordando el futuro imaginario: La escritura histórica en la década del treinta," *Sin Nombre* 14 (Apr.–June 1984): 16–35; Arcadio Díaz Quiñones, "Tomás Blanco: Racismo, historia, esclavitud," in Tomás Blanco, *El prejuicio racial en Puerto Rico* (Río Piedras: Ediciones Huracán, 1985), 15–91; María Elena Rodríguez, "Tradición y modernidad: El intelectual puertorriqueño ante la década del treinta," *OP.CIT.* 3 (1988): 45–66; Frances Aparicio, "Tato Laviera y Arista: Hacia una poética bilingüe," *Centro* 2, 3 (spring 1988): 7–13; Mayra Santos Febres, "Mapping Consciousness: Puerto Rico the Translocal Nation," in *Plebiscite: Puerto Rico at a Political Crossroad*, ed. Félix Masud-Piloto, Hector Vélez Guadalupe, and Irma Almirall-Padamsee (Ithaca, N.Y.: Cornell University Press, 1991), 71–74; Iris M. Zavala, *Colonialism and Culture: Hispanic Modernisms and the Social Imaginary* (Bloomington: Indiana University Press, 1992), 2–4, 35–36, 82–95, 112–19, 165–81; Arcadio Díaz-Quiñones, *La memoria rota* (Río Piedras: Ediciones Huracán, 1993); Efraín Barradas, "How to Read Bernardo Vega," in Torre, Rodríguez Vecchini, and Burgos, eds., *The Commuter Nation*, 313–28; Eliana Ortega, "Sandra María Esteves' Poetic Work: Demythicizing Puerto Rican Poetry in the U.S.," in Torre, Rodríguez Vecchini, and Burgos, eds., *The Commuter Nation*, 329–42; Isabelle Leymarie, "Salsa and Migration," in Torre, Rodríguez Vecchini, and Burgos, eds., *The Commuter Nation*, 343–61; Alberto Sandoval Sánchez, "La identidad especular del allá y del acá: Nuestra propia imagen puertorriqueña en cuestión," *Centro* 4, 2 (spring 1992): 28–43; Carlos Gil, *El orden del tiempo* (San Juan: Editorial Postdata, 1994); Juan Carlos Quintero Herencia, "Notas para la salsa," *Nómada* 1 (Apr. 1995): 16–34; Hugo Rodríguez Vecchini, "Cuando Esmeralda 'era' puertorriqueña," *Nómada* 1 (Apr. 1995): 145–60.

44. Some exceptions to this inclination include José Luis González, *El país de cuatro pisos y otros ensayos* (Río Piedras: Ediciones Huracán, 1980), 96–102; Julia Cristina Ortíz Lugo, "Saben más que las arañas: Arte oral y resistencia," in *La tercera raíz: Presencia africana en Puerto Rico* (San Juan: CEREP/Instituto de Cultura Puertorriqueña, 1992), 83–90; Mayra Santos Febres, "Sobre piel o sobre papel," *Piso 13* 1, 4 (Aug. 1992): 6; Mayra Santos Febres, "A veces miro mi vida," *Diálogo* (Oct. 1993): 42; Luis Rafael Sánchez, *La guagua aerea* (Río Piedras: Editorial Cultural, 1994); Arnaldo Cruz Malavé, "Toward an Art of Transvestism: Colonialism and Homosexuality in Puerto Rican Literature," in *¿Entiendes? Queer Readings, Hispanic Writings*, ed. Emilie L. Bergmann and Paul Julian Smith (Durham, N.C.: Duke University Press, 1995), 137–67; Agnes Lugo Ortíz, "Community at Its Limits: Orality, Law, Silence, and the Homosexual Body in Luis Rafael Sánchez's '¡Jum!'" in Bergmann and Smith, eds., *¿Entiendes?*, 115–36; Luz María Umpierre, "Lesbian Tantalizing in Carmen Lugo Filippi's 'Milagros, Calle Mercurio,'" in Bergmann and Smith, eds., *¿Entiendes?*, 306–14.

45. See González, *El país de cuatro pisos y otros ensayos*, 23, 33; Rodríguez, "Tradición y modernidad," 51, 54, 57–59; Díaz Quiñones, "Tomás Blanco," 162, 171; Barradas, "How to Read Bernardo Vega," 315–17, 323, 325; Quintero Herencia, "Notas para la salsa," 19, 25.

46. See, for example, Ricardo Campos, "Apuntes sobre la expresión cultural obrera en Puerto Rico" (Río Piedras: mimeographed discussion paper, Colegio de Ciencias Sociales, Universidad de Puerto Rico, 1974); Flores, *Insularismo e ideología*; Valle Ferrer, *Luisa Capetillo*; Quintero Rivera, "Socialista y tabaquero"; Campos and Flores, "Migración"; Quintero Rivera, *Patricios y plebeyos*, 23–98; Angel Quintero Rivera, "El tambor en el cuatro: La melodización de ritmos y la etnicidad cimarroneada," in Ortíz Lugo, *La tercera raíz*, 43–55.

47. For my particular conceptualization of "postcoloniality," see *"Subject People,"* 6–8.

48. Gayatri Chakravorty Spivak, "The *Intervention* Interview," in *The Post-Colonial Critic: Interviews, Strategies, Dialogues* (New York: Routledge, 1990), 120–21; emphasis in the original.

49. Talal Asad, "From the History of Colonial Anthropology to the Anthropology of Western Hegemony," in *Colonial Situations: Essays on the Contextualization of Ethnographic Knowledge*, ed. George Stocking (Madison: University of Wisconsin Press, 1991), 323–24.

50. Edward Said, *Orientalism* (New York: Pantheon Books, 1979), 40–41; emphasis in the original.

CHAPTER FIVE

Narrating the Tropical Pharmacy

José Quiroga

> *"pues tantas veces, señor,*
> *nos ha dicho la experiencia,*
> *y es cierto, que de secretos*
> *naturales está llena*
> *la medicina . . . "*
> Calderón de la Barca, *La vida es sueño*

My aim in this essay is, broadly speaking, to question whether the discourse of nationalism replicates colonialism, the very structure that it seeks to oppose. Modernist/anticolonialist writers negotiate colonialism by appealing to metaphors of disease. I question whether by extirpating at all costs the visible marks of illness from their sociologically directed texts, these authors replicate the ideological foundations that produce the taxonomy of illness by repeating a principle of univocal causation: illness, classified as such, beckons a cure. In this context, my work posits that for the nation, taxonomized as sick by colonial agents and anticolonial writers, any cure, conceived as such, actually produces another illness in the body of the patient, which then needs to be cured, in an endlessly repetitive strain. In other words, I would like to test in this essay whether, and at what point, unwittingly or not, the nationalist project colludes with colonialism.

In Puerto Rico, but also in the wider Caribbean area, nationalist projects in the twentieth century are written under the aegis of what I would call the "medical construction." What I mean by this is not, of necessity, the apparition of a doctor in a text but a position of ambivalence manifested in terms of culture and body, illness and metaphor. I can expand this construction not only to the ethnographic projects of Fernando

Ortíz in his *Cuban Counterpoint* (1940) but also to Aimé Césaire's *Notebook for a Return to a Native Land* (1939). These works set out to *diagnose* a given reality. In the case of Ortíz, the diagnosis occurs by means of a metaphor, one that reads throughout history a counterpoint of tobacco and sugar as an explication of national character by focusing on these two products as, alternatively, poison and gold, remedy and disease. In Césaire's *Notebook*, the diagnosis entails a poetic account of the "Antilles pitted with smallpox" with the consequent "parade of laughable and scrofulous buboes, the forced feedings of very strange microbes, the poisons without known alexins, the sanies of really ancient sores, the unforeseeable fermentations of putrescible species."[1] In this way (and in many others), Césaire's notebook is a laboratory that pastes together the accounts of a broken history. The illness provides the germs—disease—which can then be "cultured" for study. What I want to examine is the opposite situation: how, for example, Antonio Pedreira as the foremost essayist and nationalist critic of the 1930s excluded and extirpated from the national scene the uncomfortable gaze of texts written by colonizers by cataloging them as "other" within the discursive framework of the colony. This elision (this cure) is only the unsustained desire of a will, for upon closer inspection the discursive framework of these "other" texts metastasizes within Pedreira's narrative constructions. Indeed, the view from the colonizer's perspective is the point of origin of Pedreira's gaze upon a patient, classified as such by the foreign agent. That the point of origin of Pedreira's diagnosis is precisely the other's gaze renders its supposed excision from the nationalist discourse even more ironic. I see this exclusion to be at the heart of the failures and successes entailed in the modern attempts at dealing with an ongoing colonial situation.[2]

Culture and Evidence

As Susan Sontag's eloquent *AIDS and Its Metaphors* recalls, medicine, disease, and war have long been linked. War is part of the structural narrative of Dr. Bailey K. Ashford's *A Soldier in Science,* a counterpoint to the detective-like search for the sources of tropical disease written by a military doctor whose fieldwork was done in Puerto Rico.[3] The classical scene of colonial medicine is reenacted in the introductory scene of this work, while Ashford talks of himself with the self-effacing rhetorical mechanism of a third-person narrator:

It was a stewing hot afternoon in the Caribbean, with the sun pouring into a stuffy bare room six feet by ten; yet still he sat with his eye glued to a portable army microscope.

He had been sitting there since early morning. In fact, he had sat there most of the time since the hurricane, which had driven hordes of pallid refugees from their mountain homes to seek food and shelter in the city. Their pallor was not brought on, however, by a hurricane only three months past; *it was the pallor of years, of centuries.* It was the seal of a disease no one ever had deciphered. But of that disease they died—had for years been dying—until now, when asked of what they had lost father, mother and other kind, they answered: "De la anemia—la muerte natural" [Of anemia—natural death]. (my emphasis)

Let us place these two paragraphs under the microscope (for as hermeneuts we can only, after all, assume the position of the doctor in this scene) and notice within the rhetorical tissue a roster of deliberate silences: first, the abstraction of place, the erasure of the proper name Puerto Rico, where Ashford lived decades of his life; second, the collective orphanhood of the population (they are not individual, their voice is rendered in choral fashion); and third, the system of external and internal comparisons and contrasts: the destructive force of a hurricane counterbalances the pallid squalor of its inhabitants, a pallor due not to the forces of external nature, like the hurricane, but the "pallor of years, of centuries." Unlike the hurricane, disease is not an event for Ashford; it has no beginning, it has always already begun. We could also say that for Ashford, illness is a peculiar sort of nonevent. There is, for him, the sense of an illness, a kind of "falling sick," but inhabitants of the tropics have always been sick. They are dying of intractable, collective, and consumptive diseases whose causes medicine cannot fathom. If disease, unlike the hurricane, is not an event, nevertheless like the hurricane, disease wastes, marks, and scars the body—with pustules, outgrowths, and buboes.

When Ashford looks into his microscope (this section is called "Arms and the Microscope"—a fabulous title of epic proportions, and we should recall here Césaire's repeated attempts to have us look at his town, at his people, to keep our eyes on the "morne"), his repeated gaze, with its distance and strangeness, produces the effect of the sublime. The doctor says that the natives possessed a "tremendously interesting, fantastic blood picture"; his "[a]ppetite whetted," he tries to undo the notion of weakness as genetic and wonders "if that anemia might be caused by something else, something outside the blood." Looking into the microscope, he continues, "this afternoon, his research directed hither by his many days of examining blood, he was staring at a thin film of feces crushed between the cover-glass and glass slide," and he discovers the worm, an "oval thing with the four fluffy gray balls inside." After consulting his encyclopedia (Manson's "tropical diseases"), he has a fantastic revelation:

> His mind was definitely made up: the anemia of miners in Switzerland was the anemia from which millions had suffered and died in Puerto Rico. He began to think geographically. Of course he must be very prudent, but—the anemia pandemic in Puerto Rico could not be limited to this one little island. It was all through these latitudes. It must be. He had heard of the indolence of Mexicans, of Central Americans, of people everywhere in the old Spanish Main. He could not *say* that their indolence was caused by disease. Secretly, however, he knew now that it was, though he couldn't say so—yet. But he *could* say so for Puerto Rico, for our war ward, so newly under our Flag, and so sick.

The secret and public uses of indolence could fill countless texts of military conquest. Publicly, Ashford can state that indolence is caused by habitat, a construction that is defined by latitude but also by the culture of the old "Spanish Main." Secretly, indolence is caused by disease. Publicly, it belongs to culture; privately, it is habitat (the "insalubrious" tropics that may also be constructed as the "paradise" islands). And the two terms combine in the epistemological creation of the "war ward"—for what Anglo-Americans have inherited and have invaded is not a territory, or a strategic outpost, or even a market for goods, but a hospital of war—a locus, we should repeat, where illness becomes "cultured." Ashford leaves his microscope and proceeds to the field hospital for indigent anemics to search for the man whose feces he has been examining under the microscope:

> He looked at the expressionless face of his jíbaro (peasant) and fairly beamed. Here was the prototype of anemic millions all over the Caribbean, all round the tropical belt that girdles the portly belly of Mother Earth. That jíbaro was becoming positively beautiful to the young doctor. He would take him to town, get the local photographer to immortalize him.

But the contributor of the egg to which Ashford owes his fame as the discoverer of the cause for *anemia perniciosa* is nowhere to be found among the photographs of the book. As a medical sample, medicine insures his privacy. He is exonerated from guilt but also from representation. Because he is the passive bearer of the disease, his silence belongs to the doctor's private and inviolate memory. What is his name? How did he get sick? What is his family profile? What is his socioeconomic status? What does he eat? The patient has no face, no expression: he is not a subject but a prototype. And because he is a prototype, these questions are all erased. In the medical economy there can only be the disease, the agent, and the bearer of disease.

Hygiene

How do we classify this text that we have just put under the microscope within the canon of the nation? Should this text be included in the roster of national texts, or does it belong to some other tradition that only finds temporary articulation in a given soil? In Ashford's text, finding the disease entails looking into the microscope, but it also entails a question of taxonomy: to see the phenomenon and consult Manson's encyclopedia and then produce a catalog. Let us entertain the notion and replicate the procedure (my critical positioning is deliberate, and even perverse). The *Puerto Rican Bibliography* (*Bibliografía puertorriqueña*), published two years *before* Ashford's text, tends to isolate memoirs like these to a no-man's-land, outside of national production.[4] It is not a Puerto Rican text, but it is a text written in Puerto Rico by a non-Puerto Rican, as the editor rightly classifies. In the ongoing definition (diagnosis or descriptive dictionary) of a nation, its otherness is accounted for by language (the text is written in English) and by the national origin of the writer (he is from Virginia). But the foreignness of texts like Ashford's in this case is deceiving and should be explored in further detail.

Antonio Pedreira is the editor of the *Bibliography*, which was presented as a prophylactic endeavor aimed at a spiritual diagnostic of internal reality. Its author explains that "a bibliography, aside from being the most justified expression of the mentality of a people, prepares and simplifies its spiritual diagnosis."[5] This issue of diagnosis—with its connotation of preventive medicine—of identifying what particularly ails the native at this point, predominates in Pedreira's other project, which precedes but also informs the bibliography. From 1929 to 1931, Pedreira edited a journal titled *Indice*, actually an archive of synthetic biographies, commentaries, fragments of history, and book reviews that achieve their epiphany in the bibliographical architecture.[6] It turned its audience into experimental subjects and made the island an object of study: an insular, cellular construction fashioned with the same fictional objectivity that we find in Ashford's text. And in the same year that Ashford published his memoirs, Pedreira diagnosed the colonial situation in *Insularismo* (1934), a classic of Caribbean nationalist *kulturcritique*: "These pages will not possess the tone of admiration that our complacency has created in order to measure Puerto Rican reality. They are not the product of a scientific analysis but they . . . arose out of the sequence of facts and attitudes submitted to the most pure and disinterested meditation."[7] The sublime distance of the microscope is turned into a scientific method without science, one that focuses "our" problems as if we were looking at them from the outside. But what is the only outside gaze available? The criteria of objectivity already demands a *construction* of objectivity. Pedreira's objective argument goes as follows: no one can dispute the enormous gains that have been made in terms of civilization, brought about by the social engineering of doctors in our land. But for all that we have gained in civilization, we have lost a sense of culture. Therefore, if our civilization at this point is (physically) healthy, we suffer a cultural malaise. To put it another way, we are healthy but at the price of cultural illness.

It would take a longer hermeneutic operation to deconstruct the strands of this discourse. But what *Indice*, the *Bibliography*, and *Insularismo* have in common is not only the author but the search: first, for the causes of disease, and then for the cure. The *Bibliography*, in particular, presents us with a scene of reading: the innumerable travails at compilation of an encyclopedia. The author is the objective purveyor of a task that is beyond him. The phenomenon's origins are not unlike those narrated by Ashford: the inscription of writing given the fact that there is no inscription, or, as Pedreira would later say, that the sign of the origin is a blank page borne out of years of indolence and cultural malaise. The introduction to the bibliographical project is replete with cultural attributes that consistently threaten the parameters of objectivity. In the introduction, Pedreira exclaims:

> We will expel that effeminate curiosity with which, up until now, we
> have treated authors, books and issues, and it will establish the
> grounds in order to form the history of our cultural evolution, that is
> still to be done, and towards which we should immediately proceed
> before we achieve our definition and before we get the true orientation
> that our people should take towards its future.[8]

When is a remedy a poison? The answer is: it always is. Since we cannot say that Ashford influences Pedreira unless we engage in an anachronistic and Borgesian reading, we should frame these two texts as translations of each other. And in these acts of translation we can see the full complexity of the colonial writer and of the defining attempts at nationality. For the translation is already an interpretation that cancels the polysemy of the signifier, a network of inclusions and exclusions deliberately implicit and ideologically motivated.

Pedreira's medicine first comes in the guise of philology: a rescuing of works, archival research, and examination of documents.[9] And since Pedreira's illness is that "effeminate" curiosity that is also a lack of texts, the medicine is the bibliography or the essay. Pedreira's negotiations demand that if the nation is defined by writing, by writing the nation must be cured. But the writing that Pedreira wants to see is carefully taxonomized: literary texts, like poems or novels; essays on national character; musical compositions; and the like. This culture that Pedreira desires as an antidote to civilization (civilization exemplified by Ashford himself) relegates all other texts that are truly responsible for the structural parameters of its very construction to a no-man's-land. Ashford finds no space in the national tradition, but the national tradition cannot hold without him. He is, in all respects, a sickening supplement. For Pedreira, texts like Ashford's only belong to the taxonomy of the nation if one constantly asserts the ambivalent otherness that constitutes their appearance in this soil. But the scientific method that Ashford pursues, and the polemical distance from the source—the supposed objectivity of the diagnosis—is replicated from within, even if it becomes part of a discourse of resistance toward that very source. When we use the microscope to examine the philological projects that frame our national discourses, the ideological parameters of the colonizer and those colonized seem to structurally replicate themselves. It is not only that Pedreira offers the *Bibliography* in order to alter the "biological constitution" or the "anemic" quality of the Puerto Rican, but that, as in the interplay between the secret and public meanings of indolence, there is the impression here of a secret unveiled, of a double discourse that wants to expose that "effeminate" curiosity but at the same time explain it under the rubric of a cultural motivation. Because Pedreira defines culture at various points in the discourse as a kind of x-ray of the projection of the sensibility on the earth and on the land, the origin of Pedreira's disease, the—and I repeat Ashford at this point—"oval thing with the four fluffy gray balls inside," is insularity, the lack of vital space.

Pharmacy

And what of this space, this ovum, this cellular and insular, always fragile ecosystem that Pedreira circumscribes? If culture is sick, the space must be cultured extensively. It is true that the laboratory was already in place by the time the new colonial masters came, and that the concrete acts upon the social body combine humanitarian concerns of medicine and the public weal in order to allow the colonial invaders to say that the tropics were coming closer, bringing their diseases with them. But who is coming closer to whom? Who is moving from one place to another? It is to another way of culturing remedy and illness that we must turn—to the physical presence of the colony replete with laboratories that have subjected the population to innumerable tests in order to create medicines that the colonial masters, among others, enjoy. The manufactured culture that would cure the population of its unfathomable disease was brought in, imported and exported from 1921, when the U.S. Congress first instituted tax breaks for American companies that intended to establish themselves in Puerto Rico. And it was brought in again after 1952, when the Free Associated State or Commonwealth was created as the showcase of the Americas—where North and South contemplate each other in a fatuous embrace. This process allows for a material, physical reproduction of the same kind of procedure that is called for in Pedreira's text, but perhaps in ways not foreseen by his humanistic framework. The illness having metamorphosed into health, into economic and material "well-being," replicates itself as the site of a manufactured culture in order to provide for the health of the metropolis. The insular laboratory in recent years has incarnated its metaphor, has "grown into it," we might say. For the past twenty years, and because of the concrete sense of agency by the colonial masters, the insular locus has become the most sophisticated manufacturer of drugs for internal, national, and international consumption. "Puerto Rico, in terms of sheer concentration of pharmaceutical manufacturing plants per square mile, is considered the 'Capital of the Pharmaceutical Industry' in the world," according to Daniel Lebrón, president of the Association of Puerto Rican Industrialists; "Here, there are more than 80 medicine manufacturing plants. If we include those that produce hospital and biomedical equipment, there are more than 125."[10] According to the magazine *Drug Topics* of 1991, eight of the ten most popular medicines in the United States are manufactured in Puerto Rico, whose agricultural infrastructure has now been supplanted by the wholesale manufacture of Vasotec, Xanax, and Halcion.[11] But one should be wary of concluding with a tropism, or with a still more prototypical construction that yields Ashford's jíbaro on Prozac (manufactured in the same insular laboratory). The history of experimentation, of human experimentation within this laboratory of colonialism, is too extensive and painful for us to conclude with this kind of rhetorical flourish. The showcase of the Americas, with insidious irony, manufactures the cure for the illnesses of the metropolitan centers, but only at the expense of its inhabitants being "cured" of the wholesale destruction brought upon by the framework of colonialism.

And it is not only in and on the body of these subjects, whose very subjectivity is at the same time denied and replicated by both colonial masters and anticolonial subjects, that all metaphors are rendered into the material expression on the body; they are also inscribed within the very construction of its space. Here, two forms of culture displace each other—but their spatial relationship testifies to their linkage and bond: culture, in the colonial situation, always what supplements a lack, the place where one gives tribute to the ancestors. The main avenue of this showcase, running from east to west on a strip of land connected to the main island, full of glittering hotels and casinos, prostitutes and boutiques, is called Ashford Avenue, in homage to Ashford's labor of love at curing the population of disease. Farther out to the east, in the unperturbed isolation of the tropical enclave of the university, the building that houses the faculty of humanities is named Antonio S. Pedreira. One could say that the geographical body of the city has perversely isolated the humanist Pedreira, but also that like Josephine's statue in Césaire's *Notebook*, it has also perversely understood the invisible links between the sickness and the cure—situating precisely at its center the form of culture that has rendered to the patient an illness already beyond recognition—unrecognized by that other cultured realm that told us that culture was precisely what was to deliver us unto health.

Notes

1. Aimé Césaire, *Aimé Césaire: The Collected Poetry*, trans. Clayton Eshleman and Annette Smith (Berkeley: University of California Press, 1983), 35, 39. This edition is bilingual; the French reads: "les Antilles grêlées de petite vérole . . . " "la parade des risibles et scrofuleux bubons, les poutures de microbes très étranges, les poisons sans alexitère connu, les sanies de plaies bien antiques, les fermentations imprévisibles d'espèces putrescibles."

2. This essay is indebted to work done in Puerto Rico and the United States on Pedreira and on the intellectual context and milieu of Puerto Rico in the 1930s. The essays that I have found most illuminating in this context are the following: María Elena Rodríguez Castro, "Tradición y modernidad: El intelectual puertorriqueño ante la década del treinta," in *Boletín del centro de investigaciones históricas de la Universidad de Puerto Rico* 3 (1987–88): 45–65; Juan Flores, *Insularismo e ideología burguesa en Antonio Pedreira* (La Habana: Casa de las Américas, 1979); Arcadio Díaz Quiñones, "Recordando el futuro imaginario: La escritura histórica en la década del treinta," *Sin nombre* 14, 3 (1984): 16–35.

3. Bailey K. Ashford, *A Soldier in Science: The Autobiography of Bailey K. Ashford* (New York: William Morrow and Company, 1934). Unless otherwise noted all quotes come from pages 3–5 of this edition.

4. For the purposes of this work, as we shall see, the chronological displacement of text and bibliography is irrelevant, for Pedreira has already fashioned the category that this text would belong to. This is explored metaphorically later on. Antonio S. Pedreira, *Bibliografía Puertorriqueña (1493–1930)*, Monografías de la Universidad de Puerto Rico. Serie A. Estudios Hispánicos Núm. 1 (Madrid: Imprenta de la Librería y Casa Editorial Hernando, 1932).

5. Pedreira, *Bibliografía Puertorriqueña*, viii; translation is mine. "Una bibliografía, amén de ser la más justificada expresión de la mentalidad de un pueblo, prepara y simplifica su diagnóstico espiritual."

6. *Indice. Mensuario de historia, literatura y ciencia* (25 de abril a 28 de julio de 1931), edición facsimilar, prólogo de Vicente Geigel Polanco (San Juan: Editorial Universitaria, 1929). One is struck by the similarities between the format of this review and the work done in the Bureau de Recherche Surrealistes, which opened in Paris in 1924. Maurice Nadeau in *The History of Surrealism* (1965; Cambridge: Harvard University Press, 1989) underscores that the bureau was a kind of "laboratory" (92) where all of its participants could contribute to the creation of a new kind of life. One should also recall that the format of *La revolution surrealiste* deliberately imitated a scientific journal, and that its participants, from the beginning, scandalized the reading public by means of selective poll taking in terms of particular issues (for example, "Is suicide a solution?") accompanied by statistical data. Not only in terms of a deliberate invention of a present movement but also in terms of a past, we can compare both journals. In terms of a more immediate context, *Indice* is related to the Cuban *Revista de Avance* and its problematization of the very nature of an "island." It is important in this context to refer to Rubén Ríos Avila's "The Origin and the Island: Lezama and Mallarmé," *Latin American Literary Review* 8, 16 (1980): 242–55; and to Francine Masiello's "Rethinking Neocolonial Esthetics: Literature, Politics, and Intellectual Community in Cuba's *Revista de Avance*," *Latin American Research Review* 28, 2 (1993): 3–31.

7. Antonio S. Pedreira, *Insularismo: Ensayos de una interpretación puertorriqueño* (San Juan: Biblioteca de Autores Puertorriqueños, 1942), 9; translation is mine. "Estas páginas carecerán del tono admirativo que nuestra complacencia ha creado para medir la realidad puertorriqueña. No son producto de un análisis científico, sino que . . . fueron surgiendo de la concatenación de hechos y actitudes sometidos a la más pura y desinteresada meditación."

8. Pedreira, *Bibliografía Puertorriqueña*, xviii; translation is mine. "[se] dará al traste con esa afeminada curiosidad con que hasta la fecha hemos tratado a autores, libros y asuntos, y se pondrá en vías de formación la historia de nuestra evolución cultural, que aún está por hacer, y a la cual tendremos que ir irremediablemente antes de definirnos y antes de conseguir la verdadera orientación que nuestro pueblo ha de llevar camino al porvenir."

9. Pedreira and his circle fulfill this mission, as examined by Benedict Anderson in *Imagined Communities: Reflections on the Origin and Spread of Nationalism* (London: Verso, 1983; rev. ed., 1991).

10. As quoted in Carmen Millán Pabón, "Botiquín abierto al mundo," *El Nuevo Día*, Mar. 8, 1992, 4–5.

11. As quoted in "Hecho en Puerto Rico," *El Nuevo Día*, Mar. 8, 1992, 5.

CHAPTER SIX

Deconstructing Puerto Ricanness through Sexuality: Female Counternarratives on Puerto Rican Identity (1894–1934)

Yolanda Martínez-San Miguel

> *Oubao-moin llamaron los calibanes caníbales a la otra isla de Puerto Rico, antes de que en las márgenes del Mar Rojo, inventaran la bóveda lejana del cielo.*
>
> Manuel Ramos Otero, "La otra isla de Puerto Rico"

Sexuality and the Limits of the Nation

The main objective of this essay is to reread a group of literary texts produced in Puerto Rico between 1890 and 1934, and to identify some feminine counternarratives that questioned the notion of nationality. These counternarratives were systematically excluded from hegemonic nationalist discourses, and especially from the hegemonic discourses on national identity produced during the 1930s. The texts I discuss are the novel *Luz y sombra* (1903) by Ana Roqué,[1] and a selection of texts by Luisa Capetillo from her books *Mi opinión sobre las libertades derechos y deberes de la mujer* (1911)[2] and *Influencia de las ideas modernas* (1916).[3] Neither writer was widely published at the time they were writing, nor were their texts made available to the general public until 1991 and 1992 when Lizabeth Paravisini-Gebert (Ana Roqué) and Julio Ramos (Luisa Capetillo) collected their work.[4] I also compare their proposals with the general thesis of two books that represent the mainstream discourse on national identity of the period: *La charca*[5] by Manuel Zeno Gandía and *Insularismo*[6] by Antonio S. Pedreira. These texts maintain a continuous discursive formulation in terms of nation building as well as on the women's question within the nation.

Roqué's and Capetillo's texts propose a new representation of the body as a metaphor of the imagined community of the nation.[7] As Gayatri Chakravorty Spivak points out when reading the inscription of the female body in the nation, "The space *displaced* from the Empire-Nation negotiation now comes to inhabit and appropriate the national map, and makes the agenda of nationalism impossible."[8] In Roqué and Capetillo, the female body is represented as a strategic space from which to develop a resistance to the dominant nationalist concerns of the same period's writings that is performed through the expression of feminine sexual desires. Therefore, femaleness becomes a pervasive mark on the body of the nation, thus resisting assimilation into the national ideal of "horizontal brotherhood."[9]

In reading the female body as antinational, the notion of gender as the center of feminist and political debate becomes problematic. In a colonial context, and particularly within the constitution of nation-building projects, women are constituted in relation to a whole series of intertwined discourses and practices, such as race, class, and sexuality:

> The inclusion of other analytical categories such as race and class becomes impossible for a subject whose consciousness refuses to acknowledge that "one becomes a woman" in ways that are much more complex than in a simple opposition to men. In cultures in which "asymmetric race and class relations are a central organizing principle of society," one may also "become a woman" in opposition to other women.[10]

Therefore, there is not one single feminine perspective that proposes an alternative vision of the nation. Instead, I will propose that both Roqué and Capetillo represent in their texts different ways of "formulating a communal space" based on their diverse views of sexuality. Sexuality, not gender, will be the center of my reading since it is from this space of desire that female writers propose a new definition not only of women within the nation but also of the notions of nationality, state, and law. I will concentrate on the interrelations between what Chandra Mohanty identifies as the two levels of struggle in this process of feminist reformulation of the nation: "an ideological, discursive level which addresses questions of representation (womanhood/femininity), and a material, experiential, daily-life level which focuses on the micropolitics of work, home, family, sexuality, etc."[11]

All the texts I analyze were produced in a period (1890–1934) during which Puerto Rico's political situation was very unstable. It is important to mention that during the time from 1897 to 1898, Puerto Rico achieved political autonomy from Spain only to become a U.S. colony a few months later. The U.S. invasion dislocated various local sectors that at the end of the nineteenth century had gained control over Puerto Rico's economy through the autonomy granted to the island in 1897. As a result, these sectors were fragmented into various social groups that supported different political projects for Puerto Rico, such as political independence and statehood.

The texts of Roqué and Zeno Gandía represent the views of the decadent landholding sector. In *La charca* Zeno Gandía represents Puerto Rican society during the climax of coffee production during the late 1860s and early 1870s.[12] Roqué represents their crisis and decadence a few years after the U.S. invasion and after the emergence of urban centers on the coasts resulting from the sugar plantation system established by U.S. corporations.[13] Capetillo writes from a completely different perspective because she represents the emergence of the working sector during the first decades of this century, whose class values were opposed to the nationalist concerns presented in texts by Zeno Gandía and Roqué.[14] Pedreira proposes a nostalgic look at the nineteenth century as an idyllic past in which creole landowners achieved cultural and political hegemony. What is important here, however, is that despite their differences, both Roqué and Capetillo proposed significantly different political projects than Zeno Gandía and Pedreira did. Interestingly, these alternative perspectives were ignored by official nationalist discourses, thus helping to create an illusion of continuity between Zeno Gandía's proposal in 1894 and Pedreira's project of 1934. The reading I propose here intends to reestablish an interrupted dialogue between canonical Puerto Rican texts and marginal feminine texts of the same period, which became a proscribed zone in Puerto Rican writings.[15]

"Bodily Histories": Corporal Frontiers of the Nation

Since the late nineteenth century, and especially after the arrival of positivist ideas, the Puerto Rican nation has been represented through a series of corporeal metaphors. One of the best examples of this kind of "bodily history" is included in *La charca* by Zeno Gandía. In this novel, the history of Puerto Rico is inscribed in what I will call—following the central idea of Zeno Gandía's collection of four novels titled *Crónicas de un mundo enfermo*—the "history of a sick body":

> Imagine usted un elemento étnico venido a la colonia en días de con-
> quista para sufrir una difícil adaptación a la zona cálida.... Después
> vinieron los cruces. ¡Cuánta mezcla! ¡Qué variedad de círculos tan-
> gentes! Un cruce caucásico y aborigen determinó la población de estas
> selvas.... La hembra aborigen fue el pasto; su gentileza bravía, el único
> manjar genésico, el único fecundo claustro en donde se formó la nueva
> generación. Esa mezcla fue prolífica, ¡pero a qué precio! El tipo brioso
> de la selva cedió energía física; el tipo gallardo y lozano que pisó el
> lampo de occidente, cedió robustez y pujanza. De esta suerte, el com-
> puesto nacido, el tipo derivado, resultó físicamente inferior; organi-
> zación deprimida, que había de ser abandonado al discurrir de los
> siglos.[16]

The body of the creole is represented as the product of an illicit sexual encounter, or as an expression of barbarism, that because it took
place outside of the law, generated a mixed and degenerated offspring.
The place of women within the nation is limited to a reproductive function, so women are not seen as subjects who can participate in the public
space of the nation. Furthermore, the Indian woman is represented as
unable to establish a respectable family, and her only function is to sexually reproduce without any legal rights. In this sense, Zeno Gandía's representation of women coincides with what Partha Chatterjee defines as
the feminine space within the nation:

> But the crucial requirement was to retain the inner spirituality of in-
> digenous social life. The home was the principal site for expressing the
> spiritual quality of the national culture, and women must take the
> main responsibility of protecting and nurturing this quality. No mat-
> ter what the changes in the external conditions of life for women, they
> must not lose their essentially spiritual (i.e., feminine) virtues.[17]

Zeno Gandía privileges women as "mothers" since he defines women's
bodies as the space in which healthy national "citizens" are produced.
Therefore, female sexuality must be controlled by medical and state laws
in order to ensure healthy pregnancies that will prevent bodily degenera-
tion and the loss of national identity: "Era bestial, feroz, inicuo lo que allí
se hacía. Apenas a través de la niña se entreveía la mujer, la imponían el
decúbito. La vida genésica prematura hería de muerte a la especie; la pre-
cocidad conscupiscente la infamaba, la deprimía, diluyendo para la prole
gérmenes de miseria física."[18]

Although Roqué also represents the nation as a body, her perspective dwells on the contradiction between women as reproducers and
women as mother figures within the limits of the nation. *Luz y sombra*

narrates the lives of two couples, who represent two different and contradictory projects of nationhood. On the one hand, Matilde and Paco represent a national project based on rural agriculture as developed by Spain in the interior of the island at the end of the nineteenth century. On the other, Julia and Sevastel propose a project based on commercial development, joined to a process of modernization and the creation of cities on the northern coast of the island under U.S. domination. In contrast to *La charca*, Roqué does not represent a single project but develops both options to privilege one: the rural development. Furthermore, the most important aspect of this novel is not the national project it privileges—because Roqué seems to agree with the dominant national discourses of her social class—but the contradictions this text depicts in the production of this national project. As Homi Bhabha says, "Counternarratives of the nation that continually evoke and erase its totalizing boundaries—both actual and conceptual—disturb those ideological manoeuvres through which 'imagined communities' are given essentialist identities."[19]

The counternarrative of *Luz y sombra* is developed through the intimate friendship between Julia and Matilde. Roqué seems to emphasize not only the different options for national constitution in her representation of national frontiers but also the impossibility of establishing a single position that will include all the needs and desires of the characters. *Luz y sombra* then represents the irreducible intersections between both national projects and the notion of a single national identity. Although Puerto Rican women are inscribed in this text in the legal circuit of marriage, female sexuality is defined as an autonomous space of desire that cannot be completely subsumed by the reproductive function: "Las caricias frías y convencionales de mi esposo me exasperaban, me enardecían: y cuando contemplaba aquel ser gastado, aquel joven viejo que se dormía cuando yo, pensando en otros ojos llenos de pasión y vida, me abrasaba, una desesperación sin nombre se apoderaba de mi ser."[20] Roqué redefines the frontiers of the female body to include desires and needs that transcend the sexual economy of mainstream nationalist discourses such as Zeno Gandía's. Therefore, Julia's sexuality is not limited to a reproductive function but includes the need to satisfy her sexual desires, traditionally represented as sexual surplus in other mainstream narratives.

Another relevant feature of the text is the switching back and forth between narrative voices. In the earlier quotation, it is Julia who describes her sexual desires, but the text is also narrated by a third-person omniscient narrator who assumes scientific and medical authority to describe the nature of female sexuality:

> Lo que ocurría era lo que imprescindiblemente tenía que suceder: la esposa se abrasaba de pasión mientras el marido dormía como un bendito. Y como siempre que se infringen las leyes de la Naturaleza, éstas, al buscar su equilibrio natural, rompen por encima de todas las conveniencias sociales, y siguen su curso poderoso, siendo la voluntad y la educación débiles diques, a veces, para oponerse a esa fuerza incontrastable.[21]

Roqué also uses Matilde's voice, as the representative of traditional female values within the nationalist project, to defend Julia's behavior and, ultimately, women's equality with men in terms of sexual desire.[22] The novel also includes the final forgiveness of Sevastel, Julia's husband, who finally understands Julia's need to satisfy her sexual desire:

> Pensé que en la mujer era bastante una excelente educación moral para preservarla de sentir pasiones que no estuvieran conformes con su deber.—Eso sucedería, le repliqué yo [Matilde], si la mujer fuera un ser distinto de los demás seres, y la educación pudiera sustraerla a las leyes propias de nuestra naturaleza imperfecta.[23]

This alternation between narrative voices represents an important rupture with the continuous and homogeneous discourse of the nineteenth-century realist novel. In *Luz y sombra* we find various discourses: (1) the intimate and colloquial language used in the personal letters between the female protagonists, (2) the scientific and objective discourse of the omniscient third-person narrator, and (3) the dialogue between all the characters. The text begins as an epistolary novel, is interrupted by the third-person narrator, who authorizes the debate on feminine sexual desire, and finally returns to the letters and dialogues between various characters. This gesture of rupture with the realist and totalizing discourse of the novel is important because Roqué clearly suggests that it is impossible to "narrate the nation" from a single and coherent discursive form: "If the problematic 'closure' of textuality questions the 'totalization' of national culture, then its positive value lies in displaying the wide dissemination through which we construct the field of meanings and symbols associated with national life."[24] The multiplicity of voices, subject-positions, and levels of authority in the text emulates the diverse positions in a process of negotiation within a nation or a community. Even though Roqué tries to impose a single national project as a synthesis of Puerto Rican identity, her textual account depicts the contradictory forces that lie beneath the homogenizing forces of this project.

On the other hand, Roqué defines a female subjectivity that is able to assume the totalizing authority traditionally assigned to a third-person omniscient narrator.[25] Female sexuality is postulated as a space from which to define females as agents within the limits of the nation, and is also used as a topic from which to constitute a scientific authoritarian voice produced by a female writer. The novel goes from the intimate and domestic space of the letters between the friends to the epistemological debate, abruptly entering into a discursive space traditionally considered masculine.

Capetillo's representation of the female body and sexuality is radically different. Whereas Roqué still believes that marriage is a healthy space from which to produce the nation's offspring, Capetillo wants to transcend all legal (state) control over the bodies that constitute a community. As Julio Ramos has noted, the working sector of Puerto Rican society produced a discourse clearly distanced from the nationalist concerns of the hegemonic sectors.[26] Capetillo's writings attempt to create an egalitarian space, achieved through a general workers' strike, in which all the institutions that control human lives (state, church, judiciary) are abolished; all individuals have the same rights and receive the same benefits as a result of their work. Capitalism is also rejected as an economic system that limits women's participation within society.[27] Interestingly, Capetillo's writings are not limited to the national space. She describes situations that are shared by women from many different communities and time periods. In her essay "La mujer en la época primitiva," she tries to reconstruct a transnational history of women's role as part of the human race: "En la época primitiva, siempre fue considerada como un objeto de poco valor, hasta que se le concedió ser esclava, y de esa esclavitud surgió su reinado doméstico."[28]

In her writings, Capetillo alludes to the female body and its inscription in marriage, love, and sexual desire. She rejects the idea of arranged marriages for social convenience because she sees in that practice an official and legal form of female prostitution within the patriarchal system in which women do not participate in the process of deciding how and to whom they are going to be sold as objects. Her reformulation of this female body appears, however, to transcend the frontiers of a specific nation, and she associates this view with a "natural" law that governs all human beings:

> Yo opino que el hombre no debe pertenecer a ninguna mujer antes de su completo desarrollo y llegado este momento debe escoger a la que realmente ame con toda su alma y hacerla su mujer, y crear una familia. Si no congenian y se ven obligados a separarse puede cada uno elegir de nuevo.[29]

Although Capetillo does not include homosexual practices as part of the natural law—"y ella o se masturba o tiene 'relaciones' sexuales con otra mujer, atrofiando de este modo su cerebro y perjudicando su belleza"[30]—she defends the individual's right to control his or her body and to express freely his or her desires in order to avoid illnesses and preserve mental and bodily health: "Y la mujer actual que tiene iguales derechos, ha de privarse por una supuesta honestidad, de pertenecerle a su novio para luego martirizarse y enfermarse aniquilando su organismo, atrofiando su cerebro, envejeciéndose prematuramente, sufriendo miles achaques."[31] It is also important to note that Capetillo defines a limit between what is natural and nonnatural, but according to her views, these limits should be controlled by each individual as a subject-agent, and not by the state or the church through laws and institutional intervention.

Finally, it is important to note that whereas Roqué uses more than one narrative voice to represent her views on nation and female sexuality, Capetillo uses heterogeneous writings, including dialogues that mimic the structure of rumor within a community. In the following quotation, Capetillo narrates the story of a couple that decides to live together because they are sexually attracted to each other. After they leave, two curious men talk about them in a dialogue that reproduces two opposing views on the subject. Anjouli Janzon[32] has described this type of text as a "social dialogue," in which the official voice is eroded by the marginal voice's arguments:

> —(el otro) ¿y es alguna cosa mala, conocer a un hombre?—(uno) sí, ¿por qué lo niegan?—(el otro) lo niegan porque nosotros queremos exigirle que no vayan, pero es un crimen el que esa joven pasee con su amigo?— . . . (uno) bien, pero yo no estoy conforme, yo quiero una mujer para mí solo—(el otro) si mientras tú le gustes y ella a ti, para ti sólo—(uno) pero no quiero que haya pertenecido a otro antes—(el otro) pero si ella te exige lo mismo, que tú no hayas pertenecido a nadie?—(uno) no puede exigirlo, porque es una necesidad—(el otro) pues precisamente porque es una necesidad, ella también tiene dere-

cho a satisfacerla—(uno) pero yo no pierdo nada—(el otro) ni ella tampoco, cumple una ley natural.[33]

The structure of the text, however, is also important. Capetillo represents these two opposing views not in a dialogue between clearly identified characters but between two unknown subjects that form part of the network of rumor as described by Spivak: "Rumour evokes comradeship because it belongs to every 'reader' or 'transmitter.' No one is its origin or source. Thus rumour is not error but primordially (originarily) errant, always in circulation with no assignable source. This illegitimacy makes it accessible to insurgency."[34]

By using the structure of rumor, Capetillo inscribes her concern in the free circulation of ideas within her community. Thus, relatively radical ideas of sexuality become central rather than marginal. Her concerns are thus part of an errant and discontinuous network of knowledge that is produced by the community itself. It is also important to note that Capetillo presents the two directions of rumor: its official and repressive mode, and its marginal and insurgent mode. Rumor becomes a source of pressure that circumvents the domain of the state and its laws. In this sense, rumor is a discursive space in which natural laws function in contradiction and dialogue with a multiplicity of ideas and voices that coexist in a single space. Female sexuality is the central metaphor of a new communal organization that can include diversity without repressing its expressions and maintain the possibility of achieving communal goals.

Confronting Canons: Transcending the Limits of the Nation

In closing, I would like to present a quick overview of the essays on national culture produced during the 1930s to see how alternative proposals were repressed and silenced in Puerto Rican canonical texts. In 1934 Antonio S. Pedreira published what is considered a central text in Puerto Rican national identity formulations: *Insularismo*. As Juan Gelpí has pointed out when commenting on the central metaphors of *Insularismo*, this essay "could be read as a narration on a sick country-child,"[35] a metaphor very similar to the one used by Zeno Gandía to organize his *Crónicas de un mundo enfermo*. The voice that enunciates the whole text is constructed by fusing two authoritarian positions: the magisterial and paternal voices. The whole history of Puerto Rico is summarized in *Insularismo* as the phases of development of a child: the sixteenth, seventeenth, and eighteenth centuries are compared to a period of lactation, and the nineteenth century is the moment in which the country-child begins to crawl.[36]

Pedreira returns to many of the concerns already present in *La charca*. In *Insularismo*, however, women are not only reduced to a reproductive function but are even effaced from the account of national reproduction: "Cuando en el siglo XVIII desaparece casi totalmente el ya apagado elemento indígena, quedan en exclusiva función etnológica el blanco y el negro, alimentando el viejo cruzamiento del cual salió el *mestizo*."[37] This process of female erasure is so pervasive in *Insularismo* that it also questions the capacity of intellectual women to understand national concerns.[38] On the other hand, miscegenation is for Pedreira a central concern because it produces "confused" natives. The main thrust in Pedreira's writing is the definition of national identity through the neutralization and homogenization of diversity. This is achieved through several textual strategies: refusing to assign any historical significance to the events that took place before the nineteenth century, excluding the female subject and all alternate views on national and communal identity already discussed, and creating an illusion of continuity between the end of the nineteenth century—the moment in which Zeno Gandía is formulating his project of national identity through his novels—and the identity crisis of the 1930s, allegedly stemming from the 1898 U.S. invasion.

To conclude my discussion, I would like to return to Spivak's reading of the female body and nation-building discourses: "Woman's body is thus the last instance in a system whose general regulator is still the loan: usurer's capital, imbricated, level by level, in national industrial and transnational global capital."[39] As Spivak clearly demonstrates, in many "narrations of the nation," the female body is represented as an exchange object in the economic systems of both national and international markets. I will argue, however, that in the narrations I have just discussed, the most important feature is what Spivak identifies as a displacement of the body: "But, I am arguing that in this fiction, woman's body is apart, elsewhere."[40] And it is precisely from that elsewhere that Roqué and Capetillo rethink mainstream national projects such as Zeno Gandía's, and later the powerful reformulation performed by Pedreira, to demand the right to intervene in the national arena. Sexuality is the discursive space from which to defend the right to these new spaces.

It is also important to return to one of the concerns I presented at the beginning of this essay: why are these alternative texts being read and edited in the 1990s? During this decade Puerto Ricans have experienced a whole process of questioning and revising of concepts such as nation, national language, struggle for redefinition of the colonial status, the constitution of a state and personal law, the notion of national identity and geographical or sexual demarcations, and so forth. Events like Cerro Maravilla in 1978, the ransack of several homes and subsequent imprisonment of sixteen *independentistas* by FBI agents on August 30, 1985, the proposition of a plebiscite in 1988 followed by Bush's support of Puerto Rican statehood in 1989, the celebration of the quincentenary of the "encounter"—that is, the beginning of colonialism for Puerto Rico—in 1992, the whole debate on the official language laws that began in 1991, and the one hundred years of U.S. presence on the island (to be commemorated in 1998) have all been important in the promotion of this desire to rethink Puerto Rico's political imaginary. It is in this context that texts such as *Luz y sombra* and Capetillo's writings provide us with an opportunity to deconstruct, by reconfiguring the canon, what has traditionally been defined as a monolithic nationalist discourse based on the constitution of a Puerto Rican subjectivity that is predominantly Hispanic, white, heterosexual, and male.

Furthermore, during the last three decades (1960–90), Puerto Rican fiction has continued to "incorporate" other voices in the "nationalist" debate: Luis Rafael Sánchez, Edgardo Rodríguez Juliá, Vanessa Droz, Juan Antonio Ramos, Ana Lydia Vega, Manuel Ramos Otero, and Tato Laviera, to mention just a few examples, are trying to constitute in their poetry and fiction other Puerto Rican identities that may be organized around categories such as race, class, drug dependency, sexuality, gender, and migration histories. The process of constituting new subjectivities is inscribed within a critical debate around the crisis of intellectual production, as it no longer can produce a totalizing representation of a coherent and exclusive Puerto Rican identity.[41] These alternative voices make the agenda of nationalism impossible, thus opening cultural space to other ways of "narrating" the experiences of the Puerto Rican community.

Notes

1. Ana Roqué, *Luz y sombra*, ed. Lizabeth Paravisini-Gebert (Río Piedras: Ediciones Huracán, 1991); first published in 1903.

2. Luisa Capetillo, *Mi opinión sobre las libertades derechos y deberes de la mujer* (San Juan.. The Times Publishers, 1911).

3. Luisa Capetillo, *Influencia de las ideas modernas. Notas y apuntes. Escenas de la vida* (San Juan: Tipografía Negrón Flores, 1916).

4. Julio Ramos, ed., *Amor y anarquía: Los escritos de Luisa Capetillo* (Río Piedras: Ediciones Huracán, 1992).

5. Manuel Zeno Gandía, *La charca* (Caracas: Ayacucho, 1978); first published in 1894.

6. Antonio S. Pedreira, *Insularismo* (Río Piedras: Editorial Edil, 1968); first published in 1934.

7. Benedict Anderson, *Imagined Communities: Reflections on the Origin and Spread of Nationalism* (London: Verso, 1992), 15–17.

8. Gayatri Chakravorty Spivak, "Women in Difference: Mahasweta Devi's 'Douloti the Bountiful' " in *Nationalisms and Sexualities*, ed. Andrew Parker et al. (New York: Routledge, 1992), 127–28.

9. Andrew Parker, introduction to *Nationalisms and Sexualities*, 6.

10. Norma Alarcón, "The Theoretical Subject(s) of *This Bridge Called My Back* and Anglo-American Feminism," in *Making Face, Making Soul/Haciendo Caras*, ed. Gloria Anzaldúa (San Francisco: Aunt Lute Foundation Books, 1990), 360.

11. Chandra T. Mohanty, "Introduction: Cartographies of Struggle: Third World Women and the Politics of Feminism," in *Third World Women and the Politics of Feminism*, ed. Chandra Talpade Mohanty, Anna Russo, and Lourdes Torres (Bloomington: University of Indiana Press, 1991), 21.

12. Juan Flores, "Refiguring *La charca*," in *Divided Borders: Essays on Puerto Rican Identity* (Houston: Arte Público Press, 1993), 75.

13. Ana Roqué was an important figure in the official spaces from which an intellectual formulation of Puerto Rican political identity was constructed. She was a member of the Ateneo Puertorriqueño (founded in 1876) and also participated in the mainstream political debate through the Republican Party. Finally, she also fought in favor of women's right to vote. For more details of her life, see Miriam Montes Mock, "Ana Roqué de Duprey: Precursora del periodismo feminista," in *Precursoras del feminismo en América Latina* (Chile: Fempress, 1991); and Lizabeth Paravisini-Gebert, "Crónicas de oprobios e infamias: La escritora puertorriqueña ante la crítica," in *Subversión de cánones: La escritora puertorriqueña ante la crítica* (New York: Peninsular, forthcoming).

14. Luisa Capetillo was a reader (*lectora*) in the tobacco factories. She promoted principles from the anarchist and unionist movements. In her writings, she favored the notion of "free love," and believed that anarchism was not only a political idea but a way of life. Norma Valle-Ferrer has done the best studies available on Capetillo's life. These are included in her book *Luisa Capetillo: Historia de una mujer proscrita* (Río Piedras: Editorial Cultural, 1990), and her essay "Una adelantada a su tiempo" in *Precursoras del feminismo en América Latina*, 42–44. Valle-Ferrer identifies two trends in Puerto Rican feminism during the early twentieth century: (1) a reformist trend that defended female education and the right to vote, and (2) a working-class feminism that fought for women's union rights and defended women's equality in the working market. This two tendencies are represented by Roqué and Capetillo, respectively.

15. Paravisini-Gebert, "Crónicas de oprobios e infamias," 171.

16. Zeno Gandía, *La charca*, 35–36.

17. Partha Chatterjee, "The Nationalist Resolution of the Women's Question," in *Recasting Women: Essays in Colonial History*, ed. Kumkum Sangari and Sudesh Vaid (New Delhi: Kali for Women, 1989), 243.

18. Zeno Gandía, *La charca*, 135. Zeno Gandía's project is inscribed within a broader project proposed by Salvador Brau in his *Disquisiciones sociológicas* (Río Piedras: Editorial

de la Universidad de Puerto Rico, 1956), first published in the 1880s. According to Brau, women should be educated in order to reinscribe the rural family in a legal and sanitation network of state control. Only through education would women be made aware of their moral responsibilities toward the nation.

19. Homi Bhabha, "DissemiNation: Time, Narrative and the Margins of the Modern Nation," in *Nation and Narration*, ed. Homi Bhabha (New York: Routledge, 1990), 300.

20. Roqué, *Luz y sombra*, 65.

21. Ibid., 77.

22. Lizabeth Paravisini-Gebert, "Las novelistas puertorriqueñas 'inexistentes,'" *Cupey* 6, 1–2 (Jan.–Dec. 1989): 96.

23. Roqué, *Luz y sombra*, 122.

24. Homi Bhabha, "Introduction: Narrating the Nation," in Bhabha, ed., *Nation and Narration*, 3.

25. Lubomír Dolezel, "Truth and Authenticity in Narrative," in *Poetics Today* 1–2 (1986): 12–13.

26. Julio Ramos, introduction to *Amor y anarquía*, 42.

27. Alice Colón, Margarita Mergal, and Nilsa Torres, *Participación de la mujer en la historia de Puerto Rico* (Río Piedras: Universidad de Puerto Rico, 1986).

28. Capetillo, "La mujer en la época primitiva," in *Mi opinión sobre las libertades derechos y deberes de la mujer*, 147–48.

29. Capetillo, *Mi opinión sobre las libertades derechos y deberes de la mujer*, 28.

30. Capetillo, "El hombre y la mujer," in *Mi opinión sobre las libertades derechos y deberes de la mujer*, 34.

31. Ibid., 35.

32. Anjouli Janzon, "La ley del deseo: Forjando un espacio de legalidad femenina en Ana Roqué y Luisa Capetillo," paper presented at the Second Annual Berkeley-Stanford Graduate Student Conference on Latin American Culture: Del Fin de Siglo a la Vanguardia, Nuevos Aportes Críticos, University of California-Berkeley, May 1, 1993.

33. Capetillo, *Influencia de las ideas modernas*, 91–93.

34. Gayatri Chakravorty Spivak, "Subaltern Studies: Deconstructing Historiography," in *Selected Subaltern Studies* (New York: Oxford University Press, 1988), 23.

35. Juan Gelpí, *Literatura y Paternalismo en Puerto Rico* (Río Piedras: Editorial de la Universidad de Puerto Rico, 1993), 24. Translation is mine.

36. Ibid., 25.

37. Pedreira, *Insularismo*, 27.

38. Pedreira, *Insularismo*, 96–97.

39. Spivak, "Women in Difference," 112.

40. Ibid., 114.

41. An example of this process is Juan M. García Passalacqua's essay titled "1993: Quinientos años de formación puertorriqueña," *El Nuevo Día*, May 2, 1993, 83–87. However, although García Passalacqua includes blacks as part of Puerto Rican cultural identity, women and homosexuals are still excluded from the intellectual tradition he reviews.

CHAPTER SEVEN

"So We Decided to Come and Ask You Ourselves": The 1928 U.S. Congressional Hearings on Women's Suffrage in Puerto Rico

Gladys M. Jiménez-Muñoz

> *That some languages of liberation might be implicated in the very service of oppression, that the enfranchisement of "women" as an unmarked constituency might require and institute a different set of hierarchies, that the legal reforms in women's interests are, in the hands of the paternal state, turned against other marginal groups: these are political quandaries that call into question the adequacy of the terms of feminist political analysis.* Judith Butler, "Disorderly Woman"

In the newly acquired U.S. colony of Puerto Rico during the early twentieth century, citizenship was one of the terrains in which subaltern social subjects were being constituted and refashioned. This essay summarizes some of the transformations that unfolded in the social inscription of the category "woman" in Puerto Rico during the 1920s through a close reading of the U.S. Senate hearing on women's suffrage in Puerto Rico before the Committee on Territories and Insular Possessions on April 25, 1928. This congressional hearing revealed the extent to which the domain of political rights both included and excluded "native" women, particularly in terms of their right to vote in islandwide elections.

This hearing anticipated in a condensed manner many of the textual practices and themes prevailing in the debate on women's suffrage: the persistent question of colonial ambivalence in general, particularly the tensions within Puerto Rico's suffrage movement over the impact and onus of having "natives" appeal to the highest colonialist authorities; the looming barbarism of the "native" uneducated classes; the citizenship controversies among the colonized and within colonizer circles themselves; the contradictory codifications of patriotism; the blatant heteronormativity of positioning Puerto Rican "women" as devout partners of "their" men; and, in sum, the multifaceted issue of "woman's proper place."[1]

Approving a Limited Women's Suffrage Bill

In early-twentieth-century Puerto Rico, the category "woman" ambiguously intersected the category of "citizenship" insofar as island women were denied the right to vote within the local political scene. This prohibition gained even greater significance after the U.S. Congress passed the Jones Act of 1917 enabling every adult male "native" to elect the members of both houses of the local legislature.[2]

The rise of the women's suffrage struggle partially stems from this pivotal accumulation of political contradictions, as exemplified by the 1917 founding of an unstable women's rights confederation mainly composed of "native" women professionals from widely dissimilar social backgrounds and viewpoints known as the Liga Femínea Puertorriqueña. Although initially the majority faction had prevailed in requesting the electoral franchise for only those women who could read and write,[3] in 1920 the Liga Femínea became an organization openly struggling for a wider range of social reforms, women's suffrage included, and was renamed Liga Social Sufragista. According to the prominent suffragist Milagros Benet de Mewton, the new name and broader objectives "expressed more clearly the organization's goal,"[4] among other things indicating the rising clout and numbers of socially progressive women professionals within the Liga. In 1921 the Liga promoted several legislative bills in favor of voting rights for all the island's women, regardless of whether they were literate.[5]

In March 1924, disagreements sprung up within the Liga, overlapping with a regrouping within the island's political scene. The dispute officially arose because one Liga faction opposed pro-suffrage court actions in open association with a common working-class woman (Mariana Morales Bernard) and a lawyer (Bolívar Pagán) who was an outspoken member of the "Partido Socialista."[6] Some of the top leaders of the Liga (for example, Ricarda Ramos Casellas) became publicly recognized as straightforward Jacobinist professionals.[7] Such company was obviously anathema to women identified with patrician respectability, bourgeois high culture, and the renovated cultural nationalism of the mainstream political parties, the Partido Unión (or Unionistas) and the Partido Republicano, who joined forces that same spring to form the Alianza. The main fear of the Alianza was that if all women in the island were granted the right to vote, this would throw the election in favor of the Socialistas, who had the largest number of illiterate adherents.[8] The converging political organs of the creole propertied and educated classes rallied against what they portrayed as the Socialista "red menace" and trade union rabble, that is, the Federación Libre de Trabajadores (FLT), particularly against the last two groups' purportedly unpatriotic agenda. In June 1924, the splinter group comprised by the more refined suffragists became the Asociación Puertorriqueña de Mujeres Sufragistas.[9]

At this time, politically active working-class women were also struggling for the "emancipation of the female sex." In 1919, a FLT committee for women's organization presented a resolution at the tenth congress of the island's principal labor federation, demanding a law guaranteeing the minimum wage for women, subsequently hand-delivering this resolution to the colonial governor.[10] Two years later some of these very same trade union women established the Asociación Feminista Popular de Mujeres Obreras Puertorriqueñas, headed by Franca de Armiño and Carmen Gaetán, among others.[11] This organization was aimed at obtaining both women's suffrage and the complete recognition of all civil and public rights for island women. The ideological kinship between this association and the Partido Socialista partially stemmed from the fact that the latter was the only island electoral organization to include women's suffrage in its program.[12]

Although almost a dozen bills granting women the vote had been presented in the island's legislative assembly between 1920 and 1929, women's suffrage was hardly a burning question within local legislative polemics at this time. As the majority party in the colony's parliament (either by itself or within the Alianza), the Unionista leadership was chiefly responsible for blocking women's suffrage bills.[13] Between 1924 and 1929 the Unionistas (now known as Aliancistas) promoted and benefited from the split within the Liga by winning over the support of the splinter group (the Asociación Puertorriqueña).[14] By acknowledging the growing pro-suffrage elements among propertied and educated women, the Unionista patriarch and senator Antonio R. Barceló resurrected the 1917 project of a restricted female vote (that is, only for women who knew how to read and write), convincing the Asociación Puertorriqueña that this was the more pragmatic option.[15] Yet, despite Barceló's formal endorsement, most of the Unionista (now joint Aliancista) legislative representation basically stalled all support for even this lukewarm measure.[16]

During the Pan-American Congress of Women in 1926, the leadership of the Liga established closer links with the U.S. National Woman's Party, which, in turn, convinced U.S. Senator Hiram Bingham to submit a bill amending the Jones Act granting Puerto Rico's women the vote.[17] The short-term failure of this legislative effort led to further lobbying during 1927 and 1928 on the part of the National Woman's Party in Congress on behalf of the vote for the women of Puerto Rico.[18]

These efforts paid off because by late 1928 the bill had been passed in the U.S. House of Representatives and had almost been passed in the U.S. Senate.[19] All the while, the colony's legislature had been delaying the issue, as the Alianza became increasingly upset at yet another case of federal usurpation of the authority of Puerto Rico's official spokesmen.[20] However, the balance of forces had decisively changed by late 1928.[21] On April 16, 1929, the island's legislature finally passed a law granting educated women the vote; universal suffrage was eventually granted in 1935.

Turning Legal Reforms in Women's Interests against Different Marginal Groups

After the Sixth Pan-American Congress in La Habana in 1928, the National Woman's Party (NWP) requested a hearing before the Senate Committee on Territories and Insular Possessions in order to modify the 1917 Jones Act extending voting rights for "native" women in Puerto Rico. Unlike at the La Habana Conference, this time Puerto Rican women spoke in their own name:[22] two representatives from the Liga Social Sufragista directly addressed the committee, the first one being the creole maternity/children's physician and hospital administrator Dr. Marta Robert de Romeu.[23] Mrs. Marie E. Futer of the NWP characterized Dr. Robert's presentation as "an indication of the wish of the Porto Rican women themselves . . . to present their case before this committee."[24]

Robert de Romeu began by asking the committee to recommend the approval of the most recent legislative project submitted by Senator Bingham, the bill (S. 753) amending the Jones Act to grant women on the island "the right to vote in their own country" (2). According to Robert de Romeu, because the relevant provision in the Jones Act specified only that voters should be "citizens of the United States, 21 years of age or over and have such educational qualifications as may be prescribed by the legislature of Porto Rico," there was nothing specifically barring island women from exercising their right to vote as U.S. citizens. However, having been accorded "the right to make any discriminations they wanted, except those relating to property," the colony's legislature chose to "[limit] the voting privilege in Porto Rico to men. They did not include women" (2).

Summarizing some of the fruitless efforts made by local suffragists between 1919 and 1925 in the island's legislative assembly, Robert de Romeu recalled the advice offered by U.S. Representative Edgar R. Kiess, who, in a visit to the island, had suggested that "native" suffragists wait for the colony's legislature to grant them the right to vote. "We waited, but we wasted time," she remarked, because everything seemed to indicate that "we were getting more attention in the American Congress than we were getting in our own legislature" (3). As they waited for the colony's legislative assembly to act in their favor, Senator Bingham reintroduced his bill in December 1927, while Representative Kiess did the same in the House. Robert de Romeu expressed the Liga's reservations concerning Barceló's bill in the colony's legislature: this bill contained literacy restrictions and "was a very conservative one indeed" (3). Yet she also communicated the Liga's uneasy willingness to compromise in the interest of advancing the long-term goal of enfranchising women from the island's laboring classes. According to her, this was why the Liga "could not go against the bill": "it was just a step in our progress. . . . We had to accept it because it was a part of what we were asking for" (3). The senate in Puerto Rico approved the bill, but the colony's house of representatives refused to introduce a parallel project.

With respect to the colony's legislature, the Liga was grudgingly accepting, to borrow Judith Butler's words, "legal reforms in women's interests . . . in the hands of the paternal state" even though they knew that such reforms were "turned against other marginal groups,"[25] namely, the uneducated laboring women comprising most of the female population of the island. Robert de Romeu was evidently aware that some sectors within the creole propertied and educated classes (politically represented by the Asociación Puertorriqueña de Mujeres Sufragistas and the minority pro-suffrage Barceló faction of the Alianza) perceived the prevailing situation as a moral scandal: if ignorant and boorish men from the "native" laboring classes had been voting under the new regime since 1904, why could women not exercise the same right? This was why she took them to task by pushing their arguments to their logical and most extreme consequences. With a flair of sarcasm, Robert de Romeu suggested that if class-based imbalances between educated and illiterate "natives" were deployed against island women, then these absurd limitations should be retroactively made applicable to creole men also: "if you make this organic law in favor of women in Porto Rico, they have a perfect right to set up any qualifications whatsoever," including instituting "a standard of literacy"; however, "they have to do it for both men and women."[26]

However, the shifts within the gendered politics of colonial mimicry and the colonial-based politics of gender were even more complex and paradoxical. Acknowledging the persistent colonial ambivalence and tensions within the island's legislature, Robert de Romeu simultaneously appeared to be recognizing—to use Butler's words again—"that the legal reforms in women's interests . . . in the hands of the paternal state"— now the federal government—not only were but had to be "turned against" another and quite different "marginal group." This time the allusion was to the creole legislators being politically marginalized by colonialist authorities (in San Juan and in Washington, D.C.). "So we decided to come and ask you ourselves; having the hope that you gentlemen of the American Congress would take a little more interest in seeing justice done to Porto Rican women," (3) said Robert de Romeu.

Openly admitting that "the enfranchisement of 'women' as an unmarked constituency might require and institute a different set of hierarchies,"[27] Robert de Romeu—unabashedly—appealed directly to imperial authority and to the protection of the rights of its citizens, despite the fact that it meant overriding or even further curtailing the limited authority of the colony's (male) legislators. As a member of the Liga, many of whose leaders identified U.S. statehood for Puerto Rico as a way of blocking the continuing political ascent of the coffee hacendados and the "native" sugar land barons, Robert de Romeu would have had little compunction about appealing to the highest colonialist authorities against the Alianza legislative majority. "We feel more than justified in coming to you, because you gave us our American citizenship by an organic law," she said, asking, "Why should we not ask you to give us complete citizenship in our country?" (4). In this way, she explicitly admitted that the question of women's suffrage in Puerto Rico had long ago been transformed into an issue of colonial authority.

Although referencing colonialist contradictions, Robert de Romeu falls short of blaming the very object of her entreaty. "By our organic act, and by the nineteenth amendment to the constitution," she began, "we are allowed to come here to the United States, . . . and after six months' residence we have the right to vote, as any of our sisters in the United

States" (4). The onus falls, rather, on the shoulders of the creole men at the helm of the colony's legislative assembly: "the only thing that prohibits us from going to Porto Rico and voting . . . is just a little injustice from our men when they make the electoral law in Porto Rico" (4). In light of Robert de Romeu's and the Liga's political sympathies, these diminutives ("just a little injustice") and possessive pronouns invoking community ("our men") are probably more an indication of irony than anything else: Robert de Romeu is quite unequivocal about who is responsible for the political plight of island women.

However, how could the colony's patricians really blame her and the Liga for this strategy? After all, did the "enfranchisement of" Puerto Ricans "as an unmarked constituency" (namely, men) not also "require and institute a different set of hierarchies,"[28] this time referring not to class-based differences within the island's political scene but to gendered political inequalities? "They want us to let them act on the right of Porto Rican women to vote, but they got their citizenship" and "their political rights from an organic act of Congress," asserted Robert de Romeu. "This organic act covers all persons—men and women. The women should obtain the same right as all our citizens" (4).

Then, directly speaking to the colonizers' obligations toward their subjects, she suddenly shifted from supplication to demand. "So, gentlemen, you whose duty it is to see that Porto Rico progresses, as all the States of the United States progress," Robert de Romeu declares, "should give us the same rights as the American women of the United States, because we are part of the United States" (4). Here she appropriated the outcome of the U.S. Supreme Court's Insular Cases, inventively reworking the notion of U.S. responsibility—from pertaining to *a place* (Puerto Rico) to pertaining to *a people* (Puerto Ricans, regardless of their residence and independent of their gender)—until colonialist duties end up standing on their head. In this manner, she clearly placed herself within the realm of sheer legal audacity, at best, and constitutionalist fantasy, at worst: "You should give us the same right to exercise this privilege in our country as we have to exercise it in any part of the United States" (4).

Going to Washington, D.C., and Other Colonial Ambivalences

One of the principal features of Robert de Romeu's address was a series of challenges aimed at the masculinist arguments used mostly by her creole male counterparts (and even some Puerto Rican women) against conferring the right to vote on island women. A prominent anti-suffrage reasoning at the time was "the biological and physiological nature" of (Puerto Rican) women, a perspective populating numerous articles in the Puerto Rican press.[29] For example, G. García de la Noceda, in an article published in 1927, argued that men and women were "two sexes created by God and sustained by Nature."[30] García de la Noceda's idealized and simplified description of normal/natural masculinity and femininity was unfortunately quite emblematic of the commonplace viewpoints of the day. If "both sexes" were "created by God and sustained by Nature," then any attempts by women in Puerto Rico to expand their civil liberties and rights as citizens was pointless insofar as such attempts went against Natural and Divine designs. Robert de Romeu countered these arguments by indicating that

> our Porto Rican men cannot argue that we are not fitted to act in political affairs and have our political rights. You know, there are more than 30 countries now that have admitted woman suffrage, and we Porto Rican women are the same as all the rest of the women in the world, from the standpoint of biology. (3)

Robert de Romeu also took the opportunity to refute those who expected maternal and domestic duties to become one of the first casualties of women's suffrage—if and when it was granted:[31]

> I do not think so, because there are a lot of women in Porto Rico who have been working for a long time. They go every day and spend long hours working outside. They leave their children and they leave their homes, and yet their children and their homes are well taken care of. So, if we go to work and leave our children and our homes, why can we not go for a little while every four years and vote for the sake of our country? (3)

However, here the category "women" materialized as very contradictory and problematic because it surfaced as an "unmarked constituency,"[32] in turn giving rise to further ambivalences. Prominent women's suffrage advocates on the island, such as Robert de Romeu, perceived and framed themselves as representative of all of Puerto Rico's women. She was primarily speaking about, as well as speaking for, womanhood itself on the island, that is, many if not most women: "a lot of women." It should be remembered that the more socially progressive suffragists in Puerto Rico, such as the members of the Liga, tended to perceive themselves as also assisting the advent of a social regime in which all honest toilers (professionals and small-property owners included) could live and work in harmony on the fruits of their own labor.

Robert de Romeu, though, does not specify the class-based situation of these women who could "spend long hours working outside" and yet have children and homes that were "well taken care of." The question remains, who exactly carried out the concrete labor left behind? Where were the people that performed the corresponding motherly tasks of taking care of the children and homes of the women who could "go every day and spend long hours working outside"? Surely, not these women's husbands. Given the Jacobinism of the Liga Social Sufragista, it is possible that she was alluding to the extended-family and neighborhood networks of cooperation that usually made the rearing and supervision of children a collective and community affair among the island's laboring majorities, rather than to the responsibility of individual propertied and educated parents.

However, given the gendered social divisions of labor in Puerto Rico at this time, such domestic labor could also have been perceived as being performed by *other* women, who clearly did not belong to the same social class as those women, namely, women activists and professionals such as Dr. Marta Robert de Romeu, under whose surveillance they labored. Hence, her comments were, at best, unclear and, at worst, exceedingly contradictory in terms of what she and her comrades meant by the social category "women in/of Puerto Rico." The contradiction and ambivalence of her comments tended to resonate with many of the arguments reducing the category "women" to propertied and educated women—as in the case of those justifying "women's proper place" from an anti-suffrage position. Mrs. Carlota B. de Cabañas, for instance, claimed that Senator Bingham's bill granting Puerto Rico's women the vote "attempted to destroy woman and end the peace, tranquillity, and morality of that sacred abode that was the home. . . . Woman today has retreated, descending to a very inferior plane." According to Mrs. Cabañas, this "woman," as representative of womanhood itself in Puerto Rico, was none other than "that lady whose exquisite customs by way of dress, hair-style, gait, and behavior in society allowed her to be positioned in a very superior plane."[33]

Consequently, Robert de Romeu's unspecified and ambiguous pursuit of "legal reforms in women's interests" fell dangerously close to the social-class terrain of the more candid Mrs. Cabañas and of similar anti-suffrage arguments published in the Puerto Rican press in that this pursuit could be perceived as "turn[ing] against other marginal groups."[34]

Perceived in this way, Robert de Romeu's pursuit and the anti-suffrage arguments are summoning the category "woman" in exactly the same manner, that is, one that omitted the overwhelming majority of Puerto Rican women from "womanhood," thereby "requir[ing] and institut[ing] a different set of hierarchies"[35]—this time, class inequalities.

Robert de Romeu's class ambivalence persists when she maintains that despite the fact that before the U.S. invasion island women "were not allowed in professional affairs," nevertheless there were "great women in literature and art" (3). After 1898, women "were admitted to all the professions," there now being "doctors, dentists, lawyers, pharmacists, and a lot of women in industries," as well as "a great many women in commerce and in public offices" (3). Although the mention of "women in industries" appears to gesture toward peasant and proletarian women in Puerto Rico, her words again surface as ambiguous. She could just as well have referred to women of means who were entrepreneurs or employers—petty or large—in their own right. Although it provides no details of the dimensions of these businesses, a local newspaper article of the day offered just such a list of renowned women, including among them, interestingly enough, the then spokeswoman for the Liga, Mrs. Milagros Benet de Mewton, who owned what the article vaguely classified as a store catering to tourists.[36]

One of Dr. Robert de Romeu's most emblematic colonial ambiguities, which she shared with most creole suffragists, can be found in the way she drew on the prevailing discourses of motherhood (on the island and on the U.S. mainland) to bolster her argument that "men need us in our country in all lines of activity": "If we know what our children need, if we know what our homes need, I think that we can find out better than men what our country needs" (3–4). The Senate committee transcript indicates that this portion of her statement was followed by applause, thus revealing the obvious allure of such reasoning.

This same maternalistic narrative grounds the alleged custodial and protective disposition of women toward children and homes. In this excerpt she shifts these attributes from the domestic sphere to the political arena so as to represent women as the mothers and housekeepers of the country, the ones that would sweep out corruption and take special interest in the needs of all homes and all children. Such a shift, however, still limited these women to being "fitted to act in political affairs and have [their] political rights" only within express maternalistic boundaries (3).

Representing the righting of social wrongs as a grander-scale consummation of "motherhood" did not in any way conflict with advocating women's suffrage but was instead both its preface and its logical outcome. This problematic ambivalence, once again, was not limited to the fact that maternalistic and domestic ideological representations were being commonly deployed in favor of women's suffrage on the island.[37] Its ambivalence and discursive plasticity lay also in the fact that "motherhood" was equally being mobilized against granting the electoral franchise to Puerto Rico's women.[38]

An outstanding example of such anti-suffrage uses was a 1928 article by Sarito Roger y Nieves in which she addressed all island women in no uncertain terms: "You are, therefore, the one responsible for guiding the child, who is the man of tomorrow, to mold his feelings and to instill in him goodness and love."[39] Roger y Nieves grieved for a lapsing feminine memory and the waning of ladylike traits due to the onslaught of modernity, the latter being expressed by women demanding prerogatives understood as inappropriate to their gender: "you want to govern a people, [while] you abandon the government of your little fatherland—your home; you pretend to reign, when you have abandoned your throne." She ended by bidding women to remain true to their domestic and motherly tasks, not confusing manly callings with womanly responsibilities: "Man has another mission. He seeks the home's sustenance. He fortifies and perfects it. It is your duty to instill faith in him, encourage his aspirations, comfort him when sad, heighten his joy."[40]

Modern "motherhood," then, was perceived as creating another level of ambivalence in women, making the uses of such discourses extremely slippery and contradictory. Being a mother/woman was ontologically defined by and within the heterosexualized domestic sphere: without this sphere "motherhood"—and, indeed, "womanhood" itself—did not, and could not, make any sense. This was why Roger y Nieves could readily counterpoise "motherhood" to the public sphere, any female intervention in the public sphere being seen as "rebel[ling] against the aims of nature, violating its laws" by "want[ing] to govern a people."[41] When Robert de Romeu appealed to such narratives, her arguments had the virtue—and problem—of striking a *familiar* chord. The dilemma was that such a logic, simultaneously and heteronormatively, reinscribed "women" as the perpetually subordinate domestic partners of "men." In the home, as in the voting booth or the political party, women-as-mothers would continue to be required to perform their duties as social ancillaries, as nurturers, not only for children everywhere but also for menfolk everywhere—

even within the legislature: "instill[ing] faith in him, encourag[ing] his aspirations, comfort[ing] him when sad, heighten[ing] his joy."

The final anti-suffrage argument that Robert de Romeu rebutted was that island women allegedly would be swayed and unduly "influenced" by their husbands, brothers, or "any male relatives." She responded to these arguments by granting that women had always received political influences: "Suppose we are influenced by them" (4). But Robert de Romeu saw women as being sufficiently intelligent to make their own judgments on political matters, as having enough acumen to evaluate whatever influence they might receive, regardless of who attempted to persuade them. As far as she was concerned, the problem was not whether women were going to be politically influenced or not, but rather that women had never been able to do much about it: "I think there ought to be an intellectual balance. If the influence is a good one, well and good; and if it is not, we ought to be in a position where we can do something about it" (4).

She maintained that if the objection was based on women being trapped by being unable to make self-sufficient political decisions, then women's suffrage was not the cause of the problem but rather the solution. Granting them voting rights was a way of enabling women to exercise even greater politico-intellectual autonomy and independence of judgment. If "native" women, as women, could indeed "find out better than men what our country needs" (3–4), she asserted, then such a gendered awareness—certainly, such a moral superiority and epistemological privilege—placed women in an even better, preferred position than creole men in terms of making political decisions that affected the future of Puerto Rico.

The Deposition of Miss Rosa M. Emanuelli

Robert de Romeu's address was followed by a statement presented by Miss Rosa M. Emanuelli, another active member of the Liga, who pursued arguments similar to those of her predecessor. "I know that about 90 per cent of the teachers in the island, which number about 5,000, are Porto Rican," she began, assuming her authority as a San Juan schoolteacher (5). Immediately, her reasoning became grounded in the coupled ideologies of motherhood and colonial citizenship: "We believe that so long as we have been intrusted with the education of children to be good American citizens, we ought to have the right to vote, in addition to citizenship" (5). As teachers, "native" women in Puerto Rico were held responsible for instructing the children under their care to become reliable and obedient U.S. citizens. Therefore, how could island women, as teachers, be accountable to the state (local and federal) and how could women/teachers effectively wield this civic authority while they were simultaneously being denied all the rights inherent to the very same citizenship whose values they were called upon to instill in "native" youth? This was only a variant of the discourses of "motherhood" and "citizenship" within the island's pro-suffrage camp, the pitfalls of which we have already examined.

Emanuelli then proceeds to react to a second—and typical—antisuffrage argument, namely, the issue of women's lack of political experience. Such logic was already common among the local press, as can be seen, for instance, in a 1927 article by M. J. Mayoral Barnés, which stated that "[t]he Puerto Rican woman . . . even ignores the way a political party functions."[42] Emanuelli replied to such arguments by saying:

> Many men say that some women are capable, but not many of them. I ask you, are all men capable? Some are elected to their own legislatures, and they have no knowledge of legislature procedure, but after 10 years or so they have had quite a good deal of experience, and become good legislators. (5)

Once again, the uses of such logic proved to be very contradictory and ambivalent. Her response was mainly aimed at demonstrating that island women were no worse than creole men in such matters; that is, that one was as equally qualified—or as relatively unseasoned—as the other within the realm of politics. The problem was that calling into question the political and administrative proficiency of these men coincidentally reinforced the already existent (colonialist) narratives of "native" incompetence and immaturity in terms of self-government, regardless of the gender of the "natives." For example, in his open letter to the colonial governor of February 28, 1928, had not President Calvin Coolidge charged that the "'grave economical situation' in the finances of the government of Porto Rico" remained "exclusively the result of the exercise by the elected representatives of the people of Porto Rico of an authority granted by the present liberal organic law," the U.S. government being only responsible, "at most," for what "officers appointed by the President in Porto Rico may not have exercised"?[43] Emanuelli's statement only confirmed such evaluations of "native" (male) juridico-political inability.

She proceeded to fall headlong into the trap of colonial ambivalence when she added that "[t]he same argument can be applied to women" and that "[a]fter they get practice and experience they will be as good legislators as men are" (5). Emanuelli was obviously trying to make an argument in favor of Puerto Rican women being just as well qualified and eager to learn as Puerto Rican men were or had ever been. But insofar as derogatory colonialist appraisals of the Coolidge variety were directed at all Puerto Ricans (of whatever gender) as colonized subjects, how could Emanuelli's argument and indications exempt island women from being perceived as analogously unfit for self-government in general and for voting in particular?

Then, drawing on eighteenth-century mythologies of Euro-North American nation building, Emanuelli argued that propertied and fiscally burdened Puerto Rican women were being taxed without exercising their right to direct political representation: "We are not permitted to be elected to the legislature, and have nothing to say about how the money thus collected shall be spent" (5). Like Robert de Romeu, Emanuelli came dangerously close to conjuring visions of middle-class scandal—though this time aimed at shaming not only the colony's legislature but also the federal government. And like Robert de Romeu's, Emanuelli's entreaty was directed not at the abbreviated power embodied in the colony's legislature but at the perceived site of imperial authority—the U.S. Congress: "We have come to ask you for an act of Congress giving us the right to vote, because we want this to be considered as a national affair" (5). The women's suffrage issue in Puerto Rico continued to be referenced as a question of colonial authority, pitting Puerto Rican legislators against North American congressmen, colonized men against male colonizers.

At one level, Emanuelli surpassed Robert de Romeu, because the latter had only likened Puerto Rican women to North American women insofar as both had once been or still were relatively disenfranchised *U.S. citizens* when she asked for "the same rights as the American women of the United States, because we are part of the United States" (4). Emanuelli, on the other hand, had compared island women to North American women insofar as they both had once been or still were disenfranchised *women.* This argument made for an even more imaginative use of U.S. constitutional history, claiming that the current political predicament of "native" women in Puerto Rico—and, hence, the implied federal duty toward them—was the same as [what it had been when] woman suffrage in the United States . . . [was] considered, because we believe that as American citizens we are in the same position as women in the United States. Women in the United States were allowed to vote by an act of Congress, and we want to have our women also allowed to vote by an act of Congress, and we want this recognition of woman suffrage to appear in our constitution, enacted by Congress. (5–6)

Apparently, Emanuelli was aware that such petitions implied further eroding the limited authority of "her own" men in the colony's legislature and political parties. So, she immediately declared, "[w]e believe that in cooperation with men we can acquire more liberties for the American citizens of Porto Rico" (6).

The National Woman's Party versus the Sentinels of the Republic, the Woman Patriots, and the Emissaries of the Creole Legislature

The next presentation was delivered by Mrs. Burnita Shelton Matthews, a member of the lawyer's council who represented the legal research department of the NWP. She started by asserting that "the women of Porto Rico are citizens of the United States. . . . They are exercising a right pertaining to their American citizenship, and they come here to ask you to end the political inferiority of one-half the people of Porto Rico" (6). Here was yet another invocation of the political and civic equality of both genders within the parameters of U.S. citizenship: "The women of Porto Rico want you to write into their supreme law the provision that the right to vote shall not be denied or abridged on account of sex" (6). North American women's rights advocates, like Shelton Matthews, continued to defend the principle of women's suffrage for Puerto Rico even as they explained and debated the anti-suffrage constitutionalist arguments. The reference point for the debates over the Foraker and Jones Acts was the dispute over the rights of slave masters (6).

Shelton Matthews subsequently argued that the applicability of the U.S. Constitution transcended whatever juridical uncertainties might exist in the case of Puerto Rico's colonial condition. For her, the issue was clear: if the imperial faculties of the U.S. Congress have been repeatedly validated in the recent past for the common good of all these "natives," then why did the federal legislature not exercise these same prerogatives in favor of half of these same "natives," that is, by decreeing women's suffrage in Puerto Rico (6–7)? This was another case of the enlightened, liberal, and maternalistic racism of "white [women]" appealing to "white men . . . [to] protect brown women."[44] Such exhortations confirmed the moral superiority of (white middle-class) North American women over their male counterparts in Congress: without such (womanly) prodding, Congress would not hurry and take measures legitimizing U.S. expansionism in the Caribbean. Imposing women's suffrage in Puerto Rico would enable the U.S. government to once again verify and proclaim that it still represented the lofty spiritual values of the (Western) civilizing mission. After the passing of the nineteenth amendment, these lobbying activities were yet another "service to the empire"[45] on the part of these NWP members: "proof of their reliability as voters" (6–7).

But why did these post-suffrage, white middle-class U.S. women reformers espouse abroad a solidarity they often failed to practice at home—among African-American, Mexican, Asian, and indigenous women? Geopolitics (white petty producer and settler colonialism within the metropolis versus a colonialism based on the intensive exploitation of "native" labor abroad) seemed more important than geography (European-American colonialism in North America versus U.S. colonialism overseas). It should be borne in mind that supporting voting rights for women in Puerto Rico—like the analogous campaign the NWP advanced in the neocolonial Caribbean and the rest of Latin America—had absolutely no direct impact on the legislative composition of the U.S. Congress. Similar to the "native" populations of the U.S. protectorates (or "dependencies") of Nicaragua, Cuba, Mexico, the Dominican Republic, Honduras, Panama, Guatemala, El Salvador, Venezuela, and Haiti, the "natives" (of both genders) in the U.S. colony of Puerto Rico were barred from participating in U.S. congressional or presidential elections.

Shelton Matthews proceeded to describe the great efforts Puerto Rican women had been making to expand voting rights on the island. The obstacles and foot-dragging of the creole political leadership figured prominently within this narrative.

> For two years they have interested the Woman's Party in this movement to grant woman suffrage for the women of Porto Rico. Last year, in May, Mr. Barcelo, president of the senate, was here, and the women of Porto Rico asked that we go and interview this commission. Mr. Barcelo does not speak English, as these ladies do, and we had to speak to him, of course, through an interpreter. (7)

Again the motif of the bumbling and incompetent "native" (male) politician loomed into view. The ability of Puerto Rico's educated women to "find out better than men what our country needs" (4) became repeatedly evident: "Mr. Barcelo does not speak English, as these ladies do" (7). This type of argument had a long history within the (white) women's rights movement in the United States. Elizabeth Cady Stanton, for instance, was known for thundering against the extensive voting rights of non-Anglo-Saxon male immigrants to the North American republic in light of the better educated, English-speaking, white, and, hence, bona fide "American" women being denied such rights.[46]

Drawing on this important politico-cultural heritage, Shelton Matthews's testimony and its implications were quite clear: as "natives" who could "read and write the English language intelligently," women like Robert de Romeu and Emanuelli were considerably more equipped for U.S. citizenship and for managing the interests of the empire among the colonized than an Antonio R. Barceló, who "does not speak English, as these ladies do"—therein lay the scandal of keeping such women in a state of disenfranchisement. Through the proficiency of these "native" women, the crafting of colonialist government and enterprise could transpire much more smoothly, unencumbered by the linguistic and legislative ineptitude of these backwater, Caribbean (male) bumpkins playing with self-government. Shelton Matthews, not being under any obligation to entertain the euphemisms and qualifying statements of her Puerto Rican counterparts could, therefore, afford to be more blunt.

> He [Barceló] is not willing, nor do the politicians of Porto Rico seem willing, to deal with woman suffrage as a question in itself. They never took up that one particular question. What they all seem to do is to tie that up with some general reform in the election law. For instance, Mr. Barcelo says, "Well, we should have a literacy test," and his party is very anxious to put over this literacy test, which some of the other parties, I understand, do not favor. In that way they confuse the issue, and never at any time take up this one particular point of suffrage for the women of Porto Rico. (7)

Shelton Matthews ends by calling upon Congress (as Robert de Romeu and Emanuelli had done) to be the body ultimately responsible for righting the wrongs being committed against these "native" women, fellow U.S. citizens and loyal adherents of American democracy: "The control of suffrage in Porto Rico is in the hand of one half the people of Porto Rico, and we hope that the gentlemen of this committee will not uphold this one half of the people of Porto Rico in denying suffrage to the other half" (7).

Shelton Matthews's intervention was followed by declarations against having Congress ordain women's suffrage in Puerto Rico. The first address was delivered by Iredell Meares, speaking for the Sentinels of the Republic, an organization describing itself as "devoted . . . to the defense of the Constitution, the preservation of local self-government, and the principles upon which we think our country was founded" (8). The Sentinels of the Republic were organized in 1922 in New York City and were an extremely conservative and militantly anti-Communist organization. In addition to having ties to prominent business groups and industrialist associations, the Sentinels were associated at the time with "respectable" right-wing groups such as the American Constitutional League, the National Security League, the Association Against the Prohibition Amendment, the American Defense Society, and the Woman Patriots. Being avidly against any federal tampering with prevailing labor conditions, the Sentinels were responsible for defeating the child labor amendment during the mid-1920s and for opposing "federal encroachment on states' rights," while supporting "efforts to prevent any more amendments like those from the Fourteenth to the Nineteenth."[47]

According to Meares, at their last meeting in Baltimore the Sentinels passed a resolution opposing "pending bills to impose woman suffrage on Porto Rico and the Philippine Islands in violation of the right of self-government in this matter already conferred on these dependencies" (8). Meares found it "astonishing . . . that at a time when the whole tendency of modern legislation" was inclined toward "self-determination to the colonies of a nation," "we are reversing the policy and attempting to impose the will of this national body upon a local organization" (8–9).

At first glance, it certainly appears strange that an organization also known for its more extreme racist outlook would become the champion of "native" self-government. Such considerations seem additionally curious given that at no time did the Sentinels express remorse over the intent or results of the war of 1898, which claimed Puerto Rico as war booty for the United States and did away with the powers of the hacendado-controlled autonomous government.

The issue of "states' rights" seems to be one of the keys to this puzzle. Within the context of the federal amendment authorizing voting rights for women in the United States, states' rights meant resisting federal intervention in the more conservative areas of the country. "We had some

experience in this country in regard to attempting to force States to ac-
complish results," Meares argued. "We are involved in a terrific struggle
to-day with the nineteenth amendment" (9). In the U.S. South, this
meant defending the rights of the openly white-supremacist govern-
ments (local and regional) to preserve the apartheid conditions that
made the large concentrations of African-American labor cheaper than
white labor. "We have had it in the Southern States with the fourteenth
amendment," Meares went on, "and all the power of Congress, all the
power of this Nation, has never yet been able to overcome the intelligence
and the determination of the Saxon element of the South to govern
themselves" (9). In the case of Puerto Rico, this perspective translated
into a defense of the rights of U.S. corporations to operate on the island,
without concern about the reduced number of labor protection and tax
laws covering Puerto Rico under federal jurisdiction.[48] At that time and
despite creole rhetorical claims to the contrary, these stateside corporate
privileges were still being guaranteed by the colony's legislative assembly,
only being now and then side-stepped by congressional intervention.[49]

Consequently, when Meares declared that "[w]e have undertaken to
create a colony" and have "granted it a charter, and that charter gives the
liberty to grant woman suffrage," it appears that the initially unexpressed
motive of these words had very little to do with whether "women are superior to men in Porto Rico" or whether women there "have every quali-
fication" (9). For the Sentinels, the problem, rather, was that this or any
other matter "internal" to the colony was "not the issue here for the Congress of the United States" (9). Congress "can not become the legislature
of Porto Rico" and "can not decide the differences" within the island (9).

Only later on did Meares explicitly verbalize the strategic concerns of
his organization. "We think there is something greater here than the
granting of suffrage to the women of Porto Rico, or any other section,"
began Meares, immediately adding that the crucial issue at hand "involved . . . whether the United States Congress shall deliberately ignore the
cardinal principles of our government and impose its will upon a legislative body of Porto Rico that may or may not be in favor of this measure"
(9). Further meddling in such "native" differences by passing this or any
other federal measure regulating what was ultimately an issue of local/
regional (property) rights would "simply la[y] a train of trouble and difficulties which I think we ought to avoid in dealing with our colonies" (9).

Playing on liberal senators' anxieties about appearing to be Caribbean expansionists and gunboat diplomats, Meares adroitly coupled his

arguments against a federal law granting women's suffrage in Puerto Rico with the need to avoid charges like the ones aimed at the U.S. government as recently as the La Habana conference only a few months before:

> More than that, the position of this government with relation to all the Latin States, all of South America, is one that is rather sensitive. We are held up to criticism for a spirit of imperialism because of our dictatorial policies, as is alleged toward Mexico. We are to-day being held up to criticism and denounced even in the Senate of the United States for the attitude that we are now in Nicaragua, all of which is used to point out that this government is seeking to carry out an imperialistic policy. (9–10)

For Meares, the answer resided in learning from past empires by rejecting the type of policy "which ultimately destroyed the Roman Government" and "which came very near dismembering the British Empire," but which the British averted by "giving a greater and broader grant of autonomy to its colonies" (10). In this manner, a pro-business and extreme-racist states'-rights argument was translated into a defense of limited self-government in the overseas colonies.

Meares's exposition was followed by that of Miss Mary G. Kilbreth, President of the Woman Patriot Publishing Company, who began by stating flatly that "Porto Rico does not want woman suffrage" (10). To support her claims, she used a letter that Dr. Marta Robert de Romeu had sent to the NWP indicating that Robert de Romeu's organization had not received the support of the island's legislature on the issue of woman suffrage even though such a measure had been recommended by colonial Governor Horace Mann Towner (11). In Kilbreth's opinion, "the National Woman's Party has brought great pressure for this recommendation," counting on the assistance of Governor Towner, "an extreme feminist, as shown by his activities in Congress, before he was made governor" (11). Governor Towner's "extreme feminism" was exemplified by the fact that he was "the chief backer and introducer of the maternity act and the Federal education bill, which probably aroused as much opposition in the United States among thinking people as any two recent measures" (11). To prove the "great [and undue] pressure" that the NWP had brought to bear on this issue, Kilbreth produced copies of the letters between this U.S. women's organization and the Liga Social Sufragista in addition to a lengthy description of the NWP's files on many U.S. congressmen. For Kilbreth, such pressure had a long and sordid history, one that the Woman Patriots had brought to the attention of Congress before when her organization denounced Carrie Chapman Catt, Jane Addams, and Florence Kelley, among others, for being part of "an intricate web which joined national women's organizations together in a conspiracy to sovietize the United States."[50] On this occasion, Kilbreth disclosed not only that the NWP was "the only organization so far as I know—and I have followed it pretty carefully—that is agitating for this bill for woman suffrage for Porto Rico," but also that this sinister organization continued to be "a left wing minority faction of the feminist bloc" and a "sex party waging a sex war" (17). As far as the Woman Patriots were concerned, the NWP's advocacy of women's suffrage for Puerto Rico was but one more strand within a nefarious, anti-American, and "intricate web."

And like the Sentinels, the Woman Patriots were also adept at transforming an anti-Communist, pro-business, and extreme-racist states'-rights argument into a defense of self-government in the overseas colonies by warning that the U.S. government should not appear to be unreasonably intervening in Caribbean affairs in a time of geopolitical instability: "The repercussion of this act of tyranny, as we consider it, by the United States toward a tiny, helpless dependency throughout Latin-America, will be appreciable, at least, I think. It may jeopardize the whole of the Latin-American relations" (16).

The Resident Commissioner from Puerto Rico, Félix Córdova Dávila, also delivered a statement before the senate committee at this time. He started his presentation by saying that although he "fully agree[d] with the sentiments expressed here in favor of woman suffrage," for him "there is nothing more local to the people of Porto Rico than this question" (20). Senator Millard Tydings asked Córdova Dávila if he recommended "that the people of Porto Rico be left to deal with this question" or whether he felt that it was up to the federal government to take matters into its own hands. Córdova Dávila answered:

> I am going to say that in my opinion the Porto Rican legislature should be left to decide questions of a local nature and not the American Congress. But I want to say this: I maintain that if ever there should be an exception to that principle, this proposition comes nearer to justifying an exception to that policy than anything I know of. (21)

And then Córdova Dávila added, "I am the representative of the people of Porto Rico here, and I have to maintain the principle that the Porto Rican people are entitled to handle this matter" (21).

Here Córdova Dávila adopted a position comparable to the one Alianza leader Senator Barceló had taken when the Asociación Puertor-riqueña publicly demanded (on February 5, 1927) that he reaffirm his position in favor of restricted women's suffrage (that is, for educated "native" women only). At that time, Barceló coupled granting voting rights to illiterates with curtailing the struggle for self-government on the part of the island's mainstream politicians, saying that both measures were akin to placing the governance of Puerto Rico in the hands of "any other man who is a stranger to its customs and to its being."[51]

In a similar vein, but this time before the senate committee, Córdova Dávila declared that

> Congress should not legislate in Porto Rican local matters. To be frank, I do not believe you are qualified to legislate in local matters in Porto Rico. You do not know Porto Rico. We are better qualified than you are. So you should let the Porto Ricans handle their own local affairs. (21)

In this manner, indiscreet "native" women and their North American sponsors were forcing the representatives of the creole patricians to debate the women's suffrage issue before the empire's elected authorities. The issue of enfranchising women in Puerto Rico was unavoidably transformed into a question of the limits of the colony's administrative autonomy versus the scope of colonialist rule. And, in the end, that is what it ultimately came down to for the advocates of women's suffrage in Puerto Rico, for the island's legislative assembly, and for the U.S. Congress.

One of the crucibles of masculinist and propertied ideologies in Puerto Rico, therefore, was the capacity to demarcate "woman's proper place" in general and to determine what exactly were to be the political rights of women. As we have seen, this was a bone of contention between the colonized strata that controlled part of the island's political scene and colonialist officials (in Puerto Rico and on the U.S. mainland). Yet, even more so, women's suffrage was one of the issues that paradoxically likened two related opposing forces. On the one hand, there were the "native" propertied and educated men in general, and on the other hand, there were North American colonizers as a whole and their discourses, particularly the juridical ideologies of citizenship. Despite existing disagreements on the question of women's suffrage, both forces equally positioned island womanhood as, literally, their own territory in this crucial period of the U.S. occupation of Puerto Rico. This is the premise that the members of the Liga Social Sufragista and the National Women's Party never completely transcended during the 1928 congressional hearing.

Notes

1. See Gladys M. Jiménez-Muñoz, "'A Storm Dressed in Skirts': Ambivalence in the Debate on Women's Suffrage in Puerto Rico, 1927–1929" (Ph.D. dissertation, Binghamton University-SUNY, 1993).

2. See sec. 5 of Jones Act (Puerto Rico) 1917 in *Documentos históricos relacionados con el Estado Libre Asociado* (Oxford, N.H.: Equity Publishing Corporation, 1974), 82–86. Island "natives" were still barred from electing the colonial governor, a right that was only granted in 1948. It must be borne in mind that all of the island residents were—and still are today (1996)—barred from voting in U.S. congressional and presidential elections.

3. Angela Caldas, "Movimiento sufragista ¡Alerta señores legisladores!" *La Correspondencia de Puerto Rico*, Mar. 2, 1927, 4. The issue of allowing island women to vote had surfaced in passing since the late nineteenth century. See, for example, Rafael M. Labra, *La mujer y la legislación castellana* (Madrid: Imprenta y Estereotipia de M. Revadenegra, 1869), 11.

4. "Estamos pidiendo los derechos políticos aquí y allá," *El Mundo*, Feb. 7, 1929, 8; all translations are mine. Although Yamila Azize gives 1921 as the year in which the Liga Social Sufragista was organized, she does not disclose the source of her information. See Yamila Azize, *La mujer en la lucha* (Río Piedras: Editorial Cultural, 1985), 117.

5. See Ricarda L. de Ramos Casellas and Marta Robert de Romeu, "A la legislatura de P. Rico," *La Correspondencia de Puerto Rico*, Mar. 11, 1927, 4; "Estamos pidiendo los derechos políticos aquí y allá," 1, 8, 13.

6. Azize, *La mujer en la lucha*, 130.

7. See, for example, "El sufragio femenino y 'La Democracia,'" *La Democracia*, Mar. 25, 1929, 4; R. Rodríguez Cancel, "Las mujeres socialistas," *La Democracia*, Nov. 2, 1928, 4.

8. Between 1924 and 1929, the Socialistas joined forces with a small group of Republicano nonconformists to form the "Coalición." Nevertheless, the dissident Republicanos were not of much help to the suffragists because the former were divided over the votes-for-women issue. Angel Quintero Rivera, *El liderato local de los partidos políticos y el estudio de la política puertorriqueña* (Río Piedras: CIS-UPR, 1970), 105.

9. Isabel Andreu de Aguilar, "Reseña histórica del movimiento feminista en Puerto Rico," *Revista Puerto Rico* 1 (June 1935): 266. After 1929 the organization changed its name to "Asociación Insular de Mujeres Votantes." Some Puerto Rican women's historians have characterized the Liga and the Asociación Puertorriqueña as the collective expression of the liberal-reformist tendency within the women's movement of that period, perceiving both organizations as tacitly speaking for middle- and upper-income as well as well-educated women. See, for example, Azize, *La mujer en la lucha*, 118–19, 141–42. Here I have tried to offer a more nuanced explanation of the roles and ideological tendencies among "native" women professionals within these two suffragist organizations.

10. "Las mujeres piensan dirigirse al Gobernador para pedir el sufragio femenino," *El Mundo*, Dec. 16, 1919, 1, 3; "Las mujeres se dirigen al Hon. Gobernador Yager," *El Mundo*, Dec. 17, 1919, 1, 3. See also Alice Colón, Margarita Mergal, and Nilsa Torres, *La participación de la mujer en la historia de Puerto Rico (las primeras décadas del siglo veinte)* (New Brunswick: State University of New Jersey, 1986), 43.

11. Asociación Feminista Popular de Mujeres Obreras Puertorriqueñas, "Mujeres Puertorriqueñas," *Unión Obrera*, Feb. 8, 1921, 2.

12. The Socialistas had included this demand since the party was officially founded in 1915. Santiago Iglesias Pantín and Manuel F. Rojas, "Al electorado y pueblo en general de Puerto Rico," *Justicia* 7, 236 (Oct. 11, 1920): 9. Although I have not been able to find any leading signs of this Asociación Feminista Popular after 1922, many of its members participated in pro-suffrage activities with the Liga, before and particularly after the formation of the Coalición in 1924. This convergence between the Liga and the Asociación Feminista can once again be understood in terms of the already mentioned affinity between politically active members of the working classes and the socially progressive urban professionals.

13. Bolivar Pagán, *El sufragio femenino* (San Juan: n.p., 1924).

14. Azize, *La mujer en la lucha*, 130–31, 138–44.

15. Ibid.

16. Truman R. Clark, *Puerto Rico and the United States, 1917–1933* (Pittsburgh: University of Pittsburgh Press, 1975), 42.

17. Azize, *La mujer en la lucha*, 142.

18. "La doctora Marta Robert, embarca hoy para Estados Unidos en representación de la Liga Social Sufragista," *La Correspondencia de Puerto Rico*, Apr. 5, 1928, 1, 6.

19. Clark, *Puerto Rico and the United States*, 44.

20. Azize, *La mujer en la lucha*, 138–44.

21. Clark, *Puerto Rico and the United States*, 45.

22. For more information about the Sixth Pan-American Conference in La Habana, Cuba, in 1928 and the absence of participation by Puerto Rican suffragists in this conference, see Gladys M. Jiménez-Muñoz, "Deconstructing Colonialist Discourses: The Links between the Women's Suffrage Movements in the United States and in Puerto Rico," paper presented at the Southern Women Historians Conference, Chapel Hill, N.C., June 1991. A portion of this paper has been published under the same title in the journal *Phoebe* 5, 1 (spring 1993): 9–34.

23. See "La doctora Marta Robert, embarca hoy para Estados Unidos en representación de la Liga Social Sufragista," *La Correspondencia de Puerto Rico*, Apr. 5, 1928, 6; "La concesión del sufragio femenino a Puerto Rico fue urgido por el Comité de Asuntos Insulares," *La Correspondencia de Puerto Rico*, May 1, 1928, 9; "La 'Liga Social Sufragista' reclama para sí el honor de que se haya presentado el proyecto Bingham concediendo el voto a la mujer portorriqueña," *El Mundo*, Feb. 5, 1927, 3.

24. *Woman Suffrage in Porto Rico, Hearing before the Committee on Territories and Insular Possessions, United States Senate, Seventieth Congress, First Session on S. 753* (Washington, D.C.: Government Printing Office, Apr. 25, 1928), 1–2. Subsequent page references will be given in the text in parentheses.

25. Here I draw from Judith Butler's expressions and arguments in "Disorderly Woman," *Transition* 53 (1991): 88.

26. *Woman Suffrage in Porto Rico, Hearing*, 4. Here she seemed to be referencing the contradictions residing in the 1927 message that colonial Governor Horace Mann Towner delivered before the island's legislature. Although Towner recommended that the colony's legislators approve a restricted women's suffrage bill, his concern for the prevalent high levels of illiteracy led him to urge qualifications for all new uneducated male voters too. See "Texto íntegro del mensaje del Gob. Towner a la 11a. Asamblea," *La Democracia*, Feb. 21, 1927, 1, 5, 7.

27. Butler, "Disorderly Woman," 87–88.

28. Ibid., 88.

29. See, for example, Rafael Rodríguez, "La mujer no es igual al hombre," *La Correspondencia de Puerto Rico*, Apr. 8, 1927, 8; "Sólo aspiran al sufragio electoral aquellas mujeres fracasadas como madres o muy poco femeninas," *La Correspondencia de Puerto Rico*,

Mar. 13, 1928, 1, 10. Such masculinist arguments, of course, were not advocated only by Puerto Rican men. See, for instance, María Dolores Polo, "¡Oid Sufragista!" *La Correspondencia de Puerto Rico*, Feb. 15, 1927, 5.

30. G. García de la Noceda, "Mi voto en contra," *La Correspondencia de Puerto Rico*, Mar. 10, 1927, 3.

31. See, for example, M. J. Mayoral Barnés, "La mujer puertorriqueña no ha luchado en la política de su país e ignora sus procedimientos," *La Democracia*, Mar. 17, 1927, 3, 6; Carlota B. de Cabañas, "Deseo que en mi pobre patria las mujeres sean levantadas espiritual y moralmente," *La Correspondencia*, Feb. 15, 1928, 2. This question is scrutinized in greater depth in chapters 10 and 11 of my dissertation; see Jiménez–Muñoz, "'A Storm Dressed in Skirts.'"

32. Butler, "Disorderly Woman," 88.

33. "La señora Cabañas no es partidiaria del sufragio femenino," *La Democracia*, Feb. 7, 1927, 1, 5.

34. Butler, "Disorderly Woman," 88.

35. Ibid.

36. Alma G. Mela, "Al margen del sufragio femenino," *La Correspondencia de Puerto Rico*, Feb. 18, 1927, 7.

37. See, for example, "A la legislatura de Puerto Rico," *La Correspondencia de Puerto Rico*, Mar. 11, 1927, 4; Angel Fernández Sánchez, "El sufragio femenino," *La Correspondencia de Puerto Rico*, Mar. 24, 1927, 1, 5; Antonia Román, "El sufragio femenino," *La Correspondencia de Puerto Rico*, Apr. 6, 1927, 8; María Teresa Urquidi, "Feminismo," *La Democracia*, Oct. 11, 1927, 4; Esmeralda Sainz, "Al margen de un artículo sobre el sufragio femenino," *La Correspondencia de Puerto Rico*, Oct. 15, 1927, 3.

38. See, for instance, Carlota B. de Cabañas, "La mujer en su puesto de honor," *La Correspondencia de Puerto Rico*, June 8, 1927, 7; Charles A. L. M. Reed, "Amor de Madre," *La Democracia*, Oct. 13, 1927, 5.

39. Sarito Roger y Nieves, "¡Mujer!," *Puerto Rico Ilustrado* 931 (Jan. 7, 1928): 61.

40. Ibid.

41. Ibid.

42. M. J. Mayoral Barnés, "La mujer puertorriqueña no ha luchado en la política de su país y hasta ignora sus procedimientos," *La Democracia*, Mar. 17, 1927, 3, 6.

43. Cited in *Congressional Record*, 70th Congress, 1st Session, House of Representatives (1928), 6335. See also *Porto Rico's Case: Outcome of American Sovereignty, 1898–1924, 1925–1928* (New Haven, Conn.: Tuttle, Morehouse, and Taylor Co., June 15, 1928), 58–59; Bolivar Pagán, *Historia de los partidos políticos puertorriqueños*, vol. 1 (San Juan: Librería Campos, 1959), 268–69.

44. Here I am paraphrasing Gayatri Chakravorty Spivak, "Can the Subaltern Speak?" in *Marxism and the Interpretation of Culture*, ed. Cary Nelson and Lawrence Grossberg (Urbana: University of Illinois Press, 1988), 296. For a more in-depth analysis of the ideological representations used by the NWP vis-à-vis U.S. policies and activities in Puerto Rico and in the rest of the Caribbean, see Jiménez-Muñoz, "Deconstructing Colonialist Discourses."

45. Cynthia Enloe, *Bananas, Beaches, and Bases: Making Sense of International Politics* (Berkeley: University of California Press, 1989), 47.

46. See Elizabeth Cady Stanton, "Educated Suffrage, NASA Convention in Washington, D.C., February 12–18, 1902," in *The Concise History of Woman Suffrage*, ed. Mari Jo Buhle and Paul Buhle (Urbana: University of Illinois Press, 1979), 347.

47. J. Stanley Lemons, *The Woman Citizen: Social Feminism in the 1920's* (Charlottesville: University Press of Virginia, 1973), 219.

48. See Bailey W. Diffie and Justine Diffie, *Porto Rico: A Broken Pledge* (New York: Vanguard Press, 1931), 45–101, 166–84.

49. Under extreme circumstances, liberal government agents in Puerto Rico and creole labor leaders had appealed to federal authorities to directly investigate the cases of most blatant disregard for "native" life or well-being. This, for example, was the case for the massacres and other police excesses during the labor strife of 1915–19. See Negociado del Trabajo, *Cuarto informe del Negociado del Trabajo* (San Juan: Bureau of Supplies, Printing, and Transportation, 1916), 11–12.

50. Lemons, *The Woman Citizen*, 173.

51. "Carta: Hon. Antonio R. Barceló Presidente del Senado de P.R. a la Asociación Puertorriqueña de Mujeres Sufragistas," *La Democracia*, Feb. 5, 1927, 1.

PART THREE

The Puerto Rican Archipelago: Contested Identities

Islands at the Crossroads: Puerto Ricanness Traveling between the Translocal Nation and the Global City

Agustín Lao

On the air shuttle between the capital of the empire (Washington, D.C.) and the capital of capitals (New York City), a Latino policeman told me that he was originally "from a small part of Puerto Rico called Brooklyn," while he expressed admiration for a print on my T-shirt depicting two bridges connecting the island of Borinquen with the island of Manhattan. The bridges were named "Puente de La Salsa" and "Puente Luis Muñoz Marín," to signify both the airports and multiple threads that weave archipelago and diaspora into a transnation.

In a recent visit to the enchanted island, I attended the fortieth anniversary celebration of Cheo Feliciano's (*el gran sonero*) artistic career. This event, which reunited *sanjuanera* ladies and *politicos enguayaberados* with *cocolas y salseros*, not only violated the audience protocols at the Centro de Bellas Artes (with the *chusmagrafia* of whistling and dancing in this sacred simulacrum of "high culture") but also dared to (re)present Puerto Rican culture as (a) happening against the scenic background of Spanish colonial fortresses surrounded by palm trees and a street of Spanish Harlem. The stage, displaying our kitsch island imagery along with a New York street corner photo, evoked Cheo's trajectory: from playing *tumbadora* as an expression of the black culture of Barrio Bélgica in Ponce to being band-boy for Tito Rodríguez during the golden age of the mambo; from leading Joe Cuba's vocalizations during the times of the bolero blues/Latin bugaloo to becoming an ambassador of *salsa con feeling*. This *salsero* text, posted against the grain of official representations, reveals a history of crossing borders and traveling social worlds within a single, yet differentiated flag of "barrio y pueblo boricua" (the *salsa* bridge).

This particular gaze of Puerto Rican national geographies both coincides and clashes with another one, that of "our" financial capital(ists). The Banco Popular de Puerto Rico produced a Christmas TV special, released in 1994, called "El Espiritu de un Pueblo," which was shown simultaneously on the island and in all major U.S. Puerto Rican cities.[1] This sophisticated media product begins with a greeting to Puerto Rico, New York City, Chicago, and Miami, with footage from all of these Puerto Rican spaces and an idiosyncratic masculine voice celebrating Christmas in the name of "El Banco de Puerto Rico" and commemorating the "first year of our second century."

The emblematic song in the tune of a *salsa sensual* announces that "the spirit of a people . . . is a rumba of solitudes that walks silently in any corner of the world where our people live." Using the rhetoric of the *nueva canción*, it praises Puerto Rican natural and human landscapes as sources of poetry, faith, love, and hope. Later, nationalist poet-singer "El Topo" declares that "the tradition continues," singing to the Puerto Rican "fighting spirit, proud of his struggle in the Antillean Caribbean." This "nueva canción" sounds rather old-fashioned, now that it has been colonized into a telluric *neo-criollismo* by capitalists (creole and imperial) as well as by the state.

Music appears as the most representative expression of the national culture, the unifying substance that inscribes the Puerto Rican body: "I represent those who carry the music inside them, it doesn't matter if salsa, rumba, mambo, or flamenco, what matters is the flavor of movement . . . I represent a race of different colors that melt to become transparent and I am the living example of my people."[2] Past and present appear as a continuum of images without any spatiotemporal references ("No conoce de tiempo de ausencia ni de distancia") or mediations of power and difference.

The representational claims for an allegedly sovereign national culture under the auspices of "our" financial capital are synthesized in an interview with laureate nationalist artist Antonio Martorell. For Martorell, "universality is expressed through the particularity of nationality." The colonial question is unthinkable (or unspeakable) in this hegemonic *fiesta* of "tradition." The "spirit of Christmas" is hence represented through the nostalgia of a Puerto Rican soldier in Germany who dreams of dancing to the *sabroso* rhythm of "Puerto Rico . . . tender and pure island of great beauty," with the beautiful girl next door

The grand finale of the video is a gala night in front of the colonial capital where a musical mosaic of the diverse rhythms of the nation (with the exclusion of abject music such as Boricua Hip Hop) allegorizes the unity of the "Great Puerto Rican Family" under the patriarchal protectorate of our bank. This "carnival" of Identity ends with a "rainbow" of blondes, (lesbians?), mulattoes, (blacks?), children, boleristas, pop-raperas, pop-rockeros, salseros, baladistas, all singing univocally, "Yo soy Boricua, mi amor es Puerto Rico" in a triumphal march. The patriotism of the Banco Popular is blessed by the fluid freedoms of financial capital. Branches are booming throughout the neighborhoods of the diaspora, and the bank becomes "our" local as well as a national institution. The Creole Bourgeoisie has finally realized its cultural project without the need for political independence (the Muñoz Marín bridge).

In light of these expressions of the translocality of Puerto Ricanness, this essay intends to conceptualize Puerto Rican national formation as a translocal historical category whose boundaries shift between the archipelago of Puerto Rico and its U.S. diaspora. The purpose is not only to explore the implications of our national imaginaries of travel as articulated in literary and artistic tropes (for example, airbus, commuter nation, air bridge) and in popular signification ("jumping the pond," "allá afuera") for theorizing Puerto Rican nationality, but also to intervene in the ongoing political discussion on the fate and possibilities of anticolonial nationalisms in light of the qualitative leaps in contemporary processes of globalization.

Decolonizing the Postmodern or Colonizing the Postcolony

Puerto Rico is, by any definition, the oldest colony of the modern world. The insular territory has traveled a long historical trajectory of imperial "conquests" and "possessions," from the conversion of the island of "Boriquen" to "la isla de San Juan Bautista" along with the emergence of the capitalist world economy, to the metamorphosis of Puerto Rico into "Porto Rico" during the aftermath of the Spanish-American-Cuban War and the ascendance of the American empire. As such, it is a uniquely rich example of imperial strategies and anticolonial modes of resistance. Also, the Puerto Rican colonial experience presents some particular traits because it is the first and most enduring external colony of the United States, whose particular forms of imperial rule correspond to the "monopoly stage" of historical colonialism, and whose colonial discourses are characterized by a curiously "anticolonial" rhetoric of "Americanism."

Puerto Rico's and Puerto Ricans' location at the margins of the center as well as at the center of an imperial frontier (the Caribbean) also allows us to be heralds of modern/postmodern global changes, a laboratory for the post-World War II models of "development," "modernization," and population control, and an early example of a high-finance/high-tech semi-industrialized society becoming a peripheral postindustrial zone.

Nonetheless, most analyses of Puerto Ricans and colonialism focus almost entirely on the economic and political aspects of imperial domination, developing interpretations of the colonial condition in which colonial questions are either reduced to a function of a narrowly conceived political economy or circumscribed to formalist-legalist readings of the U.S.-Puerto Rico relationship. In these schemata, a basically essentialized cultural realm is an "inner domain" of "authenticity" that is in danger of being annihilated by the forces of "cultural imperialism," or, in contrast, is a privileged space of resistance from an indigenous "high culture" or from an often romanticized "popular culture." There is also an anticolonial stand in which colonialism is assumed to be a prime mover determining and shaping all social life. This imaginary is unable to think about the limits and contingencies of colonialism. Furthermore, its lack of understanding of (and faith in) subaltern resistance is akin to a paternalistic and vanguardist political outlook. A third (and dominant) take on the colonial question is either that it is an issue to be solved with some cosmetic legal changes, or that in light of widespread lack of support for political independence (and considering the "political freedoms" that Puerto Rico "enjoys"), there is no colonial question for Puerto Ricans. All three tendencies show an untheorized ambiguity about or a tacit exclusion of the Puerto Rican diaspora (and diasporic condition) as an important subject in the national scene.

Puerto Rico's "great transformation" in the late 1940s and early 1950s through industrialization, mass migration, urbanization, "secularization," and dissemination of the mass media also involved a "modernization" of the colonial state and a significant redefinition of the colonial relationship. After World War II, the consolidation of Pax Americana, the beginning of the formal era of decolonizations, the establishment of a liberal democratic colonial state, and the (im)plantation of colonial Fordism in Puerto Rico created a framework for a late-modern form of colonialism. A peaceful revolution constituted a modern regime of power where the (ideally) normalized self-regulated individuals were subjected by mechanisms of liberal citizenship, and (formally) rationalized state in-

stitutions submitted to rules of bureaucracy, "internal" checks and bal-
ances, and electoral accountability. This colonial "modernization" was facilitated by a populist coalition that championed a pragmatic formula of
promoting national culture, economic development, and relative political
autonomy under the auspices of the U.S. late-modern empire. This form
of "home rule," while opening real democratic space, mystified the
underlying realities of domination and exploitation that characterize the
relation with the metropolis through the fetishism of "freedom and
progress."

   This modern colonial regime resulted in, among other things a significant growth in the middle strata and working classes, a relative increase in the standards of living of considerable sectors of the population, the germination of strong local/transnational cultural industries, a
"maturely" modern differentiation of civil society, the opening of the
U.S.-Puerto Rico airbus, and finally the extension of benefits and entitlements of the U.S. national-social state. Taken together, these developments set the stage for the apparent "irrationality" of "legitimate" colonialism or the heresy of imperial hegemony.

   A massive migration mostly to the northeastern urban centers of the
United States initially displaced some of the labor pains of dependent-
peripheral industrialization and made Puerto Rican colonial-subjects
racialized ethnic minorities. However, the world economic crisis, undermining Fordism since the 1970s (*la isla del encanto*), accelerated the
falling apart (*la isla-en-cantos*) of the "unstable equilibrium of compromises," compelling the imperial-colonial state to dramatically increase
the level of transfer payments as a strategy to counter what had become a
permanent economic and legitimation crisis. A corresponding balance in
favor of the authoritarian "functions" of the state, matched with highly
volatile patterns of accumulation, contributed to the dismantling of class
solidarities and exacerbated the trends of unemployment, informal
economies, and "popular illegalities." The enormous social and cultural
distance between the *independentista* "left" and the popular sectors, together with the maturation of a late-capitalist hypercommodified consumer society, offered the conditions for the state's colonization of patriotic pride and capital's commodification of national representations. The
assignment of essential welfare "duties" to the metropolitan state, the gap
between official political discourses and popular signification, and the
prevalence in everyday life of cultural economies of pleasure and prag-

matism undermined the seductiveness of political languages of secession and separatist patriotism.

In this context, what is the meaning of colonialism and imperialism? Have Puerto Ricans transcended colonialism without the need to establish an "independent" nation-state? Is Puerto Rico the epitome of the postmodern "new world border" without frontiers? Are Puerto Ricans the quintessential hybrid, decentered, postcolonial-postmodern subjects? Or, perhaps, we are mirroring through the specter of Puerto Ricanness a dramatic case of the chameleonic character of historical colonialism.

With the current resurgence of anticolonial political rhetoric and the boom of "postcolonial" analyses, we should expect Puerto Ricans to appear in the center of the stage. However, perhaps because of our "anomalous states"[3] (colonial within an often ontologized "postcolonial condition") and our tendency to elude conventional definitions of colonialism, Puerto Ricanness paradoxically remains in the margins of the postcolonial cognitive mappings and knowledge industries. In this context, how can we inform the hermeneutics of colonialism(s) via the gaze of Puerto Rican colonial discourses? What will the possible strategies of postcolonial critique be in light of the apparent anomaly of a postcolonial colony, or what appears to be more awkward, a colonial postcolony?[4]

These riddles of Puerto Rican colonialism are symptomatic of how much "the pathological" can unveil antinomies and mirages in "the normal." Puerto Rican "colonial exceptionalism" reveals itself still more as truism and seductive fallacy when compared to the notion of the postcolonial.[5] The persistence of colonialism with a modernized "local" economy, a "democratized" liberal polity, and a hegemonic cultural politics of ethno-national self-affirmation provides us with perhaps the clearest example of the fact that "the economic, cultural, and political effects of neocolonialism are structurally colonial," that "we transcended the colonial system but not the ubiquity and primary significance of coloniality," or "that we are not yet postimperial."[6] Spatiotemporal ambiguity, semiotic-theoretical confusion, and too frequent political "lightness" and looseness of commonsensical notions of postcoloniality allow some critics to go to the extreme of classifying the United States as a postcolonial country under the name of critical theory.[7] However, we adopt the notion of postcolonial theory as a form of critique, as an anticolonial project for rearticulating histories, remapping spaces, deconstructing Americo-Eurocentric epistemes, and exploring political agendas.

Kelvin Santiago-Valles conceptualizes the condition of the Puerto

Rican subaltern majorities, both on the island and in the internal colonies in the United States, as a colonized labor force: "the product of the process of dispossession, continuous displacement, and complex subjectification . . . that characterize, classical, modern-imperial and postmodern global colonialism."[8] In this imaginary, the category of coloniality becomes a general signifier to denote conditions and situations of subalternity (based on national-cultural and racial marks of difference) that transcend the historicity of the "colonial system" and extend to all the social spaces and peoples facing forms of imperial domination and western "epistemic violence."

In the same tenor, contemporary colonial spaces of Puerto Ricanness could be represented as a "contact zone,"[9] a crossroads of unequal exchanges and uneven developments where the imperial and the colonial are intertwined in intricate economies of desire, survival, justice, and freedom, and where social actors are often difficult to delimit on one or the other side of the colonial divide. In contrast to conventional understandings of Puerto Rican colonialism, this analysis involves a critique of "colonial situations" that recognizes the materiality and hence the political centrality of cultural struggles without denying the ontologies of political-economic imperial domination.

Borinquen: The Translocal Nation

The colonial nation is conceived in the interstices of colonialism: in the political nexus between the metropolitan and the colonial state as well as around the politico-cultural paradox between "colonial mimicry" and the "incommensurable" alterities dividing imperial discourses and the subaltern. It is out of this creative tension between mimesis and alterity, westernization and anticolonial self-affirmation, and rearticulated tradition and "peripheral modernity" that the colonial nation is born as a formation of peoplehood. As such it becomes a "bounded" cultural field of exchange whose very contours are defined in relationship to its imperial (and "internal") other(s). It becomes also a political arena where subjects can negotiate freedoms, meanings, and resources against the backdrop of the metropolitan-colonial state contract.

If, then, we conceive Puerto Rico and Puerto Ricanness through the language of nationhood,[10] what are the discursive terms and conditions, imaginary webs, institutional settings, mechanisms of reproduction, and contours of this colonial nation? We can argue that Puerto Ricans constitute a nation-people both in relationship to the "institutional materiality" of the imperial-colonial state and the configuration of an insular civil society and its corresponding public spheres, and also in the dialogical duality (and colloquial multiplicity) of the social spaces between the United States and "the island" where the subjection-subjectivization of individual selves, the definition of modes of affiliation and familiarity, and the articulations of community are partially mediated by the politico-cultural rhetoric of Puerto Ricanness.

To imagine the Puerto Rican national community as a translocal social space (a transnation) is not only to acknowledge how the mutual referentiality between territory and diaspora has always constituted the national,[11] or to recognize the quotidian human flow between colony and metropolis, but more fundamentally it is to refer to the tailoring of a formation of peoplehood that, though hyperfragmented and dispersed, is netted by the web of coloniality (subordinate citizenship, racialization) and intertwined by multiple networks (political organizations, professional associations, town clubs) and flows (phone, faxes, salsanet) to constitute a deterritorialized-reterritorialized "imagined community" and a "social space."[12] As a historical product, constituted and reproduced by specific "social practices," this social space is located beyond the immediacy of place and is intersected by other spaces (subjective, local, state, societal, global) without totally losing its dimension as a locus of identity and association.

The trope of the airbus as a culture traveling between two ports of broken dreams not only does poetic justice to a continuous circular migration but constitutes a metaphoric insight into the ontology of the Puerto Rican nation-space.[13] There is a mutual referentiality between the here and there that is constitutive of Puerto Ricanness. On the island, the United States is popularly described as "out there." Many Puerto Ricans refer to traveling back and forth as "jumping the pond," and the joke of the bridge that is "still under construction" points to the continuous transit of peoples, TV programs, icons, ideologies, letters, newspapers, money, goods, festivals, dramas, conspiracies, and so on. In this spatiotemporal matrix, the chronotope[14] of Puerto Ricanness is constituted by the spatial coordinates of our peoplehood (the translocal nation that is primarily located between Boriken, which is the imaginary mainland, and the Ame-Rican-land, as opposed to Gringolandia) as well as by the politically contested temporalities of the nation and its fragments (the politics of memory/counter-memory and forgetting).

In this deterritorialized-reterritorialized nation-space, the axes of coloniality are not only the colonial state, or the second-class citizenship, but the overwhelming condition of subalternity of the Puerto Rican colonized-subjects (as colonized labor forces, increasingly idle populations, and criminalized urban dwellers) and the pejorative markers of "race" and "ethnicity." These are the threads in between that interconnect the colonial sites of Puerto Ricanness in a translocal social space, a "contact zone," or a "zone of occult instability where the people dwell."[15] In this register, the Puerto Rican colonial experience of dwelling in traveling and traveling in dwelling reveals important trends in the redefined logics of postmodern (late-capitalist) colonialism. Thus, the diversification (and differentiation) of the locales of the nation by proliferating the spaces of the colony problematizes the imaginary of the nation-state as the north of decolonization, positing the possibility of decentering anticolonial politics beyond statist nationalisms and Latin-Americanist identity politics.

The notion of translocality derives from, and refers to, a "rigorous politics of location" that corresponds to a deconstruction of the nation as categorical identity, as well as to a reconstruction of the nation as a form of difference within the context of the Ame-Rican radical politics of multiculturalism. The cutting across locations and multiple crossing of borders that define the concept of translocality refer simultaneously to the "multiple mediations" informing the individuation of a decentered subject as well as to "the transit of subjects and representations between discursive places such as gender, race, nation, community, sexuality, and classes."[16] The geopolitical/geosocietal duality of the Puerto Rican transnation simultaneously shapes a social space in between and across island and "mainland" and stresses the existence of two different (but interrelated) "imagined worlds" within the larger landscapes of the global.

Our Ame-Rica: A Federation of Diasporas?

Puerto Ricanness as a sign of membership in a translocal nation is an ID card for participating in two civil societies, from which the subjects so inscribed are "subjected" to the corresponding states (imperial and colonial state), act in the respective hegemonic fields, and exercise agency within contextually defined public spaces.

In the context of today's Puerto Rico (the island society), a historical split between "cultural nationalisms" and "political nationalisms" corresponds to a dynamics of cultural struggle where national "identity" and "culture" become reified artifacts of domination for "the powers that be." In this setting, Puerto Ricanness mostly operates as a hegemonic signifier of a categorical ethno-national identity denoting a domesticated (colonized/commodified) patriotism. These politico-cultural terms call for a "cultural politics of difference" to deconstruct dominant ideologies of nationhood, and for an engagement in a radical democratization of the insular social space.

By contrast, in the many locales of the Ame-Rican diaspora, Puerto Ricanness appears as a marker of subordinate difference (racial, ethnic, national) within an extremely complex field of hegemony, a highly heterogeneous public, and a seriously contested, multilayered, and multifaceted terrain of cultural struggle. In the United States, the struggle for Spanish is part of a resistance movement against a univocal (white male) neoracist transformative hegemony ("English Only," anti-immigrant sentiment), and an expression of collective modes of enunciation bonding strategically in order to obtain basic resources (health and educational services) and open social and political space (bilingual ballots, cultural recognition).

In Puerto Rico, the politics of "Spanish Only" represents the recycling of the Hispanophile tradition and of the colonial state's (and traditional *independentista's*) concurrent reductions of culture to language, culture to a relatively fixed organic entity, and language to a homogeneous dead vernacular. This fictive language of the "ideal nation" not only displays its Eurocentrism by defending the language of the old empire against the language of the new master but also negates that at this point in our history the various idiolects that Puerto Ricans speak oscillate between different combinations and permutations of the Spanish and English languages.

Puerto Ricans (as other racialized diasporas) function within multiple and ambiguous registers of race and racism. As colonized subjects, all Puerto Ricans are "colored" by colonial discourses. On the other hand, differential processes of racialization can either nominalize Puerto Ricans as "ethnic" and/or allow some light-skinned Puerto Ricans to "pass" as "white." Also, racial codes that are specific to the historical articulation of racist ideologies and "racial hegemonies" in Puerto Rico and that at the same time inform "racial relations" on the island often play a role in the configuration of contradictory racial practices and representations among U.S. Puerto Ricans (for example, being simultaneously against police racial violence but anti-African Americans). A single Puerto Rican "transmigrant" can be classified as *trigueña* on the island, black in Ohio, and Latina in New York.

The dialectic of traveling and dwelling configures a framework of Puerto Ricanness where the same actors often adopt similar roles in various places, writing different scripts in each scenario. The circulation of social movements (ecological, gay and lesbian, anticolonial) and forms of resistance (parodic irreverence, vindication of pleasure) also weave the imaginary and performative threads of a translocal social space populated by cultural logics in between and across tradition, modernity, and postmodernity. In these increasingly dispersed sites of the multilocal nation, the narrative of the imagined community is articulated in many different ways, from the language of neighborhood organizing in Los Sures, Brooklyn, to the persistent desire for cultural identification by Puerto Ricans in Hawaii, from the election of a Puerto Rican socialist congressman from the medium-size hometown politics of Chicago to the cultural politics of Taller Puertorriqueño in Philadelphia.

The present moment of interdependence, in which the world becomes an "ambiguous real-universal" and "worldliness" is an increasing condition of mutuality, paradoxically affirms the power of the United States as a relatively uncontested politico-military world empire, while undermining the hegemony of "imperial rulers" in the territory of "America." The dislocation of the nation (the relative liberation of the nation from the state fed by a "crisis of governability"), the existential nomadism of material and emotional insecurity, and the proliferation of global migrations account for the formation of diasporas, border and traveling cultures, that in turn deterritorialize, reterritorialize, displace, and relativize the spaces of the nation.

The emergence of new ethnicities (Latinos, Asian Americans), diasporic nations (Dominican-Yorks, Ame-Ricans), and translocal communities (Mexicans from Piaxla in New York) provide the ground for the resignification of nationalist ideologies and ethnic discourses. These new "imagined communities" maintain both an affiliation and allegiance to their mainlands at the same time that they claim and fight for their own place in America. This tendency increasingly points toward a situation of double citizenships and multiple patriotisms in which people "love America but are not necessarily attached to the United States."[17]

This duality between "empire" and "republic"[18] is profoundly dramatized in circumstances like the Cuban and Haitian "balsero crisis," where the fragility of the maritime border revealed a sharp contradiction between policing the backyard and closing the frontier. However, in spite of the great defense-offense of the racial state and the forces of nativism against colored migrations, America is turning into a crossroads of diasporas, a transnational site of unequal exchanges and unpredictable subjectivities, and an epicenter in an emerging postnational order.

Since at least the second quarter of the twentieth century, Puerto Ricans have been located in the very center of this process of the "third-worldization" of America. As a colonized labor force, Puerto Ricans shared with Blacks and Chicanos conditions of inequality within labor, displacement from work, discrimination in spheres of reproduction of everyday life (housing, education, health), invisibility and lack of recognition in the dominant public sphere, and subjection to various forms of symbolic and physical violence. In this context, Puerto Ricans understood as a "conquered minority" and Puerto Ricanness understood as a colonial-racial form of difference have framed a field of politics (mostly urban) that despite ideological/political distinctions articulates a language of community, a set of goals around ideals of collective consumption, and a political imaginary of ethno-national, ethno-racial, and pan-ethnic power. With the emergence of the "new social movements" of the 1960s as important vehicles of political agency, U.S. Puerto Rican movements, perhaps the clearest internal embodiments of U.S. colonialism, have played a key role in the fracturing of "mainstream culture" and the official narratives of Americanness.

Niuyo Rico in the Global City

Perhaps where these American postmodern antinomies between space and place, economy and polity, and ideology and culture manifest themselves in more dramatic and significant ways is through the disjuncture between the global city (New York) and the nation-state (United States). As a global city, New York is a key center in a new global economy characterized by deconcentration and centralization, where transnational capitals command operations from their headquarters located in a transterritorial system of megalopolises.[19] The path from capitalist metropolis to global city corresponds to the transition from an industrially dominated center to a "postindustrial" city, from being a financial and managerial nodal point of the multinational capital-imperial state's partnership to occupying a center stage in the transnational web of information, knowledge, and finance that constitutes the most dynamic sectors of the global economy. As such, the global city transcends (and often competes with) the borders of the nation-state. New York is a transnational enclave, a translocal crossroads whose location stands both below and beyond the U.S. nation-state.

We can also read the "Big Apple" as a microcosm of America's great conflict between a highly organized dominant minority (the traditional "white majority") and an equally diverse/divided growing majority, unequally confronting different forms and intensities of subalternity (class, racial, ethnic, gender, sexual). The codes of oppression in this "dual city"[20] (fragmentation, extreme class polarization, entire populations taken as economically idle and humanly expendable) increase and reproduce poverty and hopelessness among the most oppressed, as well as ubiquitous violence (racial, domestic, homophobic, and so on) and commonsensical fear of the "dangerous classes." In turn, colonial conditions are resisted with multiple languages of community and solidarity that often facilitate the claiming of immigrant rights, racial justice, lesbian family rights, or multicultural education against a local government with enough autonomy and resources to challenge central (federal) state policies.

This constrained freedom of New York, our U.S. capital for over a century, provides another framework of Puerto Ricanness because of the central role of Puerto Ricans in the history of this city (as central margins of the core) and in light of our largely urban form of modern/postmodern existence. The structural similarities between the island-city (Puerto Rico) and the liminal spaces of the global city serve as a passport in the journey back and forth between nation and city. The Puerto Rican subalterns, in their classification as a displaced (idle) colonized labor force, confront similar situations of chronic unemployment, abjection/criminalization, hypervisibility matched with unspeakability in the dominant regimes of representation, and material deprivation in the middle of a hyper-real supermarket of commodity signs and commodity goods in both island and mainland contexts. The discourse of the "underclass," which serves as an ideological reason for a desperately defensive-offensive U.S. "power elite" to reassert racial and class hegemony (thus informing the vilification of racialized urban space, including the entire island-city), coincides with the ideological weapons (work ethic, conservative morals, cultural elitism, a social imaginary based on fear and punishment) of the insular social war (of both the "right" and the "left") against the untouchables.

In New York, Puerto Ricanness becomes a complex marker for membership of a people variably and simultaneously defined by race, ethnicity, and nation. In the context of this global city (arguably the most central place of Puerto Ricanness), we develop another sense of allegiance. Here (and now) the postmodern alchemy of "multiculturalism" creates forms of identification for distinctive registers of domination (and various languages of self-affirmation) in a politics of multiple locations. In this context, Puerto Ricanness is a stand of enunciation that does not need to be privileged over "others." It can be a premise for the articulation of a new pan-ethnic Latino ethnicity, a referent for the formation of an Afro-American diasporic consciousness, a standpoint for a feminism of women of color, a starting point to struggle for the recognition of "ethnic difference" as a factor in a movement for trade union democracy, a marker for the organization of a Pan-Caribbean gay committee in "Queer nation," or a signifier for a community-based local movement for minority parents' representation in a school board election in the South Bronx.

To a large extent, the city displaces the nation, and Puerto Ricanness is defined as a form of citizenship of the city. In this context, Puerto Ricans become quintessential "citizens of the city," traveling dwellers and anchored nomads of the imploded postmodern megalopolis. The relative autonomy of New York allows a political dynamics of a "city-state": its uniquely diverse population, its imaginary of being an empire-city, the overwhelming character and velocity of its quotidian existence, and the highly active and seductive nature of its public spheres give New York its own dimension as a "cosmopolis." Paradoxically, our second-class citizenship finds a relatively responsive polity in the urban regime of the global city, where the political is almost ineluctably mediated by the politics of difference.

This implosion of the fragments does not erase the nation but relativizes its claims as a dominant narrative of identity. In spite of this, the island-city as both a mythical land and as a colonized territory still occupies a symbolically central place as the "real" and ultimate "mainland," an ultimate referent to the now relativized, dispersed, and displaced nation. In the "ideoscapes" of the new global cultural economy, in the multifaceted play of differences of the global city, and on the shifting and contested boundaries of the translocal nation, nationalism becomes political rhetoric with multiple meanings, and the nation a trope of identity-in-difference that can be articulated in such diverse settings as the search for Aztlan (a nation of borders) and the coalitional diversity of "Queer nations."

Conclusions without Closure: Neonationalist Projects, Postnational Identities, Postimperial Dreams

As the "fin de siècle" approaches, the ultimate territory of Puerto Ricanness is the body of a fragmented subject whose trajectories and agency, dispersed from Hawaii to the Sorbonne, from San Juan to Los Angeles, assert her uniqueness from within and against the stigma of colonialism. The avatars of decolonization become more hazy and unpredictable when the potency of a now global capital appears unshakable and "the West" has allegedly colonized even "the unconscious." Is there any possibility for politics beyond the strictly local in this disconcerting and apparently "transhistorical" present? Have colonial spaces proliferated in so many ways and the logics of capital become so pervasive that national liberation is virtually inconceivable? What possible scenarios exist for decolonizing the life worlds of Puerto Rican colonial-subjects?

The various political-economic regimes, geopolitical settings, and cultural locations that frame Puerto Ricanness are rapidly and significantly differentiating and changing. The metamorphosis of the U.S. polity through the accelerated dismantling of what remains of the "semiwelfare state," the "new federalism" accompanied by a reinvigorated white nativism (often converging with a liberal corporate multiculturalism), and the now naturalized "wisdom" of neoliberal ideologies point toward a postpartisan dominant consensus that does not leave much room for public discourses and political narratives challenging the scripts of individual self-help or the patriarchal rhetoric of triumphant empire.

Behind this drama is a growing unwillingness to continue financing a postindustrial peripheral zone turning into a welfare island-city. There is also significant opposition to the specter of an island-state populated by natives who speak Spanish. Evidently, while there are no real threats to the issues that count (markets, military bases, alliances) for the U.S. empire in Puerto Rico, imperial protagonists do not need to settle their differences, and business continues as usual, while in the internal "colonies" in the U.S. cities, the great majority of "Boricuas" dwell in "all-American" conditions of neglect for the "undeserving urban poor." Jumping the pond again, if the metropolitan state significantly cuts some basic transfer payments and capitals continue flying to more profitable "free-trade zones," what is the future of annexationist populism and modernist (postmodern) colonialism? Are there political limits to the "pleasures of culture," the "smoke and mirrors" of fear, and the national spectacle of colonial technopolitics? Is there a point of "diminishing returns" or "crash" to the consumerism of "false demand"? But if the alternatives are a pro-patria "neo-criollismo," or a nationalism of the (male) worker, are these narratives appealing to "a people" who are consuming "culture" as a matter of quotidian "enjoyment"?[21] Does "proletarian ideology" make sense when most "people" are not proletarians? Are many of us ready to fight for building a neocolonial nation-state in the Caribbean basin? Is this the "stuff" of decolonization? What could the coordinates of our liberation be?

Our new political imaginaries beyond "the insular vision" are beginning to recognize how the decolonization of the transnation entails a multifaceted politics of locations where through a variety of "wars of positions" we can challenge the institutional settings, structural patterns, dominant representations, and power practices that frame our many conditions of subalternity and experiences of oppression.

What I call a Puerto Rican neonationalist political imaginary is an emerging minimal ideology that consists of the "thematics" and "problematics"[22] that could inform our imagining of possible horizons of decolonization and (ideally) the performance of liberation strategies. This political imaginary has a nationalist edge in that it acknowledges the illegitimacy of the colonial state and recognizes the emancipatory possibilities of assuming the colonized nationality as a (partial) location of oppositional enunciation. Any politics for Puerto Rican decolonization will necessarily (although not primarily or exclusively) address the question of the colonial state. The "problem" of formal political colonialism demands at least minimal conditions of juridico-political "self-determination" for the islands and raises (on pragmatic and ethical grounds) the issue of redress for the "historical debt" of colonial domination that the U.S. imperial state owes to its colonial subject-citizens.

This projected outlook departs from nationalism insofar as the goal of the "independent" nation-state is neither its point of departure nor its north. This is not only because of the erosion of an always problematic national "sovereignty" (as formal and mythical as its "sovereign subject") in light of the increasing fracture of the nation form, but also (and primordially) because of our adherence to a political rationality of radical democracy with an accent in the freedom and autonomy of the agents of civil society. As a politics of freedom, a neonationalist project entails the exploration of ways of fostering the emergence of truly plural public spheres, the articulation and organization of grassroots forms of popular autonomy and resistance, and the engendering of a critical and active citizenry. As a politics of identity, it involves an affirmation of the national as a colonized form of difference while advocating a politics of differ-Ance to deconstruct the nation from the standpoint of its internal others and in favor of principles of tolerance and openness. As a politics of justice, it challenges us to develop new and creative ways of opposing and posing viable alternatives to the narratives of Capital (exploitation), and the institutions and practices of the Capitalist State (ruling strata institutionalized domination and hegemony). This will mean not only the integration of a practical politics of the desirable (viable utopias, concrete visions) but also a popularly grounded politics of the possible that conceived within the terms of the capitalist present (and foreseeable future), can advocate for distributive justice and for making liberal polities accountable for their promises of "freedom and equality."

In the larger context, the emerging postnational set of transnational networks and translocal social movements, forms of identification, and agency are not only challenging but also redefining the politics of the national. An unprecedented rate of intercultural intercourse is promoting a proliferation of translocal subjects, "hybrid cultures," "postnational identities," and extranational (and global) forms of citizenship. The rise of "unbounded nations" and multipeople states and the increasing power and significance of supernational (European Community) and supranational (transnational corporations) formations point toward the possibility of nonnational political bodies. The growing importance of alternative organizations with a global vision (sustainable "development," human rights) and transnational "grassroots" networks (webs of nongovernmental organizations) as well as the germination of social movements whose goals and operational terrain often transcend national territorial limits (ecological, feminist, Pan-Indian, Pan-African, new labor) are symptomatic of a relative globalization of the political. This dispersion of political energies and multiplication of democratic spaces (referred to as a "disaggregation of democracy" or the birth of "scattered hegemonies"[23]) goes hand in hand with the hyperfragmentation and relativization of the national so central to contemporary styles of Puerto Ricanness.

In "The Revenge of La Malinche: Toward a Postnational Identity,"[24] Roger Bartra mentions a 1991 survey in Mexico where 59 percent of the people indicated that they would favor becoming part of the U.S. if that meant better living conditions. Another Mexican intellectual commented recently that NAFTA, by following the economic rationality of the Puerto Rican model, can be defined as "the puertorriqueñization of Mexico."[25] This dynamics of regionalization and devastating denationalization of Latin American and Caribbean economies through the "naturalization" of "free trade" and "import-export-led growth" virtually converts Puerto Rico, to use Vargas Llosa's metaphor, to a "mirror" of "Our America."[26]

The stage clearly asks for supranational alliances and strategies (at all levels) to negotiate the best possible terms and to counteract (to the extent that is possible) imperial impulses. In this everyday more "integrated" (as well as more fragmented) hemisphere, the Puerto Rican "new" new left may advocate for a radical democratic "new americanism," free from the Monroe Doctrine and free for the blooming of thousands of Palmares and dreams of *Abiayala*.[27]

The persistence of Puerto Ricanness (beyond survival) is thus a challenge to the hegemonic rhetorics of Americanness. The historic relationship between the colonizer and "the colonized" will remain as a ghost haunting each other as "intimate enemies." The discursive and political definition of the U.S. nation as an imperial self (the home) is thus inscribed by the coloniality of Puerto Ricans as the garden of the backyard (the Caribbean).

Caribbean cosmopolitanism has since the nineteenth century included New York as one of the main stations of its metropolitan trajectories, but now with the "caribbeanization" and "Latinization" of the Big Apple, the continuous transit of Caribbean islanders has created a transinsular territory between the basin and the north continent. If the islands have always been at the crossroads of modernity, the "postmodern island" now also "repeats itself"[28] in Manhattan, in Long Island, and in all the "Calibanized" and "insularised" embodiments of the global Caribbean diaspora. The archipelagos of Puerto Ricanness (our bodies, ourselves), in so far as they serve as intersections of the crossroads, could hopefully become midwifes for the birth of postcolonial imaginaries, and (ideally and paradoxically) gates of hope for the gestation of postimperial worlds.

Notes

1. "El Espiritu de un Pueblo," television special and commercial video, produced by Banco Popular de Puerto Rico, Christmas 1994–95.

2. Ibid.

3. David Lloyd, *Anomalous States: Irish Writing and the Post-Colonial Moment* (Durham, N.C.: Duke University Press, 1993).

4. For notions of "the postcolony," see Achille Mbembe, "The Banality of Power and the Aesthetics of Vulgarity in the Postcolony," *Public Culture* 4, 2 (spring 1992): 1–30; and the essays discussing Mbembe's essay in *Public Culture* 5, 1 (fall 1992).

5. To my knowledge, the notion of the postcolonial was first articulated in relationship to the postcolonial state; see Hamza Alavi, "The State in Postcolonial Societies: Pakistan and Bangladesh," *New Left Review* 74 (July–Aug. 1972). At least since Edward Said formulated the notion of colonial discourse in *Orientalism* (New York: Vintage, 1979), and with the growing influence of poststructuralist and "postmodern" theoretical sensibilities, there has been a growing currency in the use of the signifier "postcolonial," primarily in literary studies.

6. Patrick Williams and Laura Chrisman, eds., *Colonial Discourses and Postcolonial Theory* (New York: Columbia University Press, 1994), 5.

7. For critiques of the fashionable rhetorics of "the postcolonial," see, among others, Ella Shohat, "Notes on the Postcolonial," *Social Text* 10, 2/3 (1992): 99–113; and Ann McClintock, "The Angel of Progress: Pitfall of the Term 'Postcolonialism,'" *Social Text* 10, 2/3 (1992): 84–88

8. Kelvin Santiago-Valles, "'Looking at One's Self through the Eyes of Others': Coloniality and the Utopia of Identity," paper presented at "Fixed Identities in a Moving World," Center for Cultural Studies, CUNY-Graduate School, April 1993.

9. I am borrowing from Mary Louise Pratt, *Imperial Eyes: Travel, Writing and Transculturation* (London: Routledge, 1992), 1–11.

10. It is by no means self-evident that Puerto Ricanness only, or primarily, can be articulated through the language of the nation. There are simultaneous and competing rhetorics of Puerto Ricanness, such as those based on ethnicity, country, neighborhood, race, and so on.

11. See Benedict Anderson, "Exodus," *Critical Inquiry* 20 (winter 1994): 314–27.

12. See Henri Lefebvre, *The Production of Social Space* (London: Blackwell, 1991).

13. Luis Rafael Sánchez, "La guagua aérea," in *Imágenes e identidades: El Puertorriqueño en la literatura*, ed. Asela Rodriguez de Laguna (Rio Piedras: Ediciones Huracán, 1985).

14. For the concept of the chronotope, see Mikhail M. Bakhtin, *The Dialogical Imagination: Four Essays*, ed. Michael Holquist, trans. Caryl Emerson and Michael Holquist (Austin: University of Texas Press, 1981).

15. Frantz Fanon, *The Wretched of the Earth* (New York: Grove, 1968), 174.

16. Mayra Santos Febres, "Viajes translocales, emigración y globalización de la cultura," paper presented at Cultural Studies seminar, University of Puerto Rico, Cayey, January 1992.

17. Arjun Appadurai, "Patriotism and Its Futures," *Public Culture* 5, 3 (1993): 423.

18. See James Petras and Morris Morley, *Empire or Republic? America, Global Power and Domestic Decay* (New York: Routledge, 1995).

19. See Sakia Saseen, *The Global City: New York, London, Tokyo* (Princeton, N.J.: Princeton University Press, 1991).

20. See Manuel Castells and John Mollenkopf, eds., *Dual City: Restructuring New York* (New York: Russell Sage, 1991).

21. For enjoyment as a psychoanalytical category of political displacement, see Slavoj Zizek, *For They Know Not What They Do: Enjoyment as a Political Factor* (London: Verso, 1991).

22. I borrow this methodology of reading/writing social and political ideologies in terms of the creative tension between their ethico-philosophical and epistemological premises ("the thematic") and their practical imperatives and contingencies ("the problematic") from Partha Chatterjee, *Nationalism and the Colonial World* (Minneapolis: University of Minnesota Press, 1993), 36–53.

23. Inderpal Grewal and Caren Kaplan, *Scattered Hegemonies: Postmodernity and Transnational Feminist Practices* (Minneapolis: University of Minnesota, 1994). For the notion of "disaggregation of democracy," see William E. Connolly, "Democracy and Territoriality," in *Rhetorical Republic: Governing Representations in American Politics*, ed. Frederick M. Dolan and Thomas L. Dumm (Amherst: University of Massachusetts Press, 1993), 274–94.

24. "La Venganza de la Malinche: Hacia una identidad posnacional," in Roger Bartra, *Oficio Mexicano* (Mexico: Editorial Grijalbo, 1993), 93–97.

25. In a presentation at the Institute for Puerto Rican Policy in November 1993, Juan Manuel García Passalaqua mentioned that Mexican political analyst Jorge G. Castañeda commented to him that NAFTA was the beginning of the "puertorriqueñization" of Mexico.

26. Mario Vargas-Llosa, "Puerto Rico: Espejo del mundo," *El Pais* (Madrid, Spain), Apr. 13, 1993.

27. *Abiayala* is an Aymara word that means "land of all of us." The notion has been adopted by large sectors of the pan-Indian movement to rename and reinvent the "new world." Palmares was the name of a Maroon community (the largest and most enduring of chattel slavery) in Brazil's northeast.

28. Antonio Benítez Rojo, *The Repeating Island: The Caribbean and the Postmodern Perspective* (Durham, N.C.: Duke University Press, 1992).

CHAPTER NINE

Puerto Rican Identity Up in the Air:
Air Migration, Its Cultural Representations, and Me "Cruzando el Charco"

Alberto Sandoval Sánchez

> *The classic questions which every migrant faces are twofold: "Why are you here?" and "When are you going back home?" No migrant ever knows the answer to the second question until asked. Only then does she or he know that really, in the deep sense, he's never going back. Migration is a one way trip. There is no "home" to go back to. There never was.*
> Stuart Hall, "Minimal Selves"

To Luis Felipe Díaz, who loves to fly to Chicago.

"Your attention please. Trans Caribbean Airways announces the departure of flight 123 to New York City. Passengers, please board at gate seven."

Growing up in San Juan, I always heard relatives and friends saying, "Mi primo se va p'allá fuera," "Mi hija vive allá fuera hace años," "Mi hermana viene de fuera el domingo," "Mi hijo estudia allá fuera." *Fuera* meant New York, New Jersey, Philadelphia, Florida, Illinois, California. *Fuera* became a synonym for the United States. *Fuera* was and still is a euphemism for migration. *Fuera* is that space at a distance from the speaker, that location outside, away from the island that is always conducive to spatio-geographical demarcations such as *Allá* and *Acá*, "over there" and "over here." Since mass air migrations of Puerto Ricans to the United States started in the late 1940s, the migrant's myth has been to return, to come back to the island; as the song "En mi viejo San Juan" says, "Me voy . . . Pero un día volveré, a buscar mi querer a soñar otra vez en mi viejo San Juan."[1] Unfortunately, the myth of the eternal return to the place of origin is anything but a reality; as the song says, "Pero el tiempo pasó y el

189

destino burló mi terrible nostalgia." What was supposed to be a round-trip ticket became a one-way ticket. While airline commercials glamorized Puerto Rican migration to the States as a round-trip ticket, for those who had "cruzado el charco," the phonograph that reminded them of the eternal return also blatantly warned them about the possibility of dying abroad: "Mi cabello blanqueó y mi vida se va; ya la muerte me llama y no quiero morir alejado de ti, Puerto Rico del alma."

"Irse pa' fuera" was a life journey that implied walking on the edge of loneliness, alienation, isolation, loss of identity, and ultimately death. It was not that easy to conceive of migration simply as a commercial slogan or a musical jingle: "A la ida o a la vuelta vuele por Delta" or "Vuele ahora y pague después." Indeed, migration is an awareness of death: an awareness of relatives and friends dying in the place of origin while realizing the impossibility of being there, an awareness of one's own death and the choice of burial place as there or here, and even experiencing a cultural death in assimilation.

Consequently, once many migrants were at the Aeropuerto Internacional de Isla Verde, their fear of flying coincided with their fear of not returning and, worse, with an existential fear of dying abroad. What if that flight did not make it? What if "el vuelo quiquiriquí" de la Trans Caribbean Airways ("la tranca") crashed, or if "las alas del hombre," as Eastern Airlines advertised, melted into the ocean as did Icarus's wings? Puerto Ricans have made many trips back and forth without major accidents; however, there was an airline accident in 1952, before I was born, that seems to have passed into oblivion in the Puerto Rican cultural consciousness.

Not too long ago on a New England winter afternoon as I was listening to some songs by Trio Vegabajeño (nostalgia, you know, always finds a way to take over when you are an immigrant), I heard the song "Tragedia del Viernes Santo," composed by Rafael Hernández. The song was a tribute to the victims of a plane crash on April 11, 1952. Fifty-two persons were killed and seventeen survived when a New York-bound Pan Am DC-4 crashed and sank a few minutes after its takeoff, near the San Juan harbor entrance.[2] Reading about this crash in the *New York Times*, I was surprised to learn that this accident had not been the only one, that there had been other fatal crashes: "a total of 204 persons [had] been killed in six airplane disasters in San Juan since July, 1947."[3] In fact, according to the *New York Times*, "[another] fatal crash of a passenger plane in Puerto Rico was on June 7, 1949, when a non-scheduled airliner plunged into the ocean, killing fifty three persons."[4] Why have we Puerto Ricans erased all of these fatal accidents from our cultural memory? Is the fear of flying such a silencer?

Three factors perhaps explain why the crash in 1952 was not completely silenced, and why its particular symbolism survived total cultural amnesia. First, it took place on a Good Friday; second, an entire Puerto Rican family of eight—the Brignonis—perished; and, third, the catastrophic event was immortalized in a song—"Tragedia del Viernes Santo."

The song starts by narrating the joys of flying ("Todos salieron contentos y con la esperanza de un viaje feliz") and describing mechanical trouble after takeoff ("No esperaban el momento que crueles tormentos pudieran surgir / El avión en porfía por más que quería altura ganar / Subir, subir no podía y se presentía lo que iba a pasar / Con un motor inservible ya no era posible la ruta correr / Otro motor se resiste y se hace imposible a tierra volver"). What is ironic is the fact that the accident happened on a Good Friday. Obviously it was God's punishment for flying on a sacred day. The trip to New York became a tragedy. Death interrupted the process of migration. There was no round-trip, just a fatal unfinished one-way trip to New York: "Caen en las aguas bravías y frente al vigía del morro en San Juan / Viendo a su patria querida llenitos de vida cayeron al mar / Que triste fue el viernes santo / Que horas de angustia y dolor / Ay sufrieron nuestros hermanos / Que volaban a New York." In the song the fatal calamity is translated as an elegy to the memory of the lost brothers and sisters: "Lloremos, lloremos, lloremos de nuestros hermanos la fatalidad / Que Dios acoja en su seno a los que se fueron a la eternidad." The air crash was a moment for national mourning and a call to prayer. The "not said" is that this migration to New York was detoured into a migration to the afterlife; death was the final destination.

Despite such a tragedy, Puerto Ricans kept on flying, and flying, and flying to the States. ("You know, hay que volver de vez en cuando pa' cargar la batería.") And what was supposed to be one round-trip ticket became many round-trip tickets. But, eventually, the destination on the return ticket shifted from Puerto Rico to Chicago, New York, Philadelphia, Boston, Hartford, San Francisco. I remember Christmas time at the airport, waiting for all my aunts, uncles, and cousins: Titi Gume, Titi Rate, Tío Primo, Titi Luisa, Titi Rafín, Titi Isabel, Titi Mercedes, Tío Juan, and all my cousins dancing the twist and mashed potato: Iris, Tony, Margie, Pennie, Millie, Jennie Rose, Alice (who never said "arroz con habichuelas" but "arro' con bichela"), and so on. Indeed, entire families like mine went abroad; others were totally estranged by migration.

"Your attention please. This is your Captain. Welcome aboard. We wish you a pleasant trip. Thank you for flying with us."

From the early 1950s, Puerto Rican literature started registering the wave of air migration of Puerto Ricans to New York City. As a response to the historical realities, new literary tropes materialized: the airport and the airplane. Round-trip tickets became a frequent literary motif, and characterization centered on the contradictions, ambiguities, clashes, ruptures, silences, and gaps of identity produced by air migration. As I map literary constructions of air migration, I am but tracing subjectivities in process, bilingual and bicultural identities in formation, crises of nationalist identity. Conversely, these literary representations were also the search for a total, coherent, utopian, essentialist Puerto Rican identity that was guaranteed in a round-trip ticket. And, most importantly, the appearance of characters—immigrants—who after migration were facing the reality of the impossibility of a return trip to Puerto Rico. As I search for those literary representations, a body of images start to shape a genealogy of Puerto Rican air migration. In this essay literary fragments provide the materials to constitute such a cultural and historical repertoire of Puerto Rican air migration since the early 1950s.[5]

La carreta (1952), a play by René Marqués, stages air migration as Luis, the protagonist, takes his family—his mother and sister—to New York City. His obsession is to migrate, to get in a plane, as a script direction indicates: "(Luis) sigue con su mirada el 'Constellation' de la Pan American que va rumbo a Nueva York."[6] His dream is fulfilled, but the play ends in tragedy: Luis dies in an accident at work. There is no return ticket for him, but the family returns to Puerto Rico for good. A similar tragic ending occurs in José Luis González's short story "El pasaje" (1952). The protagonist just dreams about getting a return ticket to Puerto Rico after his disillusionment with migration: "Esto aquí es la muerte."[7] Migration has turned into a nightmare, a living-dead situation for him. His only concern is to find the source to buy a ticket: "Lo malo es el condenao pasaje. No tengo la plata."[8] The story ends with the characters reading in the newspaper about a crime and recognizing him in a photo. He was killed while robbing a delicatessen. They know that the reason for committing the crime was "El pasaje": "Sí, el cabrón pasaje."[9]

What was supposed to be his escape, his dream, his happy return to his place of birth becomes a one-way ticket to death.

The ticket also means separation, termination, distancing, as in Pedro Juan Soto's short story "La cautiva" (1956), in his collection titled *Spiks* (1957).[10] "La cautiva" takes place at the Aeropuerto Internacional de Isla Verde, opening the collection and opening the doors to the migration stories that constitute the book, a whole literary interpretation of immigration to New York City. In "La cautiva," a young woman is being sent away for having a love affair with her sister's husband. Her punishment is migration, and there is no return ticket: "And live with them, Fernanda. Don't forget. I'll take care of checkin' up that you aint gone to live alone," says the mother, and the daughter responds, "Or that I ain took the plane again for Puerto Rico." And her mother echoes her words, emphasizing her exile from home: "Or that you ain took the plane again for Puerto Rico. I'll be watchin every move you make."[11]

Soto is aware of the airport as a new literary construction in placing "la acción en el umbral de viajeros que era el recién inaugurado Aeropuerto Internacional de Isla Verde."[12] The airport in the story is inhabited by passengers and voices announcing arrivals and departures. The airport is the revolving door for air migration, as well as a conglomeration of a mass of people waiting for arrivals and waiting for departures. As the plane takes off, the young woman leaving sees her sister's husband from the airplane window for the last time. He had come to the airport but did not have the courage to approach her. In the plane taxiing on the runway, all she can do is laugh and cry. There is no language but crying; there is no future return. Her departure is but a suspension. Her new life after air migration is at a threshold, and the airport is the cultural space embodying that threshold. In the rest of the book that silence will start to be verbalized in tragic stories as a consequence of migration. For these Puerto Ricans, New York becomes a dead-end situation. The door to a life of misery is the airport, and a round-trip ticket will never guarantee happiness.

As Puerto Ricans settled in New York en masse after the 1940s, the airport on the mainland became the site of return after a round-trip to the native homeland. The airport is the interstitial space where an immigrant community slips back and forth in a constant migratory circulation. In a collection of stories, or vignettes, titled *A vellón las esperanzas o Melania (Cuentos de un puertorriqueño en Nueva York)*, José Luis Vivas Maldonado captures the air migratory experience as a definite constitutive element of Puerto Rican historical reality: "Cincuenta y siete dólares y unas tres horas de vuelo. El océano es ya una charca que se cruza y se re-cruza sin esfuerzo . . . El boricua sigue el éxodo. Sin Moisés que lo guíe."[13] This collection, written in the 1950s but not published until 1971, docu-ments, like Pedro Juan Soto's *Spiks*, the misery, frustration, despair, and disenchantment of Puerto Ricans on the mainland. In the last short story, "Por Idlewild se fue Melania," the New York airport (now named John F. Kennedy) is a passageway of recently arrived emigrants and de-parting immigrants. The airport is without question a revolving door where Puerto Rican identity is at a crossroads of a nomadic journey. As migrants dwell at airports and airplanes in search for a homeland, their identities are in flux. After air migration, their identities are at a thresh-old located between departure and arrival, between one flight and the next one, between here and there. Under these circumstances, to criti-cally approach Puerto Rican emigrant identity after air migration means to define it in the context of mobility, crisscrossing, transitivity, disper-sion, errantry, discontinuity, and fragmentation, to place it within the ex-perience of a metaphorical nomadism and exile, and to understand it within the philosophical habitat of separation, uprooting, distance, es-trangement, loss, nostalgia, homelessness, and ultimately death as immi-grants realize the impossibility of returning to their homeland. This gen-eration will always be homeless: they will never feel at home in their new home, and Puerto Rico is not their home any longer. Their Puerto Rican identity is up in the air as they dream of a flight back to the place of ori-gin. Trapped in the myth of the eternal return, this generation did not re-alize the fact that they were not emigrants any longer; in truth, they missed the fact that they had become immigrants.

From the 1960s on, with the reality of a new bilingual and bicultural second generation of Puerto Ricans from New York, air migration starts to be represented as a process of transculturation.[14] Jaime Carrero's "Jet Neorriqueño/Neo-Rican Jetliner" (1964) turns the airplane into a limi-nal space of/for being.[15] The Puerto Rican is "entre dos aguas," juggling languages and straddling identities. Indeed, the plane becomes the space betwixt and between, the liminal state of being, the hyphen between being here and there, *allá* and *acá*.[16] "Cruzar el charco" is to cross borders, boundaries, and to map a new identity. Carrero's poem captures a series of conversations that articulate and constitute the formation of a new Puerto Rican subjectivity in process, the so-called "Nuyorican."

> I was born in New York new blood.
> I was born in New York
> I'm not a Jones Act Puerto Rican.
> yeah?
> I'm a Neo-Rican man new flash
> yeah?
> I known what I know no Jones Act man
> yeah?

If Carrero portrays the new identity formation of the Nuyorican in midair, Jacobo Morales in a poem titled "Pasaje de ida y vuelta" claims that even for a "jíbaro," identity is questionable after migration.[17] The poem starts with a description of his reactions to the new experience of flying:

> Fue en nave de dos motores
> que alzó su vuelo Ramón.
> ¡Y que verse en un avión,
> más alto que un guaraguao!
> El, que nunca había trepao
> más alto que el tamarindo.
> El cielo le pareció lindo
> y trató de ver a Dios,
> pero un ruido de motor
> lo sacó de sus ensueños
> y abajo en la tierra vio
> algo como un cementerio: Nueva York.[18]

Although humor sets the tone of the poem, at the moment that he sees New York as a cemetery, there is a pessimistic and morbid point of view that causes a shift of tone. The reader is led to prognosticate a future tragedy or a living-dead condition for the migrant *jíbaro* in New York.

The *jíbaro's* only dream after migration is to save money to return to his native countryside. He works only to buy a return ticket. His dream of return idealizes Puerto Rico; nostalgia is but the foundation for utopia.[19] His utopian dream nurtures his myth of the eternal return to a rural and pastoral place of origin. Fortunately he is able to return with his family, but as he looks out the plane window, he does not recognize Puerto Rico anymore.

"Pasaje de ida y vuelta" is testimony to Puerto Rican mass air migration—all social classes are aboard. It also expresses the fear that children of immigrants will speak only English. But what is most important is that migration changes the individual: past memories clash with the historical present of arrival in the native land. As a result, identity will be reconstructed between two realities, *allá* and *acá*, Spanish and English, here and there, past and present. Once the "jíbaro" lands, even he speaks English. It is obvious that he has not been immune to the linguistic "contamination" of migration: "A un guardia le preguntó: / 'Where I am? Digo, ¿dónde estoy yo?' "[20] Furthermore, the airplane has become the liminal space where Puerto Rican identity can be questioned as a floating social construction where cultural, linguistic, and personal constituencies are negotiated and reconceptualized. His crisis arises from the clash of past memories of a rural Puerto Rico with the present urban reality as the plane approaches the island: "no se ve más que concreto, / ni siquiera un arbolito."[21]

There is no doubt that in the late 1960s Puerto Rican identity became a central issue in cultural and literary representations of air migration. Both Carrero and Morales portray the process of change, transformation, and transculturation after migration. However, it is Carrero's work "Neo-Rican Jetliner" that must be considered as an embryonic literary construction for the dominant cultural paradigm for air migration and identity in the late 1980s and early 1990s, as exemplified in Luis Rafael Sánchez's "La guagua aérea."[22] In what follows we will see how Sánchez's essay exploits to its limits the trope of Puerto Rican air migration and transient identities in midair.

"Ladies and gentleman, please fasten your seat belts, it is going to be a bumpy flight."

"La guagua aérea" is an explosive, hysterical, hilarious anecdotal inventory of the occurrences and conversations of passengers in a flight from San Juan to New York. The nightly routine trip turns into a dramatic cultural event and linguistic performance of memories, jokes, incidents, anecdotes, digressions, and existential dilemmas in midair. On this particular trip, euphoric laughter erupts after two crabs are discovered running free down the aisle. The passengers' laughter is uncontrollable upon discovering that the stewardess's cry in fear is a reaction to the crabs and not a hijacking. Her cry scares the passengers who were oblivious to the crabs' escape. Once they have realized that there is no danger of a terrorist act, "the peal of laughter infects the hundreds of passengers."[23]

In the middle of all this *gufeo*, what is really at center stage is Puerto Rican identity. As fear dissipates and the outrageous discovery of the crabs is over, it is evident that the issue of identity after migration displaces the comic episode by replacing it with humorous descriptions of Puerto Ricans who place themselves between two spaces and testify to a dual selfhood. Such a circuit of migration has even erased geographical boundaries; for example, when a woman is asked which town in Puerto Rico she is from, she answers with the assertion "From New York."[24] But, as the narrator says, her precipitated response is not merely a slip of the tongue, or a joke, or a new drawing of the geographical boundaries. Such responses and anecdotes reveal the migrant condition of Puerto Ricans that primarily puts into question the coherence, stability, and homogeneity of their national identity. In this way, "La guagua aérea" embodies a discursive and ideological analysis of Puerto Rican identity in its fluid, transitive, floating, betwixt and between phase in the duration of the flight. As a result of such a floating and transient state of being, the narrator concludes that such splitness, doubleness, confusion, and flux of geographical territories and mental and psychological spaces are but "reality's current, leveling and dazzling in its pursuit of a new space, furiously conquered. It is a course of a nation afloat between two ports where the contraband is hope."[25] What is at stake in Sánchez's conclusion is that the so-called "floating identity" of Puerto Ricans is articulated not only between two geographical spaces but also in the creation of a space in midair where identity intersects, overlaps, and multiplies. The fact is that this identity is a subjectivity-in-process that recognizes, appropriates, and reaffirms its doubleness, multiplicity, heterogeneity, plurality, and dissemination. Clearly, the airbus metaphor makes it possible to expose the experience of migration as a site of/for hybrid cultural production and identities. The airbus, as a creative space of/for the process of transculturation started after migration, exemplifies identities in transition, as dislocated, alienated, uprooted passengers interact and intersect through experiences in midair.

Consequently, Puerto Rico is not a "divided nation" but a nation that is afloat, reconciling, negotiating, and reconceptualizing contradictions, differences, discrepancies, hesitancies, oppositions, and dilemmas for its own survival as a migrant nation. In this way, Puerto Rico is "a nation afloat between two ports,"[26] that is, between "two air-ports." The air flight has made possible the articulation and configuration of a new identity at a crossroads in midair as a result of the circuit of migration. And the passport that confirms that new identity formation is a round-trip ticket, which also validates a new politics of identity and a new form of agency produced by the circuit of migration. The Nuyorican identity inaugurated by Carrero in "Jet Neorriqueño" is consolidated in "La guagua aérea" as migrant identities are acted and transacted in back and forth flights between New York and Puerto Rico. By wanting and being able to be here and there, in between, and in a state of perpetual transience, Puerto Ricans inhabit the air flight as the ultimate creation of a bicultural/transcultural interstitial zone where identity is but oscillation, flux, fusion, elusiveness, ambivalence, ambiguity, and contradictions: "Puerto Ricans who are confused, annoyed and disturbed by their inability to live uninterrupted in Puerto Rico and who become needlessly irritated and needlessly uncomfortable, become captives of their own needless explanations."[27] Unquestionably, for the Puerto Rican "nomadic being" his place to be and his raison d'être can only be concretized in the "guagua aérea" per se.

When considered, both airports (in Puerto Rico and New York) constitute a borderland that makes border crossings possible. Given that there is no border and no borderland between Puerto Rico and New York, but a vast ocean, the site of the airports as well as the airbus in flight incarnate an imaginary border zone or border town like Tijuana or El Paso in the United States. Having an American citizenship and no required passports or visas, Puerto Ricans can cross the borders freely to the States, unlike other migrants from the Caribbean and Latin Americans from South of the Border. What "La guagua aérea" magnificently depicts is an imaginary border zone for Puerto Ricans as an "imagined (migrant) community" in transition.[28] Such a figurative border zone floats above the ocean and is inhabited by "Puerto Ricans who are permanently installed in the wander-ground between here and there."[29] For Puerto Rican migrants, the airplane inaugurates a border zone where identities are always going to be in transition and negotiated. Indeed, in this "living border" in midair, identity is hyphenated between two geographical spaces, cultures, languages, and histori-cities.[30] The hyphen itself is materialized in the verticality of the airplane, which duplicates at the same time an imaginary borderline/*la frontera*. The airplane, as well as the airports, materializes a bicultural and bilingual border zone that becomes a site of "creative cultural production" and transculturation. In this sense, Puerto Ricans have invented their own "border" trope.[31] If for Mexicans the border/*la frontera*, a tangible and horrible reality, is both a dream to cross over and a nightmare if caught or deported, for Puerto Ricans it is a figurative one where tragedy is translated into humor and always mediated through sarcasm, cynicism, mockery, parody, and irony. In the literary territory of the metaphorical borderland between Puerto Rico and New York that is "la guagua aérea," Sánchez, by making migration into a comedy show à la Saturday Night Live, a postmodernist spectacle and performance, redefines Puerto Rican culture and national identity. What is staged is identity formation not only for the U.S.-born Puerto Rican generations, the so-called Nuyoricans, but also for the Puerto Ricans themselves on the island. Their displacements, replacements, dislocations, relocations, alienation, uprooting, separation are mediated and negotiated through "el gufeo, el vacilón, el relajo, el desorden, la bachata, la chabacanería" in the only way for Puerto Ricans to cope with their deterritorialization and reterritorialization.[32] As Juan Flores and George Yúdice have stated, "But as a cultural practice, 'el gufeo' clearly harkens to 'el vacilón,' that long-standing Puerto Rican tradition of funning and funning on, fun-making and making fun."[33] In this "signifyin' process," it is the Puerto Rican nationalist identity that is ultimately questioned through continuous joking and laughter.[34] Consequently, nineteenth-century political and nationalist paradigms of identity are reconceptualized and redefined. The text testifies that a nationalist identity is not valid anymore: a residual nineteenth-century nationalism is obsolete, not sufficient for the postmodernist diversified migratory experience. This means that Puerto Ricans are in a figurative borderland where identity is a place of confusion, contradictions, ambiguities, ambivalences, and multiple and shifting subject positions. In these terms, "la guagua aérea" is the floating paradigm, a floating nation, inhabiting a metaphorical border zone in the duration of the nightly flight. As a "nación flotante," Puerto Ricans echo, rather reflect and refract, the hybridity of the Chicano bicultural and bilingual reality, as Gloria Anzaldúa has defined the new mestiza: "The new mestiza copes by developing a tolerance for contradictions, a tolerance for ambiguity. . . . She learns to juggle cultures. She has a plural personality, she operates in a pluralistic mode. . . . Not only does she sustain contradictions, she turns the ambivalence into something else."[35]

Furthermore, Sánchez's text must be read alongside Guillermo Gómez Peña's performance work of *Border Brujo*, which centers on border identity: "Border Brujo [like "La guagua aérea"] puts a mirror between the two countries then breaks it in front of the audience."[36] Sánchez does the same in his essay and breaks that mirror in a flight in midair at the moment of migration. In that instant, up in the air, identity is fractured, fragmented, discontinuous, and transgressive. In that border-land/airport/airplane zone Puerto Rican identity is up in the air as the migrants perform their subjectivities in process in the circuit of migration.

In the 1990s "La guagua aérea" trespassed out of its literary representation into art. By being translated into art, it captured the Puerto Rican cultural imagination.[37] It is not pure coincidence that El Museo del Barrio in New York commissioned Antonio Martorell, one of Puerto Rico's most prominent artists, to create a work of art based on "La guagua aérea."[38] In the exhibition, titled "A House for Us All/La casa de todos nosotros," an airplane cabin is included as a house that Puerto Ricans inhabit in their cultural imagination. Other houses are House of Maps, Silk Cotton Tree of Ponce, House of Fire, White House, Kamikaze, Rilkehaus, the Green House, and Singer House. In the installation of the "House in Mid-Air," fragments of Sánchez's essay are written over the seats and walls of the cabin with the purpose of using it as a motif, whose winged words push and pull our own House in Mid-Air. Once again the space of the airplane defers to the issue of identity, that is, the "House in Mid-Air" is a metonymical representation of the Puerto Rican diasporan and colonial condition:

> the "House in Mid-Air," the one that is neither here nor there, shooting star, make-believe house, house to make believe, suspended, imaginary and lettered, tunnel of the voice, like a long-distance phone call, homestead between two vacancies, the conveyor belt of a national body rooted in a diverse terrain. The house that wants to be a palpable echo of the richest and most resounding echo of the "Boricua" voice, a luscious uncoiling of the sharpest tongue in the island.[39]

The "House in Mid-Air" is a new space of possibilities for new identities formation: "the house is a provocative emblem of the suspended identity of millions of Puerto Ricans as they live their lives between the 'acá' and 'allá' of two islands, Puerto Rico and Manhattan."[40] According to the artist, "'House in Mid-Air' offers them a home—a portable one they can take wherever they go. It is, at last, a house they understand, one that accords with their needs, with their internal geography, rather than their external circumstances."[41] With the installation, the imaginary passengers

> should "recharge the batteries" easing the pain of the split existence many Puerto Ricans experience, living between "acá" and "allá," here and there. Ultimately, "House in Mid-Air" celebrates those qualities of Puerto Ricans, and of emigrants everywhere; those qualities that keep

the flying bus, the suspended identity shuttle, aloft thirty thousand feet: resiliency, humor, resignation, pride, strong cultural roots, and endless, inexhaustible hope.[42]

Over and over again, the work of art in its iconic and visual dimension is, as is Sánchez's literary piece, a creative manifesto of/for Puerto Rican national identity as a migratory process, a transcultural crossroads, a border zone. The wandering airbus, now a midair house, is but a paradigm to Puerto Rican national identity as a "floating nation," not a divided nation.

If Martorell's goal was to materialize a new conceptualization of "home-ness" for new identities with the "House in Mid-Air," it is clear, however, that traditional definitions of "home" and "nation" are not valid anymore. The issue here is: what is "home" for the migrant Puerto Ricans? Is there a "home" to return to after migration? Is it that easy to believe that "There is no place like home" and to just shake your heels like Dorothy and just be there? Where is "home" after you migrate? Are we all migrant aliens like E.T., always saying "E.T. phone home" and reaching out to get a round-trip ticket in order to touch a national identity? Or is "home" portable, as Martorell says, and all we have to do is to carry it within us whether we are *acá* or *allá*, or in midair? Martorell's work of art and declarations blatantly insinuate that we, Puerto Ricans, as a migrant nation in the postmodern world order, carry our own suitcases of identity, our cultural baggage, and our internal geography of identity in our own bodies and cultural imaginary; as Gloria Anzaldúa, a Chicana, has prophesied, "I am a turtle, wherever I go I carry 'home' on my back."[43]

But such a new image of "home" and an existential definition of be(long)ing in the borderland become problematic and conflictive when one takes into consideration that Puerto Rican migrants do not want to die and be buried abroad. In these circumstances, what happens in the 1990s when with the pandemic of AIDS, a new circuit of migration between Puerto Rico and New York, has joined the midair flight?

In the final part of this essay we shall see how with AIDS air migration attains a new meaning and reinstates the presumed return to the island, the moribund being expected to die in his or her "homeland" because of the myth of the eternal return to the place of origin, "La Isla del Encanto." Most pressing, he or she is expected to be buried in Puerto Rico. No one is supposed to escape from being buried on the island no matter how conflictive his or her relationship was with the homeland. Such is the case of Puerto Rican writer Manuel Ramos Otero, who died of AIDS. He problematizes his exile with the following defiant poetic image and rebellious voice: "Y si al llegar, Borikén es la misma / que te obligó al exilio, sacrifícala; / sólo de cuna y tumba te ha servido la tierra."[44] But at the end he returned to die and be buried in Puerto Rico. For Ramos Otero, who always lived in exile because of his homosexuality, his Puerto Rican identity was always a central preoccupation. His existentialist agony was to be an emigrant and to endure a spiritual exile from his homophobic "homeland," which forced him to migrate and obliged (and seduced?) him with the myth of the eternal return at the moment of death; as "La guagua aérea" enunciates, "nor will there be burial in a foreign land."[45] "En mi viejo San Juan" reverberates: "Ya la muerte me llama / y no quiero morir alejado de ti / Puerto Rico del alma."

"Ladies and gentleman. This is your Captain. We are now at 30,000 feet of altitude. We are here to make your trip pleasant. Let us know if you need anything. Enjoy your trip. In a few minutes we will be showing the film *Philadelphia* with Tom Hanks and Antonio Banderas for your entertainment."

AIDS has been a devastating tragedy for Puerto Ricans in our native land and in the United States. Since the late 1980s, Puerto Ricans and other Latinos have been increasingly infected by AIDS and affected by the alarming proliferation of cases among the population in the inner city ghettos and *barrios* in the United States. As of December 1994, there were 13,900 cases of AIDS reported in Puerto Rico. Among the Latino population in the United States as of December 1994, there were 62,934 reported cases. And the numbers keep on growing.[46]

As a result of the high percentage of AIDS among Puerto Ricans, *allá* and *acá*, a new air migration has developed. The pattern is the following: Those who get infected in Puerto Rico come to New York and other U.S. cities for treatment. As American citizens they can get on a plane and qualify for Medicaid in the United States. And those who are in a terminal state go back to Puerto Rico to die with their families and to be buried in their native land.

Even Sánchez's "La guagua aérea" was not immune to AIDS, although it was written in 1982, a time when the fatal virus's name was only starting to appear. AIDS intrudes in the text silently when Sánchez alludes to Victor Fragoso's terminal illness and his mother's trip for a deathbed reunion: "and with a certain Gloria Fragoso who is off to New

York to keep her dying son Vitín from dying."[47] Victor Fragoso, a Puerto Rican poet and intellectual residing in New York, was one of the first to die of AIDS. Since then, many mothers have made the trip to their children's deathbed in a hospital, or have made a round-trip to bring home the moribund or to pick up the ashes of the deceased. Indeed, AIDS has been so devastating that in the 1990s, the airbus trope has been metamorphosed into a "floating cemetery" while the metaphors of the airport or the midair flight as a deathbed have become prominent. The "guagua aérea's" ultimate metaphorical representations during the AIDS crisis will be registered as a return trip for a deathbed reunion or as a floating cemetery.

AIDS is not only redefining Puerto Rican air migration and its cultural and metaphorical representations in Puerto Rico and among the Latino communities in the United States; the mainstream Anglo culture also has had to invent its own air-migration-with-AIDS trope. If for Sánchez the appropriate metaphor to capture air migration was the "guagua aérea," for the Anglo cultural imaginary the metaphor is an "air bridge." An article in the *New York Times* on June 15, 1990, has a headline that reads, "AIDS Travels New York-Puerto Rico 'Air Bridge.'" The metaphorical construct of an "air bridge" constitutes a space of continuity and contiguity that makes possible the passage of those condemned by Puerto Rican society: the sick, the infected, the contaminated, the marginal (IV drug users, homosexuals, gay tourists, prostitutes). They even blame Nuyoricans for the transmission of AIDS: "Some Puerto Ricans believe AIDS was imported by those returning from the mainland—those they call 'New Yoricans,' and gay tourists."[48] The air bridge metaphor is logically and solidly constructed as an imaginary structure connecting New York and Puerto Rico given that there is a body of water in between—the Atlantic Ocean—and the "air bridge" provides passage over it. This air bridge, by connecting Puerto Rico to New York, allows for the constant flow of migrant populations increasingly affected by AIDS.[49]

The air bridge is not floating like "la guagua aérea": it is securely anchored, should I say politically and economically, at each end in the cities of San Juan and New York. But this bridge is a transitional passage mainly for people with AIDS, according to the *New York Times*:

> For half a century, millions of Puerto Ricans have crossed back and
> forth over the "air bridge" linking New York and San Juan. These days,
> the air bridge also joins New York and its southernmost "suburb" in

the devastating epidemic of AIDS. . . . The Puerto Rican AIDS epidemic . . . is now being exchanged back and forth across the air bridge in a growing cycle of disease. . . . Air travel "made it one epidemic," said Dr. Nicholas A. Rango, director of the New York State Health Department's AIDS Institute.[50]

With AIDS, there are no borders. Air travel has made AIDS "one epidemic," which has disseminated and is being contained in the body of the Puerto Rican nation, that floating nation *entre el allá y el acá.*

"Passengers and crew, please prepare for landing. Thank you for flying with us. We wish you a happy stay wherever your final destination is."

Twenty years ago I migrated from Puerto Rico to the United States to attend college. As the years went by, I became an immigrant without a round-trip ticket. The typical existentialist dilemma of Puerto Rican immigrants about the possibility of returning to their "home/land" never disconcerted or perturbed, rather disturbed, me. I was never concerned with the dilemma of "to be or not to be here, or there, where?" Going back home was not, however, my main preoccupation. My energies went into inventing home here, constructing a historical reality and a bilingual and bicultural Latino identity in the United States. In other words, home was not located for me in the realm of an eternal return to a mythical "home/land" called *la isla del encanto.*

Home for me is w/here I am. The myth of the eternal return is not going to trap me in an obligatory reactionary nostalgia, a patriotic dead-end imposition rooted in nineteenth-century nationalist ideology. I was born in Puerto Rico, but I do not have to die and be buried in San Juan: "Mi cuna no es mi tumba." I am not taking "la guagua aérea" to attend my own funeral.

Five years ago when I was diagnosed with AIDS, I had to decipher and confront the enigma of the myth of the eternal return to my "home/land." AIDS has become my ultimate migration. Why? Because with AIDS a one-way ticket back to San Juan meant to die, not to live. I asked myself, should I now go home sick when I have never been "home-sick"? Being gay with AIDS, and having death around the corner, does not convince me at all that I have to get an airline ticket to return *para bien o para mal* to a homophobic and chauvinist society. Besides, in my final days, I am not going to put up with Catholicism dictating to me to repent.

I have not lived in sin. "Mea culpa, Mea culpa" will not be my final words on my deathbed. "Silencio = muerte." Home is not where silence is death.

I have made it very clear: I am not getting in "la guagua aérea" to go to die in my "home/land." There will be no round-trip ticket. No final destination. My home in my "home/land" was where I started from. After migration, life has been a long journey away from home with many homes. I have had many homes with my friends, my community, my relatives, my lover—my guardian angels here and there, everywhere. After AIDS, home is w/here I am surviving day by day. To wake up on a new day is a "home run": "la vida continua . . . gracias a la vida."

I am in a race with the clock. I am running out of time. I live on borrowed time, and my days are counted. They are precious. I do not need any nationalist and patriotic dogma telling me how to live my life, where to die and be buried. I do not have to replay over and over again, like a broken record, the lyrics to "En mi viejo San Juan": "ya la muerte me llama / y no quiero morir / alejado de ti / Puerto Rico del alma." I say "a los cuatro vientos," like Nuyorican poet Miguel Piñero, who died of AIDS: "scatter my ashes thru . . . / There's no other place for me to be / . . . so please when I die . . . / don't take me far away / keep me near by / take my ashes and scatter them thru out / the Lower East Side" ("A Lower East Side Poem").[51]

Lately, when my friends and relatives ask me, When are you going home? When are you flying home? I just say, "I am home." When my parents ask me, When are you coming home? I just say, "un día de estos menos hoy." For a fact, I know, that I am not "home-less." Home is w/here I am, within me. For me, to "cruzar el charco" meant once and for all that home was going to be portable, on the other side, at a crossroads, in the borderlands.

You know, with AIDS, home is very much like death. On the one hand, death is always at your side. Ironically, life is always a death threat. On the other hand, home is where you live, and death can knock at your door any time. Once you migrate, once you cross the borders, exiled with AIDS, there are other places called home. Once you are diagnosed with AIDS, death feels at home within you, makes itself at home within your body. You must make room for it. Negotiate with it. Feel at home with it. Homecare.

After an AIDS diagnosis, like after migration, home is where you live until you die. Home is w/here you are with your past and present, memories and dreams, language and culture, pain and hope, health and sickness, life and death. Life, home, and death are where you are. When I migrated in "la guagua aérea" twenty years ago, I carried home "on my back" like a "cobito," and home has been my baggage in my heart since then. When you have home within, once you are t/here, there is no place like home. Hogar dulce hogar. Home Sweet Home.

Notes

I would like to thank Luis Felipe Díaz and Arnaldo Cruz, who encouraged me to write this essay. A first version of this essay was read at Brown University in April 1993, on a panel titled "Puerto Rican/Latinos in the Arts: A Celebration." The panel was organized by Suzanne Oboler. The participants included Sandra Maria Esteves, Frances Aparicio, and Efraín Barradas. This is an abridged version of a longer critical study.

 1. "En mi viejo San Juan," words and music by Noel Estrada. The song was composed in 1947 and interpreted by Trío Vegabajeño. Disco Hit compact disk XX6, Digital Recording Services, Santurce, Puerto Rico.

 2. See "52 Die, 17 Survive in U.S. Plane Crash at San Juan, Puerto Rico," *New York Times,* Apr. 12, 1952, 1; "Plane Falls in Sea; 17 Rescued, 52 Lost," *Washington Post,* Apr. 12, 1952, 1; "Mueren 52 en accidente aéreo / Avión cayó tres millas de San Juan / Iba hacia Nueva York lleno de Boricuas," *El Mundo,* San Juan, Apr. 12, 1952, 1; and "Police Bar Visits to Air Crash Pilot, Delay Reunion with Jane Froman," *New York Times,* Apr. 13, 1952, 1.

 3. "Police Bar Visits to Air Crash Pilot," *New York Times,* Apr. 13, 1952, 26.

 4. "52 Die, 17 Survive," *New York Times,* Apr. 12, 1952, 20.

 5. The most important studies on Puerto Rican literary representations of migration are Rafael Falcón, *La emigración a Nueva York en la novela puertorriqueña* (Valencia: Albatros, 1983); and Rafael Falcón, *La emigración a Nueva York en los cuentos de José Luis González, Pedro Juan Soto y José Luis Vivas Maldonado* (New York: Senda Nueva de Ediciones, 1984). For a sociocultural reading in the theater of the crisis of the Puerto Rican family after migration, see my article, "La puesta en escena de la familia inmigrante puertorriqueña," *Revista Iberoamericana* 162–163 (Jan.-June 1993): 345–59.

 6. René Marqués, *La carreta* (Río Piedras: Editorial Cultural, 1969), 78.

 7. José Luis González, *20 Cuentos y Paisa* (Río Piedras: Editorial Cultural, 1973), 173.

 8. Ibid.

 9. Ibid., 14.

 10. Pedro Juan Soto, *Spiks* (Río Piedras: Editorial Cultural, 1973), 13–26.

 11. Pedro Juan Soto, *Spiks,* trans. Victoria Ortiz (New York: Monthly Review Press, 1973), 27.

 12. Soto, *Spiks* (Río Piedras: Editorial Cultural, 1973), 13.

 13. José Luis Vivas Maldonado, *A vellón las esperanzas o Melania: Cuentos de un puertorriqueño en Nueva York* (New York: Las Americas, 1971), 5.

 14. On transculturation, see Fernando Ortiz, *Contrapunteo cubano del tabaco y la azúcar* (La Habana: J. Montero, 1940); and Angel Rama, *Transculturación narrativa en América Latina* (Mexico: Siglo XXI, 1982). Ortiz defines transculturation as follows: "Entendemos que el vocablo transculturación expresa mejor las diferentes fases del proceso transitivo de una cultura a otra, lo que enrigor indica la voz anglo-americana aculturación, sino que el proceso indica también necesariamente la pérdida o desarraigo de una cultura precedente, lo que pudiera decirse una parcial desculturación, y además, sig-

nifica la consiguiente creación de nuevos fenómenos culturales que pudieran denominarse neoculturación" (103).

15. Jaime Carrero, "Jet Neorriqueño/Neo-Rican Jetliner," in *Notes of Neorican Seminar*, ed. Jaime Carrero and Robert Muckley (San Germán: Inter-American University, 1972), 47–49. The poem is reprinted in *The Puerto Ricans: A Documentary History*, ed. Kal Wagenheim and Olga Jiménez de Wagenheim (New Jersey: Waterfront Press, 1988), 276–81.

16. See Victor Turner, *Drama, Fields, and Metaphors: Symbolic Action in Human Society* (Ithaca, N.Y.: Cornell, 1984); and Arnold van Gennep, *The Rites of Passage* (Chicago: University of Chicago Press, 1960).

17. Jacobo Morales, *100 X 35/Poesía* (Río Piedras: Editorial Antillana, 1975), 7–10.

18. Ibid., 7.

19. See Efraín Barradas, " 'De lejos en sueño verla . . . ': Visión mítica de Puerto Rico en la poesía neoyorrican," *Revista Chicano-Riqueña* 8, 4 (1979): 46–56, for his analysis of how Nuyorican poets in their effort to return to their roots mythify their vision of Puerto Rico as an Edenic paradise.

20. Morales, *100 X 35/Poesía*, 10.

21. Ibid.

22. Luis Rafael Sánchez, "La guagua aérea," in *Catalog: Exposición La Casa de Todos Nosotros/A House for Us All*; English translation, "The Airbus," by Diana L. Vélez, El Museo del Barrio (1992), 24–39.

23. Ibid., 25.

24. Ibid., 35.

25. Ibid., 39.

26. Ibid.

27. Ibid., 37, 39.

28. See Benedict Anderson, *Imagined Communities* (London: Verso, 1991), 6.

29. Sánchez, "The Airbus," 39.

30. Following Juan Bruce Novoa in works such as *Retrospace: Collected Essays on Chicano Literature* (Houston: Arte Público Press, 1990), 178, I suggest that such hyphenated space is not schizophrenic. It is a space for contested territorialities and positionalities, a potential site for subversiveness where intermediary, emergent, and alternative subject positions produce new identity formation and new consciousness. When migrants inhabit a borderland, they can challenge the privileged site of nationalist identities as they juggle bilingual/bicultural realities.

31. I am indebted to Renato Rosaldo's *Culture and Truth: The Remaking of Social Analysis* (Boston: Beacon Press, 1989), for this reading's formulation. Also, see José David Saldívar, ed., *The Dialectics of Our America: Genealogy, Cultural Critique, and Literary History* (Durham, N.C.: Duke University Press, 1991); Héctor Calderón and José Saldívar, eds., *Criticism in the Borderlands: Studies in Chicano Literature, Culture and Ideology* (Durham, N.C.: Duke University Press, 1991); and D. Emily Hicks, *Border Writing: The Multidimensional Text* (Minneapolis: University of Minnesota Press, 1991); as well as the work of Gloria Anzaldúa and Guillermo Gómez Peña.

32. I am using the term *deterritorialization* as used by Gilles Deleuze and Félix Guattari in *Kafka: Toward a Minor Literature* (Minneapolis: University of Minnesota Press, 1986), 18.

33. See Juan Flores and George Yúdice, "Living Borders/Buscando América: Languages of Latino Self Formation," *Social Text* 8, 2 (1990): 57–84.

34. See Henry Louis Gates Jr., *The Signifying Monkey: A Theory of African-American Literary Criticism* (New York: Oxford University Press, 1989).

35. Gloria Anzaldúa, *Borderlands/La Frontera: The New Mestiza* (San Francisco: Spinsters/Aunt Lute, 1987), 79.

36. Guillermo Gómez Peña, "Border Brujo," *Drama Review* 35, 3 (T131) (fall 1991): 49.

37. "La guagua aérea" was also made into a film. The film, directed by Luis Molina, had a gala premiere aboard a flight from San Juan to New York City on August 6, 1993. At least 400 passengers attended the event. The happening can be read as a postmodernist performance and simulacrum.

38. The exhibition took place from September 1992 to January 1993. I am grateful to Antonio Martorell for providing me with a catalog and reviews of the exhibition: Guy Trebay, "Deep Houses," *Village Voice* Feb. 23, 1993; and Holland Cotter, "Homelessness Explored at El Museo del barrio," *New York Times*, Jan. 1, 1993, C16.

39. *Catalog: Exposición La Casa de Todos Nosotros/A House for Us All*, El Museo del Barrio (1992), 13.

40. Ibid., 19.

41. Ibid.

42. Ibid., 21.

43. Gloria Anzaldúa, *Borderlands/La Frontera*, 21.

44. Manuel Ramos Otero, "Kavafis," in *El libro de la Muerte* (Puerto Rico: Waterfront Press/Editorial Cultural, 1985), 60.

45. Sánchez, "The Airbus," 37.

46. These statistics were provided by the Centers for Disease Control/National Center for Infectious Diseases/Division of HIV/AIDS, Atlanta, Georgia. According to the Centers for Diseases and Prevention, Puerto Rico has the second highest per capita rate of AIDS in the United States. Some observers have predicted that by the year 2000, one third of the island's population will be HIV positive.

47. Sánchez, "The Airbus," 37.

48. "AIDS Travels New York–Puerto Rico 'Air Bridge,' " *New York Times*, June 15, 1990, B1.

49. There are 3.5 million residents on the island and 2.5 million living on the "mainland." Many of the people with AIDS are drug users. The disease is spreading faster among women and children. Given that homosexuality is a taboo in Puerto Rico, the number of homosexuals/bisexuals with AIDS is unknown.

50. "AIDS Travels," *New York Times*, June 15, 1990, B1.

51. Miguel Piñero, "A Lower East Side Poem," in Efraín Barradas, ed., *Herejes y mitificadores* (Río Piedras: Ediciones Huracán, 1980), 96–98.

CHAPTER TEN

"Pa' La Escuelita con Mucho Cuida'o y por la Orillita": A Journey through the Contested Terrains of the Nation and Sexual Orientation

Manuel Guzmán

"Una noche como un loco mordió la copa de vino . . ."[1]

It was 1984, shortly after my arrival to New York City, and I still felt strongly intimate with those foreigners who never miss an opportunity to announce their foreignness lest they be confused with one of the local sort. I was one of those foreigners who tread on enchanted ground when the target of their announcement, during one of many deployments of small talk in any one of New York City's typical gay bars, reveals the smallness of a life that has never had the experience of being foreign and says, "I'm from New York." The grandiloquent smallness of the local target signifies to the foreigner not only a geographical and national location but the inner workings of a "Great White Way," a "Disneyfied" imagination, *la gingería total.* Confronted by the sign and its significations, the foreigner feels scorn, remembers his arrival, and a much slower version of the famous tune "I wanna be in America." Of course, the enchantment of the ground is no longer. However, as the tune lingers, fades, and dies, the foreigner gleefully rehearses in *his* imagination the last measures of the famous tune, for he knows that Chita—*Ms. Rivera herself*—no longer screeches from *los rufos del barrio* but thrives and connives from within the murderous strings of a most pleasurable web.

A few years later, still quite young, and, as always, very Puerto Rican, I decided one summer evening to go to one of those New York City rituals where urban folk all dressed in black rent a locale undergoing construction, set up one or two neon signs, and partake in one of those social events that only those able to pump beer out of a keg while balancing themselves on the edge of cultural and urban sophistication are capable of apprehending as a festive occasion called a party. Unable to balance myself in the requirements of the ostensibly social occasion, utterly bored, I wandered off into the night of our garment district, where I noticed a less than conspicuous stream of "serious *loquitas* down" making their way into my stream of consciousness, compellingly guiding me to follow their steps. They were not wandering and knew exactly where to go.

The lack of windows, signs, or markers of any sort immediately signaled to me that down those steps off the corner of 39th Street and 8th Avenue I was to find not only a Latino club but a "gay" Latino club. It had been years since my first gay club. Hence, I had already had ample opportunity to understand how gay liberation had liberated me to go in pursuit of my homosexual desires down into the darkness of basements without windows outside the view of the outside world.

At once, I knew exactly the place where I had arrived. Years before, and again shortly after my arrival in New York City, following a trip with other Puerto Ricans to the Midwest for a much preferred undergraduate education in the United States, another group of Puerto Ricans, a group of bourgeois *sexiles*,[2] had successfully convinced me that I would not like the place where I now found myself. Without doubt, I knew I was at the place that I had first heard about in San Juan's now defunct Stars Disco. I knew I had arrived at *La Escuelita*.

"Les diré que llegué de un mundo raro ..."

La Escuelita, not quite perfectly rectangular in shape, is made up of one large space divided into two contiguous, semi-open areas where patrons gather for the purpose of socializing, and a number of smaller enclosed spaces (that is, DJ booth, dressing room, rest rooms, coatroom, and the kitchen). I will ignore the enclosed spaces and focus my observations on the contiguous, semi-open areas, which, for lack of a better signifier, I shall refer to as the "hall." These semi-open areas each have their own bar. Toward the center, in the larger of the two semi-open areas is the stage, the rectangular dance floor, and tables arranged along two of its sides. Forming an L-shaped margin around the larger of the two parts is the other semi-open area of the hall, where near the entrance to the site and decorated with pictures of Mirta Silva, Flor de Loto, a famous New York City immigration lawyer, and others, the larger and busier of the two bars in the club stands prominently.

The semi-openness of the hall—the division between its two areas—

is achieved by means of a low wall, close to the entrance of the site, and two similar walls across from the stage and the smaller bar. These low walls create a structure that produces an effect similar to that produced by windows in the rear of orchestra seats in the standing-room section of a theater. Patrons always stand behind these low walls to watch the drag show. These low walls, opposite the stage and the smaller bar, are arranged to permit passage and entrance onto the dance floor and those tables in front of the smaller bar.

Inside the inner space of the hall, in the larger of the two semi-open areas, lit "fuck me red" chandeliers hovering over the entirety of the hall, as well as tables and booths all dressed in red, without excuse, capture the beauty of it all. The glaring vivaciousness of this less than perfect attempt to snatch at the nocturnal extravagance of a Latin American nightclub never had or never to be enjoyed again strikingly emphasizes, by comparison, the austerity found in the region adjacent to the inner space of the hall, the starkness of the margin of the hall.

The inner space of the hall is structured so as to discourage people from standing. In this area, people may sit or dance. In fact, during the show, while female impersonators perform, standing is prohibited. In the margin, however, people have no choice but to stand, and dancing is not allowed. It is prohibited.

"I could have danced, danced, danced ... all night"

My fellow sexiles were proven wrong. I went native, perhaps. Regardless, my sudden discovery lead to an endless string of ritualistic forays to La Escuelita's treacherous dance floor, wanting sound effects and motley decor. Incorporating the jolting effect of a needle skipping over the records of a DJ's poorly suspended turntable was made rather easy considering the less than gracious, haltingly spasmodic displacement of one's body over the capriciously irregular, if not missing, wooden slats of an erratic dance floor. Ill-mannered waiters and the dangerous libations of less than civil bartenders, whose greatest offense was not necessarily the potentially poisonous traces of mercury in the bottles of "Ron Castillo," were not enough to keep me away. Neither my less than successful venture into the sexual economy of the space nor the indignation I felt when two of their always brutish heterosexual bouncers scrubbed the floor with the face of an ill-behaved drunken patron, dragged him past me and up the cement steps of the club's entrance, and threw his body off

onto the street—none of this—was successful in keeping me away. Years
went by, and my attendance achieved the excellent regularity that facilitated my access, on a Sunday evening, to the club's kitchen. There I *formally* transgressed a line the boundaries of which had already been
blurred in my intellectual attempts to figure out why I would go to such a
dreadfully unpleasant place with such regularity. Equipped with concepts
such as resistance, hegemony, and subversion, I dedicated myself to a
more systematic appraisal of the space. In 1992, I interviewed Raúl, the
club's co-owner, regarding the origins of La Escuelita, while he prepared
espagetis con pollo for a poorly attended Sunday ritual that save for the
club's entourage of cross dressers, transsexuals, and female impersonators is virtually unknown to most of the patrons of the club.

Although I repeatedly tried to convey to Raúl that the purpose of my
interview was in no way connected to a journalistic endeavor for any of
the newspapers of the region, in all likelihood I failed. His presentation
was quite well managed, and his narrative regarding the history of La Escuelita was laced with assertions regarding the sanctity of the space and
its respect for traditional values. I still wonder about the motivation behind his notably diligent efforts to portray the space as one amenable to
tourists and free of weapons, illegal drugs, and sexual activity. Also, during the month following the interview, I never paid a cover charge.

Like many of us, Raúl arrived in the United States due not to his own
will but to that of his family, who sent him to Florida because of their
tacit suspicions regarding his homosexuality. There, in 1957, Raúl came
out. He then moved to New York City, where he lived until 1960 before
returning to Cuba to manage "Night & Day," the cabaret of his recently
deceased brother-in-law. Because of political reasons bearing little relationship to his sexual orientation, shortly thereafter Raúl came back to
New York, leaving Cuba—for what has been up until now—*forever*.[3]

Not long after the Stonewall Riots, which for Raúl trigger no relevant
memories, a group of people including Raúl were interested in opening a
nightclub where *men could dance with men and women with women*.
During our interview, Raúl preferred to protect the anonymity of his
partners and thus withheld the names of the people in the group, which
included two other men and a woman. They lacked the necessary licenses
and permits and hence decided, like other gay club managers at the time,
to open up a social club instead of a bar.

The club has always been located on New York City's West Side. Its
first location was on Broadway Avenue across the street from New York's

Lincoln Center for the Performing Arts. Rent for the space was rather inexpensive. The building where it was located was soon to be demolished. The partners could not reach a decision regarding a name for the new place; hence the woman in the group suggested skipping the idea of a name altogether and directing new patrons to a huge, three-story-high banner outside of the building that read "The School." The original patrons of the club were mostly Spanish-speaking immigrants, who wrote love notes on the blackboards that remained from the days when the building was a school for dental hygienists. Puerto Rican patrons, specifically, wrote the lyrics of "Mi Escuelita," a famous Puerto Rican song for children extolling the virtues of children's love for knowledge—an ironic event, given the old biblical debate regarding the meaning of the verb "to know."

"El piso se pandeaba," said Raúl as he remembered the crowd of three hundred or so regulars who paid a cover charge of three dollars to dance to the music of an orchestra and a juke box on Friday and Saturday nights. Rather quickly, the new social club managed to make a reputation for itself not only among its patrons but among its neighbors as well. Raúl still remembers receiving a letter from the administrators of Lincoln Center, who asked the management of "La Escuelita" to please keep the noise level down until midnight and complained about how their dancers no longer danced classical ballet but so-called Spanish "cha-cha."

Patrons no longer went to the place with the big sign outside of the building—"The School." They now felt like they owned a space that they and no one in particular had named La Escuelita. The club still did not have a liquor license, but it did have a name. One night, two or three years later, the police closed the social club.

Raúl's partners moved to Miami, and he moved the club farther uptown where the ravages of gentrification had not yet been felt. Here, at the Hotel Lucerna, on Broadway and 79th Street, Don Paco and Dolores held all the necessary permits and licenses for a club that was not doing well financially. Dolores, an Italian-American woman married to Don Paco, a Puerto Rican man from "la calle Loiza," remained partners with Raúl until her death a few years ago. Don Paco, together with Raúl, still manages La Escuelita. It was Don Paco and Dolores who facilitated the space that led to the development of the club's current greatest attraction, its drag show.

"Drag," according to Raúl, "caught people's attention." The first production by Raúl, "Las Tuti Fruti Revue," featured a troupe of about thirty-five performers in a parody of the famous Cuban *zarzuela* "Cecilia Valdez," a *zarzuela* about the illegitimate child of an African slave and a Spanish plantation owner, who unknowingly marries the son of her father.[4] The jocular trivialization of Latin America's obsession with racist, romantic *hacienda* narratives was a kind of humor the audience at La Escuelita could not resist. According to Raúl, the histrionic and reportedly hysterical event led to local reviews on network television. These reviews represented merely the beginning of a trend toward the exoticizing coverage of the locale by a number of mass media, including various newspapers from Israel, Italy, and France, American magazines and newspapers like *Vogue*, *Newsday*, and the *Village Voice*, as well as "Noticias y Más" and "Ocurrió Así," two syndicated television shows in Spanish transmitted throughout most of Latin America and the United States.

The location of La Escuelita at the Hotel Lucerna lasted a little over one year. At the end of its lease, the club temporarily relocated to 48th Street. Six months later it moved to its current location in the garment district, the place where I found it. Here, in the lanes of an old bowling alley, La Escuelita found a home.

"Yo tengo ya la casita . . . "

Allow yourself a less than strenuous intellectual exercise and entertain the thought that conspiratorial fantasies are held not only by the oppressed but the oppressors as well. If this were the case, and it would be the case if the history of contestation over the sites of antihegemonic discourse were to be taken into account, would it not make all the sense in the world for subordinates to conceal their antihegemonic discourse exactly *at* the site *in* which such discourse is supposed to be hidden? Would not such a tactic turn compulsively paranoid strategies of containment upon and against themselves, forcing those in search of the tree to lose sight of the forest? This, I suggest, is exactly the case at La Escuelita—a social site that no matter how socially distant from dominant elites, will forever be far from perfectly distant, that is, socially homogeneous.

Arbitrary cultural provisions, according to Pierre Bourdieu, are acquired through simple familiarization, precept, prescription, or structural exercises provided by the culture, which tend to transmit a wide range of these provisions in their practical state, that is, "in practice . . . without attaining the level of discourse."[5] In his book *Outline of a Theory of Practice*, Bourdieu discusses a number of these structural exercises and writes:

> It is in the dialectical relationship between the body and a space struc-
> tured according to the mythico-ritual oppositions that one finds the
> form par excellence of the structural apprenticeship which leads to the
> embodying of the structures of the world. . . . In a social formation in
> which the absence of the symbolic-product-conserving techniques . . .
> retards the objectification of symbolic and particularly cultural capi-
> tal, inhabited space—and above all the house—is the principal locus
> for the objectification of the generative schemes.[6]

The gay Latino community is characterized by an absence of traditional texts. Consequently, for this community, inhabited spaces should
become the location par excellence for the objectification of its generative schemes—the principles on which the production of thought, perception, and action are based. If one entertains the possibility that given
the demographics of the city, New York might be the urban center with
the largest concentration of gay and "differently homosexualed" Latino
men and La Escuelita *the* gay Latino club in the city, then La Escuelita
might be considered the house of gay Latino men in the city of New York.
However, at La Escuelita patrons find their bodies engaged not with homologous, mythico-ritual oppositions but their inversion. Isn't it funny,
the "inverted" playing a game of inversion?

At La Escuelita, the division made between practices allowed and
prohibited on different sides of the divide, that is, the differential regulation of practices in the two main areas of the hall—the inner space and
the margin—homologously resemble differences between practices typical of Latin American "nite-clubs"—*the ambiance of which Raúl sought to
emulate through his choice of what he described as "very Latina" chandeliers*—and those practices typical of that American institution, rarely
found in Latin America, the "gay bar."

While at the margin, patrons may "stand, stare, and cruise." In the
center, however, the articulation and the negotiation of sexual desire
must perforce blend in the matrix of social interactions found there.
While sitting or dancing, men must negotiate their sexual desires in the
presence of homosexual women, heterosexuals, and their relatives.
Mothers and their mothers, *nuestras abuelas*, are members familiar to the
audience. According to Raúl, "we, Hispanics, do not have any shame or
complejos with regards to our children. We love them as they are. They
[Hispanic families] have heard so much about La Escuelita that they
come to see where it is their children go to. I know that is the case because
I receive them at the door where they always ask for a table." Thus,

through the division of sexual and social practices set up by the socio-physical structure of the site, one finds, in homologous resemblance, those culturally idiosyncratic differences found between the sexual economies of Latin America and the United States.

The social construction of "gayness," the incarnation of homosexuality in the hegemonic regions of the North American cultural landscape and the physically marginal regions of La Escuelita, responds to those individuals seeking to arrange their lives around a homosexual identity. The concept of "gayness" in the Anglo world has achieved normative proportions such that the articulation of a homosexual desire independent of an identity or a countercultural movement, as well as the ability of some to whimsically transmogrify the experiences of others into so-called "fields of study," has resulted in the fascination of some North Americans with the homosexual practices of those other Americans perceived to be less northerly—Mexicans. In his book *Homosexuality: Society and the State in Mexico*, Ian Lumsden reports having found "no residential concentration of the homosexual population"[7] and describes a situation where the lives of homosexuals are conspicuously characterized by a lack of specifically gay locales or institutions. Confronted with the inability to impose or make his observations conform to his cultural expectations, Lumsden also finds that unlike the case with "North American" communities of homosexuals, in Mexico, homosexuals integrate, to a greater extent, with larger sectors of the heterosexual community. In fact, according to Lumsden, "only a small minority of homosexuals in all probability would place their sexual orientation as their main priority in terms of organizing their lives."[8]

The sexual economies of many Latin American cultures are characterized by a number of sexual subjectivities, discussed later, that do not function as organizing existential principles. In this regard, the remarks of Tomás Almaguer should be noted:

> In the Mexican/Latin American context there is no cultural equivalent to the modern gay man. Instead of discrete sexual personages differentiated according to sexual preferences we have categories of people defined in terms of the role they play in the homosexual act.[9]

Although the assertion that there are no gay men in the Latin American context is incorrect and fails to adequately assess the impact of mass communication media and, its close relative, transnational capitalism on the relationship between Latin American cultures and the rest of the world, particularly the Anglo world, a less reductive version of Almaguer's assertion that takes into account that "cultures do not hold still for their portraits" and that "attempts to make them do so always involve simplification and exclusion"[10] would provide a more adequate approach to our exploration of differences between the organization of sexuality in Latin America and the United States.

These partial sexual identities, that is, sexual identities that do not act as the organizing principle in the complex of identities that often characterizes multiply-identified subjectivities, are also evident in the Puerto Rican cultural landscape. Puerto Rican *bugarrones*, like Mexican *mayates*,[11] articulate their sexuality within a sexual economy where sexual activity with another man does not necessarily constitute a homosexual identity or act. Sexual economies such as these result in social locations that are part and parcel of the culture itself. They do not constitute a riposte to cultural standards and, unlike the social construction of "gayness," do not represent a countercultural trend, let alone a political movement or a thread easily pulled from the social fabric itself.

The negotiation of sexual pleasure at La Escuelita, particularly those gestures preceding the act of copulation, the conquest, is organized in similar fashion. At the center of the social site, patrons, like other Latin American homosexuals, engage in rituals of sexual exchange enmeshed in the matrix of social relations—homosexual, heterosexual, and othersexual—produced in and by the space. No matter how discrete the exchange of sexual rituals, ventures into the sexual economy in the margin of the social site will never be as successful. In the margin, speculators must delay the gratification of their desires. Like speculators in the sexual economy it resembles—an economy obsessed with the elimination of homosexual pollutants and the marginalization of the homosexual through what Almaguer has aptly described as "discrete sexual personages differentiated according to sexual preferences"—patrons who situate themselves in the margin of the social site must always deal with a greater level of risk in their investments of sexual capital. Investments in the sexual economies of both regions, the margin as well as the center, are characterized by variable rates of success. At the center, however, one may obtain, if nothing else, the benefit of immediate returns. Anyone familiar with the pleasures of a Mexican sauna or "crunching the crotch" while dancing merengue—the most popular form of dance at La Escuelita—will know exactly what I mean.

La Escuelita is a space structurally arranged around the inversion of that mythico-ritual opposition between the First World and the Third World, the Anglo and Spanish-speaking worlds. The displacement of the center toward the margin and vice versa is achieved through the physical inversion of this mythico-ritual opposition. This structural arrangement of the social site surreptitiously constitutes, as object, and promotes, in overly determined practices described earlier, the subversive response of this cultural community to the arbitrary provisions of a dominant culture where the immigrant is relegated to the margins of the dominant culture's landscape, where both immigrant and native-born members of the Latino minority in the United States must contend with the perplexity of an identity much disdained.

The generative scheme behind this form of thought, that of violent symbolic displacement and (re)appropriation, is not exclusive to Latino homosexuals and has already made more public appearances. Recently, it crossed over, as it were, and made its public New York City debut in the play *Mambo Mouth* by John Leguizamo. During its 1992 on- and off-Broadway productions, one of its characters, Pepe Vázquez, an undocumented Mexican immigrant, delighted its mostly Anglo audience. While affecting violent pelvic thrusts behind prison bars, speaking to "gabachos pendejos," he unerringly stated, "Go ahead and try, and try to keep us back because we're gonna multiply and multiply so uncontrollably 'til we push so far up you're going to be living in Canada."

"Se oye este lamento por doquier ... "

In *Domination and the Arts of Resistance*, James C. Scott wrote "that an individual who is affronted may develop a personal fantasy of revenge and confrontation, but when the insult is but a variant of affronts suffered systematically by a whole race, class, or strata, then the fantasy can become a collective cultural product."[12] La Escuelita is one of these collective cultural products, a venture realized jointly by scheming entrepreneurs and consumers engaged in symbolic acts of emancipation, that is, having "fun."

For people with limited access to the means of violence, resistance may take more subtle forms and find articulation in a symbolically violent "critique of power spoken behind the back of the dominant."[13] "Hidden transcripts," Scott's term for such critique, are "typically expressed in disguised form" and "insinuate [themselves] . . . while hiding behind anonymity or behind innocuous understandings of their conduct."[14] In the absence of those resources necessary for the successful enactment of a violent act, the articulation of direct violence, at best, amounts to the wasteful exertion of precious energy or, at worst, self-annihilation. Hidden transcripts serve cathartic purposes that may also conceal a preparatory function. Thus, the location of the hidden transcript represents, at once, the possibility for release and subversion.

The ways in which the oppressed experience their subordination as well as the emergence of the social spaces where hidden transcripts are constituted and maintained should be made specific. Knowledge of the intimate experience of an individual with his or her subordination will facilitate our decoding of a hidden transcript whose constitution depends on forms of domination that are extended beyond mere material appropriation. The location of these social spaces should be specified in relation to "a continuum of social sites ranged according to how heavily or lightly they are patrolled by dominant elites."[15] Finally, one should specify the social genesis of a hidden transcript since such specification will make "it possible to move from the individual resisting subject—an abstract fiction—to the socialization of resistant practices and discourses."[16]

While Scott's ideas regarding the nature of those social sites where counterhegemonic ideologies are forged make room for discursive and practical forms of speech not readily discernible by the dominant elites, Scott seems to privilege socially homogeneous, physically sequestered locations. The possibility of a sequestered, socially homogeneous, and politically effective site for Latino gay men still remains an idea to be fulfilled. No matter where one looks on the continuum of predominantly homosexual not to mention heterosexual social sites within which La Escuelita may be included (for example, "The Center," ACT-UP NY, Latino gay groups like LLEGO, HUGL LLGMNY, and other mainstream gay bars), the ability of gay Latinos in New York City to assemble privately has been either outrightly denied or curtailed through contestation.

Because of his pecuniary interests, Raúl, La Escuelita's entrepreneur, is in no position to emulate the exclusionary practices at the doors of clubs in the gay mainstream or ignore laws regulating discrimination in public accommodations; the entrance to La Escuelita is closed to none and open to all. Nevertheless, and perhaps because of its sociogeographically sequestered location south of 42nd Street's Port Authority terminal, La Escuelita somehow manages to maintain a level of social homogeneity close to that which Scott believes necessary for the cathartic and preparatory functions served and produced by the social sites wherein hidden transcripts might be found.

The everyday lives of working-class Latinos in New York City are fraught with the indignities that the ethnocentricity of the American cultural landscape provides for immigrants unable to reverse the journey of their migration. Shunned, in the margins of the landscape, these immigrants must contend with the perplexity of an identity that until the moment of their arrival to the United States was no reason for disdain by oneself or others. According to Murray Davis,

> during ordinary interaction, the inconsistent identities imposed by others and the latent identities unactualizable with others may weaken the coherence of the self as a whole. The accumulation of these imposed or unactualized identities may eventually motivate a person to attempt the self-work or self-maintenance necessary to achieve psychological reunification.[17]

Although Davis suggests that such interactional "waste products" might be consumed in the dissolution of ego boundaries during the sexual act, our concern is not merely with individuals, and La Escuelita is not a sex club. Hence, we should return to Scott, while retaining the insight gained from our interactional detour, and remember the sociogenic origin of the motivations behind the cultural products of social groups whose members systematically confront what may be understood as variants of the same affront—the same disdainful identity—and begin to explore the dynamics through which the social homogeneity of La Escuelita is achieved.

The social homogeneity is achieved through what amounts to an inversion of strategies employed for the exclusion of the marginal in the mainstream of the outside world. According to Scott, the creation of a secure site for the development of a hidden transcript does not require physical distance from the dominant elements of society but might be achieved through the implementation of gestures not understood by the dominant. One such gesture is the requirement that patrons be frisked for weapons before entrance into the social space. At the most concrete level, frisking serves a function of safety. At the same time, it functions as a gate-keeping device at the club's entrance, where dangerous elements of all sorts must be screened. Danger lurks not only in the form of potential physically violent horizontal or vertical attacks from working-class Latino patrons but also in the form of emotionally violent vertical attacks from Anglo or middle-class Latino slummers. According to Raúl, "gringos" go to the club "a mirarnos de arriba 'abajo con la nariz pará." I can assure the reader that such a contemptible attitude at La Escuelita is held by slummers of *all* sorts.

Working-class Latinos everywhere know firsthand about the tyranny of police states and other systems of surveillance and control. Opposite working-class Latinos stand the Anglo and not so Anglo middle-class slummers for whom the frisker represents not the assurance that weapons will be of no concern in the eventuality of a hostile social encounter but reassurance that the "other" is in fact as dangerous and noxious as he or she assumes it to be. Consequently, the frisker acts to discourage the possibility of an extended stay and, by extension, the likelihood of any future visitations. Thus, the frisker effects the protection of the social site from hostile extraneous elements of class, race, and ethnicity through the implementation not of physical distance (clearly impossible) but the inversion of hegemonic strategies of containment now reconfigured in patterns that remain obscure from "epistemologically disadvantaged" social positions, which find their social privilege inadvertently turned against them in topsy-turvy sites of cultural contestation.

Most certainly, if questioned, none of the patrons of La Escuelita would report going there for the purpose of release, the rehearsal of future negations, or the disposal of interactional "waste products" generated by inconsistent or unattainable identities in their interactions with others in the outside world. It is also safe to assume that working-class Latino patrons at La Escuelita do not enjoy the filthy bathrooms, the heat and smoke that collect inside the poorly ventilated basement, or any of the nuisances that have also failed to keep me away. In all likelihood, they would agree with the club's owner and report that they come to see the show.

Every Saturday night—as in busy, rush-hour, midtown intersections where the advantages of avoiding "gridlock" are all but appreciated—at the first hour past midnight, the space reaches the most enjoyed disorder of its first climax. In the midst of the chaos, as if ordered to a halt by a mischievous "Cenicienta" gone AWOL, the human "gridlock" achieves order to the tune of the theme from *The Empire Strikes Back.* Promptly, all participants gather on and around the dance floor to witness the celebration of form. Although not the only performance of the evening, the drag show at La Escuelita is the focal performance. As the histrionic event of the evening progresses, all patrons, as on every other Saturday night, delight and enchant themselves with *mechanically reproduced works of art.*

"Pushed out of the tribe for being different," we have developed *facultades,* a "capacity to see in surface phenomena the meaning of deeper realities."[18] Somewhere between New York City, San Juan *y la Habana de los "50,"* caught in *operations* having nothing and everything to do with *bootstraps* tied around *los sueños y los desengaños de Mariel,* otras "*manos*" se entregan "*a la obra*" de abrazarle los bordes a la grieta doloroza de un exilio cultural. At the cultural border, while we apprehend the subversive potential inherent in the appearance of "the material girl," "Madonna," between the contortions of "La Lupe y La Chacón," we see absolutely no irony in our playful exchange between cultural systems that more often than not are played against each other. Our spectacle contains no irony, for we have realized not only that "we are a synergy of two cultures"[19] but that the nature of our ultimate identity defies fixity in the movement of its dialectic. The second-nature quality of our keen playful activities, *facultades* that Bourdieu has described as a system of dispositions objectively adjusted to the material conditions of their constitution and our existence (Bourdieu's habitus), prevents us from naming the unnameable. Thus, the word dialectic itself comes as a surprise, and its sound conjures up images of a red-sequined diva "press-on" nailed to some fake microphone, lip-synching the torch of our sexile. The voluptuous one, *desgarra el negro manto de la noche* in the margin of a dingy New York City basement. *Después de tanto soportar la pena de sentir tu olvido,* in the world of our contradictions and competing demands, the irrelevance of the signifier, because redundant, brings us to the inevitable conclusion that dialectic is not that which defines the movement of our identity but the Anglicized stage name of the latest Latina drag queen rage—*Ms. Día Léctica.*

In an orgiastic celebration of form, drag queens, and more specifically *transformistas,* non-men armed with techniques of reproduction, some of which Walter Benjamin would never have imagined—breast implants and hormonal inductions—go back in time and regale their bodies with a history rich in feminine glamour. Like a technical reproduction, female impersonation "detaches the reproduced object from the domain of tradition. . . . And in permitting the reproduction to meet the beholder or listener in his own particular situation, it reactivates the object reproduced."[20] Thus, *transformistas* mediate for their audience the attainment of that desire identified by Walter Benjamin long ago: "the desire of contemporary masses to bring things closer spatially and humanly."[21]

No matter how precariously glued by a sense of ethnicity forged in the border of its "Made in the USA" marginality, this community, one torn by chasms of class, gender, race, and nationality, finds itself able to come together and coalesce. For a performance at La Escuelita is not solely the product of its producer or its performers but of the financial rewards slipped by the audience into the bosom of its performers as well; producers, drag queens, and audience alike, literally, facilitate the reincarnation of long-disembodied images of Latina divas dead long ago. But, more significantly, all participants find respite and release from the interactional "waste products" of inconsistent or unattainable identities in their interactions with others and the outside world by effecting the closure of that wound, *cerrando la grieta*, between the margin of their First World exile—*the skin, flesh and bones of their cheap labor-producing bodies*—and their Third World origins—*the romanticized memories, the carcass, of a Latin American spirit left behind*. Thus (re)constituted, the Latin American exile, as well as its "US"-born counterpart, symbolically subverts the ostensibly inevitable, hence unabashedly perverse needs of capital to extract cheap labor from the spiritless bodies of living dead migrants.

"Adios muchachos compañeros de [la] vida . . . "

Since my interview with Raúl in the winter of 1992, I have fallen in Love and temporarily, at least, suspended my ritualistic Saturday evening forays to La Escuelita. I left not without first realizing the impact such forays have had on the haughtiness of my foreignness and the relationship of its hegemonic safety to the products of its diaspora—its "Nuyorican" other.

I must explain the nature of this haughty foreignness—the insolent posture with which I opened the initial pages of this essay—specify the meaning of that hegemonic safety referred to earlier, and, most importantly, expand on the impact these forays to La Escuelita have had on that hegemonic safety and the relationship of that safety to the "other" of the Puerto Rican diaspora, Nuyoricans.

According to George Herbert Mead, the realization of the self is contingent on the maintenance and development of some sense of superiority in relation to other people. This sense of superiority is required. One must distinguish one's self from others. This distinction, according to Mead, "is accomplished by doing something which other people cannot do, or cannot do as well."[22]

The insolence and the haughtiness with which I approached the initial pages of this essay are simply a manifestation of the form of superiority that Mead characterized as assertive. A disdainful attitude, a mere device, as Mead would have it, to keep myself going in a social situation void of social integration.

This disdainful attitude is one that I may sustain with insignificant effort. My national identity was not forged in the margins of a hostile dominant culture but within the hegemonically safe center of a Puerto Rican culture and the margins of its political left. That centered hegemonic safety requires the production of a violent relationship to a marginal other, the Puerto Rican "other," Nuyoricans.

Mead argues that these debatably temporary attitudes of hostility help individuals navigate through hostile social situations. This hostile attitude allowed or allows me to "keep going" outside a mainstream to which I have always felt I belong, but, more importantly, it kept me or keeps me out of a margin with which I doubt I will ever fully identify.

My regular Saturday night trips to La Escuelita have not been the only factor in the reappraisal of my relationship to the products of the Puerto Rican diaspora. I doubt I would have ever changed my mind had it not been for the manner in which debates with other "real" Puerto Ricans around the issue of political sovereignty and my right to cast an opinion, let alone a vote, on the issue have threatened my hegemonically safe identification as a Puerto Rican. These debates have been many. I will provide you with some examples in what follows.

During the Latin American Congress held two years ago at the International Lesbian and Gay Association conference in Acapulco, I found myself in a painful, though vitriolic, argument with a "real" home-based Puerto Rican lesbian activist struggling to convince me about the absurdity of the political sovereignty debate given that only 5 percent of the "real" Puerto Rican population, those living on the island, felt the need for such sovereignty. Perhaps, I placed too much hope on my ability to convince her of the absurdity of *her* argument by noting how few people are concerned with the rights of women on the island. Perhaps. She seemed to be convinced that concerns with political sovereignty were characteristic of those Puerto Ricans who left the island and forged lives somewhere else, and, according to her, should now simply move on. I think of the lives of Emeterio Betances, Pedro Albizu Campos, and others currently wasting their lives away in American prisons. I feel the abandonment and think that perhaps she is right.

On even more familiar ground, I believe I have failed as well. Arguments with my "real" Puerto Rican sister, at the beach while on vacation on the island, have likewise proven futile in their ability to convince her that as a "real" Puerto Rican, I have more of a right to cast my vote on matters of political sovereignty than other non-Puerto Ricans living on the island. I seriously doubt my "real" Puerto Rican sister is right.

I have confronted Puerto Rican "realness" from within the newness of my less than genuine performance and the birth of new meanings for resistance, hegemony, and subversion, the concepts with which I began this investigation. I no longer wander. I successfully followed the steps of those serious Nuyorican loquitas down who, that summer evening years ago, knew exactly where to go. Thus, I now better understand the meaning of the site of the popular as a site of resistance, a shield and weapon against the violent deployment of noxious and foreign cultural elements.

In the hostile condescension of the foreignness with which I approached the initial pages of this investigation, I now recognize a self not simply concerned with being identified with locals of the generic sort but with locals of that Puerto Rican sort—Nuyoricans. Fortunately, following healthy dosages of pleasurable forays to La Escuelita, strenuous repetitions in its cultural gymnasium, and the bitter aftertaste of unhealthy encounters with others vested in the "realness" of their Puerto Ricanness, I now find that the symptoms of this social malaise—Puerto Rican purism—have gone into remission.

My sense of superiority endures, however. As I mentioned earlier, there is a sense in which superiority refers to that which one witnesses when an individual or oneself is able to positively change the world around him or her by utilizing capacities that others do not have. Previously, I made reference to Gloria Anzaldúa's concept of "la facultad," that is, "the capacity to see in surface phenomena the meaning of deeper realities."[23] According to Anzaldúa, people who do not feel psychologically or physically safe in the world are more likely than others to develop this capacity. The queer, according to Anzaldúa, are among the people most likely to develop this capacity.

As a citizen of the American nation, I do have lots to complain about. However, I am not a citizen of the nation's center but rather a citizen of its border. I was born an American citizen, but I have always remained a foreigner and will always be so. As a foreigner, I am hardly ever disappointed by the American nation from which I expect very little in the way of recognition.

Although I have expressed a personal progression away from notions such as a Puerto Rican essence, I have not fully divorced myself from notions such as the nation or nationalism. In fact, I still hold dear to some of their ideological derivatives, for example, the notion that the resources of a nation belong first and foremost to the citizens of that nation, a notion that serves both as a most effective shield against any possible disappointment and the heat emanating from the cauldron where I keep a lot of my rage.

Spanish, my first language, is no longer my dominant language, and I have learned some of the puritanical ways of the American nation. I am never late. *Calibanes de Oro y Pigmaliones de Plata*, for the right price and dues paid in the currency of lost memories and permanent dislocation, I have enjoyed the resources of the American nation to an extent larger than many "legitimate" American citizens have and will. As an American citizen, I may, albeit reluctantly, have lots to be grateful for or, at least, lots about which I should have absolutely no complaints.

An assessment of my relationship to American society or the American nation that fails to take into account the possibility of complaints as an heir to the nation as well as the possibility of my gratitude as a foreigner would be an oversimplification. An oversimplification of this sort could preclude the realization or the identification of the ways in which I stand both inside and outside of this nation/society, as well as the realization of that potential alluded to earlier: the potential for a playful exchange between cultural systems that more often than not are played against each other, as well as the ability to apprehend the subversive potential inherent in the appearance of "the material girl" between the contortions of "La Lupe" and "La Chacón." Any appraisal of my social reality that precludes the realization of the potential for such playful or subversive activity would render ineffective the source of my enduring sense of functional superiority, that capacity to communicate through and between cultures, a capacity that others do not have and that Anzaldúa has sought to capture through the concept of "la facultad."

I no longer go to La Escuelita. *Me fuí por la orillita y con mucho cuida'o* to gather and arrange the feathers of a nest where I spend beautiful Saturday evenings watching *Picket Fences* and *Deep Space Nine* with my beloved boyfriend, who happens to be North American. Thus, better than ever, I am finally able to understand and master, even enjoy, the fine and delicate balance required at those festive occasions where urban folk, all dressed in black, manage that incredible ability to pump beer out of a keg while standing on the thin and slippery edge of cultural and urban sophistication.[24]

Notes

1. The subheadings in this essay are fragments of popular songs. With the exception of the subheading that makes reference to the musical *My Fair Lady,* all of these fragments are extracted from popular Latin American "boleros" from the 1940s and 1950s. I was introduced to all of this music, without exception, by an incredibly gifted singer, my mother.

These subheadings serve the obvious purpose of indicating significant ruptures in the text. More importantly, these fragments of songs are meant to evoke an emotional text parallel to the main text. Of course, this emotional text is not available to everybody. The discursive, politically suave strategy assumes a knowledge that is far from universal.

Those of you who have access to the pathos of this emotional repertoire do well to enjoy it. This cathartic evocation is my way of welcoming you home (my home) and the manner in which I have chosen to reenact, to share, in the midst of this text what "La Escuelita" meant to me, how it felt.

If these fragments mean nothing to you, are less than evocative, then consider them a strategy meant to share with you, to show you, what it feels like to navigate, certainly uncertain, through a cultural terrain that never yields all of its secrets. All culture is ultimately unyielding. However, some navigators can lean and prop themselves up against assumptions of universality, thus embarking upon their voyages with the comforting illusion of certainty. People in exile cannot lean or prop themselves up in similar fashion. Theirs is not a voyage of comfort but of struggle to master the disorientation brought about by the certainty of disillusion, which itself requires other kinds of illusion.

2. A *sexile* is a neologism of mine that refers to the exile of those who have had to leave their nations of origin on account of their sexual orientation.

3. I have purposefully avoided a discussion regarding the particularity that Raúl's national origin might represent for the current analysis. While differences of national origin are not irrelevant to the social reality of Latinos in the United States, this essay, in fact, deals with the erasure of such differences and the products of such erasure.

4. *Zarzuela* is a kind of dramatic performance of alternate declamation and singing.

5. Pierre Bourdieu, *Outline of a Theory of Practice* (Cambridge: Cambridge University Press, 1977), 87.

6. Ibid., 89.

7. Ian Lumsden, *Homosexuality: Society and the State in Mexico* (Mexico City: Solediciones, 1991), 76.

8. Ibid.

9. Tomás Almaguer, "Chicano Men: A Cartography of Homosexual Identity and Behavior," *Differences: A Journal of Feminist Cultural Studies* 3 (1991): 78.

10. James Clifford, "Partial Truths," introduction to *Writing Culture: The Poetics and Politics of Ethnography,* James Clifford and George E. Marcus, eds. (Berkeley: University of California Press, 1986), 10.

11. *Bugarrones* like *Mayates* are sexual subjectivities that the more "social scientific" discourse on AIDS produced by psychiatrists, psychologists, and social workers in the research and human services industries have erroneously described as "men who have sex with men." This way of representing this form of homosexual practice has been characterized as homophobic. However, this is not its main theoretical limitation. "Men who have sex with men" is not an adequate representation since it fails to take into account the man-

ner in which the actors involved in the sexual act experience and apprehend their sexual act. Although an adequate objective representation of the sexual act in question, the representation of such a sexual act as "men who have sex with men" fails to convey the fact that even if the two actors "look" like men, the ways in which these two or more men experience themselves in such a sexual act is far from the way they look. Often one of the partners is not only emasculated by his partner but by himself as well. Therefore, the sexual act would be more adequately represented as "men who have sex with non-men." As Almaguer and others have indicated, the active or masculine partner in the sexual act is bestowed a certain degree of leniency on behalf of the culture at large. Nevertheless, this leniency should not be confused with a romantic denial of homophobia in Latin American cultures. If the homosexual character of this sexual activity was publicly known, both partners to different degrees, of course, would suffer from stigmatization.

12. James C. Scott, *Domination and the Arts of Resistance/Hidden Transcripts* (New Haven, Conn.: Yale University Press, 1990), 9.

13. Ibid., xii.

14. Ibid., xiii.

15. Ibid., 120.

16. Ibid., 118.

17. Murray Davis, *SMUT: Erotic Reality/Obscene Ideology* (Chicago: University of Chicago Press, 1985), 98.

18. Gloria Anzaldúa, *Borderlands/La Frontera: The New Mestiza* (San Francisco: Spinsters/Aunt Lute Book, 1987), 38.

19. Ibid., 63.

20. Walter Benjamin, "The Work of Art in the Age of Mechanical Reproduction," in *Illuminations*, ed. Hannah Arendt, trans. Harry Zohn (New York: Schocken Books, 1969), 221.

21. Ibid., 223.

22. George Herbert Mead, *Mind, Self and Society* (Chicago: University of Chicago Press, 1967), 208.

23. Anzaldúa, *Borderlands/La Frontera*, 38.

24. Late in the summer of '95, La Escuelita closed. I spent that night at home, just "hangin' out." Others, more fortunate, were there and have lived to tell about the sadness, the tears, and the end. All of the drag queens, *transformistas*, and impersonators—so the fortunate tell me—gathered on stage for the grand finale. They sang "America the Beautiful." They cried. Their makeup ran. An American flag unfurled . . . *upside down.* "Paid it no mind." A little matter of inversion, which demands "no mind," I say.

Reportedly the old crowd now parties at Krash, a club in Astoria, Queens. I am a bit more cynical, and while I have not been to Krash, Queens is Queens, the garment district at night *is* the garment district at night, and La Escuelita, forever, even if no longer, La Escuelita will be. Really, the crowd dissipated. It is gone.

Flowers, mostly yellow and white chrysanthemums, were left, anonymously, on the sidewalk by the door for weeks later. The flowers were often accompanied by candles left burning. For whom, what purpose, or "wish" the candles burned, I do not know, but I am happy to think they burned in memory and for the well-being of all those who have been displaced, those who have had no choice but to move on.

For myself, I continue making feather arrangements in a nest that does not include a boyfriend anymore. I no longer watch *Picket Fences* and *Deep Space Nine*, well, that too came to a crashing end. " 'Taluego an' gubai."

PART FOUR

Culture Wars in Contemporary Puerto Rico

Contending Nationalisms: Culture, Politics, and Corporate Sponsorship in Puerto Rico

Arlene Dávila

This chapter considers the involvement of commercial interests and their public relations and publicity officers in the development of nationalist ideologies and conceptions of national identity in Puerto Rico. I will argue that companies dealing in such consumer goods as liquor, soft drinks, food, and tobacco have emerged as important elements affecting the growth of nationalist ideologies both through their use of Puerto Rican folklore, history, and scenes depicting "Puerto Rican life" in their advertisements and through their support of folk-art fairs, festivals, and grassroots activities. Thus, not solely homogenizing agents or threats imparting Western ideas of modernity,[1] the media and transnational corporations are also emerging as important supporters and contributors to the "marketing" of culture. In their search for consumers they are turning to culture and tapping into local events, from folk–art fairs to salsa and merengue concerts, thereby contributing to representations of Puerto Ricanness and to ongoing debates about the scope and nature of the "national" community.

Nationalism as the Forging of a Cultural Identity

As ethnic and cultural identities attain greater importance in present-day political movements, cultural nationalism comes to the forefront of contemporary social analysis. Yet cultural nationalism, which emphasizes the cultural rather than the politically defined boundaries of a nation, constitutes one of the least understood forms of nationalism. It is often seen as a transient ideology, as a "lesser" kind of nationalism, or as a strategy designed by state bureaucrats and intellectuals. In the literature, cultural

231

nationalism has often been differentiated from political nationalism, the latter referring to the classical conception of the nation as a political community bounded by a state. Cultural nationalism has also been devalued in relation to separatist nationalism, involving the classical conception of the nation as a political community bounded by a state, or represented as a transitory form that would be superseded by a political entity in which ethnic identity would wither away with modernization.[2]

What remains constant in the analysis of cultural nationalism is the recognition that the forging of a cultural identity from an ethnic past[3] or from recent inventions[4] is an effective basis for political mobilization among people seeking to establish themselves as national entities, irrespective of any objective state or territorial boundary. This is evident in the case of Puerto Rico, where cultural nationalism is elaborated by a variety of interests to emphasize the cultural aspects of Puerto Rico as a nation and a distinct community.

Departing from approaches taking territorial boundaries and political legitimacy as objective bases for defining a nation, recent studies emphasize elements of cultural construction involved in the development of a national cultural entity.[5] This focus points to the processes through which nations are modeled, imagined, and communicated through state institutions, cultural policies, or official versions of history, and to the ways in which "nationals" receive and manipulate official constructions of nationhood. As a result, we are now more aware of the different arenas, such as popular festivals and corporate advertising, in which national ideologies and identities are being forged and contested.[6]

In Puerto Rico views of national identity had been disseminated in the cultural nationalistic literature since the late nineteenth century, but it was in the 1950s that an official view of Puerto Rican culture became popularly disseminated through the cultural policies initiated by the government. After the establishment of the Commonwealth in 1952, which gave the island autonomy over local affairs, the government initiated policies to boost cultural nationalism while also maintaining the political and economic dependency on the United States that ensues from commonwealth status. The founding of the Institute of Puerto Rican Culture (ICP) in 1956 to "study, promote and enrich Puerto Rican culture" was an important aspect of this process, as it provided a vehicle for the consolidation and propagation of an official view of Puerto Rican culture. This view presented the Indian/Spanish/African components in society as "harmoniously" integrated under the rubric of Hispanic tradition, and developed a folklorized view of the nation whose main manifestations were the rapidly disappearing agrarian society with its customs and folklore.

While these "foundational" ideas helped objectify and delimit the national community in response to U.S. colonialism, their development also entailed the dissemination of an essentialist view of nationhood predicated on racist and classist biases. In this view, a folklorized peasant tradition and Puerto Rico's Hispanic heritage are exalted while Puerto Rico's popular culture and Afro-Caribbean heritage are largely excluded. Also excluded from this view of Puerto Rican identity is the transnational community of Puerto Ricans who are constituted as the "other" against which exclusive conceptions of Puerto Ricanness are constructed. True Puerto Ricans are perceived to speak a "purer" Spanish and to be more virtuous, less crime-ridden, more politically organized, more knowledgeable of their culture, more conscious of "proper" gender roles, and less "chabacanos" (cheap) than their New York, Philadelphia, and Chicago counterparts.

The authenticated view of Puerto Rican identity has, of course, not been free from criticisms or from contentions.[7] Yet, the relevance of the island's cultural distinctiveness against the continued economic and political dependence on the United States has historically limited critical evaluations of the content and definition of Puerto Rican cultural identity and has thwarted more inclusive definitions of identity. Thus, the old myths of Puerto Rican nationality continue to be defended by many Puerto Rican intellectuals while the Institute of Puerto Rican Culture is still regarded by many as the most legitimate representative of Puerto Rican culture and the "battleground for Puerto Rican nationality." In fact, Awilda Palau, the former director of the ICP (1993–95), was forced to resign because, among other things, she questioned the relevance of having "legitimate" representatives of Puerto Rican culture in light of the growth of grassroots cultural groups and private cultural organizations on the island.

It is against this context that the involvement of corporate sponsors in Puerto Rico's cultural politics appears as a complex and contradictory issue. This became evident while I undertook research on the local-level elaborations of nationalist ideology and the interaction of local organizers of cultural activities with state and private funders at the local and national levels. For instance, it soon became evident that corporate sponsors have evolved as an element against which "authenticity" is defined by many intellectuals, who fear them as extraneous influences on Puerto Rican culture. However, a closer look at the commercial appeal to culture disclosed that corporate sponsors are often shunned by the same government elites that help give credibility to their work. Moreover, corporate sponsors appear to be serving as unwitting catalysts for the promotion of aspects of contemporary popular life that are rejected by the official standards of national identity, thus adding a new dimension to Puerto Rico's cultural politics.

A Nation for Sale

The turn to culture by corporate sponsors has become a highly visible trend in contemporary Puerto Rican society. However, foreign and local companies have shown an interest in using Puerto Rican culture in their advertising since the origins of Puerto Rican radio and TV.[8] Ads for Corona beer in the 1960s identified the beer with a Puerto Rican national who outwits his competitors, the latter represented by Spanish, American, and "Nuyorican" characters. In the 1970s Don Q Rum associated its product with the traditional peasant wedding, and Mazola oil linked its product with Puerto Rico's indigenous population. As these culturally oriented advertising campaigns yielded substantial profits, the identification of products with Puerto Rico became a requirement for the successful introduction of products into the local market.

Several factors have contributed to the cultural turn in marketing since the 1970s. Among these are brand competition, the growth of the publicity industry on the island, and governmental restrictions on advertising by liquor and cigarette industries, which increased competition and grassroots promotions. Transnational public relations conglomerates had been opening offices in Puerto Rico and creating mergers and partnerships with local offices since the 1940s. By the 1960s, the most important transnational advertising agencies in the world, such as Leo Burnett Worldwide, Saatchi and Saatchi Advertising, and J. Walter Thompson, had established themselves on the island. Since the mid-1970s, however, there has been steady growth in the industry: over sixty out of the seventy-three advertising agencies included in an industry profile study were founded in the mid-1970s.[9] Although these new agencies are much smaller and accrue less than $1 million in annual billings, they have added vitality to an industry that is now perceived as one of the fastest growing on the island, generating over $770.8 million annually and creating 11,680 direct and indirect jobs.[10] The government, for its part, has also contributed to this growth by facilitating the internationalization of the island's economy through Section 936 of the Internal Revenue Code and the Industrial Incentive Law 26 of 1978, which extended tax exemption to export services such as consulting services and public relations agencies.[11] These advantages led to the restructuring of different industries (including finance and advertising) along transnational lines and to the opening of many transnational public relations conglomerates on the island.

Another important factor in the turn to culture by publicity strategists was the nationalization of the publicity industry through the recruitment of local artists and intellectuals. Most agencies, regardless of whether they are owned by local or transnational interests, are dominated by a Puerto Rican staff that brings local knowledge to the publicity process. Among the local staff are important Pro-Independence leaders, some of whom have been involved in the development of many of the most "Puertorricanizing" campaigns in the media.

While the use of Puerto Rican culture in the advertising and promotion of products has been a successful tactic for many products on the island, the case of R.J. Reynolds Tobacco Co., one of the first companies hitting the "national nerve" in Puerto Rico, provides one of the clearest evidences of this success. Since the 1960s, the company has marketed Winston cigarettes by openly drawing on feelings of national pride among Puerto Ricans. The slogan "Winston y Puerto Rico No Hay Nada Mejor" (Winston and Puerto Rico, there is nothing better) sung or written with a backdrop of Puerto Rican landscapes and music has associated the product with Puerto Rican artisans and national icons relating to the "autochthonous" culture. In addition, R.J. Reynolds has been an active funder of promotional events ranging from art events (R.J. Reynolds is one of the major sponsors of the Casals Festivals featuring classical music) to grassroots promotions, including sports events, rock concerts, and cultural festivals. While the company's promotions are fairly varied, their smaller contributions to grassroots activities have further furnished this company's main image as a pro-Puerto Rico company, concerned with Puerto Rican culture and the "gente de pueblo" (popular masses). This image is strengthened by their annual prize, the "Winston Medal for Culture," established in 1983, which constitutes the only national award for cultural activity on the island, and by their now popular "Noches Borincanas," a series of public concerts showcasing Puerto Rican artists, featured throughout different towns, especially those rating low on product sales. These activities benefit from and feed into the common cultural nationalists' preoccupation with hiring Puerto Rican "artistas de patio" over foreign artists.

R.J. Reynolds's nationalistic approach has indeed reached the local public. Knowing this company to be "culturally concerned," local-level organizers of cultural activities constantly submit proposals seeking its support in exchange for exclusive advertisement rights. Winston advertisements decorate the smallest bars and cafeterias in the farthest regions of the island, and according to public relations officers, Winston remains the best-selling cigarette in Puerto Rico.

R.J. Reynolds's emphasis on the promotion of events and activities follows advertising trends by tobacco companies worldwide, which are gradually shifting from print advertisement to promotion and sponsorship of entertainment and sport events.[12] This shift allows them to circumvent an increasing banning of direct cigarette advertisement while building a constituency of thankful and financially dependent recipients.[13] Besides their sponsorship of mass-appeal sports activities, tobacco companies have been known to concentrate on funding a variety of cultural and artistic activities. These range from museum exhibits and classical music concerts to grassroots and increasingly cultural activities as part of global trends toward culturally specific marketing. However, it is the corporate sponsorship of activities that are normally out of the reach of the average consumer and their use of slogans that associate products with modernity and the West that have gained most attention, especially as examples of the old malaise of cultural imperialism. It has been noted that whether or not the sponsored sports and activities actually touch on the lives of the people, the sense of festivity they imply fosters the association of cigarettes with the West and with happiness and leisure living.[14] Yet, companies are turning to culture, and as seen in the case at hand, it is not only the classical music concert or the nationally broadcasted sports events but also the community cultural festivals that draw mass audiences on the island, to which companies have staked claims through their sponsorship. In addition, it is worth recalling that Winston's message in Puerto Rico is not "Join the West" but "Winston y Puerto Rico, No Hay Nada Mejor." In fact, it is campaigns and slogans such as "Pepsi es Puerto Rico" and "Territorio Schaeffer" that public relations workers, interviewed during this research, deem responsible for the great advantage of their products over their competitors'. Thus, in their view, going to "el pueblo" sells, or as the popular motto states, "la Puertorriqueñidad vende" (Puertorricanness sells).

As tobacco, beer, and soft drink companies increasingly capitalize on the booming cultural nationalism of Puerto Rican society, the question arises: what kind of cultural nationalist ideology are R.J. Reynolds and other private companies advocating and for what specific purpose? This is particularly important considering that in contemporary Puerto Rican society, as has been noted, adherence to or departure from traditional views of Puerto Rican culture is often interpreted as a sign of people's commitment or lack of to Puerto Rican culture. In this context, corporate sponsors become one of the many different actors involved in the constitution of Puerto Rico's national identity, often voicing a different conception of what is a "culturally relevant" program. Their views on culture ultimately respond to what is popular and attractive to the greater public, which is not always congruent with the views of Puerto Rican culture advocated by the government's cultural institutions.

For instance, corporate support of the popular rhythms of salsa, merengue, rap, and reggae for cultural activities has defied the government's disapproval of these genres, a disapproval directly inferable from the cultural policies of the Institute of Puerto Rican Culture. This departure, in turn, has generated a discussion about which musical styles can appropriately represent Puerto Rican culture. Since salsa is not "original" to Puerto Rico, but rather is still associated by many with Nuyoricans and expatriated Puerto Ricans, both of whom are subject to racism and classism by island Puerto Ricans, this genre, although greatly popular, is still not deemed a proper representative of "authentic" Puerto Rican culture by government officials. Thus no funding is available in the ICP budgets for salsa groups to participate in ICP-sponsored cultural activities. Interestingly, although salsa remains excluded from the context of the ICP, it has already made inroads into some governmental domains. The last pro-Commonwealth administration presented salsa rather than the traditionally favored peasant music during the "day of Puerto Rico" at the recent International Expo 92 in Seville, where the then governor capitalized on the popularity of salsa music among Europeans. Other examples include the use of salsa in the Pro-Statehood Party's campaign jingles and in the official celebrations of the Central American and Caribbean Olympic games held in Puerto Rico in 1993.

Yet, salsa and other popular rhythms remain excluded from "proper" representations of Puerto Rican culture, according to the official cultural policy, which always highlight Puerto Rico's peasant past. Salsa, however, is less critically received than merengue, another Afro-Caribbean rhythm, which is criticized for being an "inferior rhythm" and an example of *chabacaneria* (that which is cheap and inferior). This rejection is closely tied to the racism to which Dominicans, the originators of this rhythm, have been exposed since their immigration to the island. On many occasions I heard cultural organizers expressing fear of merengue as evidenced by their request, unsuccessfully, that it not be played at cultural activities because doing so would "turn the festival into a Dominican rather than a Puerto Rican festival."[15]

Also cheap programs (*chabacanos*) are believed to be the most popular TV shows, which are heavily sponsored by the same corporate interests that invest in and promote cultural festivals throughout the island. These shows, which are locally produced, often employ nationalistic elements in their settings and dialogues and always draw from Puerto Rican popular culture, satire, and humor.[16] In these shows, and in a very Bakhtinian sense, hierarchies are played with when politicians are debased, clientelism is exposed, gender roles are altered, and sexual double meanings inundate dialogue. Consider, for example, *Que Bacilón*, recently rated the number one show on Puerto Rican television, which proudly presents itself as "Puro de aquí" and "Hecho en Puerto Rico" (authentically Puerto Rican), as well as the program *El Kiosko Budweiser*, whose setting is the popular *kiosko* or outdoor food stand, and the new *El Gran Bejuco*, whose main character's uniform is a T-shirt prominently displaying the Puerto Rican flag. While it is not my purpose to analyze the content of these TV shows, it is important to note that they are an important forum in contemporary discussions about "Puerto Ricanness." For it is in opposition to representations such as occur on these shows that conservative sectors of Puerto Rican society define the "true character" of Puerto Rican culture.

The impact of private corporations in the cultural realm has created controversy among governmental officials about the role of commercial interests in sponsoring cultural programming. The dilemma lies in the fact that the same companies that sponsor events considered to be examples of consumerism, social decay, and disintegration by conservative sectors of Puerto Rican society ("fiestas patronales" [patron-saint festivities], beach festivals, and the most popular TV shows) also sponsor more traditional cultural activities. The companies' flexible approach surfaces in their different strategies for advertising and promotions. In mass advertising campaigns companies often reinforce images and ideas that have been institutionalized as representative of Puerto Rico by the government cultural institutions, whereas in their promotional strategies they often foster a different conception of what is a "culturally relevant" program, which greatly relies on popular culture. This flexibility of promotional and publicity strategies seems inconsistent to many intellectuals, who, irrespective of their political ideology, are concerned with rigidly delimiting and securing what should rightfully represent Puerto Rican culture.

Welcoming the financial assistance of some major corporations, the government has praised and recognized the cultural work of companies such as R.J. Reynolds and Bacardi, which hold large-scale annual activities on the island. Recent examples are the letters of praise and recognition to R.J. Reynolds sent by the then governor Hernández Colon and the President of the Senate, Miguel Hernández Agosto, published on January 1992 in "Las Artes," an annual bulletin published by R.J. Reynolds to announce its cultural work throughout the year. The present governor, Pedro Rosselló, whose focus is on the "reinvention of government" through increased privatization, has also encouraged the role of private corporations in the funding of cultural festivals and cultural work within the communities.

Moreover, private corporations assure the government's positive evaluation of their work by maintaining close personal ties and good relations with government cultural officials. What is more, some of the same governmental sectors that shun the involvement of corporate sponsors are associating themselves with corporate sponsors who for their part enlist the help of cultural officials in order to legitimize the cultural content of their own promotions. For instance, the jury panel for Winston's annual "Medal for Culture" is always coordinated with the help of the ICP office. At least two of the five awards to cultural groups are always granted to government-affiliated cultural centers, and the awarding committee often includes a government cultural representative. Winston's criteria for selecting the most renowned cultural institutions also adhere to the highest standards about authentic folk art and traditions and international art as stipulated by the different political officials. Bacardi's annual National Folk Art Fair invites only artisans affiliated with and recommended by the ICP, and the awarding of the 1993 Budweiser Prize to a Master Artisan gathered a group of directors and officers of the government's folk-art institutions on the island and included as a main speaker a renowned ex-director of the ICP. These activities fail to include the salsa and popular musical groups that these same companies sponsor heavily in local activities and festivals.

At the local level, cultural centers affiliated with the ICP continually try to reach compromises between the requirements of the governmental cultural policy for educational programming and the funding conditions of commercial companies. The government's educational bent, as represented by the ICP, is constantly obstructed by corporate funders' display of banners, whose corporate logos, according to a local leader, "tend to turn the cultural festivals into a Schaeffer or Budweiser beer activity." Another critical issue is how to reconcile or find a compromise between the government's preference for a no-alcohol policy for cultural activities and the corporate sponsors' preferences, especially beer and soft drink companies, which always require a commitment of massive sales.

Whereas some organizers of cultural events and activities have chosen to remain at the margin and to reject government and corporate funding as a means of avoiding both governmental and corporate regulation, people's relationships with nonstate funders are secured by their unavoidable dependency on these sources for the popular entertainment aspect of their activities. For although the government endorses folk music and troubadours, it is salsa and more often merengue music that draw and lure people to the "cultural" programming. Thus, folk music and troubadours are often featured during the day, but the night belongs to rum drinks, salsa, and merengue. As a leader of a local cultural center stated, "through salsa you bring people in so that they participate in the cultural activities," thereby openly voicing the official discourse that distinguishes salsa from the legitimate "cultural" activities.

Instead of rejecting either government or corporate funding, many organizers of cultural activities manipulate their funding conditions at the local level. One common strategy is covering the most prominent festivity areas with the activity's distinctive banners before the corporate staff has a chance to put up their logos and announcements. Another strategy involves concentrating all advertising around the drinking areas, leaving the food and artisanal *kioskos* free from advertisements. Oftentimes, however, people involved in organizing popular festivals are not troubled by companies inundating them with their advertisements, as these are also believed to give a more festive and contemporary feel to the activities. This attitude should also be seen in light of the importance that these cultural activities attain for people in the informal economy, for whom printed ads, posters, and publicity paraphernalia are an important way of attracting consumers.

Considering that rejection of corporate financial support is almost inconceivable for most groups interested in organizing cultural activities, corporate sponsorship of cultural activities will continue and is likely to increase. The corporations continue to benefit from this publicity strategy, and even the government is encouraging the participation of private corporations as funding for cultural work has once more been cut. In 1993, the ICP experienced a cut of over $2 million, and most legislative assignments to cultural groups for local festivals and cultural activities are being discontinued.

Yet, far from eroding national culture, these companies are another source that local groups tap in the ongoing struggle over defining and representing Puerto Rican culture. In this process, people draw on corporate funding to highlight aspects that are officially excluded because of their more popular and less "cultural" content, thereby creating a venue for the validation and recognition of different elements of Puerto Rican culture. In this way, discussions of Puerto Rican culture are refurbished with new materials that can potentially broaden the discourse of what can rightfully represent Puerto Rican culture. The many grassroots events that draw on popular culture and local regional histories rather than on officially recognized national symbols, or showcase mass-mediated cultural expressions along with folk music attest to how contemporary Puerto Rican society is less identified with strict nationalist rhetoric and more eager to embrace everyday forms of expressions to communicate their Puerto Ricanness beyond traditional modes.

It remains to be seen whether this trend will translate into a more inclusive definition of Puerto Rico's national identity that fits in with the island's changing sociocultural conditions, and whether it will evoke a positive evaluation of alternative voices. The current discussion, however, points to the existence of alternative visions about "Puerto Ricanness" that are not predicated on old recycled myths of a racially homogeneous society, on the no longer existing peasant culture, or on some conclusive solution to the island's political fate.

Notes

1. See Armand Mattelart, *Transnationals and the Third World: The Struggle for Culture* (South Hadley, Mass.: Bergin and Garvey, 1983); and Henry Giroux, "Consuming Social Change," *Cultural Critique* 26 (1993): 5–32.

2. Ernest Gellner, *Nations of Nationalism* (Ithaca, N.Y.: Cornell University Press, 1983).

3. Anthony Smith, *The Ethnic Origins of Nations* (New York: Blackwell, 1987).

4. Benedict Anderson, *Imagined Communities* (London: Verso, 1983).

5. See Robert Foster, "Making Cultures in the Global Ecumene," *Annual Review of Anthropology* 20 (1991): 235–60, for a review of this literature.

6. For the purpose of this article, national ideologies will be defined as "cultural productions of public identity." (See Richard Fox, *Nationalist Ideologies and the Production of National Cultures*, AES Monograph Series, no. 2 [1990]: 4.) See Arlene Dávila, "Making and Marketing National Identities: Culture, Politics, and Corporate Sponsorship in Puerto Rico" (Ph.D. diss., City University of New York, 1996), for a more detailed definition of this term in relation to the construction of views of national identity.

7. This discussion is elaborated in my dissertation, "Making and Marketing National Identities."

8. This trend has been noted in the works of L. M. González, "Cultura y grupos populares en la Historia Viva de Puerto Rico Hoy," *Centro* 1, 8 (1990): 98–113; Antonio Lauria, "Reflexiones sobre la cuestión cultural y Puerto Rico," in *Crisis y crítica de las ciencias sociales en Puerto Rico*, ed. Rafael Ramírez (Río Piedras: Centro de Investigaciones Sociales, 1980); and most recently by Carlos Pabón, "De Albizu a Madonna: Para armar y deasarmar la nacionalidad," *Bordes* 1 (1995): 22–40.

9. "Puerto Rico's Advertising Agencies," in *Caribbean Business Book of Lists, Caribbean Business* (1996): 24–33.

10. Sandra Rodríguez Cotto, "Puerto Rico's Marketing Industry," *Caribbean Business*, Nov. 10, 1994, 1–2.

11. Emilio Pantojas, *Development Strategies as Ideology* (Boulder, Colo.: Lynne Rienner, 1990).

12. Simon Chapman, *Great Expectations: Advertising and the Tobacco Industry* (London: Comedia, 1986).

13. Ibid. See also Michael Jacobson and Laurie Mazur, *Marketing Madness* (Boulder, Colo.: Westview Press, 1995).

14. Uma Ram Nath, *Smoking, Third World Alert* (London: Oxford University Press, 1986), 190.

15. For a discussion of the government's love/hate relationship with salsa, see Juan Flores, "Cortijo's Revenge," *Centro* 3, 2 (1991): 8–21.

16. See Emilio Colón-Zayas, "Sunshine's Café y el poder del espectador," *El Mundo Domingo*, Apr. 1, 1990, for a discussion of cultural transgressions in Puerto Rican television.

CHAPTER TWELVE

Rapping Two Versions of the Same Requiem

Raquel Z. Rivera

Hip-hop is inverse capitalism.
Hip-hop is reverse colonialism.
Hip-hop is the world the slaveholders made, sent into nigga-fide future
shock.

Greg Tate, "What Is Hip-Hop?"

Rap music has been evolving in Puerto Rico for nearly ten years. Beginning as an underground, though widespread, artistic expression of young people, it became a great commercial success after 1989. Today this musical genre is one of the most popular among Puerto Rican youths.

Rap, as a phenomenon of mass communication, has a considerable audience. Still, it continues to be a cultural expression, mostly developed by and identified with young people of poor urban communities. Given the social imaginary of fear, which views poor youths as a threat to society, it is not surprising that rap is frequently perceived as a musical expression that promotes juvenile delinquency. In addition, the commitment of rappers to describing their daily lives in poor communities adds to this perception. The lives and experiences of these young people, who are viewed as scapegoats of the rhetoric and repressive policies of the state, make their stories reflect a crude and explosive reality that few people wish to acknowledge.

There are two main factors that fuel the hostility toward and distrust of this genre. In Puerto Rico, as in many other countries, social status is closely associated with race. This helps explain why the majority of rappers and their audiences are both poor and black. Through rap, performers not only question the existing class structures but also elaborate a racial discourse that clashes with the prevailing views on race. While the existing discourse is based on a myth of racial harmony, rap identifies and explores racial disparity.

Another factor that contributes to the poor acceptance of rap is its status as a cultural expression that surfaced outside of the island's boundaries and that was not predominantly influenced by "traditional Puerto Rican music." Still, this is a sensitive issue considering that Puerto Rico has been a territory of the United States since the invasion of 1898.

The nationalist discourse was formulated, in great part, in response to the colonial-state discourse. Both of these ideologies are presented in Puerto Rican politics as opposites. Therefore, it is extremely interesting that both ideologies view rap as a cultural expression of a fringe group that cannot redeem itself in either of the two discourses. For the state, this segment of the population is the most socially defiant of all and, hence, in dire need of an "effective" anticrime policy ("Mano Dura Contra el Crimen"). Nationalism, on the other hand, views rap as an indicator of the alienation and dependency of youths, the result of colonial politics.

Those who participate in rap culture are keenly aware of the social prejudices they face. Their music is an act of creation, deconstruction, and reflection. Rap is also a result of the varied processes of defiance, negotiation, and communion between prevailing social structures and discourses and a large number of Puerto Rican youths.[1]

This essay will focus on the elements of defiance found in rap music. This defiance seems to have emerged as a result of the class and race structures of Puerto Rican society.[2] The inability of both the nationalist and the colonial discourses to effectively address the needs and concerns of a large segment of the population is clearly evidenced in rap.

Nationalism: Representin' Whose Cultura?

Although rap music is an important element of contemporary Puerto Rican culture, enjoying commercial success and widespread acceptance both in and outside of Puerto Rico, it continues to be perceived by many with great suspicion and contempt. Since its beginnings, rap has been characterized by its constant quest for cultural acceptance and artistic recognition.

The nationalist discourse views rap as a threat to the culture of Puerto Rico for at least two reasons. First, since rap originated in the United States, it is perceived as a manifestation of the "values and cultural models of the oppressing country," thus "contributing to the cultural uprooting and materialistic values of our youth."[3] Second, it is considered a marginal manifestation of a subculture that cannot aspire to become part of the national culture. Let us analyze both of these views separately.

Fernando Clemente, a columnist for *Claridad*, points out that the popularity of rap and the consumer goods that follow serves to reaffirm "our colonial condition and the vulgar influence of the United States' economic power."[4] Clemente views this genre as another import that strengthens imperialism and corrupts the true culture of Puerto Rico.

Clemente's statements are in tune with the concept of cultural imperialism proposed by theorists such as Herbert Schiller. This theory establishes that the political and economic subordination of the Third World is extended to the field of cultural production. First World nations, through transnational communication and technology, have been able to undermine the cultural production of the Third World and its potential for alternate forms of social resistance and development.[5]

It is true that rap is promoted by large commercial interests as a consumer good, and that these commercial entities have little interest in the historical origins and cultural purpose of rap. However, rap was not created by either commercial interests or dominant sectors to alienate gullible youths. On the contrary, this musical culture was created by young people and was capitalized on later by commercial interests.

The concept of cultural identity, on which many theories of cultural imperialism are founded, should also be reexamined. National culture is neither a natural nor absolute category but a human creation. This definition, which changes with time, cannot be objective. It is always colored by ideological constructs. Furthermore, national culture has been historically defined by the national elite through the integration of folk culture, popular culture, traditional culture, and elite culture—all categories that are questionable in themselves.[6]

In the contemporary context *lo nacional* is particularly elusive. Internal cultural conflicts, migration, the influence of transnational communication, and the deliberate construction of identities and traditions are all factors that make difficult the definition of national cultures. The meaning of this constantly evolving category is challenged by the same elements that form it.

Many of the ideas about national culture are based on nostalgia and a conservative view of cultural identity. The thesis of cultural imperialism can be limiting if class relations and other local cultural dynamics, which turn national identity into a site of struggle, are ignored.[7] When traditions are portrayed as the most effective form of resistance, when faced with imperialism, they serve to conceal the true nature of a term that has been mostly defined through the perspective of dominant social sectors.

The term *traditional culture* is as much a creation of the dominant sectors as the term *national culture*. Several popular manifestations of the twentieth century that have been described as the pillars of national culture were considered vulgar and expressions of the lumpen in their time. This was the case with the *plena*, the *son*, the calypso, jazz, and the blues.[8]

In the name of tradition, the most conservative sectors of society have fought and have tried to silence the expressions that threaten their privileged position. According to Dick Hebdige, any cultural manifestation that defies the myth of cultural unity constitutes an attempt against cohesion and national consensus.[9] This is precisely the case with rap, which deals with a series of issues involving identity, culture, and art that challenge the conception of unity promoted by the nationalist discourse.

Rap places more emphasis on class, generational, and racial identity than on national identity. For example, rapper Vico C. recognizes the subjective nature of the concept of national culture. In his rap "Tradición," he makes reference to the traditions of the barrio and the *caserío* rather than to the national homogeneous tradition:

> I am a common man with a street perspective
> Not a politician with first class ways
> I use every day language
> Huh! with the dictionary of the barrio
> We are all the same, different social class
> But you know, the point of my song
> My motto is everyone with his/her own tradition.[10]

The need of purists to preserve national culture is not shared by rappers. Their understanding of national concepts is quite ample. Culture is not "lost" even if it changes with time; it merely evolves. This understanding is shared by Vico C., for whom "there is an established culture and an evolving culture." Vico C.'s comments are remarkably similar to Jose Luis González's views about culture. González believes that most Puerto Ricans do not share the elite's sentiment that the culture of Puerto Rico has either deteriorated or has been lost completely.[11]

Cultural purity, as defined by the thesis of cultural imperialism, has virtually no place in the contemporary context. Our modern world is a place for cultural exchange and global dissemination.[12] Therefore, cultural cannibalism, or adopting aspects of different cultures to enrich one's own, is seen in rap as a common process. For this reason, D. J. Carlos, a member of Three to Get Funky, states—without feeling the need to explain or justify himself—that among his major influences are James Brown, Celia Cruz, Boyz II Men, and Michael Jackson.[13]

Puerto Rico is not the only country where the concepts of tradition and culture have created so much controversy. Given rap's status as an international commercial product, it has been accused of corrupting the traditions of several countries, from Guinea to Brazil.[14] Self-proclaimed advocates of national cultures fear that products promoted by the transnational communication industry may serve to corrupt and replace national culture. However, these products are not reproduced in all societies in the same way. They are molded according to the culture and particular historical conditions of the country.[15] This has definitely been the case with rap.

Although rap has become an international product, it still continues to address local issues, as it did in its beginnings. Geographic specificities manifest themselves through the issues that rap lyrics address and by the type of music sampled. The events that are described in Puerto Rican rap, for example, cannot be reproduced in any other part of the world.

What would provide more insight into the history, politics, and culture of Puerto Rico than the remarks made by Vico C. during the 1994 Fourth of July celebration in old San Juan?

> To the kid who asked me to autograph the
> American flag, I apologize. It's nothing
> personal, but I rather autograph those
> with only one star.

The irony in this statement is scandalously beautiful: the same rapper who participates in a Fourth of July celebration declares that as an *independentista*, he can only autograph the Puerto Rican flag. The dichotomy between *lo nacional* and *lo colonial*, as proposed by the nationalists, cannot explain in its entirety this young rapper's participation in a Fourth of July festivity and his pro-independence beliefs.

Contemporary Puerto Rican culture will continue to evolve even if the nationalist discourse, academia, and the government bureaucracy do not acknowledge the cultural value of rap. Puerto Rock and Krazy Taíno, as well as many other rappers, believe that through their art, they are "representin' [their] cultura." This statement serves to prove that the only recognition these rappers seek is their own:

> I'm into hip-hop as well as plena
> And as for those who want to battle
> Bendito que pena . . .
> I'm representin' my cultura
> Represent! Representa![16]

The Colonial State and Its "Mano Dura"

Rap, as a cultural discourse, serves to describe the personal experiences of urban youths during the latter part of the twentieth century. This generation has been affected not only by a recession but also by an official discourse that has targeted the poorest sectors. The present socio-economic crisis is often attributed to the alleged erosion of traditional values, which is thought to have caused a rise in crime rates and drug trafficking. In Puerto Rico, the so-called "Mano Dura Contra el Crimen" (anticrime policy of the Pedro Rosselló administration) is linked to a worldwide government trend that favors restricting civil rights to fight crime. The latest efforts to control Puerto Rican youths include establishing a curfew, limiting the right to bail, and censoring underground rap-reggae.[17]

Marginalized youths are the most affected by these repressive policies. Their guilt is inscribed in the state's definition of violence. James W. Messerschmidt's analysis of "criminal" violence in America also applies to "criminal" violence in Puerto Rico:

> The criminal law defines only certain kinds of violence as criminal—namely, one-on-one forms of murder, assault, and robbery, which are the types of violence young marginalized . . . males primarily engaged in. The criminal law excludes certain types of avoidable killings, injuries and thefts engaged in by powerful white males, such as maintaining hazardous working conditions or producing unsafe products.[18]

Given the biased definition of "criminal" violence, it is not surprising that the average Puerto Rican convict is nineteen years of age or younger.[19] The majority of penal facilities do not provide the best environment for the rehabilitation of most convicts. Young people also face a future with few or no employment prospects, considering that the rate of unemployment among youths is above 40 percent.[20] Ironically, those with the most economic independence are young convicts whose main source of income derives from selling drugs.[21]

However, the limited social prospects facing youths in Puerto Rico are a mere reflection of the general state of the economy. According to the 1990 U.S. census, 2.1 million people on the island (59 percent of the population) live under the poverty level. These official figures indicate that 18.1 percent of the work force was unemployed as of February 1993.

It was this social context that gave way to the rise and development of rap. This dynamic and innovative artistic expression evolved in spite of and because of the social inequalities present in our society. Rap is a counterhegemonic project that challenges different social structures by undermining the dominant discourse on violence and social inequality.

Philosophers of the Barrio: "Humble, but not Stupid"

> *I am a philosopher without a Ph.D.*
> *'cause, I graduated from the streets*
> Vico C., "El Filósofo"

As stated earlier, most youths who participate in rap culture come from poor communities. Some of the best-known interpreters of rap are Brewley M. C. (from Tras Talleres), Vico C. and Lisa M. (Puerta de Tierra), Big Boy (Barrio Obrero), and Wiso G. and Ranking Stone (Barrio Jurutungo). Vico C. explains that rap is "a product of the ghetto, and all of us who rap, whether in Puerto Rico or in the United States, come from the *caserío*."[22]

Through rap, marginalized youths offer their version of reality, which differs greatly from the "official" version provided by mass communication. For this reason, many rappers believe that their music carries on the social role of the *plena* as the "newspaper of the people." These youths, by declaring themselves the official narrators and critics of their communities' history, are defying a society that only recognizes academic historicism.[23] Rap, in response to this limited understanding of intellectual life, makes reference to the wisdom and knowledge that is acquired on the streets. Rappers who have addressed this issue include Puerto Rock, who says that "being a teenager on the streets of the Bronx in the late 70s, that was college for me";[24] Vico C., who states that he is "a philosopher without a Ph.D."; and Lisa M., who calls herself "the queen and the captain." The members of Fat Pocke's call themselves "the teachers," Prince Komazshi thinks of himself as "admirable," Alma considers that "with knowledge I wreck a nigger's behind," and Wiso G. concludes he is "the genius."

The historical approach taken in Puerto Rican rap is usually of a personal nature. The history of the community revolves around personal, everyday experiences. By narrating their everyday experiences, rappers take on the role of contemporary historians. Most of the lyrics center on the *gufeo* and the *jangueo*. The aspects of everyday life that receive the most attention are fun and desire. This discourse on pleasure is part of "conquering the present." María Milagros López explains that "this conquest entails abandoning self-sacrifice as the mediation necessary to achieve pleasure."[25]

The absence of a work ethic defined by personal sacrifice in most rap lyrics is a response to the terrible socioeconomic prospects facing most poor youths. Personal sacrifice seems pointless—given the high levels of unemployment, police brutality, restriction of civil rights, and the lack of many government services. Many rappers, for example, Wiso G., prefer to enjoy and to poeticize the pleasure that can be derived from idleness:

> I wake up on Sundays, and I want to pee
> I look out the window and see, that the sun is
> perfect for a tan
> I invite my friends, they're a bunch of thugs
> who like to trip
> We take our folding chairs and coolers
> And a little marihuana[26]

Rap, particularly underground rap, has been strongly criticized for its representation of violence. Rap has been accused of being an expression of alienated youths and of "promoting" violence and crime.[27] This simplistic view of reality and representation, however, tends to ignore the complexity of human behavior and artistic creation.

The violence present in rap music is sometimes the result of cathartic fantasies, metaphors, "sales gimmicks," everyday experiences, or simply different combinations of all the above. This "violence" usually responds to the violence of the society at large and also of many poor communities in particular. According to Tricia Rose, "the ghetto badman posture-performance is a protective shell against real unyielding and harsh social policies and physical environments."[28] In a hostile environment, being an *hijoeputa* (son of a bitch), as stated by the group N.B.H., can be both a defense mechanism and a way of proving oneself in society:

> 'cause I'm an *hijoeputa*, and fuck the rest
> 'cause we're the teachers N.B.H. and that's it[29]

The use of vulgar language (for some, "obscene") in rap is considered another form of individual and collective affirmation. Brewley M. C. comments that this type of language is necessary to reproduce accurately the crudeness of the oral expression and the harshness of life in the ghetto.[30] Artistically reproducing everyday life on the streets with accuracy means being true to the community and to oneself. However, this particular view of life in the ghetto has not been a constant in the development of Puerto Rican rap. During 1989–91, when "positive rap" hit the market, lyrics that supported the state discourse on crime, idleness, unemployment, and drugs abounded.

While positive rap remained supportive of the "Say No to Drugs" campaign, more contemporary rap has focused on ridiculing the antidrug campaign and celebrating the use of marihuana. Marihuana, as a result of this different perception, became another symbol of the marginal culture that rap sought to vindicate.

In rap, acquiring street smarts, reconstructing daily life in the margins, and celebrating marginal culture (the use of marihuana, violence, and vulgar and sexually explicit language) are presented as a collective response to a socioeconomic predicament. Puerto Rican rap has developed in a violent context where social inequalities, prejudices, and police brutality prevail. Just as in the 1980s young *cocolos* (salsa fans) were considered *títeres robacadenas*[31] (jewelry thieves), in the 1990s rappers symbolize juvenile delinquency.

The particular way in which rappers dress and carry themselves reveals a great deal about their social origins. Rappers realize that the state authorities take those outward markings of social class as a label of criminality. According to Ivy Queen:

> Us rappers are victims of discrimination
> We are also put in jail
> Just for being who we are
> Us rappers are victims of discrimination
> We are also put in jail
> Just for showing people a good time
> and getting them real high[32]

Unlike previous generations, who felt the need to validate themselves in society as "humble but decent," rappers view themselves—as graffiti on Domenech Avenue, Hato Rey, says—as "humble, but not stupid." For rappers, being "humble but decent" translates into working hard for low pay. Being "humble but smart," however, allows the possibility to earn respect as well as one's livelihood in the local community. Not sharing the ideal of previous generations that a better life awaits those who work hard, these young people prefer the life that marginal culture offers them.

In rap, the streets, as a symbol of marginal life, represent social unity. The nation and the state are not as important in defining cultural and class identity. For rappers the streets constitute the "basis" of their creativity and expression.[33] However, by describing marginal life, rappers address not only social and class issues but also racial ones. Race has been found to be an important element in class and social relations in Puerto Rico. In light of this relation, rappers address both class and race issues in their music.

"Race" and the Poetría of Identity

> *Fabrícale un casito al negro de Tomasa*
> *Que al rico no le importa lo que al pobre le pasa*
> Irie Boy, "Acapella"[34]

Since its beginnings, rap music in the United States has been characterized as questioning the existing racial and socioeconomic power structures. As in the United States, rap in Puerto Rico is a class-conscious cultural expression, where "class" is defined by both economic and racial factors. This genre, which originated in urban ghettos, seeks to validate two of the most evident elements of marginal culture—poverty and race.

The concept of race is highly controversial because of its questionable nature. Moreover, "race" is viewed differently in Puerto Rico than in the United States. This serves to prove that it is far from being a universal concept. The dominant racial discourse in Puerto Rico places more emphasis on skin color and other racial markings than on heredity. This is mostly due to the higher proportion of interracial unions (relative to the total population size) in Puerto Rico than in the United States. For example, a white-skinned person whose father happens to be black would be considered black in the United States, but probably white in Puerto Rico, where physical traits are given more weight than heredity. Moreover, in the United States there are only two major skin-color categories, black and white, whereas in Puerto Rico, there are a number of intermediate categories.[35]

Although racial prejudices exist in Puerto Rico, these have been hidden under a discourse of interracial harmony. In grade school we are taught that Puerto Ricans are the product of three unions: Spanish (white?), African (black?), and Indian (red?). However, this alleged acceptance of our interracial heritage has been used to elaborate a myth of racial harmony, where differences are constantly ignored and denied.

The fact that Puerto Rico is a racially diverse country is thought to be proof enough of our racial tolerance: "we are not racist because we are incapable of being racist." Allegedly no one can be racist because anybody's grandmother could turn out to be black ("y tu abuela ¿adonde está?"). However, when examined closely, the discourse on racial tolerance is partial in favor of Hispanic culture. Puerto Rock, a Niuyorican rapper, expresses his objection to the dominant racial discourse:

> Everything that's positive the Spaniards [supposedly] created. The Africans created the little negativity, the cooking, this and that, the music . . . nothing "important." . . . Everybody over here, the Niuyoricans, is more or less up-to-date on all that. We realize our roots lead back to Africa.[36]

Thus, I agree with Mayra Santos's remarks that the great acceptance of rap in Puerto Rico is greatly due to its acknowledgment of racial diversity:

> This is precisely the problem, not establishing [racial] differences when there are differences. The "invisible" people [of our society] found other mirrors in which to seek their reflection: those of Afro-American culture and Malcolm X t-shirts, or in the commercialized image of the Rastafari, stripped from his rebelliousness and his third utopia of escaping Babylon.[37]

Since the "official" history is partial to Hispanism, rap culture proposes a new discourse that emphasizes African culture. This new discourse, which originated in the comparatively more segregated U.S. society, fights the effects of the Puerto Rican discourse on racial integration and assimilation. The latter discourse sought to whiten the African heritage of Puerto Rico by emphasizing our tri-racial heritage.[38]

As mentioned before, there is a close relation between the phenotype of Puerto Ricans and their social origins. In poor communities the majority of the population are dark-skinned while in more affluent communities there is a stronger presence of whites.[39] As a consequence, in the popular social imaginary there is an inherent relation between being black and being poor. The concept of race in Puerto Rico depends not only on phenotypic characteristics but also on social markers, such as clothing, general appearance, attitude, and verbal and nonverbal communication.

Most rappers are considered and consider themselves black. This is due both to their dark skin and their lower-class origins. Rapper Ranking Stone, for example, has commented that in our prejudiced society, being black, poor, a rapper, and a criminal are considered interchangeable categories. He says,

> In San Juan, people from the suburbs have a different meeting place than those from the barrio. Few of them socialize, and that causes problems. . . . I see a lot of rejection. It has happened to me and my friends, just for being black and for dressing a certain way we were not allowed to enter a discotheque. They said "this is a respectable place and look how this guy from the *caserío* expects to come in here."[40]

The dominant racial ideology has been used to further the concept of an interracial society by assimilating and silencing all elements of African culture and highlighting anything white or at least "nonblack." The concept of an interracial society has been used to support racism. For this reason, rappers have ditched the interracial symbolism in favor of blackness as symbol and metaphor.

One of the strategies adopted by rappers and *diyeis* (DJs) in this process of reassigning identities is to create artistic names that have a racial connotation. Rappers such as D. J. Negro, Prieto M. C., Black Mail, Blackie D., and O. G. Black have adopted this strategy. In addition, other rappers such as Eddie Dee, Latin Empire, Twice as Much, and Three to Get Funky have used the word *nigger* in a nonpejorative way. Thus, as in North American rap, the word *nigger* has been redefined in Puerto Rican rap to allow other, more positive interpretations.

In the United States, hip-hop culture has served to analyze the racial dilemma of Puerto Rico from a different perspective. Following Mayra Santos, hip-hop culture has been the mirror of the "invisible ones."

Reflections (Remix)

Rap is the poetic and musical genre with the largest audience of Puerto Rican teenagers and young adults in their twenties. Young people, particularly from poor communities, have used this genre to articulate experiences and identities. For rappers, their marginalized communities represent a source of pride and identity. Through rap these youths can express their views about a colonial-state discourse that blames them for all the social havoc created by neoconservative and neoliberal policies. In addition, rap rejects the exclusionary definition of Puerto Rican culture proposed by the nationalist discourse.

I must admit that the title of this chapter is somewhat hyperbolic. As of yet, no one has signed a death sentence for either the state-colonial discourse or the nationalist discourse. But what is undeniable is that we continue to rap as both discourses continue to rant incoherencies.

Translated from Spanish by Marianne Negrón

Notes

1. It is of great importance to note that rap produced in Puerto Rico is neither monolithic nor homogeneous. This genre is in constant struggle, dialogue, movement, and change.

2. Rap music is highly argumentative where racial and social issues are concerned. However, it is as homophobic and misogynic as our society. On the one hand, it participates in the reconstruction of social and racial identities, but on the other, it takes part in repressing nonheterosexual identities. The preponderance of a sexist discourse in rap is also not surprising. Male chauvinism, however, is challenged by rappers such as Ivy Queen, Yezimer Carrero, Lisa M., and Sharon.

3. Jesús Delgado Burgos, "Del cable TV a la cultura del 'heavy metal,'" *Claridad*, Jan. 21, 1994, 38.

4. Fernando Clemente, "Entrando por la salida," *Claridad*, Feb. 18, 1994, 10.

5. Herbert Schiller, *Communication and Cultural Domination* (New York: M. E. Sharpe, 1976), 5.

6. Arjun Appadurai and Carol A. Breckenridge, "Why Public Culture?" *Public Culture* 1, 1 (winter 1988): 6.

7. Nicholas Garnham, "The Mass Media, Cultural Identity and the Public Sphere in the Modern World," *Public Culture* 5, 2 (winter 1993): 256.

8. Juan Flores, *Divided Borders* (Houston: Arte Público Press, 1993), 94.

9. Dick Hebdige, *Subculture: The Meaning of Style* (London: Methuen, 1980), 18.

10. Vico C., "Tradición," on *Hispanic Soul*, Prime, 1991, sound recording.

11. José Luis González, *El país de cuatro pisos y otros ensayos* (Río Piedras: Ediciones Huracán, 1989), 35.

12. George Yúdice, "We Are Not the World," *Social Text* 31/32 (1992): 208.

13. Jorge Meléndez, "La casualidad y la suerte," *El Nuevo Día*, Apr. 13, 1993, 60.

14. George Yúdice, "The Funkification of Rio," in *Microphone Fiends: Youth Music and Youth Culture*, ed. Andrew Ross and Tricia Rose (New York: Routledge, 1994), 206.

15. Néstor García Canclini, "Cultural Reconversion," in *On Edge: The Crisis of Contemporary Latin American Culture*, ed. George Yúdice, Jean Franco, and Juan Flores (Minneapolis: University of Minnesota Press, 1992), 34.

16. Puerto Rock and Tony Boston, rappers of the Latin Empire group, interview by the author, May 6, 1994, South Bronx, N.Y.

17. During the month of February 1995, the Vice Control Squadron of the Puerto Rico Police Department raided six commercial establishments in the metropolitan area for selling underground music. The sale of this music allegedly violates obscenity laws in Puerto Rico.

18. James W. Messerschmidt, *Capitalism, Patriarchy and Crime: Toward a Socialist Feminist Criminology* (Totowa, N.J.: Rowman and Littlefield, 1986), 52.

19. Trina Rivera de Ríos, "Derechos humanos y civiles: Juventud, trabajo y criminalidad," *Claridad,* Apr. 29, 1994, 9.

20. Mario Edgardo Roche, "Desempleo y falta de orientación afectan a la juventud puertorriqueña," *Diálogo,* Jan. 1994, 9.

21. Ibid.

22. Sofía Ortiz, "Más allá del enfiebre de rap," *Claridad,* Mar. 15, 1991, 20.

23. Terry Williams and Bill Kornblum, *The Uptown Kids: Struggle and Hope in the Projects* (New York: G. P. Putnam's Sons, 1994), 81.

24. Lecture by Puerto Rock and Krazy Taíno, rappers of the Latin Empire group, City College, Manhattan, N.Y., May 6, 1994.

25. María Milagros López, "Post-Work Selves and Entitlement 'Attitudes' in Peripheral Postindustrial Puerto Rico," *Social Text* 38 (spring 1994): 124.

26. Wiso G., "Me levanto los domingos," on *Sin Parar,* NRT #1012, 1994, sound recording.

27. See Yolanda Molina, "Un llamado contra el rap," *Diálogo,* Mar. 1995; José Luis Ramos Escobar, "Rap underground: Entre la censura y la ingenuidad," *Diálogo,* Mar. 1995.

28. Tricia Rose, *Black Noise: Rap Music and Black Culture in Contemporary America* (Hanover, N.H.: Wesleyan University Press, 1994), 12.

29. Underground recording by N.B.H., 1994.

30. Héctor I. Monclova Vázquez, "Los comienzos del abogado Brewley," *Claridad,* Oct. 8, 1993, 23.

31. See Ana María García, documentary film, "Cocolos y roqueros," 1993. *Cocolo* is a term used to identify those who prefer salsa. Most people who identified themselves as *cocolos* came from poor backgrounds. Given the social prejudice that allows the use of both "poor" and "delinquent" interchangeably, the term *cocolo* took on a pejorative connotation.

32. D. J. Joe, *Underground Masters Vol. 2,* Nuvo Records #0003, 1995.

33. Vico C., "Base y fundamento," on *Xplosión,* Prime, 1993, sound recording.

34. "Fabricate a case to Tomasa's *negro* / That the rich don't care what happens to the poor."

35. F. James Davis, *Who Is Black? One Nation's Definition* (University Park: Pennsylvania University Press: 1991); Clara Rodríguez, *Puerto Ricans: Born in the U.S.A.* (Boulder, Colo.: Westview Press, 1991).

36. Puerto Rock and Tony Boston, rappers of the Latin Empire group, interview by the author, May 6, 1994, South Bronx, N.Y.

37. Mayra Santos, "A veces miro mi vida," *Diálogo,* Oct. 1993, 42.

38. Halbert Barton, "The Drum-Dance Challenge: An Anthropological Study of Gender, Race and Class Marginalization of Bomba in Puerto Rico" (Ph.D. diss., Cornell University, 1995).

39. Sidney Mintz, *Caribbean Transformations* (Chicago: Aldine Publishing Co., 1974), 35.

40. Ranking Stone, interview by Patricia Vargas, *TeVe Guía,* Jan. 14, 1995, 65.

CHAPTER THIRTEEN

English Only Jamás but Spanish Only Cuidado: Language and Nationalism in Contemporary Puerto Rico

Frances Negrón-Muntaner

> *Through that language encountered at mother's knee and parted only at the grave, pasts are restored, fellowships are imagined, and futures are dreamed.* Benedict Anderson, *Imagined Communities*
>
> *Como si fueran pocas las cosas que nos dividen, volverá a dividirnos el "problema del idioma."* René Marqués, *Ensayos*[1]

At the time of the U.S. invasion of 1898, the creole elites in Puerto Rico were increasingly savoring political power over local affairs. As expectations of home rule under the incoming colonial power quickly withered away, segments of these groups discursively upheld their "Hispanic" heritage and Spanish language as a way to symbolically encase their opposition to the English-speaking "Anglos" (and their Puerto Rican pro-statehood allies) who quickly became major obstacles to their political project. The seizing of language as a metaphor by a suddenly disempowered elite should not, however, be confused with the majority's recognition of the pragmatic need and desirability of learning English.[2] This state of affairs inaugurates one of the paradoxes of language nationalism in Puerto Rico after 1898: the majorities tend to support the coexistence of both languages as the "ideal" state of affairs while using Spanish as the undisputed vernacular; at the same time, pro-autonomist and *independentista* politicians and intellectuals are bilinguals defending a Puerto Rican monolingual "essence." At the heart of both proposals is a seemingly opposed project with a substantial investment in language as a metaphor for imagining political arrangements and power alliances. Within this context of contestation, resistance to an opposing version of language metaphorization is often enacted through performances of compliance or difference. In this essay, I will become both a spectator to and critic of the language histrionics played out in Puerto Rico during the past five years, as language surfaced once more as a politically mobilizing force.

The Tongue of Citizenship: May U.S. Citizens Speak Spanish?

In the first four decades of U.S. direct rule of Puerto Rican affairs, colonial administrators experimented with diverse policies regarding language. From assuming that Puerto Ricans spoke a "patois" to recognizing the value of Spanish, from using hastily translated textbooks to using Puerto Rican writers to generate culturally "appropriate" ones, from imposing English as the medium of instruction in the first grade to making English a special subject, the ultimate policy of using Spanish as the medium of instruction was an intense struggle involving diverse sectors and interests. American policy on English acquisition was a complex, often coercive, and desperate process of producing bilingual Puerto Ricans who were to be loyal subjects (later "citizens") of the colonial state apparatus as well as disciplined laborers.

The design and implementation of language policy by people who often knew little about Puerto Rico or education but had a "moral imperative" toward the "natives" reached such absurd levels as Commissioner Edwin G. Dexter's (1907–12) education policy. Dexter proposed to teach monolingual Puerto Rican children English composition and reading skills in the first grade, even when they had never experienced English before entering the classroom. The language law of 1902 stating that both English and Spanish could be used indistinctly as "official languages" thus had several effects: it allowed the English monolingual colonial rulers to insure their right to govern without learning Spanish, it assured pro-American allies that the U.S. presence was permanent, and it served as a performance of successful assimilation for the U.S. government authorities.

From the chaos of these four decades, contemporary language nationalists have constructed at least four widely held premises that deserve a brief examination. These include that U.S. linguistic policy was aimed at destroying Puerto Rican nationality and ethnicity, that Americanization was a clear-cut and almost triumphant policy carried out in schools, that resistance to these policies was a life or death struggle between Puerto Ricans and Americans for the soul of Puerto Ricanness, and that

"Americanization" was never successful because Puerto Ricans heroically held on to their vernacular.

With few exceptions, most colonial language policies implemented in the schools were not aimed at destroying Puerto Rican nationality or ethnicity per se (that they were ignored would perhaps be a better assessment) but at fostering loyalty to the U.S. colonial project through instilling admiration for "American" history, polity, and symbols. In relation to language, education commissioners such as Martin G. Brumbaugh saw the acquisition of English as a necessary condition for rapid political integration into the United States as a state. Others acted out of an imperial sense of entitlement that prescribed that a newly acquired "territory" and thus its "natives" must speak English as the language of a higher civilization. Most, however, saw themselves as having an obligation to uplift the population through American ideals of democracy and citizenship disseminated through the public school system.

Although the extension of the school system was thought to be the means to "Americanize" the population, more than twenty years after the Americanization policies were in place, education commissioners continued to note limited school attendance. Poor attendance was primarily due to inadequate roads, illness, rain, poverty, undernourishment, double enrollment, erratic language policies, lack of funds and trained personnel, and low rates of promotion between grades.[3] In 1934, only 295,495 of 600,000 school-age children were officially enrolled.[4] Most of these children lived in urban areas, leaving the rural population (75 percent of the total) with limited access to public education.

Instead, what the rural/urban schooling dichotomy initially reinforced was the reproduction and radicalization of class differences. Given the fact that most rural children dropped out of school after the third grade, perhaps the only limited success of schooling was the enforcing of new forms of discipline, obedience, and basic literacy. Among the mostly urban children that attended school on a more regular basis, Americanization was an attempt to generate loyalty to U.S. national and imperial narratives while circulating a citizenship discourse, which ultimately backfired. Culturally speaking, "Americanization" during this period had a limited impact; the policy never had the massive resources needed to fully implement it, nor did the process rely on a set of politically sophisticated strategies to effectively counteract "native" resistance.

Despite the relative failure of the Americanization policies, those schoolchildren and teachers who formally submitted to it quickly came to resist under the guise of performance. Pedro Cebollero, a witness to the "patriotic" exercises imposed on the schools, wrote that these attempts were, at best, "naive." In a widely quoted passage usually used to point to the effectiveness of Americanization, Cebollero instead questions its impact:

> The writer saw groups of second and third grade pupils conducting meetings which Commissioner Huyke calls "English Clubs," where parliamentary rules were "*observed*," meetings called to order, motions made and seconded, in *parrot-like* fashion. Teachers were forced to give extra time to the oral English exercise in order to make a *good showing* before supervisors; distinguished visitors were taken to observe special classes where pupils went through their *stunts; special drills* were prepared at the central office to secure phrasing and intonation in the spoken English of the pupils.[5]

Considering that during the most intense Americanization process (first four decades), most children were still not in school all day nor were their teachers "properly Americanized," one can only read these successful reports with suspicion. Not only were administrators under considerable pressure to demonstrate significant "improvement" toward the goal of literacy, bilingualism, and Americanization, but also the supervisor's reports often narrated performances acted out exclusively for them and not reflective of any "progress" in the policy's twin goals of English competency and loyalty to "America."

Along with the most transparent aspects of the "Americanization" policies (English, patriotic exercises, compulsory education) was the irony that the schools were designed to produce secular, patriotic *citizens* capable of sovereign action. As Commissioner Paul G. Miller suggested in 1915, the duty of the rural school was to "convert our rural people into citizens capable of maintaining the sovereignty of the state. . . . We cannot hope to establish democratic institutions upon a safe and lasting foundation without first reducing that enormous mass of illiterates."[6] Unlike the concerns of the local elites, who battled for the founding of a university under Spain to no avail, the United States' main concern was with primary education geared to restructure the labor force. High schools, normal schools, vocational schools, and the first Puerto Rican university (1903) quickly followed, however, soon becoming a colonial battleground.

Despite the claims of contemporary nationalists, the language war at the beginning of the century was not a confrontation between Puerto Ricans and Americans embodying opposing interests among *nationals*. It is important to note that some of the most retrograde linguistic policies were designed and carried out by pro-statehood Puerto Ricans, while some of the most level-headed curriculums were proposed by American academics. Juan B. Huyke, for example, opposed a 1913 bill that sought to make Spanish the language of instruction in Puerto Rico, and as education commissioner in 1915, he later claimed that under his leadership, "our schools are agencies of Americanism. They must implant the spirit of America within the hearts of our children."[7]

Furthermore, it was also Huyke who started the chapters of the School Society for the Study of the English Language, which required members to wear a small American flag in the buttonhole and to speak English among themselves. The commissioner was also responsible for the English clubs (where parliamentary procedure was "observed"), a pen-pal project where Puerto Rican children would correspond with U.S. children (beginning their letters as "Dear Sisters and Brothers"), the prohibition of school papers written in Spanish, and the intensification of the teaching of English. Under pressure to please Washington and to not create any obstacles to political incorporation, he also dismissed a study by Columbia University suggesting that Spanish should be the primary medium of instruction until the seventh grade.[8]

Unlike many contemporary nationalist versions of past language struggles, the increased tension around the imposition of English had less to do with popular resistance to the English language and more to do with a multiplicity of conditions created by U.S. colonial rule. In addition to the deep resentment of certain local elites, the massive expansion of the school apparatus created an unprecedented number of relatively educated Puerto Ricans who became critical of the status quo. These sectors included both radicalized high school students and teachers. Because of the often punitive measures taken toward teachers, forcing them to show immediate willingness to learn English, this sector became restless, although they never opposed the teaching of English itself. From 1899 onward, local teachers were mass reproduced only to be exploited, monitored, and disciplined. The humiliations endured by the teachers were many, including higher pay for U.S.-born teachers, a requirement that the English examination grades be printed on a teacher's certificate (1902), the unconditional adherence to the regime (1918), and the solidification of the rural/urban dichotomy, which meant different salaries, prestige, and upward mobility opportunities (finally abolished in 1931). Although those who accommodated the demand for English were compensated with training, trips to the United States, and the promise of up-ward mobility, the Teachers Association, formed in 1911,[9] sought politi-cal remedies for the situation. Among the demands were that Spanish should be the medium of instruction and that English should be taught as a special subject.

Many Americans saw the acquisition of English as a precondition to U.S. citizenship. Puerto Ricans, however, were made citizens not only without consultation but also without this requirement.[10] While the im-position of citizenship polarized the political leadership (autonomists expressed ambivalence, *independentistas* rejected citizenship, and social-ists and republicans welcomed it), what was at stake was not the issue of saving the Puerto Rican "vernacular" but whose interests were to be served by the local state apparatus, as embodied by the public school system.

If "good American citizenship" was understood at the time as the willingness to support the colonial status quo and to submit to state mandates such as war, modernization, compulsory schooling, and hy-giene, then most Puerto Ricans became "better" U.S. citizens when the local elites were allowed some degree of home rule and a populist coali-tion brought on a modernization project with tangible benefits for a sub-stantial number of Puerto Ricans. The elite's home rule also brought a Spanish policy that satisfied most political sectors and pragmatically re-defined Americanization not in "cultural" but in "political" terms. With the implementation of the Villaronga policy in 1949, allowing Spanish as the medium of instruction with English as a special subject (first pro-posed by José Padín in 1934 but resisted in Washington), the acquisition of English became a "linguistic" issue and not one of transmitting "American" culture. This is an important distinction since the policy un-settled the equivalencies between American citizenship, English, and democracy. At the same time, "American values" such as high consump-tion rates, home ownership, literacy, and representative democracy effected a broad-based consensus around the commonwealth option as these values took on concrete meaning in people's lives. Thus, under Muñoz Marín, Puerto Ricans—in Spanish and reproducing state-sanctioned cultural nationalism—became more effectively "American-ized" than in the first fifty years of U.S. rule, when it was carried out as a matter of "policy" in the schools.[11]

Simultaneously, as the general welfare of many Puerto Ricans began to improve slowly, most tended to associate English with upward mobility, resisting any attempt to curtail access to learning English. A Brookings Institute study published in 1930 supports this claim:

> An opportunity to learn English, no matter how imperfectly and adequately, is one of the magnets that draws the children of the poorer classes to the public schools. To tens of thousands of the disinherited in Puerto Rico, a knowledge of that language seems to promise—perhaps fallaciously—a better economic future. Popular willingness to make sacrifices for the schools is in some degree due to this pathetic faith.[12]

A second example of the popular faith in English was the attack on parts of Padín's 1934 proposal, which sought to provide English according to the perceived "need" of the child. This policy would have potentially blocked access to rural children, who allegedly did not "need" to master English.

In sum, even though language can be mobilized as a way of creating solidarities, these can also be effected through the metaphorization of languages one may not speak or read well or at all. Today, it can be argued, many of the new social identities challenging the status quo in Puerto Rico are made possible by the globalization of culture (in English or in translation), while defenders of language nationalisms—in Spanish or English—are proposing more effective ways to perpetuate the existing power inequities at the expense of most of the population.

Performing the Republic: The "Spanish Only" Revolt Is in/for English

Unlike the earlier chapter of the language war, when the outcome of the debate affected specific sectors such as teachers and rural students, today's debate is mostly a simulacrum. Despite its symbolic importance and cultural impact, the Spanish First legislation (1991) produced little change. It excluded the school system and trade transactions, thus making Spanish the official language only of the "government." Conveniently, government agencies and professional organizations adversely affected by the law could seek exemption (although only the governor could dispense these), annulling the law's impact. Given this paradox, the political meaning of a law that did not seek to change anything must be looked for elsewhere.

In order to fully understand the Spanish First spectacle, it is important to mention that one of the most relevant contexts for the signing of the legislation was the aborted 1989 congressional plebiscite bill. For multiple reasons, including debates around the binding nature of the plebiscite as well as fiscal and cultural questions, the bill was ultimately forgotten. However, during the two years of negotiation between the Energy and Natural Resources Committee and the three major political parties in Puerto Rico, some widely circulated premises of both the statehood and independence proposals were critically challenged. Senator Bennett Johnson clearly stated that any insistence on cultural autonomy was best left out of any plebiscite discussion since it would kill the statehood option in Congress. It was also made clear to the *independentistas* that the United States would not be obligated to invest in an independent national economy, nor would Congress recognize the republic's full autonomy (Puerto Rico would remain a U.S. military zone). Because of the dramatic increase of pro-statehood sentiment in Puerto Rico after the 1967 plebiscite, and the political and/or fiscal resistance in Washington, autonomist and pro-independence sectors assumed that statehood only needed one more fatal blow—language nationalism.

Despite the political expediency of this strategy, the process leading to the signing of the Spanish First legislation was riddled with ironies. Not only were some of the legislation's proponents defending it by making rhetorical alliances with anti-Spanish/Latino language nationalists in the United States, but the law itself created mayhem for many government administrators and employees, who thought the law was not, as it proposed to affirm, a reflection of Puerto Rico's "Spanish" reality.

In making alliances with the rhetoric of the English Only movement in the United States, the language nationalists proposed that both nations had the "right" to defend their vernaculars and national values against intrusion. That in the mainland context those "intruders" included a significant number of Puerto Ricans and other Latinos and that those "values" might be racism and intolerance were a marginal part of the discussion. This tactical alliance clarified that for language nationalists, the symbolic construction of Puerto Rico as a nation equal to the United States is more relevant in the consolidation of a "postcolonial" national power base than questioning the oppressive power relations between Puerto Rico and the United States or among Puerto Ricans.

In a strategic move by the anti-Spanish officialization press, many opponents of the legislation named it "Spanish Only" (in English) as a way of ridiculing the measure and mockingly linking it to English Only efforts in the United States. This political move was important since the official Spanish legislation became discursively defined by its opponents. Even when the administration attempted to popularize its own conception of the legislation as "Spanish First,"[13] the Spanish Only label stuck in part by its repeated use in the popular media and the press and the readership's familiarity with the U.S. English Only movement. Some "Spanish First" proponents attempted to counter the image made by this significant symbolic victory by suggesting that referring to the legislation as Spanish Only was a gross translation that only showed the colonization of the island and its deformities:

> Es una transposición del inglés que pretende dar a las rosas el olor que no tienen. Revela, además, el fracaso del bilingüismo entre nosotros, porque tomada de la frase "English Only", resulta a todas luces una pésima traducción, puesto que se trata de cosas distintas en su significación y alcance.[14]

> [It is a transposition from the English language that aims at giving roses a smell they do not have. Furthermore, it reveals the failure of bilingualism among us, because it is borrowed from the "English Only" phrase, which is ultimately a terrible translation, since (each law) refers to very different things in both their meaning and scope.]

"Translation," however, is a misreading of a self-conscious strategy to limit the measure's reception as "progressive" by associating it with a reactionary movement. In this sense, "Spanglish" was an important resource during the controversy, acting as a source of creativity, parody, and political alignment (on both sides). Thus, for example, many press headlines and punch lines used Spanglish to stress a point. Examples include the headline "It's Official" for the day Pedro Rosselló reversed the law and Lola Aponte's conclusion in a newspaper column: "El inglés, según nos promete *Peter* Rosselló, nos igualará a los norteamericanos." (English, according to Peter Rosselló's promise, will make us equal to the Americans.)[15] It was perhaps this unnoticed detail that best captured the fact that most readers of the press could be effectively interpellated as bilingual interlocutors and not exclusively monolingual. Without this bilingual competency, the political parodies of the press would have been incomprehensible and unconvincing and ultimately an argument in favor of what Spanish First claimed.

The Spanish First legislation also partly constituted a performance for a U.S. audience, already receptive to its message. Despite the fact that not all Congress members understood Spanish First as Spanish Only, the measure had its desired effect among the most conservative sectors. The pro-autonomist and independence forces were counting on this response, as they (correctly) believe that conservative interests in the United States constitute their strongest allies against congressional approval of statehood for Puerto Rico. This anti-democratic strategy seeks to mobilize the most bigoted and racist mainland political sectors to crush popular sentiment in favor of permanent U.S.-Puerto Rico association.

Within this calculation, it is not surprising that some members of Congress immediately sought to punish the *malagradecidos* who do not want to "speak English." Legislators such as Congressman Richard Schulze, Republican representative from Pennsylvania, for instance, sent letters to all House members condemning the Spanish law as "a harsh slap in the face to American taxpayers"[16] and immediately found five cosponsors to eliminate Section 936 of the Internal Revenue Code. The English First organization also publicly advocated for Puerto Rico's right to be separate and independent. Privately, the group also asked members to donate money to impede statehood efforts.[17]

Finally, while it is possible to read the Spanish First as a progressive nationalist strategy against colonial domination (particularly from the United States), the many layers of the process suggest that it was an attempt made by pro-autonomists, *independentistas*, and intellectuals to gain symbolic power and test the strength of political alliances against the statehood project and its supporters, many of whom are poor and black. A closer look at the language used to imagine the nation in relation to Spanish and English provides critical ways to engage with the question of how each of these discourses proposes to create (or limit) spaces for broader political participation by Puerto Ricans.

The Tropes That Bind: Spanish in the Nationalist Imagination

Many of the most circulated sets of tropes for Spanish among the writings of language nationalists uphold racial, sexual, and gender hierarchies. This tendency is not surprising since as Doris Sommer has written in the context of Latin American national romances, "the language of love, specifically of productive sexuality in the domestic sphere, is remarkably coherent despite the programmatic differences among the nation-building novels."[18]

Within the context of the metaphorization of Spanish in Puerto Rico, imagined sexual exchanges are represented as historically inevitable and pleasurable. The "pleasure" of these encounters is made possible by the assumption of symmetrical social relations where hierarchies along the lines of race, gender, and class do not exist. Writer Luis Rafael Sánchez, for instance, defines Puerto Rican Spanish as "Puertorriqueño del hablar dulce y cadencioso, hablar del viejo amor entre las negritas dingas y los peninsulares retóricos" (a sweet and rhythmic Puerto Rican form of speech, a way of speaking about the old romance between the little black dingas and the rhetorical Spaniards).[19] The idea that the "origins" of Puerto Rican Spanish are to be found in the "love" between white men and African (and native women) is consistent with the nationalist tendency to view the nation as a horizontal relationship between equals.[20] Nonetheless, in Salvador Tió's formulation of the "miracle" of Spanish, his language betrays the violence through which Spanish—understood as a "biological" attribute—was imposed on the bodies of the colonized, signified as women: "La letra con sangre entra y el español la entró en el cuerpo de la india y de la negra, sin miramientos y sin aspavientos. ¿Y cómo pensar que lo que se hizo por amor se pierda por decreto?" (Blood takes the word in, and the Spaniard, without shame or fuss, entered it through the bodies of native and black women. So, how can we lose by decree that which was created by love?)[21]

Ironically, despite the generalized acceptance of the *mestizaje* implicit in the sexual metaphors, many commentators do not accept the notion that Puerto Ricans are also racially and culturally *mestizos* or that various articulations of Puerto Rican cultures and ethnicities coexist. Severo Colberg, for example, wrote: "El idioma no es un café con leche. De origen hispánico, somos desendiente de una civilización, la hispánica, a la que Lope de Vega, Cervantes, De Hostos y García Márquez añadieron gloria." (Language is not like a cup of coffee and milk. Hispanic in origin, we are descendants of a civilization, the Hispanic civilization, to which Lope de Vega, Cervantes, De Hostos, and García Márquez added glory.)[22] In this case, "café con leche" can also be read as a racial designation for the mulatto, in opposition to the "pure" claim to Hispanic ancestry. The hostility of considering racial conflicts as legitimate areas of political intervention is summarized in Juan Manuel Carrión's defense of Hispanic ethnic (national) identity as opposed to a politicized "racial" (i.e., black) ethnic identity:

> Es necesario que hagamos una distinción entre mitos y rituales que promueven la cohesión nacional y el proyecto independentista y mitos

y rituales para la disolución nacional y a través de la participación
como miembro en las luchas políticas de las minorías étnicas
norteamericanas. Al proyecto nacional que Puerto Rico necesita no le
hace falta que le agraven las fisuras raciales.[23]

[It is necessary to distinguish between myths and rituals that promote
national cohesion and a pro-independence project, and myths and rituals toward national dissolution through participating as members in
the political struggles of ethnic minorities in the United States. The
national project that Puerto Rico needs can do without the deepening
of racial fissures.]

Despite the hegemony of the image of Spanish as *la letra* (feminine),
which in turn is offered to the creole male through the *mestiza's* milk,[24]
the feminization of Spanish should not be confused with the patriarchal
implications of the metaphor (best signified by its Spanish designation of
el español). Women are the vehicles for the reproduction of the nation,
but its spaces are the privileged arenas for "intercourse" among male nationals. Given this discourse's investment in Spanish as simultaneously
the language of the beloved past empire, the embodiment of the elite's
cultural/ethnic matrix, and the sign of their claims to political power, it is
not surprising that another cluster of metaphors refers to the fear that
Spanish will become, under certain political arrangements, the language
of the "kitchen" (i.e., of women).

Furthermore, the "kitchen" becomes a fearful image, not only because it refers to feminine confinement, but because it connotes (vamp)
sneakiness. An example of this usage is Victoria Muñoz's critical claim
that the statehooders were "entering statehood through the kitchen."[25]

Antilanguage nationalists also deployed sexual tropes in writing
about language, although with significantly less frequency. Jesús Hernández suggested that Puerto Rican culture and language are so strong that
legislating them can only be read as a sign of weakness where the legisla-
tor (identified as male) acts out of a fear of "acostarse con una mujer por
temor a salir impotente" (sleeping with a woman for fear of revealing
himself to be impotent).[26] Although Spanish (*la lengua*) is again feminine, the Puerto Rican language has such virility that there is no need to
legislate it, that is, to protect it. At the same time, Hernández is quick to
point out that his decline of sleeping with the "mother tongue" does not
mean that he makes "genuflexiones al coloso del norte" (gives a blow job
to Uncle Sam). In both formulations, the phantom of weakness (homosexuality) and female virility (lesbianism) are sources of anxiety through

denial (maleness is not threatened), rather than condemned under the sign of "ambiguity."

In the context of the bilingual Puerto Ricans, particularly the ones raised in the United States, feminization comes packaged in the notion of the *medio hombre* (half man). Popularized by Epifanio Fernández Vanga and Antonio S. Pedreira during the 1930s, this position holds that "un niño que vive dos idiomas no llega a ser nunca un *hombre doble*; se queda siempre en *medio hombre*" (a child that lives two languages never grows up to be a double man; he always remains a half man).[27] In this scenario, bilingualism becomes a metaphor for ambiguity, cultural disorders, and political passivity:

> Muchos de ellos [puertorriqueños en EU] han descubierto en carne y sangre como la presión desmesurada y ala trágala de la lengua inglesa ha resultado en el desorden comunicativo que en el mejor de los casos solemos llamar "Spanglish": una especie de media lengua que frecuentemente corta el acceso humano, comunicativo y expresivo no sólo con otros congéneres hispanohablantes sino con los angloparlantes.[28]

> [Many of them (Puerto Ricans in the U.S.) have experienced in their own flesh and blood how the excessive pressure of the English language has resulted in the communicative disorder that in the best of cases we refer to as "Spanglish": a sort of half tongue that frequently cuts communicative, expressive, and human access to other Spanish- and English-speaking people.]

The notion that only standardized language practice can produce "ideas" is another major premise of a discourse that unambiguously constructs the intellectual as the caretaker of language and, hence, a privileged political figure in the building of the nation. Rafael Castro Pereda, an educator and one of the most invested voices in this debate, explicitly claimed the relationship between the capacity to think and master standard language practices in his "master lecture" at the Cayey College:

> La falta de dominio en el idioma nacional produce en amplias capas de nuestra sociedad una enorme incapacidad para el pensamiento abstracto, fundamental para una adecuada percepción de las complejidades de la vida y el mundo actuales.[29]

> [The inability to master the national language produces among broad segments of our society an enormous incapacity for abstract thought, a fundamental skill for the adequate perception of the complexities of today's life and world.]

Because intellectuals are the self-proclaimed guardians of language, popular linguistic practice can also be taken as a challenge to their authority. Intellectuals thus tend to thrive on the "problem" of language since, in their eyes, they are the only ones who can truly "heal" it. Thus, the insistence on schooling by intellectuals is often coupled with fears about social and political upheaval among the disenfranchised, underlining the intellectual sector's close ties to the state, its ideological project, and apparatus:

> La lengua es lo que la gente debe hablar. Si no lo sabe, se le enseña.... Evitar ese desastre [corrupción de la lengua] debe ser labor conjunta de la conciencia de los hombres individualmente considerados, y sobre todo del Estado.[30]

> [Language is what people should speak. If they do not know how to, it should be taught to them.... The prevention of this disaster (the corruption of language) should entail the labor of each individual man's consciousness, and, above all, the state.]

Generally, what nationalist characterizations of popular and bilingual language practices attempt is to stigmatize these forms of speech as inferior and hence in an uncanny replication of colonial discourses to signify the incapacity of self-representation, cultural autonomy, and political action by subordinated social groups. Central to the articulation of this fear is the ironic and obsessive repetition of a single word: *tartamudo* (stutterer).

Tar-tar-tar-tar-tar-ta-mu-do: Stuttering Clashes

According to most defenders of the official Spanish legislation, Puerto Ricans who have been raised bilingual in Puerto Rico or the United States are a race of *tartamudos*, unable to communicate either in English or Spanish:

> La ambiguedad linguística, como bien señala el autor recién citado, podría terminar convirtiéndonos en una sociedad tarada por una terrible tartamudez idiomática, por una especie de gaguera colectiva que terminase sumiéndose en el triste universo de unas generaciones que no hablan ni escriben con propiedad y corrección ni una lengua ni la otra, y permanecen engomadas ante la pantalla del televisor, viendo y escuchando, en inglés—gracias a la magia del Cable TV—la última canción que les trae quién sabe cuál de los últimos intérpretes del rock norteamericano.[31]

[Linguistic ambiguity, as the former author so well indicates, could well end up transforming us into a society incapacitated by a terrible linguistic stuttering, by a form of collective tongue-tiedness, which would end up by confounding itself with the sad universe of generations who neither speak nor write with propriety or accuracy Spanish or English, and instead remain stuck to a TV screen, watching and listening in English—thanks to the magic of cable TV—the last hit song of the latest American rock singer.]

Interestingly, the word *barbaroi* in its classical Greek usage also meant "stutterer,"[32] thus supporting the notion that she or he who cannot speak "properly" must be a barbarian. A critical element in the use of this metaphor is the notion that he or she who cannot speak correctly cannot properly organize reality, construct value hierarchies, or think intelligently:

Tengo por verdad como la catedral que la raíz de ese fenómeno [crisis de valores] está en la falta de dominio de nuestro idioma, porque al perder el dominio de la realidad—la exterior a nosotros y la interior—se acaba perdiendo la capacidad de jerarquizar los sentimientos, las ideas, las personas y las cosas.[33]

[I hold to be as true as the cathedral that the root of this crisis of values is the lack of mastery over our native language, because once mastery over reality is lost—both in the exterior and interior—one ends up losing the capacity to hierarchically organize feelings, ideas, people, and things.]

The emphasis on good Spanish also represents an attempt to stop the creation of new intellectual competencies (for example, the Spanglish specialist, the hip-hop critic, the postmodern guru, the English dominant Puerto Rican intellectual) and the rapid transformation of Puerto Rican Spanish into a vernacular that these elites cannot understand, identify with, or master. However, in opposition to this proposition, an engagement with some of the cultural production of the so-called stutterers suggests that far from being unilingual, atrophied, or alienated, forms such as rap and graffiti are extremely sophisticated poetic and musical constructs using and understanding language in precise and politically astute ways.

Within this context, it is provocative to note that one of rap's most distinctive lyrical strategies is the repetition of sound, analogous to the "stutterer" way of speaking. As Tricia Rose remarks, "African melodic phrases 'tend to be short and repetition is common; in fact, repetition is one of the characteristics of African music.' "[34] In taking rap as a counter-metaphor to the "stutterer," I intend to suggest that the *tartamudo* is in sync with significant Puerto Rican cultural realities for which the language nationalists have no vocabulary for, and that they are, in fact, speechless.

Ventana Window y Pluma Pen

Puerto Rican rap is a product of the globalization of culture, black diasporic cultural production, the valorization of slang and popular speech, the blurring of strict language boundaries, and the open proposal of other cultural solidarities based on class and race.[35] Contrary to the obsession with origins, rap is concerned with making the past present, as part of the texture of everyday life, resistance, and creativity.[36] Its dissemination is often underground, and its function that of consolidating urban poor, (mostly) black identities.

Even a superficial brush with Puerto Rican bilingual raps, poetry, and everyday exchanges points not only to their "grammatical" use of English and Spanish,[37] but to the creative and binding possibilities of "Spanglish" (or *inglañol*) as a linguistic practice:

> Indeed, the most important contributions of US Latina/o writers to American literature lie not only in the multiple cultural and hybrid subjectivities that they textualize, but also in the new possibilities for metaphors, imagery, syntax and rhythms that the Spanish subtexts provide literary English.[38]

Furthermore, and perhaps more terrifying to some, exchange between languages can create challenging expressive possibilities for the "dominant" languages that incorporate the experiences and desires of other groups. As performance artist Gómez Peña says, "I am interested in subverting English structures, infecting English with Spanish and in finding new possibilities of expression within the English language that English-speaking people don't have."[39] Within these formulations, "Spanglish" is not a language or "dialect" but a resource, a practice of destabilizing and multiplying meanings, a form of articulating hybrid personal and social experiences.

It is important to note that the negative connotation attached to bilingualism as a "half tongue" refers not to bilingualism itself but to linguistic exchange between practices considered not "standard." Thus, he or she who speaks and writes "perfect" English and Spanish is enriched by having access to the Western canon through the "classics" (Shakespeare, Cervantes, and García Márquez), while those who speak and write variants of Puerto Rican/Black English and/or popular Spanish are considered illiterate. Simultaneously, speakers with diverse levels of bilingual competence are confused, rather than just competent at different levels.

The intellectual's sorting of competencies is a way to reinforce their power over contestation by dictating what language use is "correct" and what types of speech can produce an intelligent "thought." It is not unusual—when commenting on the "poverty" of young bilingual speakers in the United States and Puerto Rico—to note how badly they do in standardized tests. Yet, standardized tests do not "measure" language competence but rather skills in a specific domain of language use. "Uneducated" speakers can deploy equally sophisticated linguistic strategies as evidenced by comparing a "high-culture" short story such as "Pollito Chicken" by Ana Lydia Vega[40] to "Puerto Rican in the U.S.A.," a rap written by English-dominant KMX Assault.[41]

In both cases, frequent (and grammatically correct) code switching, puns on English and/or Spanish pronunciation, and the juxtaposition of both languages generate parody, humor, and political commentary. Through these textual strategies, both texts assume and help create a bilingual, bicultural reader/listener who is competent in sorting these codes. The difference between the texts does not reside in their "quality" (the effective literary use of English and Spanish) but in their radically different political proposals. For Vega, "Spanglish" is equivalent to assimilation, self-hatred, and buying into the American dream:

> Aprender a hablar good English, a recoger el thrash que tiraba como
> savage en las calles y a comportarse como decent people era lo que
> tenían que hacer y dejarse de tanto fuss.[42]

Yet, for KMX, Spanish, English, and Spanglish are different ways to articulate a U.S.-Puerto Rican location and generate solidarities:

> We do our thing with much respect
> we speak two lingoes and have our own dialect
> In effect, don't you know
> We swing low con mucho orgullo
> Despierta boricua, defiende lo tuyo . . .
> My abuelita says la vida es dura
> Levántate, Boricua! wakin' up es la cura

Orgulloso, proud of my heritage
Echar pa'lante with my people is my imperative . . . [43]

While for Vega, Spanish is inevitably linked to independence through the body—as Suzie Bermiudez comes at the hands of the "local specimen" bartender in "Pollito Chicken," she screams, "Viva Puerto Rico Libre"—"Puerto Rican in the U.S.A." makes use of a mix of left and U.S. minority pride discourses to resignify the notion of "making it" in terms of community survival and ethnic solidarity.

The Future of the Past: Laws That Perform

In addition to generating press coverage as a stage for circulating alternative narratives regarding language legislation, the signing of each of the laws (Spanish First and English Also) constituted scripted performances that broadened the audience and were intended to consolidate alliances around specific political proposals. In each case, language policy played a significant role in imagining Puerto Rico as either an autonomous republic or state of the union.

The Partido Popular Democrático's administration proceeded with the signing of the 1991 legislation on the basis that Spanish had been Puerto Ricans' mother tongue for the past "500 years." Given that Puerto Ricans were not constituted as Puerto Rican "nationals" until the late nineteenth century (distinctions were made between *criollos* or *del país* and *peninsulares*), that the inhabitants of Puerto Rico spoke different languages during the disputed 500 years, and that today a substantial number of Puerto Ricans have English as their native tongue, this construction is, at best, inaccurate. In this sense, rather than an attempt to "reflect reality," the Spanish First legislation was a staging of a possibility and at best a rehearsal where a potential change (the Associated Republic?) was given what Eric Hobsbawm calls "the sanction of precedent, social continuity and natural law as expressed in history."[44] Interestingly, the legislation itself contained a historical inaccuracy: it suggested that Puerto Ricans had been speaking Spanish since 1492, when in fact the island of Borikén was claimed by Columbus in 1493.[45]

The signing of the Spanish First bill was staged in a luxury environment, the Performing Arts Center, on April 5, 1991.[46] It was a black-tie "solemn" event[47] for which the stage (significantly) included the following artifacts: podium, U.S. and Puerto Rican flags, and the U.S. and Puerto Rico shields.[48] A quartet opened the act with a composition by Mozart, and *jíbaros* (the mythic white peasants of the countryside) sang *décimas*, a Spanish literary and oral form. Because the main hall could not seat a large gathering, "minor" supporters were provided with monitors in more modest nearby halls. The attendees were mostly well-known local and international politicians and intellectuals, including the president of the Real Academia Española de la Lengua, and the directors of the language academies of Venezuela, Colombia, and the Dominican Republic. Spanish writer and Nobel Prize winner Camilo José Cela also was in attendance.[49]

The bill was not taken to popular vote; it was passed by a Partido Popular Democrático legislative majority. Outside of the Performing Arts Center, the Police Association staged a "symbolic" demonstration against the new law. The governor's message proclaimed the event as one of national definition/performance: "nos definimos ante nuestros ciudadanos de los Estados Unidos y ante el mundo . . . [como] un pueblo culturalmente diferenciado" (we define ourselves to our fellow U.S. citizens and to the world . . . as a culturally differentiated people).[50] Because of this cultural difference, Hernández Colón claimed to "thunderous applause" that the United States would not grant Puerto Rico statehood. Within this discourse, U.S. citizenship became a contingent part of Puerto Rican identity against biology, race, and culture. The relative disdain in which U.S. citizenship was treated here contrasts with its defense in an ad written in English and carried in the *New York Times* "explaining" the Spanish First legislation as one consistent with U.S. citizen loyalty, as "over 15,000 Puerto Ricans in American uniforms" were returning "from the Middle East." Most importantly, Colón summarized the pitfalls of both the statehood and U.S. hegemonic independence projects: "What we have found is a dignified and respectful relationship in which economic integration and national security are shared, while our cultural differences are celebrated, protected and enjoyed."[51] Thus, in between both performances and targeted audiences, the pie is so divided: the U.S. military and exploitative economic interests can "have" Puerto Rican labor and bodies in exchange for federal transfers fostering relative social peace. Puerto Rican intellectuals only ask for symbolic hegemony, free of U.S. "cultural" intervention.[52]

English Also

A year after the signing of the Spanish First legislation, the Partido Nuevo Progresista won the 1992 election. One of Governor Rosselló's campaign promises was the elimination of the official Spanish law through partisan legislation. In contrast to the signing of the Spanish First legislation, the English Also bill was signed in a "popular" setting: the Luis. A. Ferré Parque de las Ciencias. Ferré is the founder of the pro-statehood New Progressive Party and one of its major ideologues, responsible for the *estadidad jíbara* formulation. Rosselló's performance was without the solemnity characterizing the earlier ceremony and was for a different audience: the Puerto Rican poor. Journalist Jorge Luis Medina described the ceremony:

> Rosselló signed his law under a tarp, flanked by his wife Irma and the child Belén Rubio, 8, who a year-and-a-half ago gave him a pen and made him promise that he would sign the law with it. Instead of singers, Rosselló had the National Guard band playing. Instead of the Policemen's Association, members of the Teacher's Federation picketed outside. . . . And while the party faithfuls also made an appearance at Bayamón, they took second place to the children.[53]

Although some criticism was voiced regarding the "use" of children as props during the ceremony, the casting of children was essential to Rosselló's performance. Despite the fact that the school system was never affected by Spanish First, pro-statehood associations seized upon the fear that upward mobility through the school system would be curtailed to critique Spanish First as an elitist measure. Pro-statehood leader Miriam Ramírez de Ferrer savored the opportunity to stress that "Jaime Fuster, quien teniendo que utilizar el inglés en su trabajo, no le importa que los niños puertorriqueños no puedan aspirar a esa posición por no hablar inglés" (Jaime Fuster, who has to use English as part of his job, does not care that Puerto Rican children will not be able to aspire to his position because they do not know English).[54] Although these claims were groundless—at least in the short term—the seizing of children and the schools as metaphors for assured prosperity was consistent with the statehooders' equation of English, technology, modernization (and therefore statehood) as a formula for assuring the well-being and progress of future generations. As Luis Ferrao has written, it is the association of these historical transformations with English and the United States that allowed Rosselló to simply conclude that "'El inglés es progreso'" (English is progress).[55]

At face value, it seems evident that the Partido Popular Democrático's proposal is "elitist" and the Partido Nuevo Progresista's "popular" (or perhaps more accurate, "populist"). Yet, both attempted to consolidate monolithic notions of language and power while avoiding any critique of the intricacies of colonialism. The Spanish First ceremony stressed Hispanic "roots," thus glossing over the black heritage of a substantial number of Puerto Ricans. It also sought international recognition and increased autonomy but understood only as "power" over the island's "cultural" affairs, leaving actual colonial relations intact.

The English Also signing pointed to an unfounded faith in the "unfinished" project of modernity where federal transfers and assured high consumption standards would guarantee a high quality of life. Because of current reshiftings in the global economy and U.S. responses to this restructuring, "progress" under these terms can only be translated as intensified policing aimed at "protecting" the shrinking middle classes from *la chusma*. Not only do these scenarios not constitute "progress," but as the U.S. congress proceeds to destroy the welfare state and construct Puerto Rico as a fiscal burden and political headache, these premises are far from assured during the next decade.[56]

The statehood movement's assumption that the mastery of English will result in increased material possibilities for Puerto Ricans as well as the enjoyment of the "plenitude of our rights as American citizens"[57] is critically misleading. At the heart of these premises lies the notion that "citizenship" is a purely judicial concept that is not already embedded in a web of inequities, including those based on class, race, gender, and sexuality.[58] Not only is the exercise of full citizenship inaccessible to many English-speaking Americans (African Americans, Latinos, gays and lesbians, and poor whites), but political participation requires social transformations that include the claiming of economic, cultural, gender, racial, and sexual rights. As in the autonomist proposal, the statehooders also refuse to challenge the ways in which Puerto Rico, under statehood, could remain in a subordinate position to hegemonic regional U.S. interests. Finally, consistent with a restricted sense of the political sphere, both parties engaged in public simulacra and private negotiation with Washington instead of advocating for popular and mass participation. This position was evidenced when all parties had little trouble agreeing to exclude U.S. Puerto Ricans, who under United Nations decolonization guidelines are entitled to vote.

The fragility of both political proposals can be evaluated by looking at the several immediate reversals that each party suffered. The Partido Popular Democrático's efforts created alliances not only with local intellectuals but also with intellectual elites from other countries, most notably Spain. Symbolically recovering their former colony,[59] the Spanish gave the "people of Puerto Rico" the Príncipe de Asturias award for their courage in defending and nurturing the Spanish language. It was the first time that the award had been given to "a people" (the award is usually given to writers), and it constituted a dress rehearsal for some sectors in testing the international waters of prestige as a potentially sovereign national elite. For the first time in many years, politicians and intellectuals were, in effect, princes for a day. Only two years later, Rosselló's pen turned royalty into toads.

The notion that Puerto Rico's relationship to the United States is mostly a matter of "law" was also put to question when from 1991 to 1993, a number of government agencies and trade groups asked to be exempted from the law to avoid the extra work and hindrance it created. The president of a market research firm, Nestor Beron, was quoted as saying, "Culturally speaking, we're Latino . . . But we get paid in English."[60] This sentiment was echoed by the Engineers and Surveyors Association, among many others, who commonly write their technical specifications in English for federal approval and funds.[61] The practical failure of the Spanish First legislation clearly supports the notion that not only is there no Puerto Rican "economy" but that there is no autonomous Puerto Rican "government" either.

A second blow for the autonomist/*independentista* coalition was the 1991 "Law of Democratic Rights" referendum, which proposed the amendment of the constitution to protect certain basic rights in case of a change of status. These included the right to maintain culture, language, and identity regardless of the resolution of the status question, and the maintenance of U.S. citizenship.

This attempt to dictate some parameters for a change in status met an unexpected defeat (by a margin of 100,000 votes). As multiple surveys suggested, the referendum revealed not a lack of attachment to language or culture by Puerto Ricans but instead the state's failure to seduce a majority of the population into jeopardizing what may be perceived as "real" change (permanent association to the United States) by protecting a "national culture" that is not endangered.

The statehood forces, who rejoiced at the 1991 referendum defeat and their 1992 electoral victory, misread popular sentiment against the officialization of Spanish and culture as unequivocal support for state-hood. With this false sense of confidence, the Partido Nuevo Progresista launched a nonbinding plebiscite in 1993, which they lost by 2 percent (commonwealth won 48 percent; statehood, 46 percent; and independence, 4 percent). Given the massive opposition that statehood faces in Washington, the lack of a significant majority in Puerto Rico assures that regardless of the relative strength of the statehooders locally, Congress may impose independence without hesitation. Despite the minority status of the language nationalists, these sectors are culturally very powerful. In 1993, 100,000 Puerto Ricans marched in defense of the vernacular, and the Movimiento Afirmación Puertorriqueña conducted a vigil in defense of Spanish.[62] In sum, the combination of all these consultations reflects a generalized distrust of limiting political options, particularly those created by political association with the United States, without any clear "political" mandate as embodied by the three status options. This "productive vacillation"[63] is ultimately a refusal to the "political" as framed by dominant discourses.

Fear of a Spanglish Planet

For many intellectuals on the island, U.S. Puerto Ricans serve as a "futuristic" projection of what all Puerto Ricans will/have become: culturally "impure" or hybrid, racially *mestizo* and bilingual (that is, having two "national" loyalties). The notion of "hybridity" is important since given the nation-building narratives' concern with reproduction, a hybrid cannot reproduce; it is sterile. The possibility that the elite's destiny will be explicitly tied to the U.S. diasporas (the *hampa*) or be displaced by the "lower classes" partly fuels these groups' writing off of two-thirds of the Puerto Rican population. Within this discourse, the insistence that Spanish is the only Puerto Rican language acts as a border that has, however, already been crossed. Puerto Ricans are no longer a monolingual nation, nor is the island the only referent of Puerto Rican ethno-national definitions and political claims.

The obsession with purity is a reaction to an already transformed reality of not being able to control the frontiers of the nation. As Arturo Torrecilla has written, "en este presente escenario una pléyade de letrados, con pretensiones principescas, pierde esta vez de modo irreversible su capacidad policial para autentificar la substancia de lo nacional y, con ella, el estrechamiento del espacio de su propia funcionarización discur-

siva" (in the present stage, a group of *letrados*, with royal pretensions, ir-
reversibly loses its ability to authenticate the substance of the national,
and with it, narrows the space of its own discursive functioning).[64] It is
no coincidence, then, that words such as "frontier" and "border" are frequently used by supporters of language nationalism. For writers like Luis
Rafael Sánchez, there is no need to worry about the "frontier" since the
Spanish language has been upheld for one hundred years.[65] Others, however, are concerned that things in fact have changed: "En esta frontera
lingüística, los aduaneros hace tiempo que se están haciendo de la vista
gorda. Y yo les digo que hay palabras a las que hay que revocar el pas-
aporte. O que si se cuelan hay que deportarlas." (In this frontier, the cus-
tom officers have been avoiding this situation for a long time. And I tell
you that there are words whose passports should be revoked. Or if they
manage to sneak in, they should be deported.)[66] In an attempt to uphold
the frontier allegedly separating the island from the United States, and is-
lander elites from U.S./lower-class Puerto Ricans, it becomes imperative
to distinguish "real" Puerto Ricans from impostors, thus activating the
policing function of the "patriots": "Vamos a ver quiénes son puertorriqueños 'de a verdad,' quiénes los son a medias y quiénes menosprecian
el hecho de haber nacido aquí y haberse criado con el español como
vernáculo" (We will see who the "real" Puerto Ricans are, who are only
halfway, and who looks down upon having been born here and being
raised with Spanish as their native tongue).[67]

The fact that U.S. Puerto Ricans share space and cultural practices
and forge political alliances with "other Americans" makes harsh di-
chotomies between groups harder to sustain on the basis of the national,
positioning U.S. Puerto Ricans as a threat to a traditional notion of the
national. Thus, it comes as no surprise that even when the almost 3 million strong Puerto Ricans in the United States are mentioned within the
context of the language debates, they are represented as not part of the
story. U.S. Puerto Ricans are perhaps often represented as mute supporters of a diversity of positions, ranging from an *independentista* stating
sympathy for the *pobre* U.S. Puerto Ricans to a statehooder claiming that
English (statehood) is the key to a more prosperous future. Puerto Ricans
in the United States are well aware that command of "Puerto Rican English" does not translate into upward mobility but instead stigmatizes the
speaker as inferior. The denial that there are many *ingleses* and relations
to "English" understood as the U.S. standardized cultural and economic
norm obscures the more relevant discussion of decolonization as a com-

plex process that will not take place under any status option if not addressed beyond the fetishism of nationalism as the "cure" to colonialism.

A growing number of Puerto Ricans have ties to the United States beyond strictly administrative structures, unlike the constructions of most island nationalist intellectuals. Different from the abstract concept of *la gran familia puertorriqueña* as the nation's paradigm or the American melting pot myth, specific Puerto Rican family networks live between the United States and Puerto Rico, creating an investment in the survival possibilities offered by the air bridge. The legal mechanism allowing for this state of affairs is, ironically, American citizenship, which allows Puerto Ricans to migrate freely to and from the island at will. This ease of travel has created a Puerto Rican political and cultural territory that does not coincide with linguistic homogeneity or political identity. It is instead, a survival route, where the state's construction of the citizen as a culturally homogeneous, territorialized patriotic subject is replaced by a demanding nomad, a nomad subjected to two states but always moving, a transoceanic gatherer redistributing resources.

Although in the United States Puerto Ricans are legally "first"-class citizens, they are often perceived as a racialized minority group and treated as such. On the other hand, in Puerto Rico Puerto Ricans are second-class citizens of the United States with little decision-making power, but islanders tend to think of themselves as an autonomous region and/or a separate country. Conversely, in the United States an increasing number of Puerto Ricans are English-dominant bilinguals, but in Puerto Rico the majority of bilingual Puerto Ricans are Spanish dominant. Unlike the commonwealth and statehood discourses that stress English as only necessary for trade and commerce, I would argue that English, in both its standard and popular forms, is increasingly more important for speaking not to Washington but to fellow travelers, both Puerto Ricans and others.

Native command of Spanish does not signify or contain Puerto Ricanness. As a metaphor, Spanish can be claimed as a way of affirming Puerto Ricanness, but the democratizing potential of these claims is contextual. In the United States, affirming language rights when they may be under siege and when Spanish speakers are a minority can constitute a transgressive proposition. In Puerto Rico, where Spanish is the undisputed vernacular and the issue is instead one of politically powerful elites claiming Spanish within a hegemonizing and marginalizing discourse, language nationalism is a farce.

Political forces, assuming that a monolingual nation would be "easier" to govern, overlook not only that all Puerto Ricans are not monolingual, but that governability and monolingualism do not have a causal relationship. The insistence that Spanish is the only language Puerto Ricans speak and should be so "forever" hegemonizes the future by ignoring the political options of the present. Spanglish, or *inglañol*, may indeed be the language of the future inhabitants of the island formerly called Puerto Rico. However, whether Puerto Ricans speak Spanish, English, Spanglish, or another language in the future is much less important than that today's Puerto Ricans have the most open and fair society possible. In proposing this, I do not deny that language metaphors can be mobilized toward a democratizing goal; I only question this use in that so far they have been deployed for different ends.

Rather than attempt to confine the borders of the nation to the island, I suggest that any attempt to decolonize Puerto Rico (and Puerto Ricans) take into account that decolonization is partly about multiplying spaces for intervention, not reducing them. In this sense, creating the conditions for cultural and political intervention in every part of Puerto Rico (where the island is one of several) would point to the need to continue the process of appropriation of English by Puerto Ricans, as well as a struggle for a broader definition of citizenship that transcends rigid definitions of nationhood.

A *cobito* notion of citizenship that allows all Puerto Ricans to intervene wherever they may live may be a more radical notion than arguing for a Puerto Rican citizenship that would exclude millions of Puerto Ricans. Getting beyond nationalism and colonialism is, then, a matter not of avoiding or dismissing each discourse's effects but shifting the questions so as to imagine new solidarities that foster autonomy, active citizenship, and more equitable access to wealth in a space beyond current hegemonic versions of "America," perhaps on a "Spanglish" planet.

Notes

1. René Marqués, *Ensayos* (Río Piedras: Editorial Antillana, 1972): "As if there were not enough things already dividing us, the 'language problem' will come to divide us once again." Unless otherwise noted, all English translations are mine.

2. Juan José Osuna, *A History of Education in Puerto Rico* (Río Piedras: Editorial de la Universidad de Puerto Rico, 1949).

3. Ibid.

4. Ibid.

5. Pedro Cebollero, as quoted in Aida Negrón de Montilla, *Americanization in*

Puerto Rico and the Public School System, 1900–1930 (Río Piedras: Editorial Universitaria, Universidad de Puerto Rico, 1975), 215; my emphasis.

6. As quoted in ibid., 153.

7. As quoted in ibid., 181.

8. See Juan José Osuna, *A History of Education in Puerto Rico* (Río Piedras: Editorial de la Universidad de Puerto Rico, 1949); Negrón de Montilla, *Americanization in Puerto Rico and the Public School System*; and Ada Muntaner, "The Language Question in Puerto Rico" (Ph.D. diss., State University of New York at Stony Brook, 1993).

9. Osuna, *A History of Education in Puerto Rico*.

10. Juan Manuel García Passalacqua and Carlos Antonio Torre, "Plebiscite, Migration and the Role of Puerto Ricans in the United States," in Carlos Antonio Torre, Hugo Rodríguez Vecchini, and William Burgos, eds., *The Commuter Nation* (Río Piedras: Editorial de la Universidad de Puerto Rico, 1994), 365–81.

11. For a well-argued essay on this transformation, see Carlos Pabón, "De Albizu a Madonna: Para armar y desarmar la nacionalidad," *Bordes* 1995: 22–40.

12. Osuna, *A History of Education in Puerto Rico*, 362–63.

13. "El idioma del gobierno es el español," advertisement, *El Nuevo Día*, May 26, 1991, 53.

14. Rafael Castro Pereda, "El español primero," *El Nuevo Día*, Apr. 5, 1991, 61.

15. Lola Aponte, "Los que dicen 'Yes my dear' esos no son de aquí," *Claridad*, Feb. 29–Mar. 6, 1993, 16; my emphasis.

16. Harry Turner, "Schulze Letter Slaps RHC over Spanish-Only Law," *San Juan Star*, July 19, 1991, 3.

17. Delinda Karle, "'English First' Wants Island to Remain 'Separate,'" *San Juan Star*, June 22, 1991, 3.

18. Doris Sommer, "Irresistible Romance: The Foundational Fictions of Latin America," in Homi Bhabha, ed., *Nation and Narration* (London: Routledge, 1990), 76.

19. Luis Rafael Sánchez, "Puertorriqueño," *El Nuevo Día*, Apr. 20, 1991, 57.

20. Benedict Anderson, *Imagined Communities* (London: Verso, 1987).

21. Salvador Tió, "Palabras sin argumento," *El Mundo*, Oct. 1, 1989, 6–7.

22. Severo Colberg, "El español: Idioma oficial," *El Mundo*, Sept. 3, 1990, 27.

23. Juan Manuel Carrión, "Etnia, raza y la nacionalidad puertorriqueña," in Juan Manuel Carrión, Teresa C. Gracia Ruiz, Carlos Rodríguez Fraticelli, eds., *La nación puertorriqueña: Ensayos en torno a Pedro Albizu Campos* (Río Piedras: Editorial de la Universidad de Puerto Rico, 1993), 13.

24. Salvador Tió, *Lengua Mayor* (Madrid: Editorial Plaza Mayor, 1991).

25. Andrea Martínez, "Intento de asimilación," *El Nuevo Día*, Jan. 20, 1993, 13.

26. Jesús Hernández, "Miopía nacionalista," *El Nuevo Día*, May 23, 1991, 63.

27. Antonio S. Pedreira, *Insularismo* (Río Piedras: Editorial Edil, 1973), 91.

28. Pedro Juan Rua, "'Spanish Only' y los boricuas ausentes," *El Mundo*, Aug. 30, 1990, 29.

29. Lizette Cabrera Salcedo, "Reiteran urgencia de fortalecer el español," *Diálogo*, Mar. 1991, 10.

30. Tió, *Lengua Mayor*, 37, 47.

31. Manuel Maldonado Denis, "Con la lengua española," *El Mundo*, Aug. 21, 1990, 28.

32. Dennis Barron, *The English Only Question* (New Haven, Conn.: Yale University Press, 1990).

33. Rafael Castro Pereda, as quoted in Ada Muntaner, "Política pública y planificación en el sector privado en Puerto Rico," *Revista de Administración Pública* 24, 2 (June 1992): 121.

34. Tricia Rose, "Rhythmic Repetition, Industrial Forces and Black Practice," in Adam Sexton, ed., *Rap on Rap* (New York: Dell Publishing, 1995), 45–55.

35. Juan Flores, "Latin Empire: Puerto Rap," *Centro* (spring 1991): 77–85.

36. George Lipsitz, "We Know What Time It Is: Youth Culture in the 90's," *Centro* (winter 1992–93): 10–19.

37. Juan Flores, *Divided Borders* (Houston: Arte Público Press, 1993), 163–64.

38. Frances Aparicio, "On Sub-versive Signifiers: U.S. Latina/os Tropicalize English," *American Literature* 66, 4 (Dec. 1994): 797.

39. As quoted in Coco Fusco, *English Is Broken Here* (New York: New Day, 1995), 157.

40. Ana Lydia Vega and Carmen Lugo Fillipi, *Vírgenes y Mártires* (Río Piedras, Editorial Antillana, 1981), 75–79.

41. Quoted in interview by Blanca Vázquez, "Puerto Rican in the U.S.A." *Centro* (winter 1992): 49.

42. Ana Lydia Vega, "Pollito Chicken," in Vega and Fillipi, *Vírgenes y Mártires*, 77.

43. "Puerto Rican in the U.S.A." *Centro* (winter 1992): 49.

44. Eric Hobsbawm, "Inventing Traditions," in Eric Hobsbawm and Terence Ranger, *The Invention of Tradition* (Cambridge: Canto, 1992), 1–14.

45. Obed Betancourt, "Revive el 'fantasma' del idioma," *El Mundo*, Aug. 11, 1990, 12.

46. The Performing Arts Center was the subject of much controversy when a proposal to name it after a black popular musician met great resistance from many intellectuals and politicians. See Juan Flores, "Cortijo's Revenge," *Centro* (spring 1991): 8–21.

47. Jorge Luis Medina, "Law Signing Provides Chance for Kids to Party," *San Juan Star*, Jan. 29, 1993, 3.

48. Nilka Estrada Resto, "De gala el idioma español," *El Nuevo Día*, Apr. 6, 1991, 4.

49. Waldo D. Covas Quevedo, "Grandes figuras en la firma del 'Spanish Only,' " *El Nuevo Día*, Apr. 4, 1991, 20.

50. Estrada Resto, "De gala el idioma español," 4.

51. "Ad in *New York Times* Defends Spanish Only," *San Juan Star*, Apr. 10, 1991, 2.

52. Carlos Gil, *El orden del tiempo* (Río Piedras: Editorial Postdata, 1994), 170.

53. Medina, "Law Signing Provides Chance for Kids to Party," *San Juan Star*, Jan. 29, 1993, 3.

54. As quoted in Agencia EFE, "Firme rechazo al movimiento 'Spanish Only,' " *El Nuevo Día*, Aug. 10, 1990, 13.

55. Luis Ferrao, "Puerto Rico: Fin de un siglo que termina en 1998," *Hoy*, May 3, 1995, 20.

56. See Miriam Muñiz, "Más allá de Puerto Rico 936, Puerto Rico USA y Puerto Rico INC: Notas para una crítica al discurso del desarrollo," *Bordes* (1995): 41–53; and Roberto Otero, "Modernidad, educación y razón," *Bordes* (1995): 54–66.

57. Luis Ferré, "Una fusión hermosa," *El Nuevo Día*, Feb. 25, 1993, 70.

58. T. H. Marshall, "Citizenship and Social Class," in *Class, Citizenship and Social Development* (London: Doubleday and Co., 1964), 65–122.

59. Arcadio Díaz Quiñones, *La memoria rota* (Río Piedras: Huracán, 1993).

60. Eneid Routte-Gómez, "A Second Look at Language Law and Its Meaning," *San Juan Star*, Apr. 21, 1991, 17.

61. Doreen Hemlock, "Law Sends Engineers Back to the Drawing Board," *San Juan Star*, Apr. 27, 1991, 3.

62. Nilka Estrada Resto, "Alianza intelectual contra el proyecto de Rosselló," *El Nuevo Día*, Jan. 14, 1993, 14.

63. Juan Flores and Milagros López, "Introduction: Dossier Puerto Rico," *Social Text* 38 (spring 1994): 93–95.

64. Arturo Torrecilla, *El espectro postmoderno* (Río Piedras: Publicaciones Puertor-riqueñas, 1995), 128.

65. Luis Rafael Sánchez, "El cuarteto nuevayorkés," in *La Guagua Aérea* (San Juan: Editorial Cultural, 1994), 23–24.

66. Tió, *Lengua Mayor*, 101.

67. Severo Colberg Ramírez, "En defensa del español," *El Mundo*, Aug. 27, 1990, 24.

Contributors

Jaime E. Benson-Arias is an assistant professor in the economics department of the University of Puerto Rico at Mayagüez. He is also assistant director of the Institute of Socioeconomic Regional Research and chief editor of *Ceteris Paibus*, Puerto Rico's journal of socioeconomic research at the University of Puerto Rico, Mayagüez.

Arlene Dávila is an assistant professor of anthropology at Syracuse University. She is currently working on a manuscript on the making and contesting of national identities in contemporary Puerto Rico.

Chloé S. Georas studied economics and anthropology. She has published articles on race, culture, and the identity of Caribbean migrants in the United States. She is also a creative writer and has been an activist against AIDS and gender-related discrimination. Currently she is a graduate student in art history at State University of New York, Binghamton, and is working on a research project about the social/cultural construction of Paris as a Eurocentric space.

Ramón Grosfoguel has published many articles on Caribbean migration, global cities, and the sociology of international development. He has been a visiting professor in the Department of Sociology at the Johns Hopkins University, a Ford Foundation Postdoctoral Fellow at the Fernand Braudel Center, a visiting scholar at the Maison des Sciences de l'Homme in Paris, and a Rockefeller Fellow at the Center for Puerto Rican Studies at City University of New York-Hunter College. He is a senior research associate of the Fernand Braudel Center and an assistant professor in the Department of Sociology at State University of New

York, Binghamton. Currently he is finishing a book on colonial Caribbean migrations to France, the Netherlands, England, and the United States.

Manuel Guzmán is a graduate student in the Sociology Program at the Graduate Center of the City University of New York. He has lectured on social and historical aspects of gender and sexuality at the Sociology Department and Women Studies Program at Hunter College. Before entering the Sociology Program, he worked as a psychotherapist and advocate for lesbian, gay, and transsexual youth at the Hetrick-Martin Institute in New York City.

Gladys M. Jiménez-Muñoz is an assistant professor of women's studies at the State University of New York at Oneonta. Her recent publications include "Joining Our Differences: The Problems of Lesbian Subjectivity among Women of Color," in *Moving beyond Boundaries: Black Women's Diaspora*, vol. 2; "Rethinking the History of Puerto Rican Women's Suffrage," *Centro de Estudios Puertorriqueños Bulletin* 7, 1 (winter 1994–95/ spring 1995); and guest editor, "Interrogating Intersections: Women's Studies/Ethnic Studies," *Phoebe: An Interdisciplinary Journal of Feminist Scholarship Theory and Aesthetics* 7, 1/2 (fall/spring 1995).

Agustín Lao is a Ph.D. candidate in sociology at the State University of New York, Binghamton, and is working on a dissertation on the Latinization of New York. He has been a political activist and community organizer for more than twenty years.

Yolanda Martínez-San Miguel is an assistant professor at the Departamento de Español, Facultad de Estudios Generales, Universidad de Puerto Rico. She recently finished her dissertation, "Engendrando nuevos sujetos del saber en Sor Juana Inés de la Cruz: Estrategias para la construcción de una subjetividad epistemológica desde una perspectiva femenina, colonial y criolla." She has published various articles on the following subjects: Puerto Rican and Brazilian literature, Caribbean diaspora, colonial and postcolonial theory, cultural studies, and studies on epistemology and literature.

Frances Negrón-Muntaner is a scholar, writer, and filmmaker. She is currently a Ph.D. candidate in comparative literature at Rutgers University. She is the recipient of several professional and academic fellowships, most recently the PEW Fellowship in the Arts. Among her media works are *Homeless Diaries, Puerto Rican I.D., Brincando el charco: Portrait of a Puerto Rican,* and *AIDS in the Barrio* (co-directed with Peter Biella). She has published creative literature and critical essays on film, cultural politics, literature, and gay and lesbian studies in many journals and newspapers. She also edited the book *Shouting in a Whisper: Latino Poetry in Philadelphia.* Her first collection of poetry, *Anatomy of a Smile, Prose and Poetry,* is forthcoming.

Mariano Negrón-Portillo is a researcher and professor at the Social Sciences Research Center of the University of Puerto Rico. His main areas of interest are slavery and urban social history. He has published several books, including *El Autonomismo Puertorriqueño, Las Turbas Repulicanas,* and *La esclavitud urbana en San Juan* (in collaboration with Raúl Mayo).

José Quiroga is an associate professor of Spanish at George Washington University. He has published extensively on poetry and poetics in Latin America and is the author of essays on Octavio Paz, Vicente Huidobro, and Virgilio Piñera. He is currently working on a manuscript tentatively titled *Homosexualities in the Tropics of Revolution.*

Raquel Z. Rivera is currently a graduate student at the sociology department of the City University of New York Graduate Center. She received a master's degree in Puerto Rican studies from the Centro de Estudios Avanzados de Puerto Rico y el Caribe. Her thesis is titled "Para rapear en puertorriqueño: Discurso y política cultural" (1996). She has had the joy of conducting research on hip-hop culture in Puerto Rico and New York for the past four years. Her work in this area has been published in *Boletín del Centro de Estudios Puertorriqueños, Post-data, Claridad, Diálogo,* the *San Juan Star,* and *Against the Current.*

Alberto Sandoval Sánchez is an associate professor of Spanish at Mount Holyoke College. He is both a creative writer and a cultural critic. His bilingual book of poetry, *New York Backstage/Nueva York Tras Bastidores,* was published in Chile. In 1993 Mount Holyoke College produced his theatrical piece *Side Effects,* based on his personal experiences with AIDS. He has just edited a special issue of *Ollantay Theater Magazine* on U.S.

Latino theater and AIDS. He has published numerous articles on U.S. Latino theater, Latin American colonial theater and identity, Spanish baroque theater, Puerto Rican migration, and images of Latinos in film. He is currently working on two books: *José Can You See? Essays on Theatrical and Cultural Representations of Latinos* and *Stages of Life: Latinas in Teatro* (in collaboration with Nancy Saporta Sternbach).

Kelvin A. Santiago-Valles is an associate professor of sociology at State University of New York, Binghamton, and author of *"Subject People" and Colonial Discourses: Economic Transformation and Social Disorder in Puerto Rico, 1898–1947*. He is currently researching U.S. racialization practices in relation to Puerto Ricans vis-à-vis Puerto Rican racial codes after the Spanish-American war.

Index